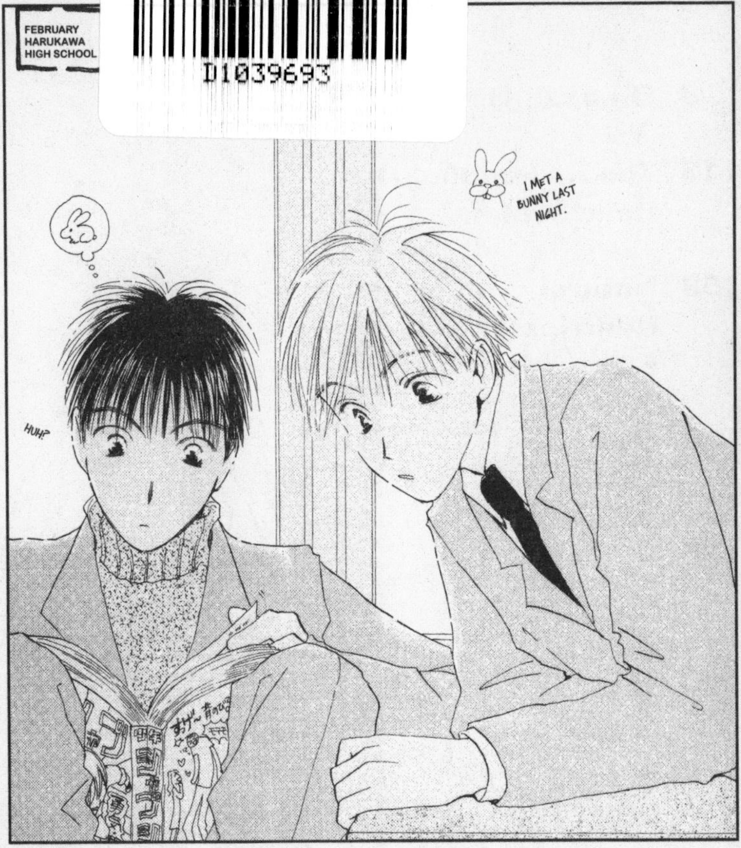
FEBRUARY
HARUKAWA
HIGH SCHOOL
I MET A BUNNY LAST NIGHT.
HUH?

OMUKAE desu.

By Meca Tanaka

Volume 2

CONTENTS

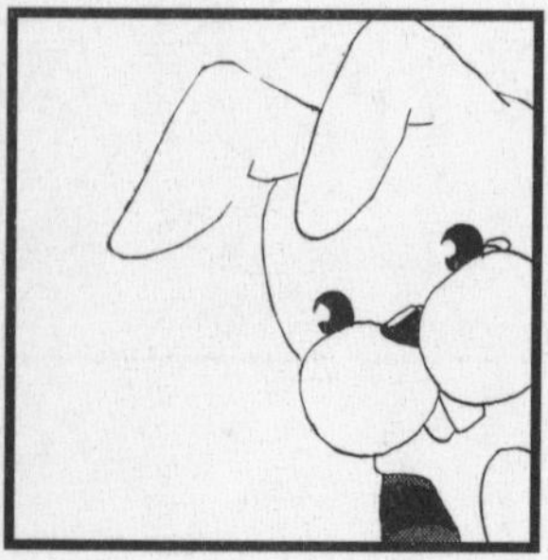

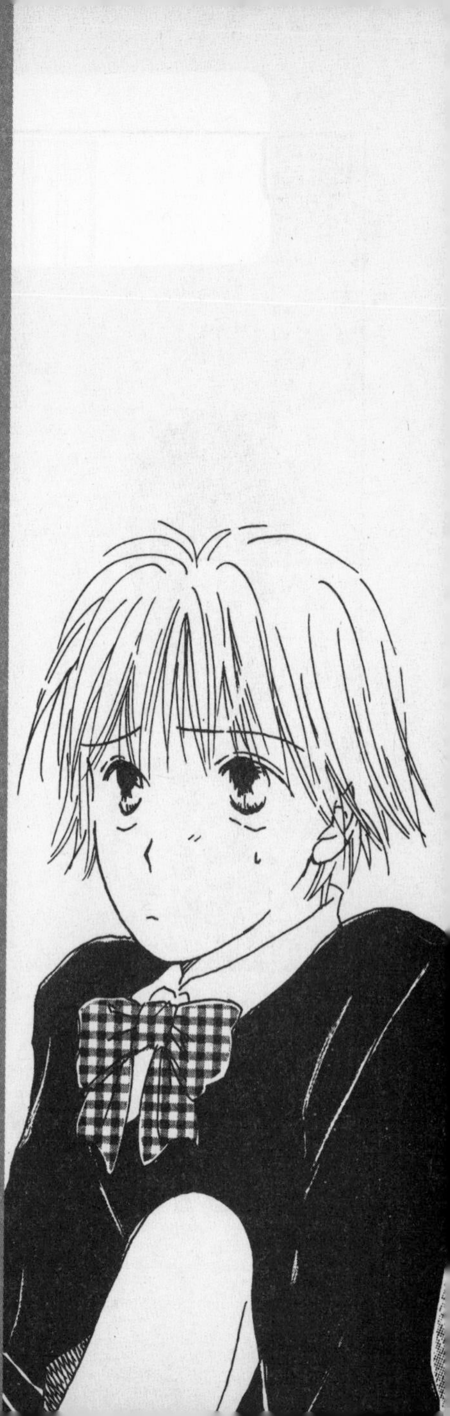

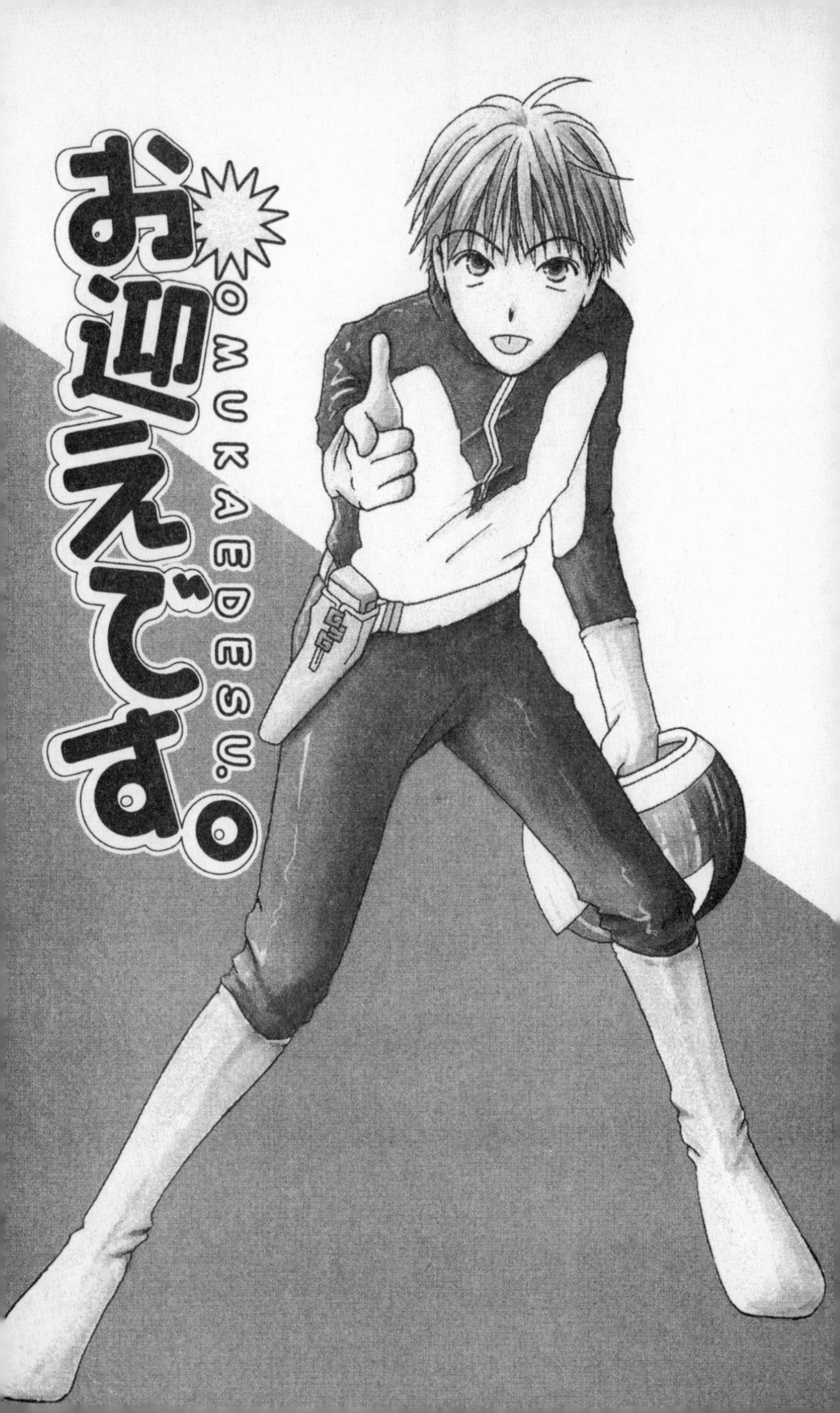
お迎えです。
OMUKAEDESU.

GREETINGS

WELL, WHADDA YA KNOW? "OMUKAE DESU." HAS MADE IT TO A SECOND VOLUME! AND YOU MADE THE RIGHT CHOICE PICKING IT UP, TOO, 'CAUSE JUST LIKE LAST TIME, WE'LL HOOK YA UP!

● NABESHIMA ●

GSG'S MONTHLY THEMES SCARE ME, BUT THEY'RE ALSO A LOT OF FUN. ♥

● YUZUKO ●

THIS TIME AROUND, IT GETS KINDA CHAOTIC, ALL BECAUSE OF NABESHIMA-SAN!

● AGUMA ●

HELLO... THINGS ARE PRETTY MUCH THE SAME.

......

NOTHING LEFT FOR HIM TO SAY. →

● THE MAIN CHARACTER

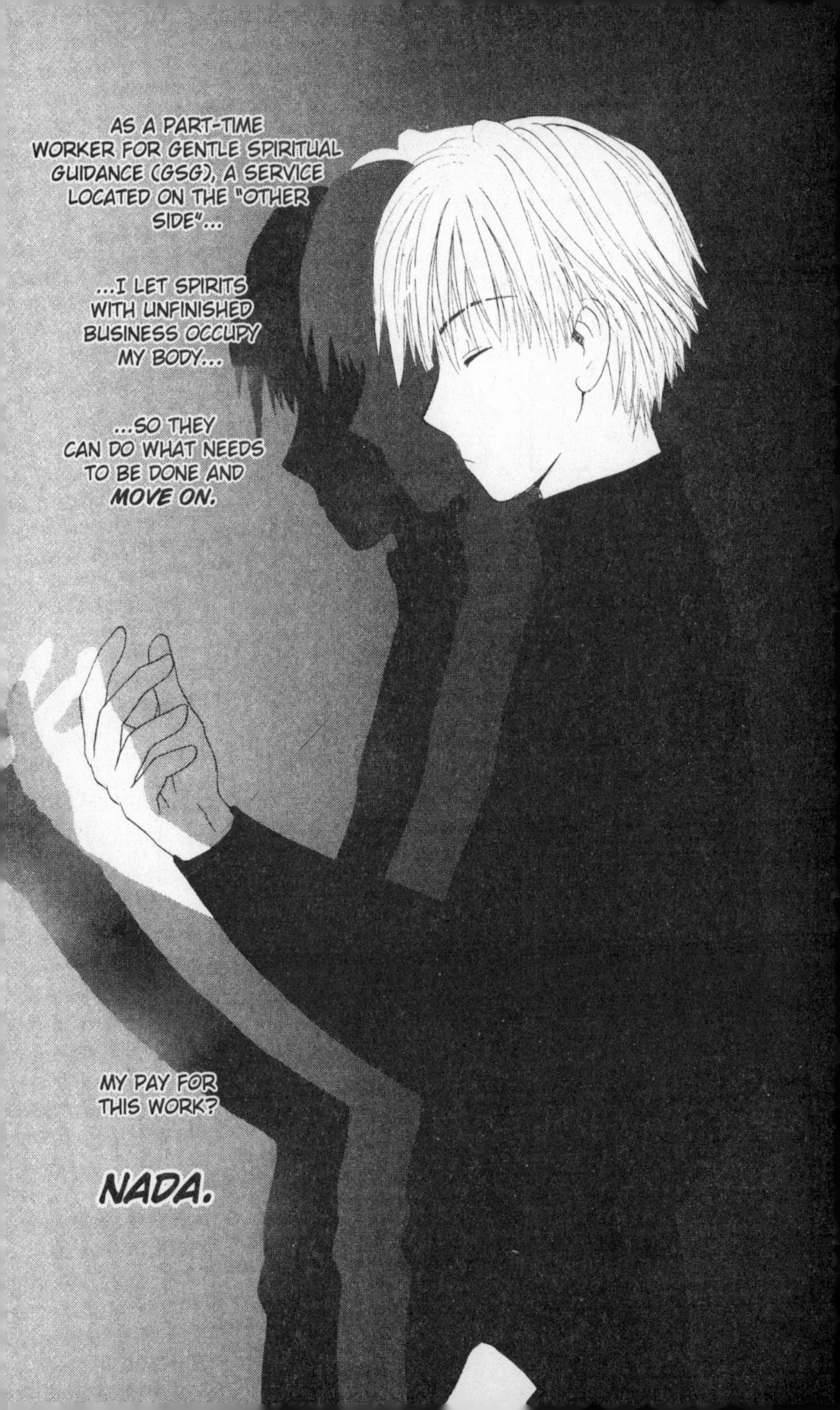
AS A PART-TIME WORKER FOR GENTLE SPIRITUAL GUIDANCE (GSG), A SERVICE LOCATED ON THE "OTHER SIDE"...
...I LET SPIRITS WITH UNFINISHED BUSINESS OCCUPY MY BODY...
...SO THEY CAN DO WHAT NEEDS TO BE DONE AND *MOVE ON.*
MY PAY FOR THIS WORK?
NADA.

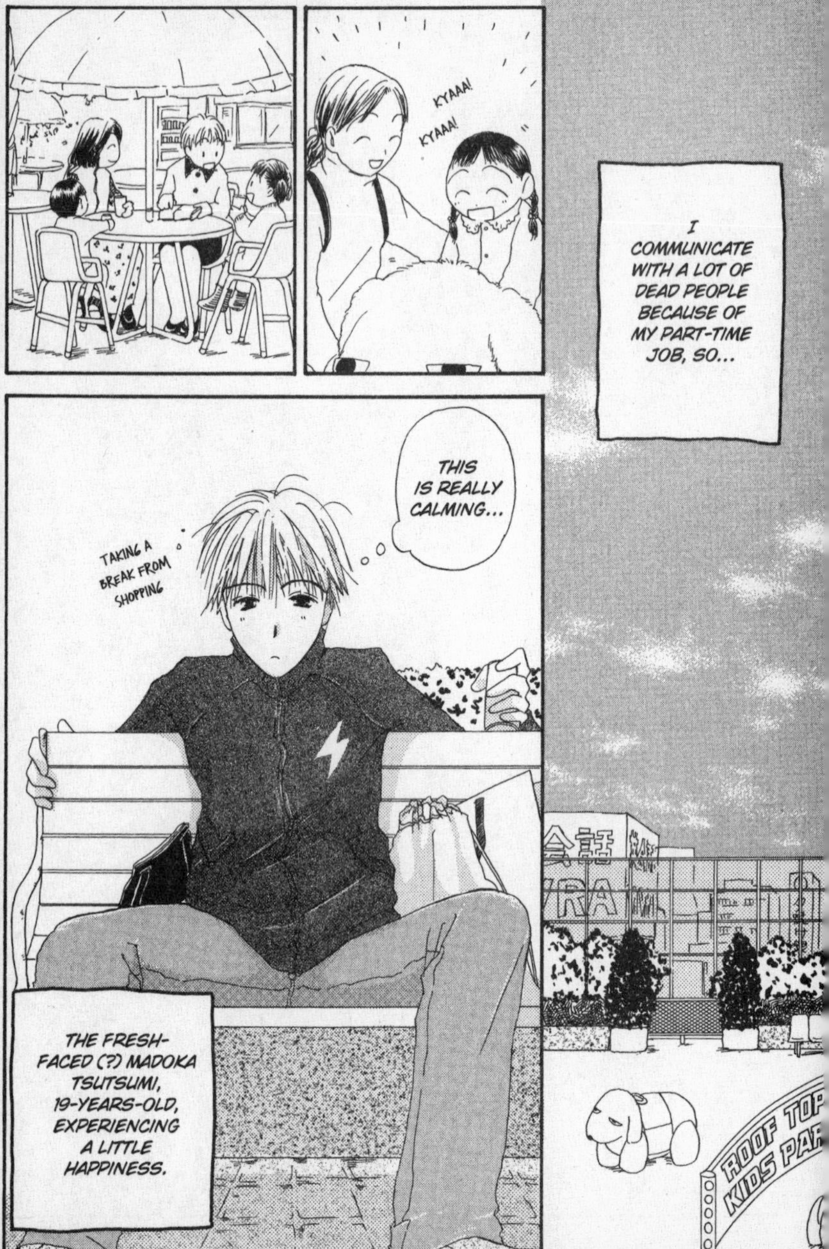
I COMMUNICATE WITH A LOT OF DEAD PEOPLE BECAUSE OF MY PART-TIME JOB, SO...
KYAAA!
KYAAA!
THIS IS REALLY CALMING...
TAKING A BREAK FROM SHOPPING
THE FRESH-FACED (?) MADOKA TSUTSUMI, 19-YEARS-OLD, EXPERIENCING A LITTLE HAPPINESS.
ROOF TOP
KIDS PAR

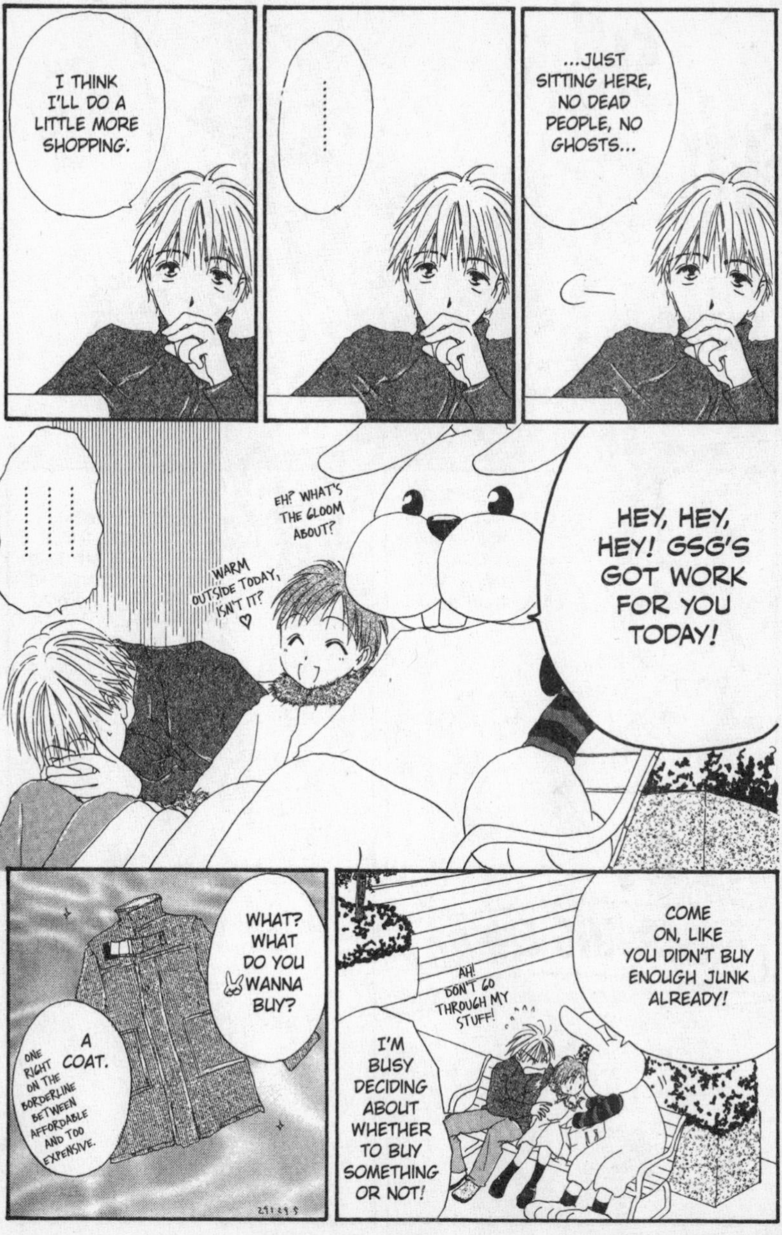
...JUST SITTING HERE, NO DEAD PEOPLE, NO GHOSTS...
......
I THINK I'LL DO A LITTLE MORE SHOPPING.
HEY, HEY, HEY! GSG'S GOT WORK FOR YOU TODAY!
EH? WHAT'S THE GLOOM ABOUT?
WARM OUTSIDE TODAY, ISN'T IT? ♡
......
I'M BUSY DECIDING ABOUT WHETHER TO BUY SOMETHING OR NOT!
COME ON, LIKE YOU DIDN'T BUY ENOUGH JUNK ALREADY!
AH! DON'T GO THROUGH MY STUFF!
WHAT? WHAT DO YOU WANNA BUY?
A COAT.
ONE RIGHT ON THE BORDERLINE BETWEEN AFFORDABLE AND TOO EXPENSIVE.

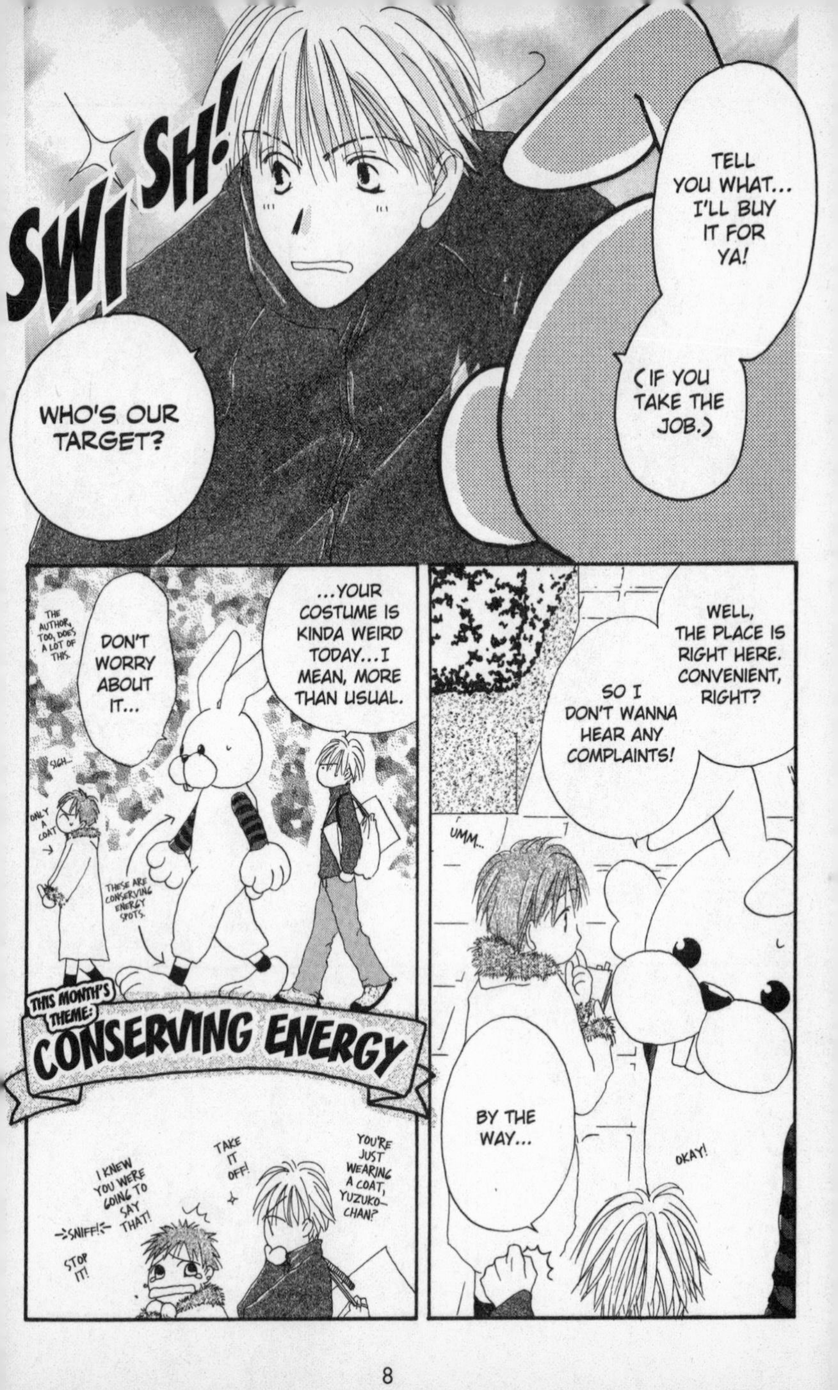
SWISH!
TELL YOU WHAT... I'LL BUY IT FOR YA!
(IF YOU TAKE THE JOB.)
WHO'S OUR TARGET?
WELL, THE PLACE IS RIGHT HERE. CONVENIENT, RIGHT?
SO I DON'T WANNA HEAR ANY COMPLAINTS!
UMM...
OKAY!
BY THE WAY...
...YOUR COSTUME IS KINDA WEIRD TODAY...I MEAN, MORE THAN USUAL.
DON'T WORRY ABOUT IT...
THE AUTHOR, TOO, DOES A LOT OF THIS.
SIGH...
ONLY A COAT
THESE ARE CONSERVING ENERGY SPOTS.
THIS MONTH'S THEME: CONSERVING ENERGY
YOU'RE JUST WEARING A COAT, YUZUKO-CHAN?
TAKE IT OFF!
I KNEW YOU WERE GOING TO SAY THAT!
SNIFF!
STOP IT!

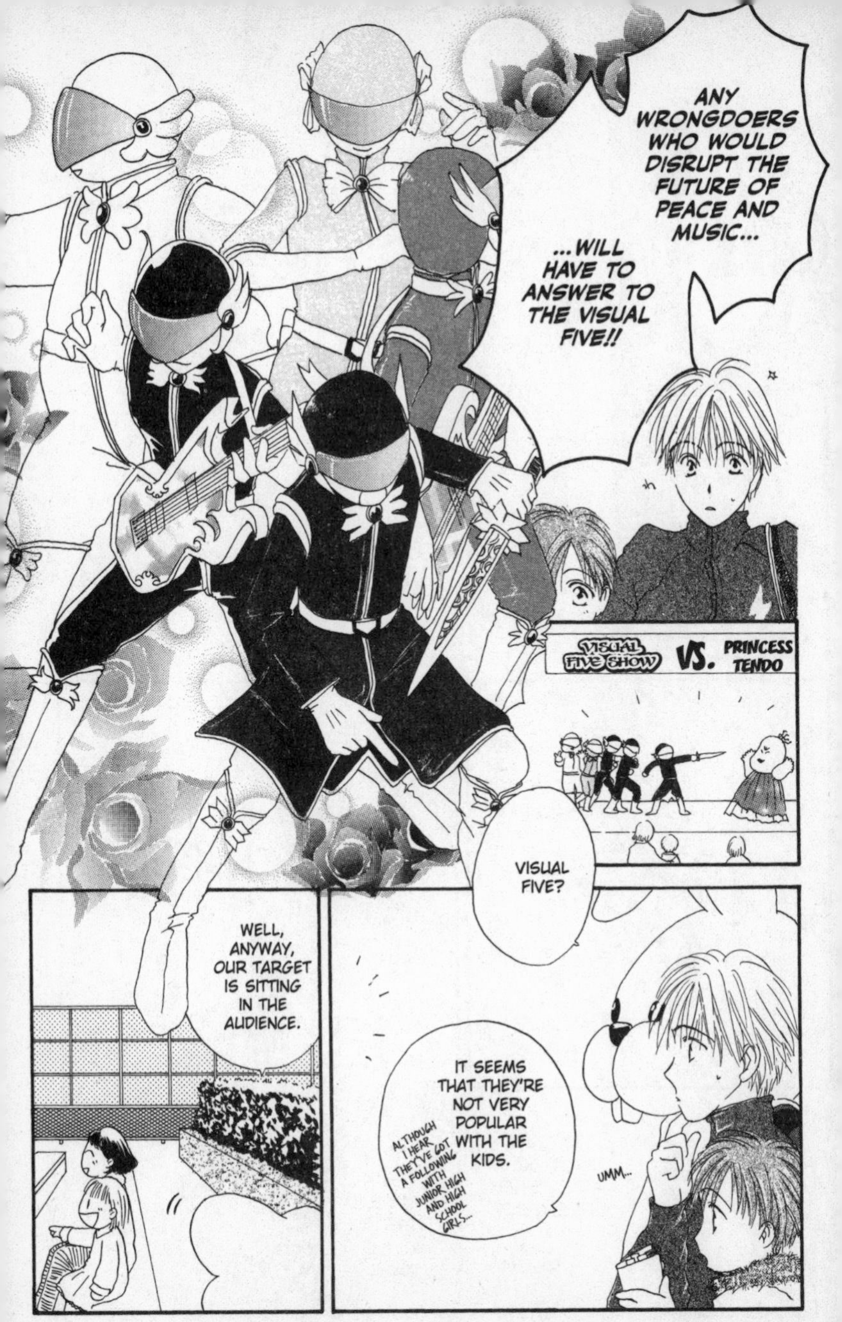

ANY WRONGDOERS WHO WOULD DISRUPT THE FUTURE OF PEACE AND MUSIC...
...WILL HAVE TO ANSWER TO THE VISUAL FIVE!!
VISUAL FIVE SHOW VS. PRINCESS TENDO
VISUAL FIVE?
IT SEEMS THAT THEY'RE NOT VERY POPULAR WITH THE KIDS.
ALTHOUGH I HEAR THEY'VE GOT A FOLLOWING WITH JUNIOR HIGH AND HIGH SCHOOL GIRLS...
UMM...
WELL, ANYWAY, OUR TARGET IS SITTING IN THE AUDIENCE.

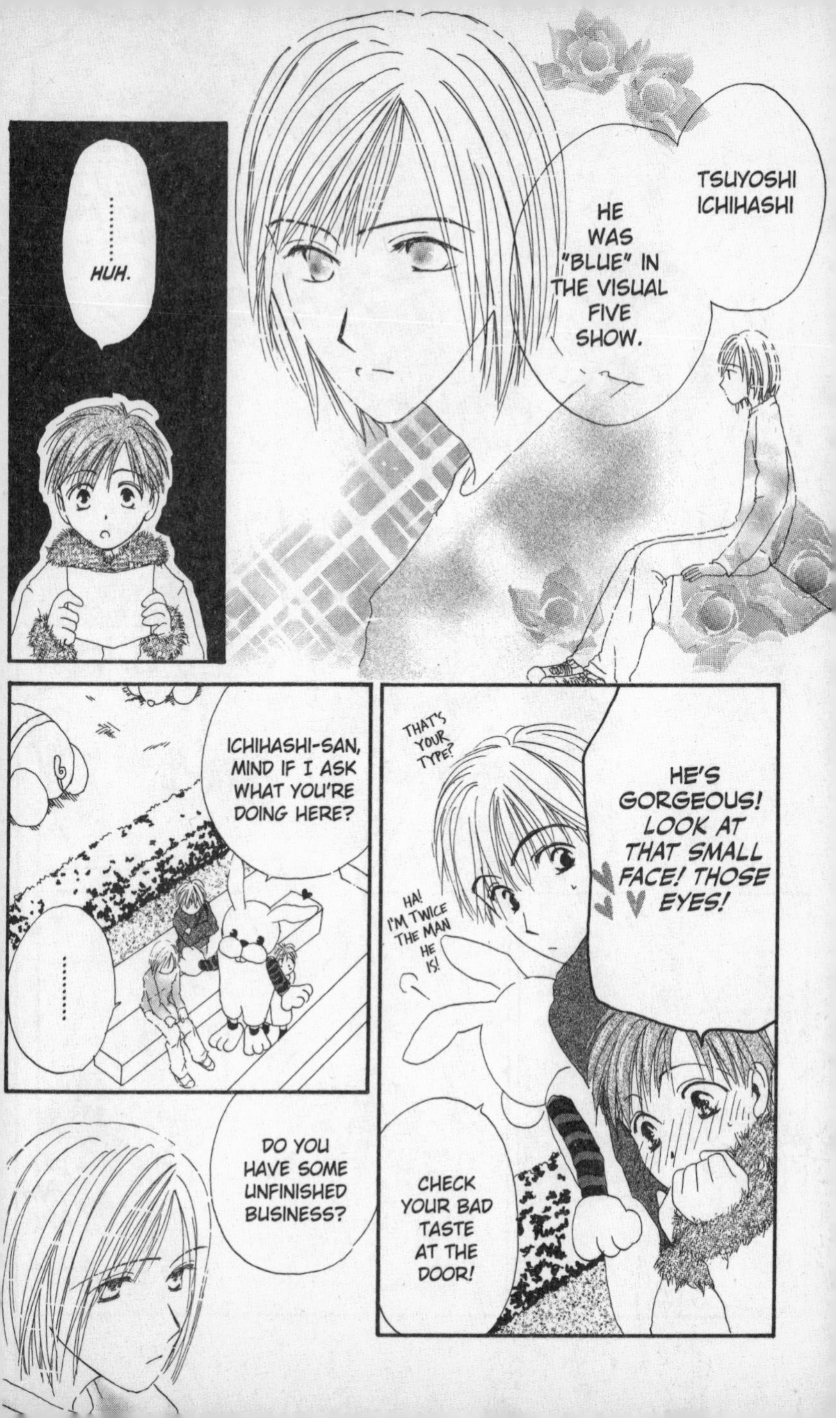
TSUYOSHI ICHIHASHI
HE WAS "BLUE" IN THE VISUAL FIVE SHOW.
...... HUH.
HE'S GORGEOUS! LOOK AT THAT SMALL FACE! THOSE EYES!
THAT'S YOUR TYPE?
HA! I'M TWICE THE MAN HE IS!
CHECK YOUR BAD TASTE AT THE DOOR!
ICHIHASHI-SAN, MIND IF I ASK WHAT YOU'RE DOING HERE?
......
DO YOU HAVE SOME UNFINISHED BUSINESS?

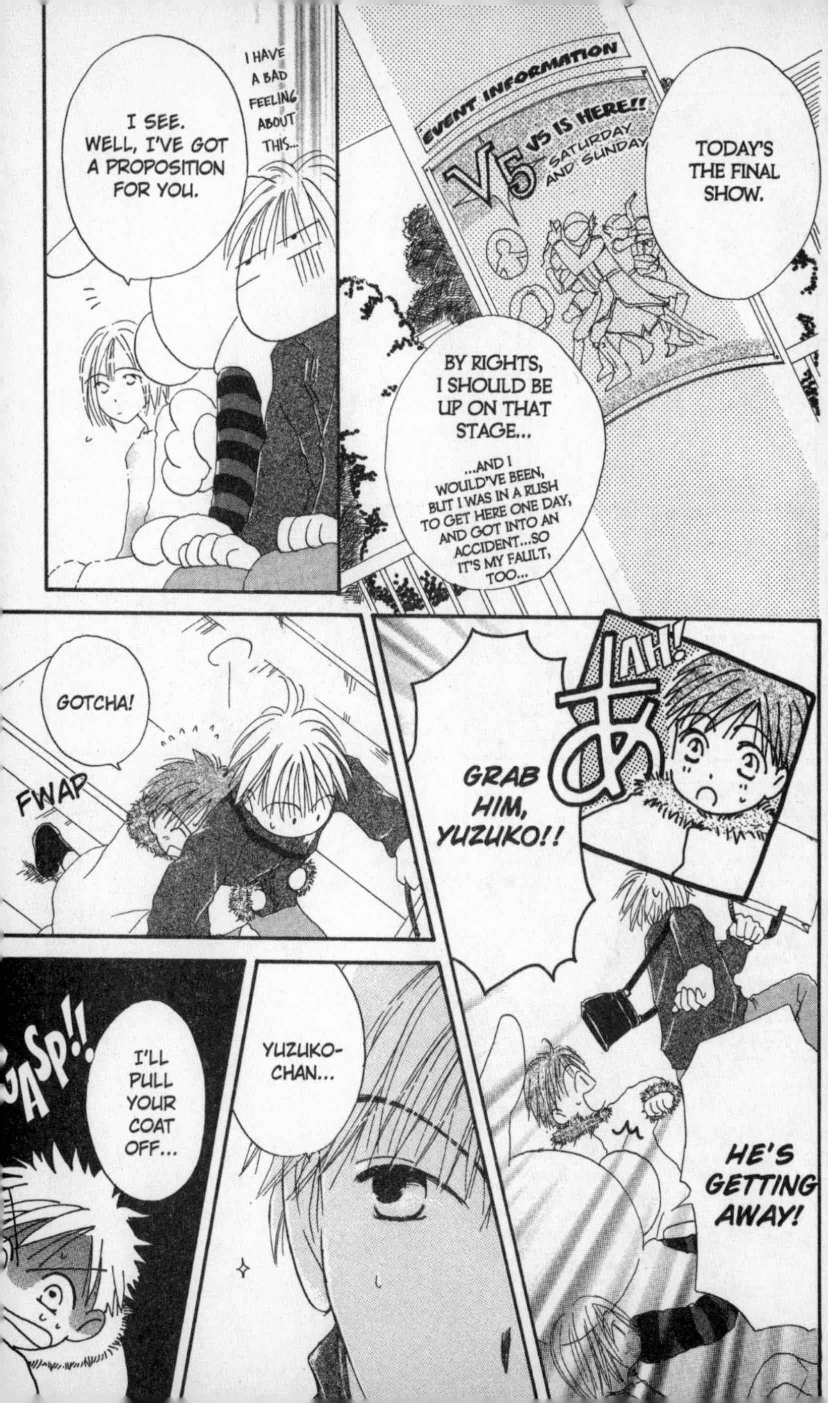
EVENT INFORMATION
V5 IS HERE!!
SATURDAY AND SUNDAY
V5
TODAY'S THE FINAL SHOW.
BY RIGHTS, I SHOULD BE UP ON THAT STAGE...
...AND I WOULD'VE BEEN, BUT I WAS IN A RUSH TO GET HERE ONE DAY, AND GOT INTO AN ACCIDENT...SO IT'S MY FAULT, TOO...
I HAVE A BAD FEELING ABOUT THIS...
I SEE. WELL, I'VE GOT A PROPOSITION FOR YOU.
AH!
あ
GRAB HIM, YUZUKO!!
HE'S GETTING AWAY!
GOTCHA!
FWAP
YUZUKO-CHAN...
GASP!!
I'LL PULL YOUR COAT OFF...

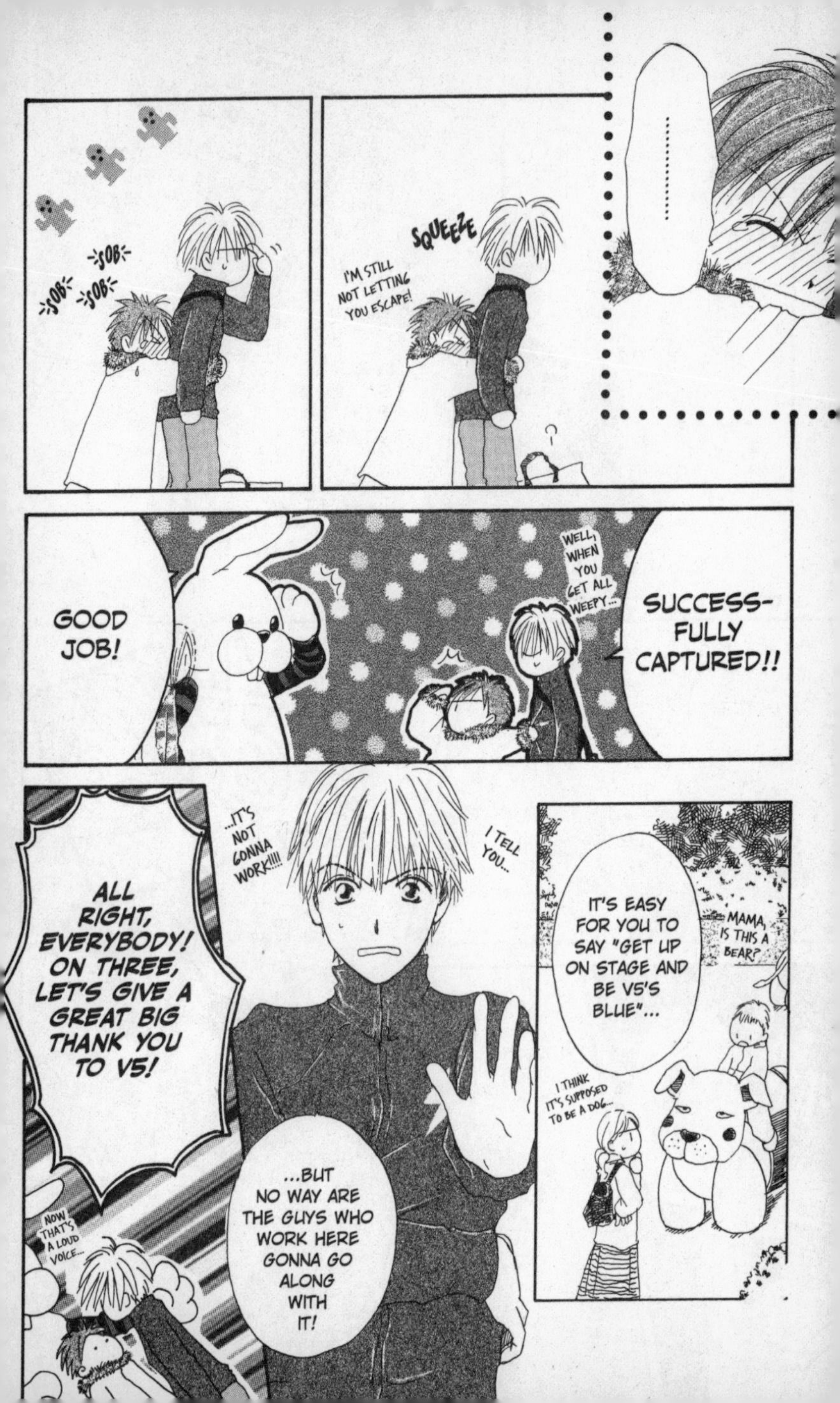
……
SQUEEZE
I'M STILL NOT LETTING YOU ESCAPE!
SOB
SOB
SOB
SUCCESS-FULLY CAPTURED!!
WELL, WHEN YOU GET ALL WEEPY...
GOOD JOB!
IT'S EASY FOR YOU TO SAY "GET UP ON STAGE AND BE V5'S BLUE"...
MAMA, IS THIS A BEAR?
I THINK IT'S SUPPOSED TO BE A DOG...
...BUT NO WAY ARE THE GUYS WHO WORK HERE GONNA GO ALONG WITH IT!
ALL RIGHT, EVERYBODY! ON THREE, LET'S GIVE A GREAT BIG THANK YOU TO V5!
NOW THAT'S A LOUD VOICE...
I TELL YOU...
...IT'S NOT GONNA WORK!!!!

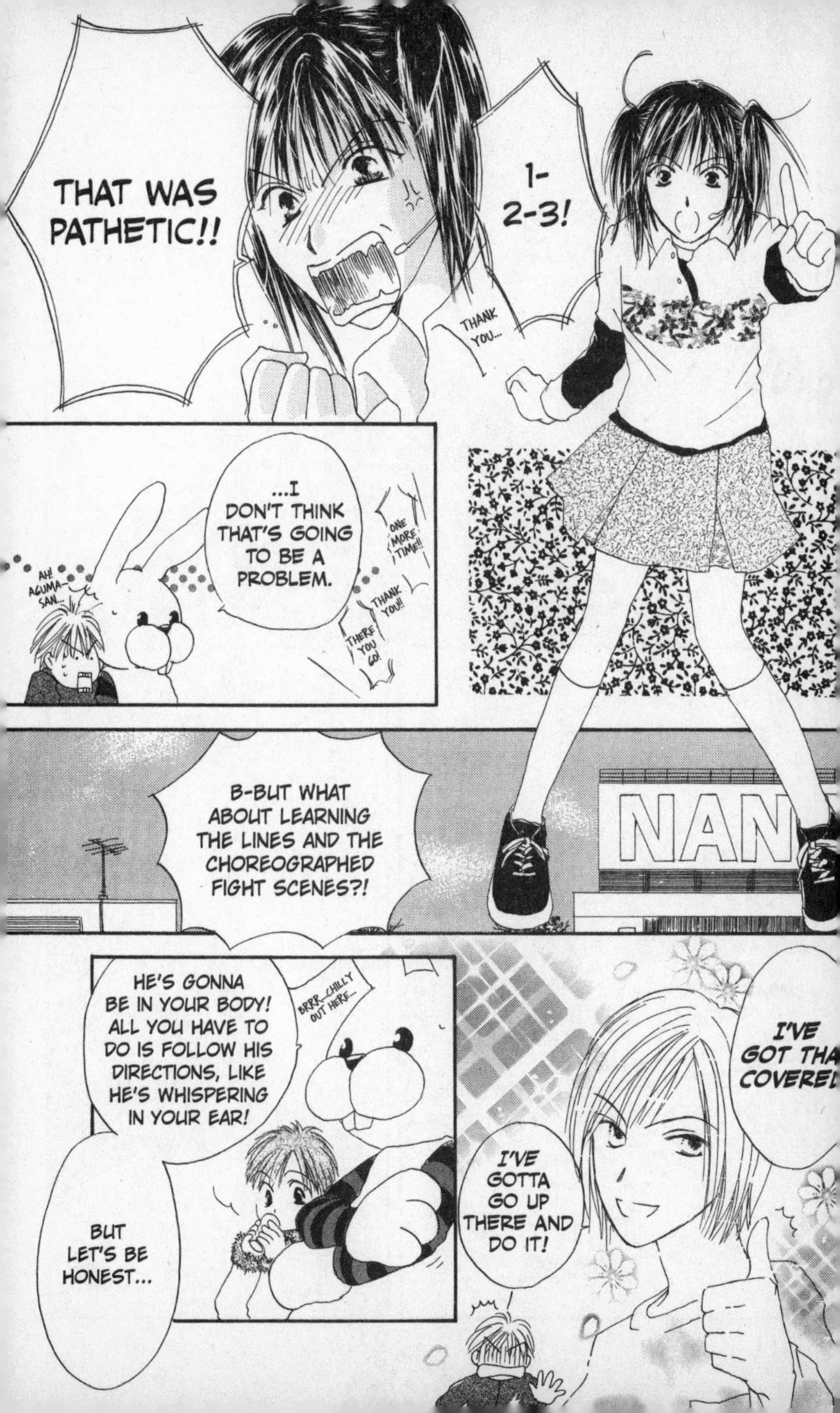
1-
2-3!
THAT WAS PATHETIC!!
THANK YOU...
ONE MORE TIME!!
THANK YOU!!
THERE YOU GO!
...I DON'T THINK THAT'S GOING TO BE A PROBLEM.
AH! AGUMA-SAN...
B-BUT WHAT ABOUT LEARNING THE LINES AND THE CHOREOGRAPHED FIGHT SCENES?!
NAN
I'VE GOT THA
COVEREI
I'VE GOTTA GO UP THERE AND DO IT!
BRRR...CHILLY OUT HERE...
HE'S GONNA BE IN YOUR BODY! ALL YOU HAVE TO DO IS FOLLOW HIS DIRECTIONS, LIKE HE'S WHISPERING IN YOUR EAR!
BUT LET'S BE HONEST...

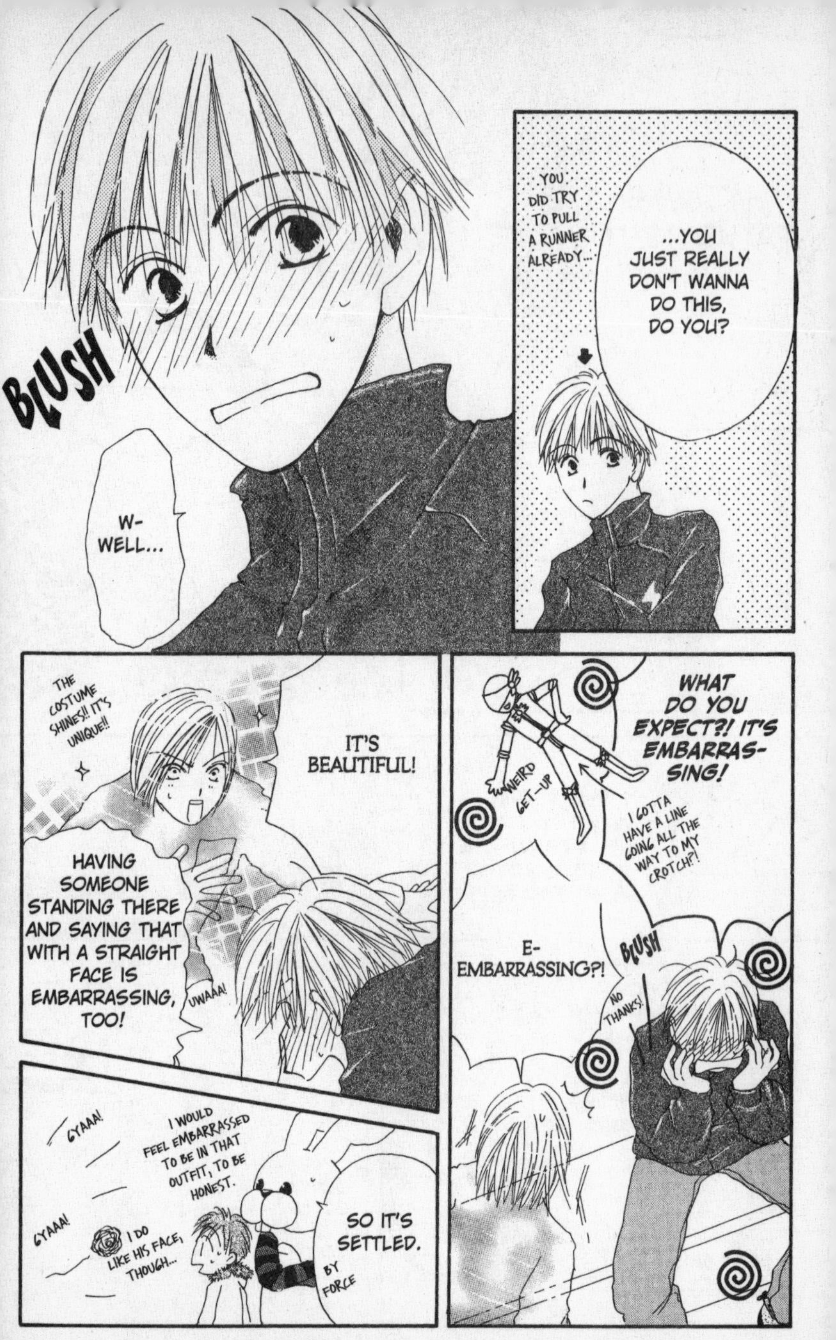
...YOU JUST REALLY DON'T WANNA DO THIS, DO YOU?
YOU DID TRY TO PULL A RUNNER ALREADY...
BLUSH
W-WELL...
WHAT DO YOU EXPECT?! IT'S EMBARRASSING!
WEIRD GET-UP
I GOTTA HAVE A LINE GOING ALL THE WAY TO MY CROTCH?!
E-EMBARRASSING?!
BLUSH
NO THANKS!
IT'S BEAUTIFUL!
THE COSTUME SHINES!! IT'S UNIQUE!!
HAVING SOMEONE STANDING THERE AND SAYING THAT WITH A STRAIGHT FACE IS EMBARRASSING, TOO!
UWAAA!
SO IT'S SETTLED.
BY FORCE
I WOULD FEEL EMBARRASSED TO BE IN THAT OUTFIT, TO BE HONEST.
GYAAA!
GYAAA!
I DO LIKE HIS FACE, THOUGH...

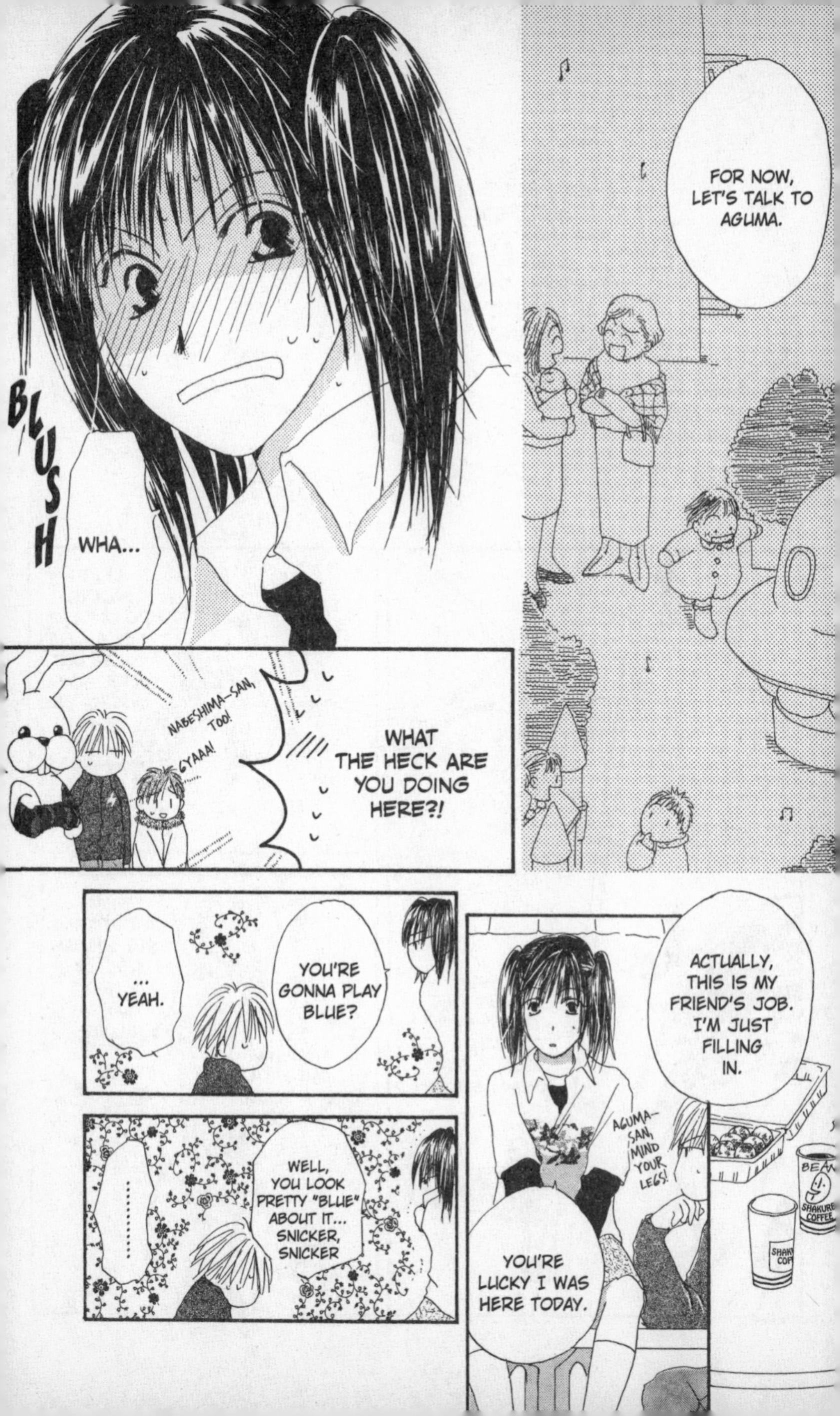
FOR NOW, LET'S TALK TO AGUMA.
BLUSH
WHA...
WHAT THE HECK ARE YOU DOING HERE?!
NABESHIMA-SAN, TOO!
GYAAA!
ACTUALLY, THIS IS MY FRIEND'S JOB. I'M JUST FILLING IN.
AGUMA-SAN, MIND YOUR LEGS!
SHAKURE COFFEE
YOU'RE LUCKY I WAS HERE TODAY.
YOU'RE GONNA PLAY BLUE?
... YEAH.
WELL, YOU LOOK PRETTY "BLUE" ABOUT IT... SNICKER, SNICKER
......

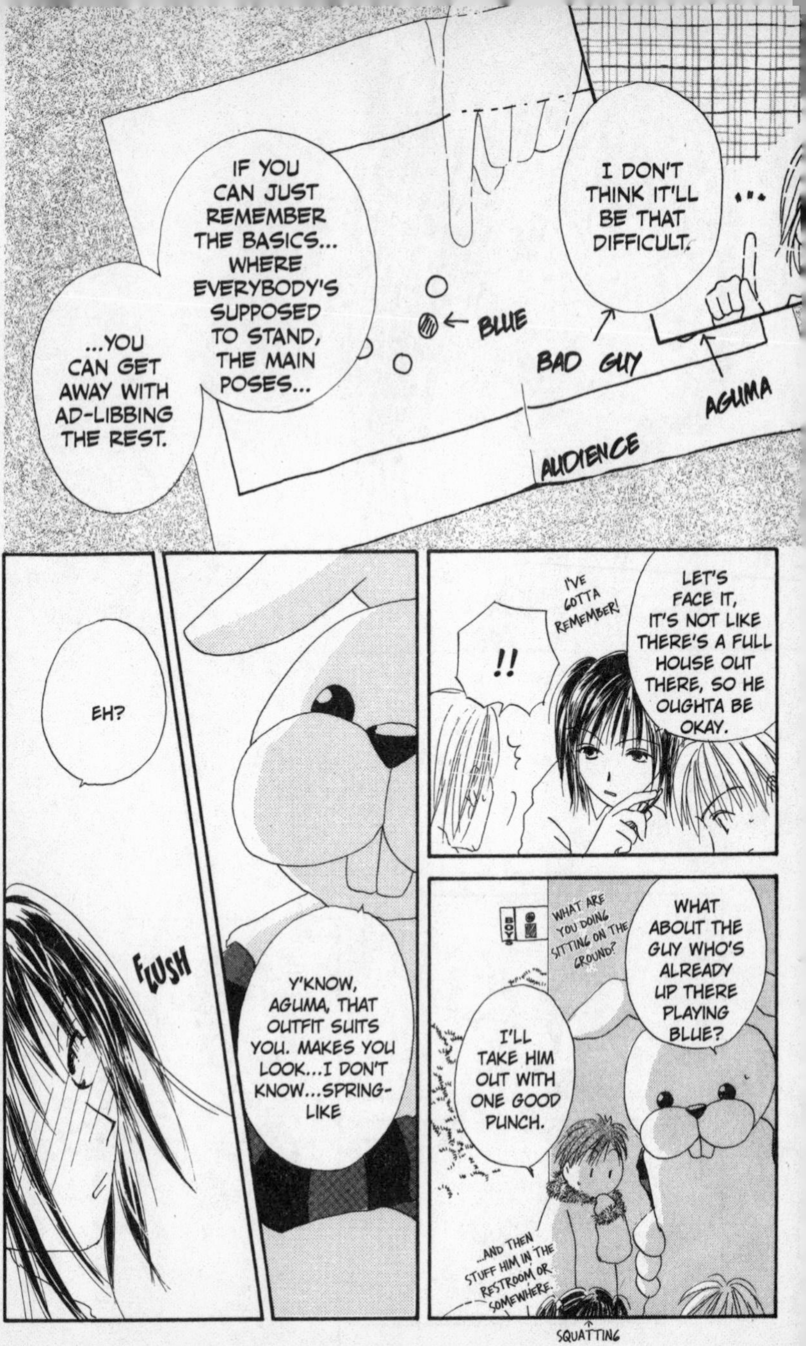
...
I DON'T THINK IT'LL BE THAT DIFFICULT.
BLUE
BAD GUY
AGUMA
AUDIENCE
IF YOU CAN JUST REMEMBER THE BASICS... WHERE EVERYBODY'S SUPPOSED TO STAND, THE MAIN POSES...
...YOU CAN GET AWAY WITH AD-LIBBING THE REST.
LET'S FACE IT, IT'S NOT LIKE THERE'S A FULL HOUSE OUT THERE, SO HE OUGHTA BE OKAY.
I'VE GOTTA REMEMBER!
!!
WHAT ABOUT THE GUY WHO'S ALREADY UP THERE PLAYING BLUE?
WHAT ARE YOU DOING SITTING ON THE GROUND?
BOYS
I'LL TAKE HIM OUT WITH ONE GOOD PUNCH.
...AND THEN STUFF HIM IN THE RESTROOM OR SOMEWHERE.
SQUATTING
Y'KNOW, AGUMA, THAT OUTFIT SUITS YOU. MAKES YOU LOOK...I DON'T KNOW...SPRING-LIKE
FLUSH
EH?

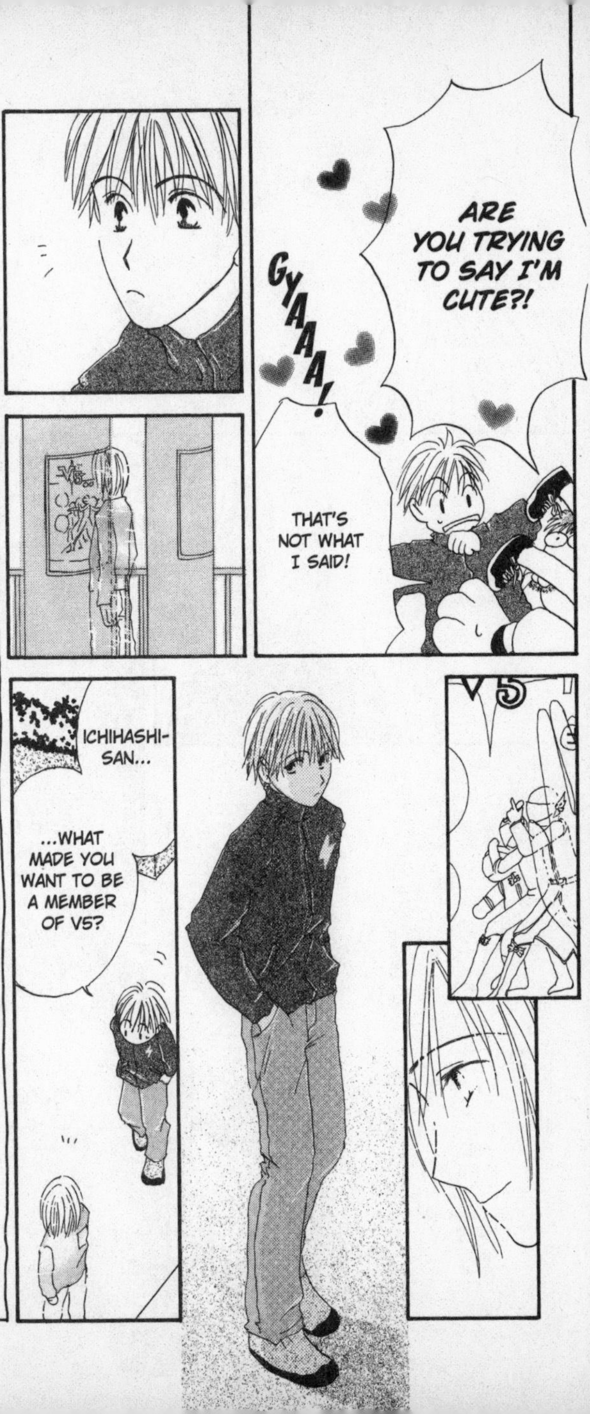
GYAAAA!
ARE YOU TRYING TO SAY I'M CUTE?!
THAT'S NOT WHAT I SAID!
ICHIHASHI-SAN...
...WHAT MADE YOU WANT TO BE A MEMBER OF V5?
V5

SIDEBAR!

****

HELLO, TANAKA HERE.

IN THIS SPACE FOR THE FIRST VOLUME, I DESCRIBED CREATING THIS MANGA AS NOT UNDER MY OWN POWER BUT LIKE I WAS BEING DRIVEN.

AND I DREW A LITTLE PICTURE OF A CART(?) TO SHOW THE SIMILE, BUT A FRIEND OF MINE SAID I SHOULD'VE DRAWN SOMETHING MORE LIKE I WAS RIDING SOMETHING REALLY FAST AND SHINY...

LIKE THIS?

LIKE I'M BEING POWERED UP BY A LUCKY SERIALIZED STORY CRAFT?

BUT IT LOOKS LIKE IT'S GOING SO FAST THAT I'D BE THROWN OFF.

EEEYAA!

...I'LL TRY TO WORK HARD.

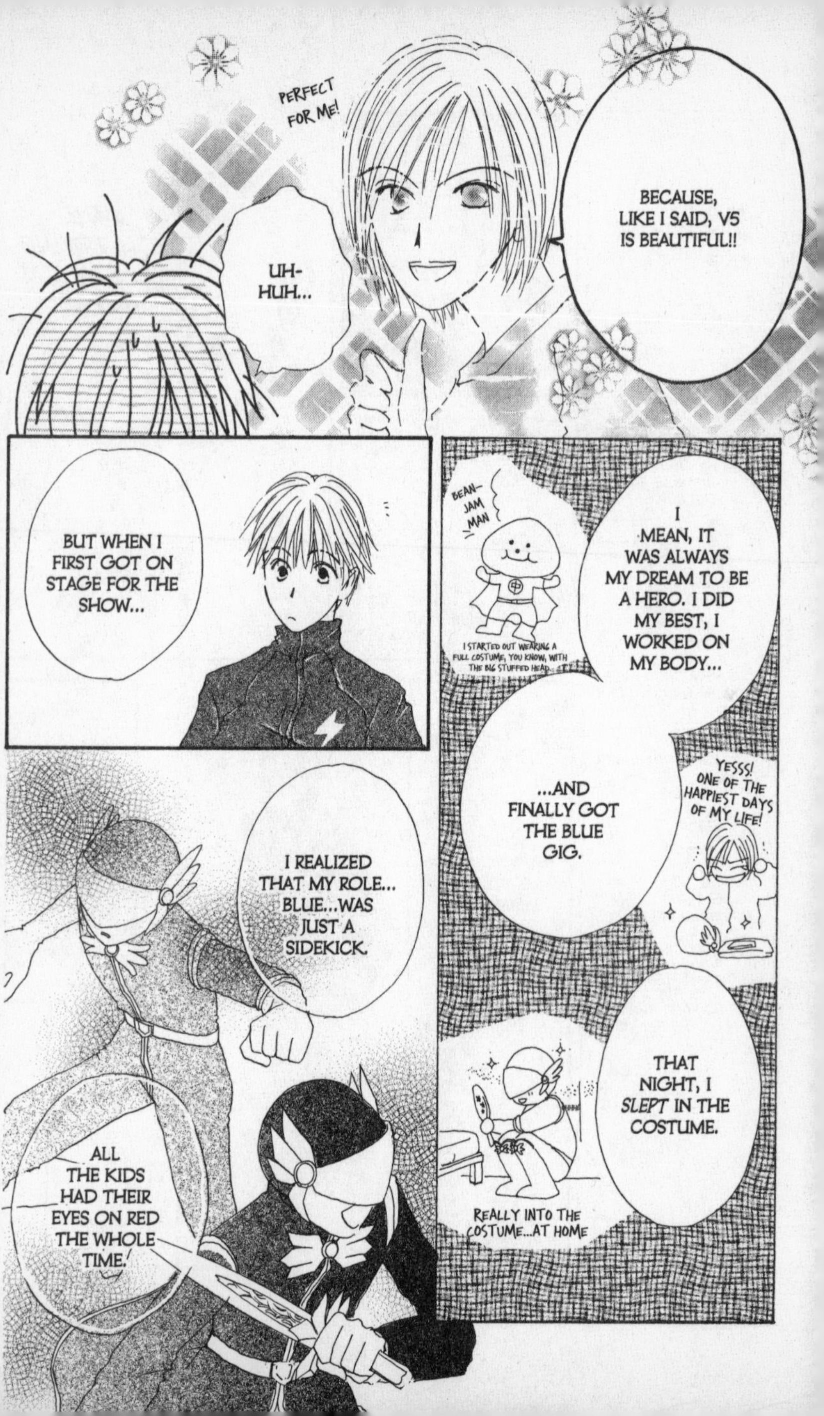
BECAUSE, LIKE I SAID, V5 IS BEAUTIFUL!!
PERFECT FOR ME!
UH-HUH...
I MEAN, IT WAS ALWAYS MY DREAM TO BE A HERO. I DID MY BEST, I WORKED ON MY BODY...
BEAN-JAM MAN
I STARTED OUT WEARING A FULL COSTUME, YOU KNOW, WITH THE BIG STUFFED HEAD.
...AND FINALLY GOT THE BLUE GIG.
YESSS! ONE OF THE HAPPIEST DAYS OF MY LIFE!
THAT NIGHT, I *SLEPT* IN THE COSTUME.
REALLY INTO THE COSTUME...AT HOME
BUT WHEN I FIRST GOT ON STAGE FOR THE SHOW...
I REALIZED THAT MY ROLE... BLUE...WAS JUST A SIDEKICK.
ALL THE KIDS HAD THEIR EYES ON RED THE WHOLE TIME.

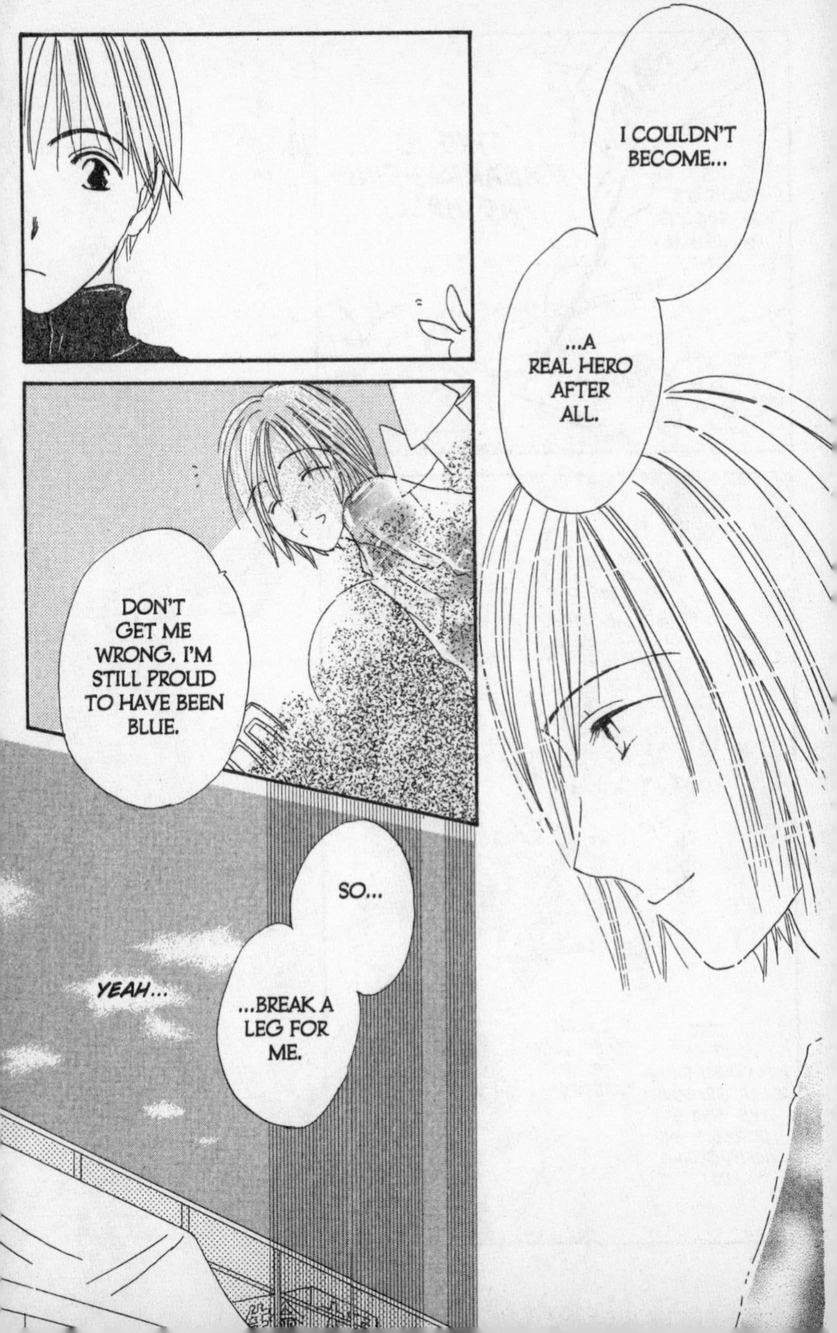
I COULDN'T BECOME...
...A REAL HERO AFTER ALL.
DON'T GET ME WRONG. I'M STILL PROUD TO HAVE BEEN BLUE.
SO...
...BREAK A LEG FOR ME.
YEAH...

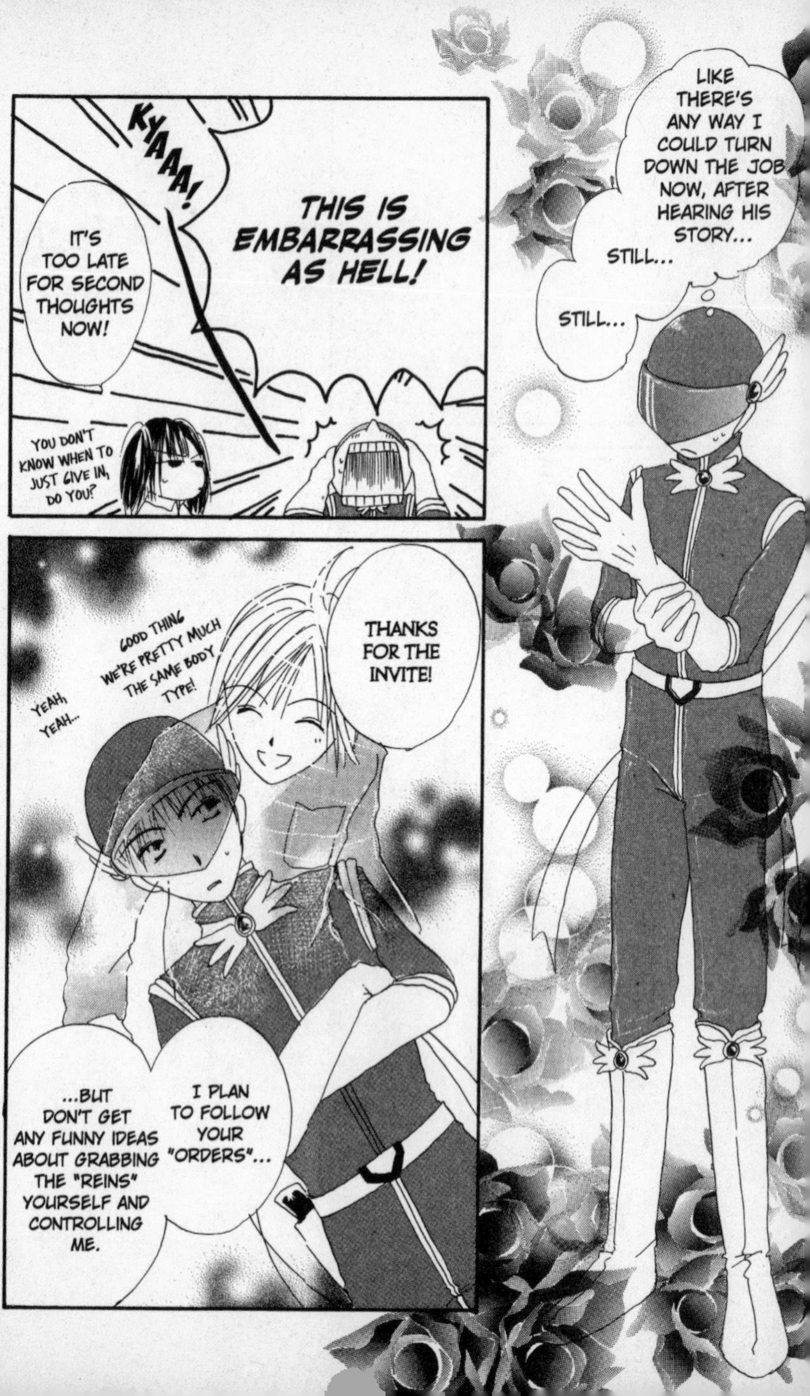
LIKE THERE'S ANY WAY I COULD TURN DOWN THE JOB NOW, AFTER HEARING HIS STORY...
STILL...
STILL...
KYAAAA!
THIS IS EMBARRASSING AS HELL!
IT'S TOO LATE FOR SECOND THOUGHTS NOW!
YOU DON'T KNOW WHEN TO JUST GIVE IN, DO YOU?
THANKS FOR THE INVITE!
GOOD THING WE'RE PRETTY MUCH THE SAME BODY TYPE!
YEAH, YEAH...
I PLAN TO FOLLOW YOUR "ORDERS"...
...BUT DON'T GET ANY FUNNY IDEAS ABOUT GRABBING THE "REINS" YOURSELF AND CONTROLLING ME.

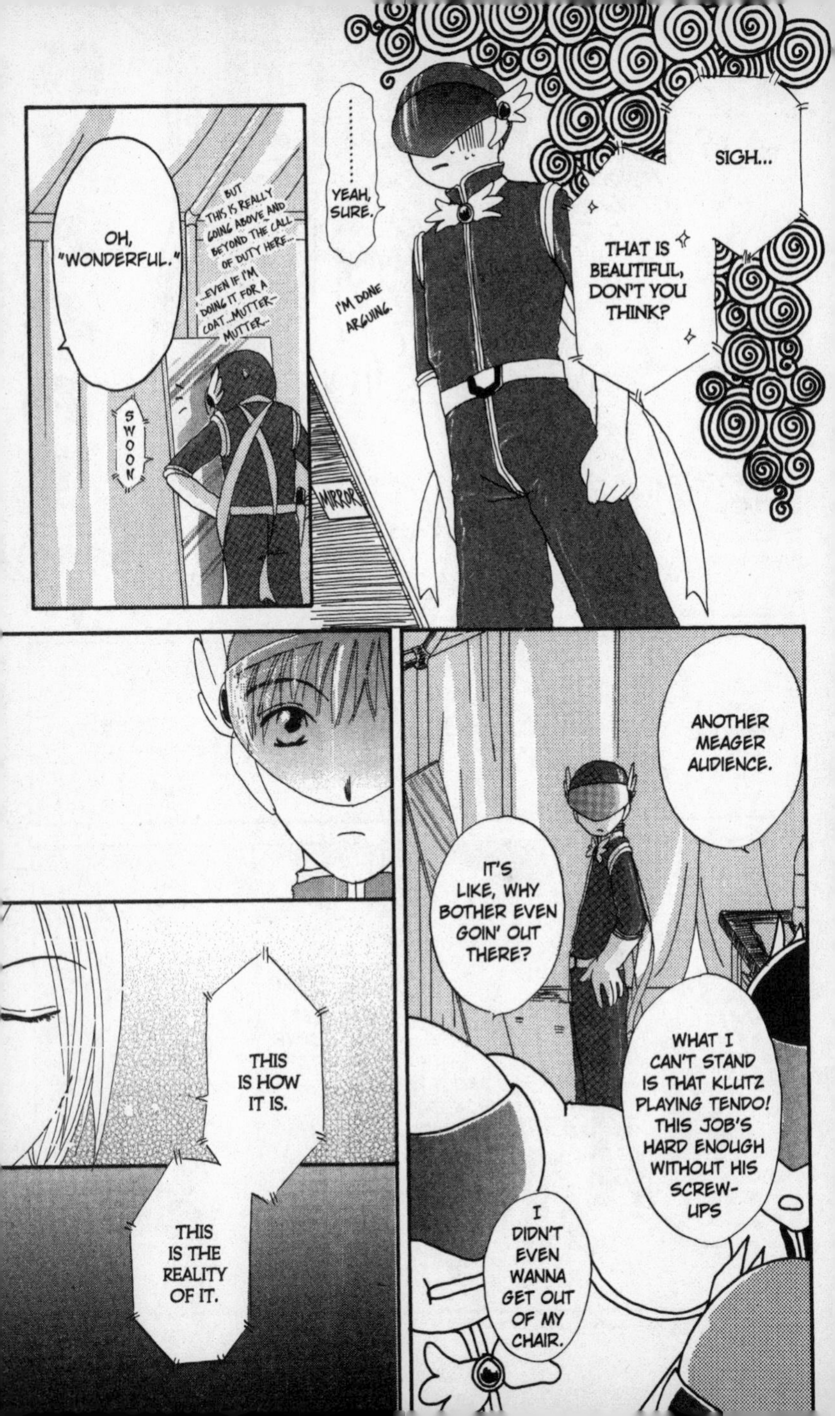

SIGH...
THAT IS BEAUTIFUL, DON'T YOU THINK?
......YEAH, SURE.
I'M DONE ARGUING.
OH, "WONDERFUL."
BUT THIS IS REALLY GOING ABOVE AND BEYOND THE CALL OF DUTY HERE...
...EVEN IF I'M DOING IT FOR A COAT...MUTTER-MUTTER...
SWOON
MIRROR
ANOTHER MEAGER AUDIENCE.
IT'S LIKE, WHY BOTHER EVEN GOIN' OUT THERE?
WHAT I CAN'T STAND IS THAT KLUTZ PLAYING TENDO! THIS JOB'S HARD ENOUGH WITHOUT HIS SCREW-UPS
I DIDN'T EVEN WANNA GET OUT OF MY CHAIR.
THIS IS HOW IT IS.
THIS IS THE REALITY OF IT.

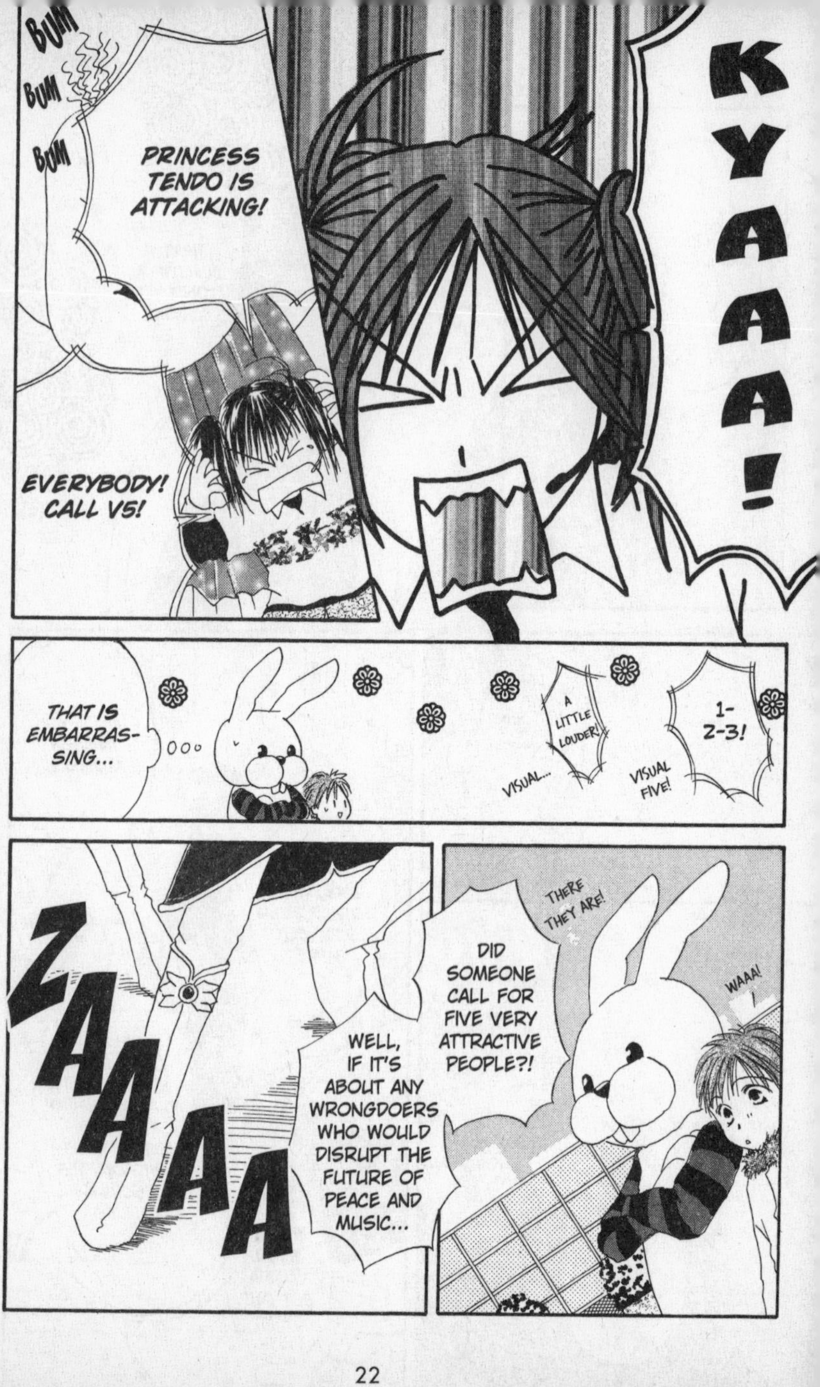
KYAAAA!
PRINCESS TENDO IS ATTACKING!
BUM
BUM
BUM
EVERYBODY! CALL V5!
1-2-3!
VISUAL FIVE!
A LITTLE LOUDER!
VISUAL...
THAT IS EMBARRAS-SING...
THERE THEY ARE!
WAAA!
DID SOMEONE CALL FOR FIVE VERY ATTRACTIVE PEOPLE?!
WELL, IF IT'S ABOUT ANY WRONGDOERS WHO WOULD DISRUPT THE FUTURE OF PEACE AND MUSIC...
ZAAAAA

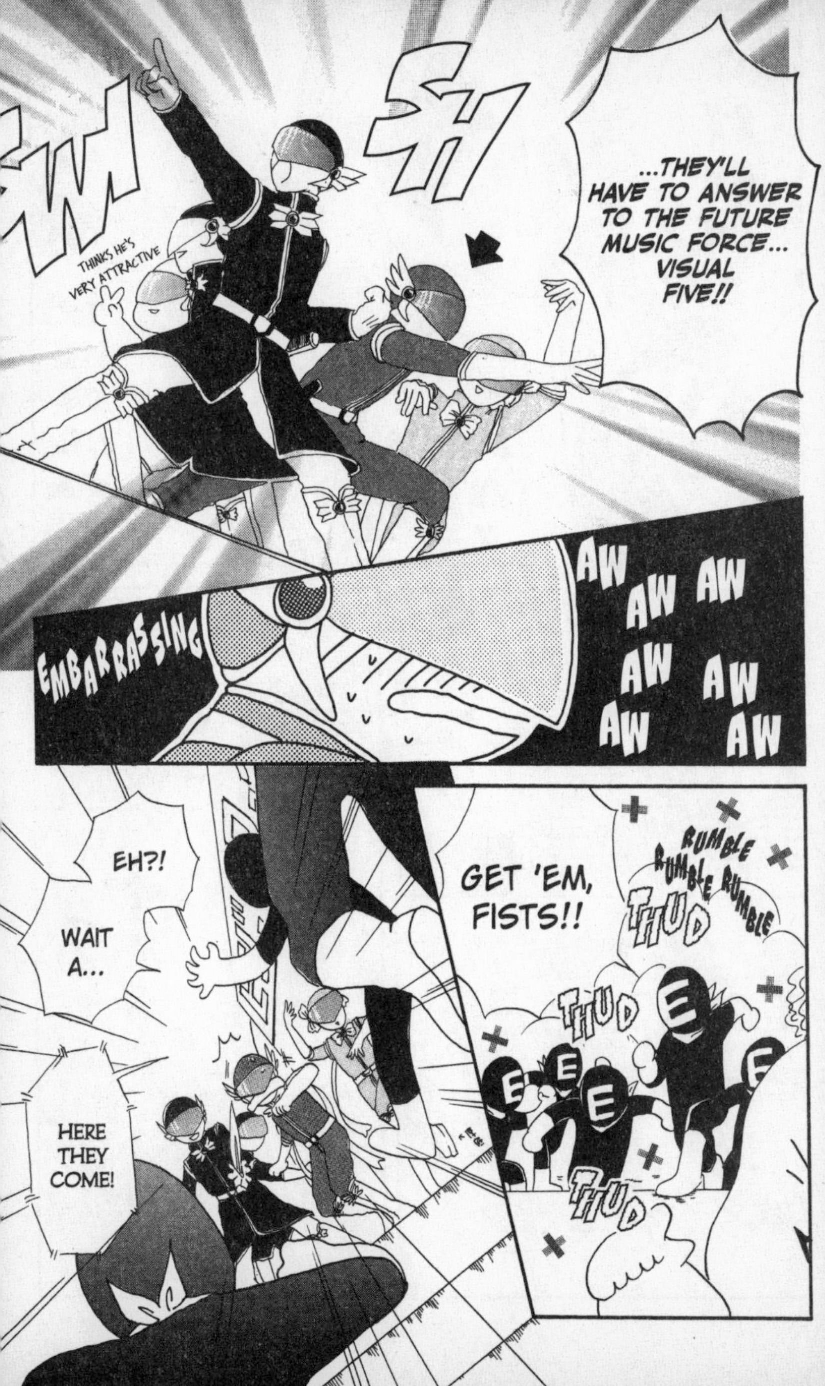
...THEY'LL HAVE TO ANSWER TO THE FUTURE MUSIC FORCE... VISUAL FIVE!!
SH
WM
THINKS HE'S VERY ATTRACTIVE
AW AW AW AW AW AW AW
EMBARRASSING
GET 'EM, FISTS!!
RUMBLE RUMBLE RUMBLE
THUD
THUD
THUD
EH?!
WAIT A...
HERE THEY COME!

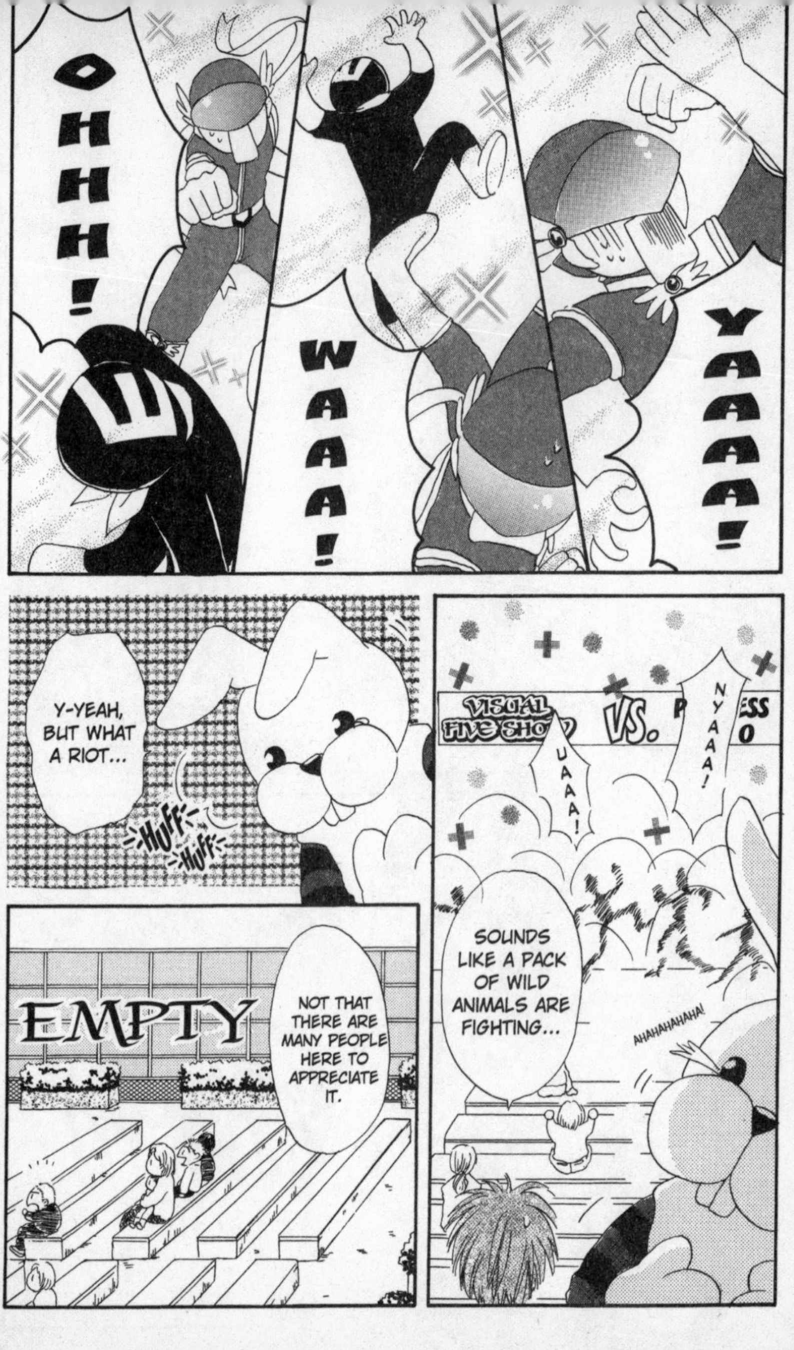

YAAAAA!
WAAAA!
OHHHH!
VISUAL FIVE SHO
VS.
NYAAAA!
UAAAA!
SOUNDS LIKE A PACK OF WILD ANIMALS ARE FIGHTING...
AHAHAHAHAHA!
Y-YEAH, BUT WHAT A RIOT...
HUFF HUFF
NOT THAT THERE ARE MANY PEOPLE HERE TO APPRECIATE IT.
EMPTY

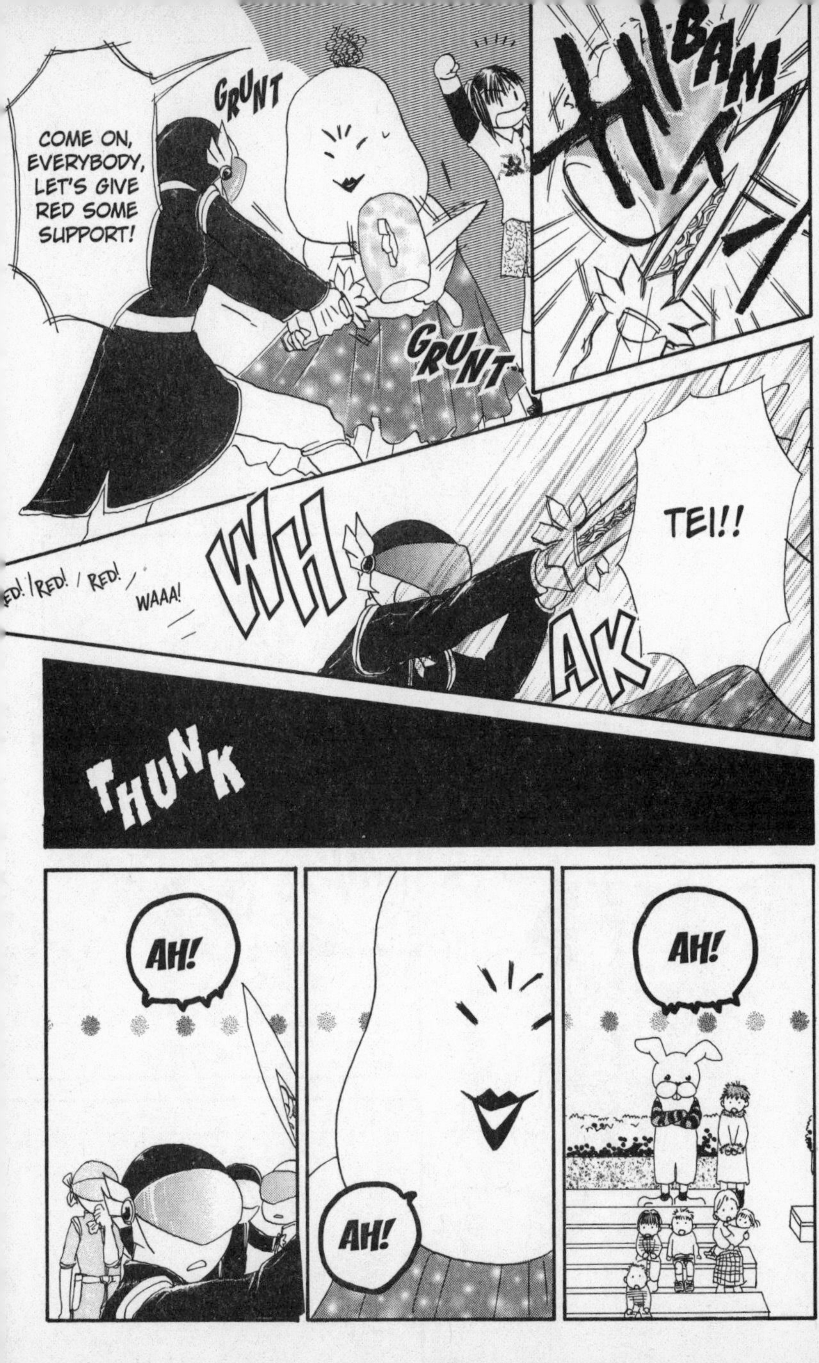
BAM
GRUNT
COME ON, EVERYBODY, LET'S GIVE RED SOME SUPPORT!
GRUNT
TEI!!
WH
AK
WAAA!
ED! RED! RED!
THUNK
AH!
AH!
AH!

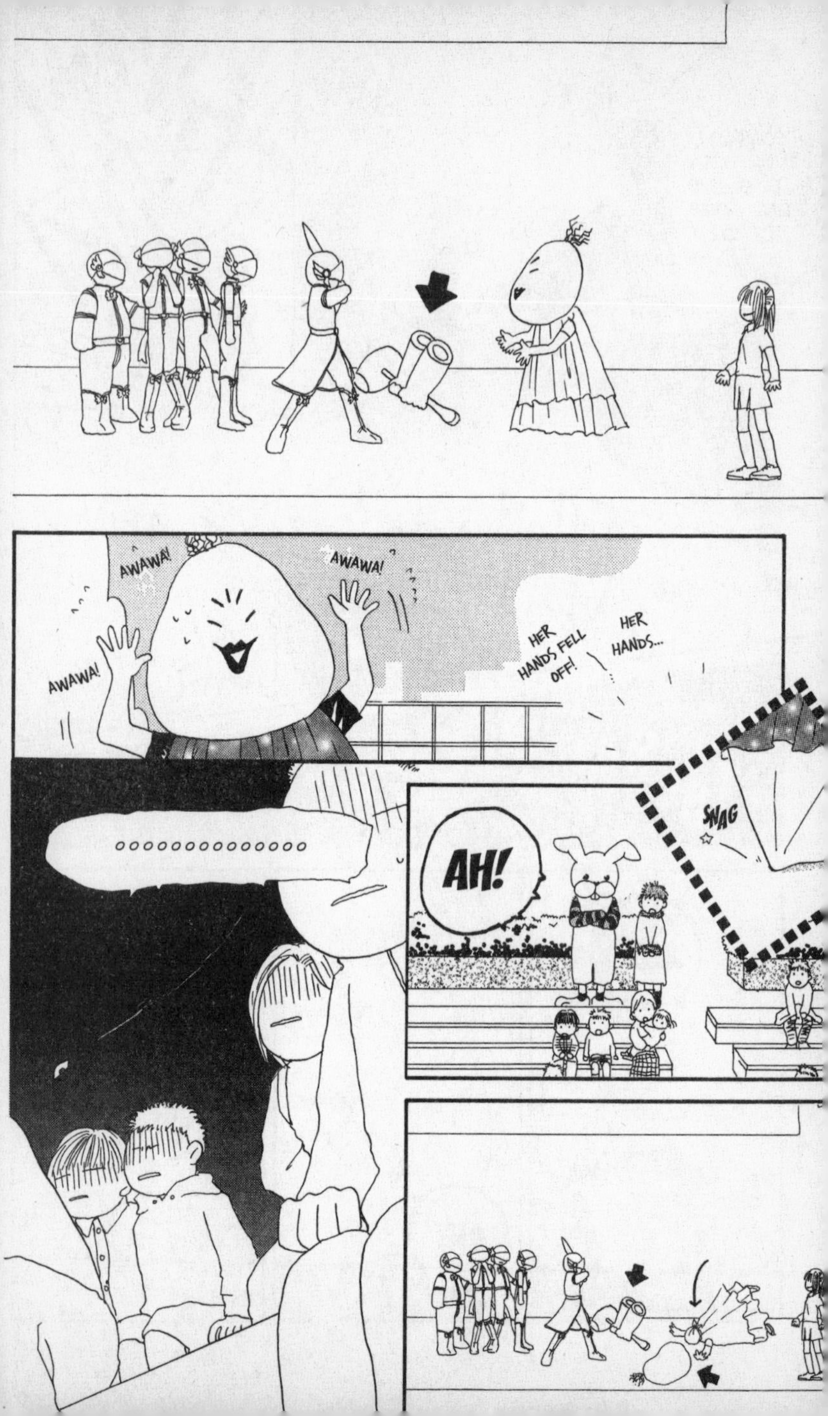

AWAWA!
AWAWA!
AWAWA!
HER HANDS...
HER HANDS FELL OFF!
SNAG
AH!
OOOOOOOOOOOOOO

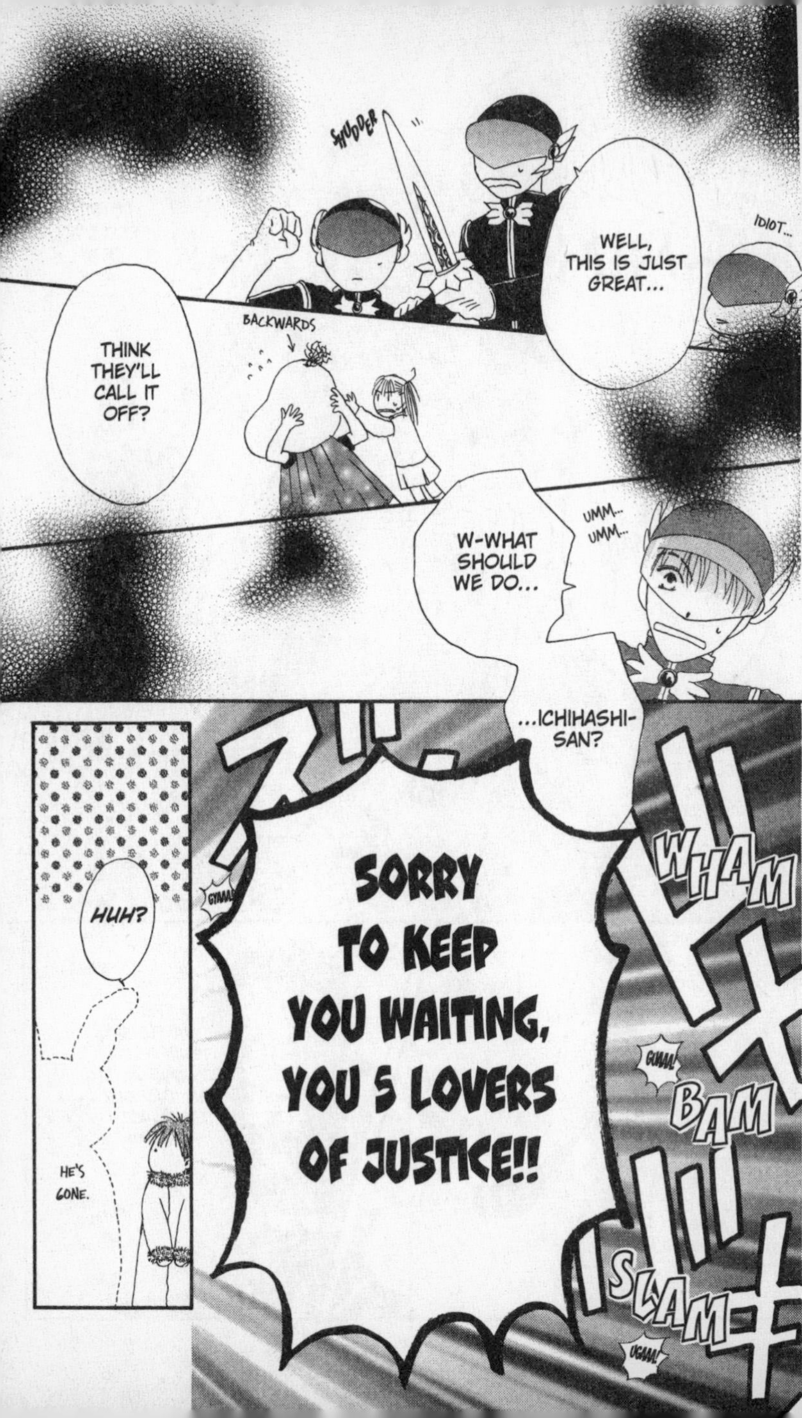
SHUDDER
IDIOT...
WELL, THIS IS JUST GREAT...
BACKWARDS
THINK THEY'LL CALL IT OFF?
UMM... UMM...
W-WHAT SHOULD WE DO...
...ICHIHASHI-SAN?
WHAM
GUAAA!
BAM
SLAM
UGAAA!
SORRY TO KEEP YOU WAITING, YOU 5 LOVERS OF JUSTICE!!
GYAAA!
HUH?
HE'S GONE.

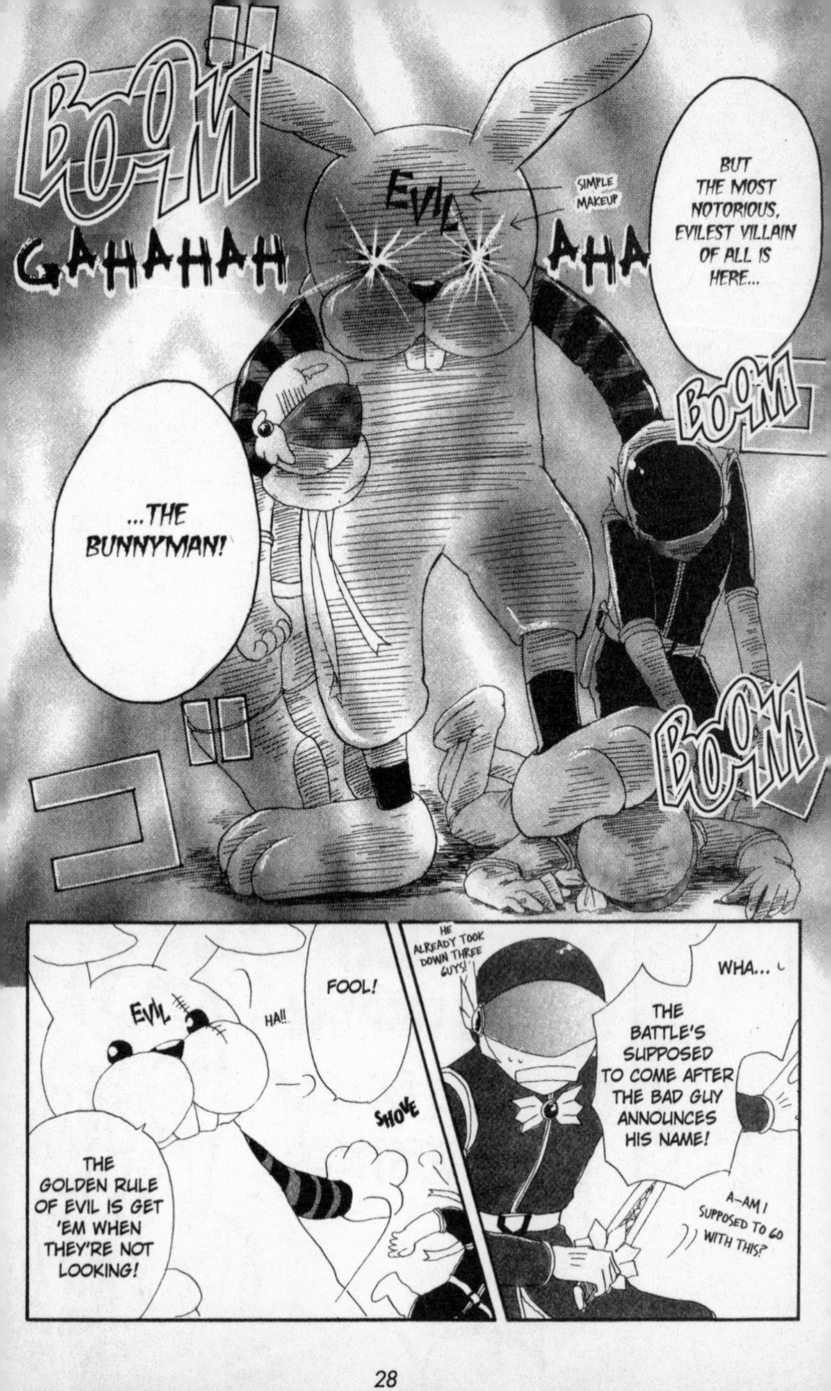
BOOM
GAHAHAH AHA
EVIL
SIMPLE MAKEUP
BUT THE MOST NOTORIOUS, EVILEST VILLAIN OF ALL IS HERE...
BOOM
BOOM
...THE BUNNYMAN!
WHA...
THE BATTLE'S SUPPOSED TO COME AFTER THE BAD GUY ANNOUNCES HIS NAME!
HE ALREADY TOOK DOWN THREE GUYS!
A-AM I SUPPOSED TO GO WITH THIS?
FOOL!
HA!!
EVIL
SHOVE
THE GOLDEN RULE OF EVIL IS GET 'EM WHEN THEY'RE NOT LOOKING!

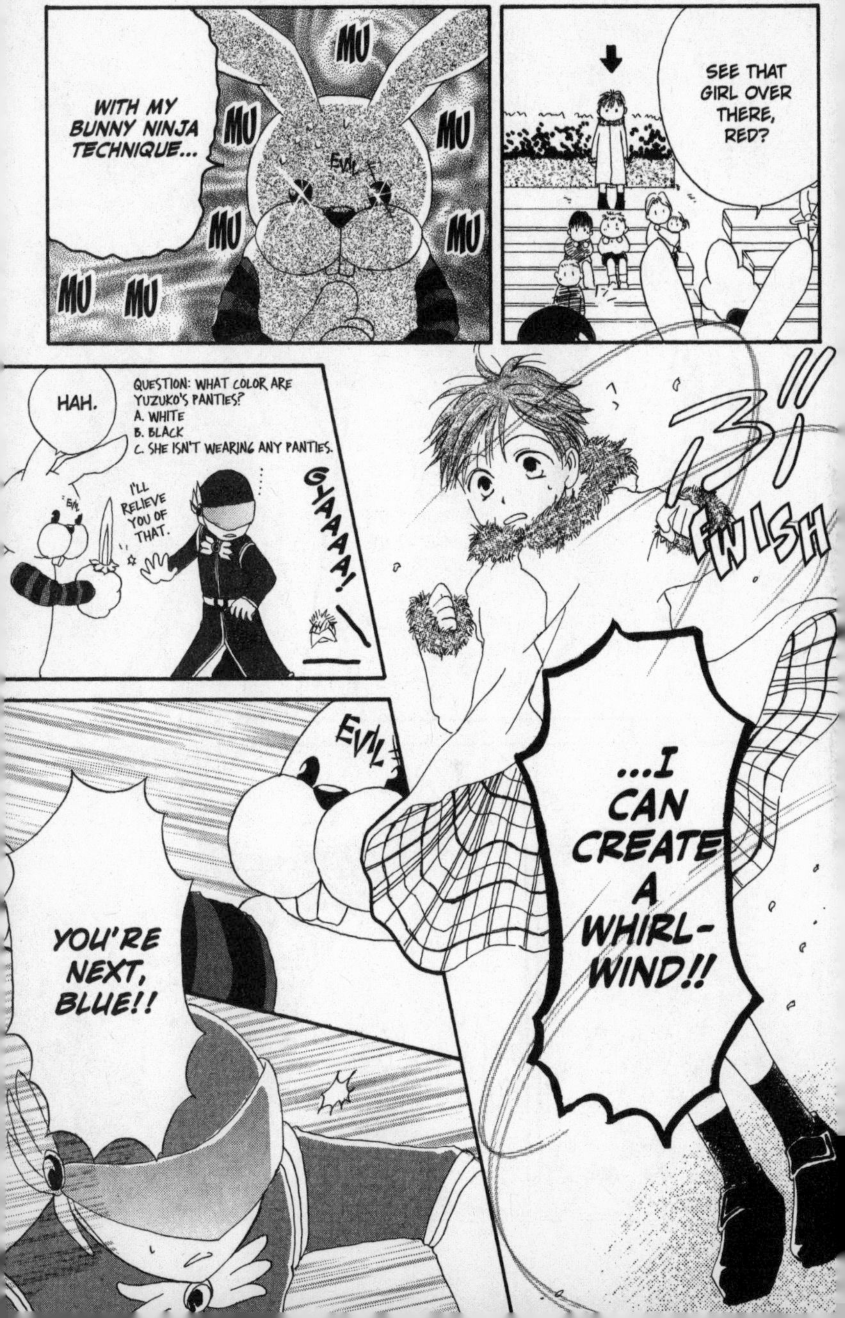
SEE THAT GIRL OVER THERE, RED?
WITH MY BUNNY NINJA TECHNIQUE...
MU MU MU MU MU MU MU MU
EVIL
FWISH
...I CAN CREATE A WHIRLWIND!!
GYAAAAA!
I'LL RELIEVE YOU OF THAT.
HAH.
QUESTION: WHAT COLOR ARE YUZUKO'S PANTIES?
A. WHITE
B. BLACK
C. SHE ISN'T WEARING ANY PANTIES.
EVIL
EVIL
YOU'RE NEXT, BLUE!!

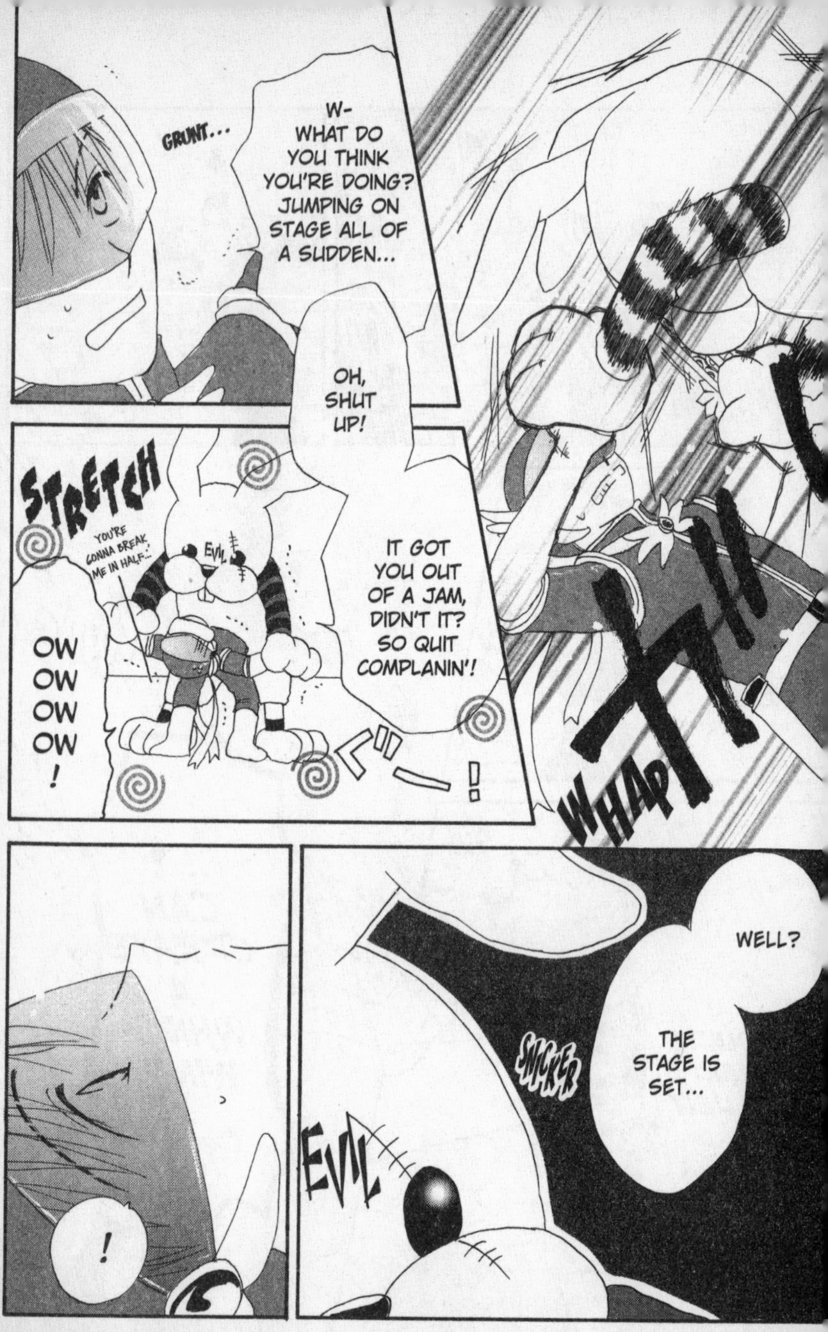
WHAP!!
GRUNT...
W-
WHAT DO YOU THINK YOU'RE DOING? JUMPING ON STAGE ALL OF A SUDDEN...
OH, SHUT UP!
IT GOT YOU OUT OF A JAM, DIDN'T IT? SO QUIT COMPLANIN'!
STRETCH
EVIL
YOU'RE GONNA BREAK ME IN HALF...
OW OW OW OW!
WELL?
THE STAGE IS SET...
SNICKER
EVIL
!

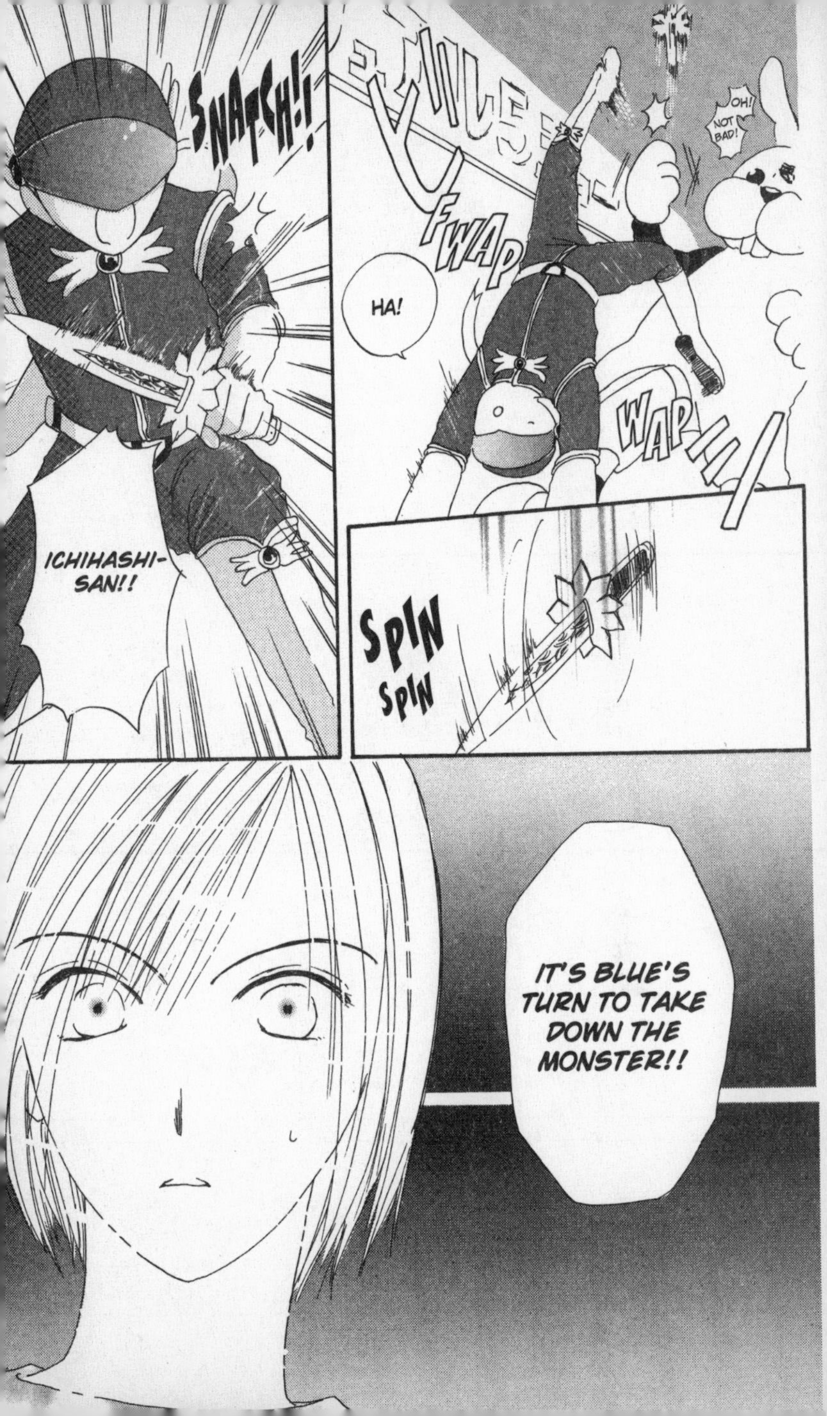

OH! NOT BAD!
FWAP
HA!
WAP
SNATCH!!
ICHIHASHI-SAN!!
SPIN
SPIN
IT'S BLUE'S TURN TO TAKE DOWN THE MONSTER!!

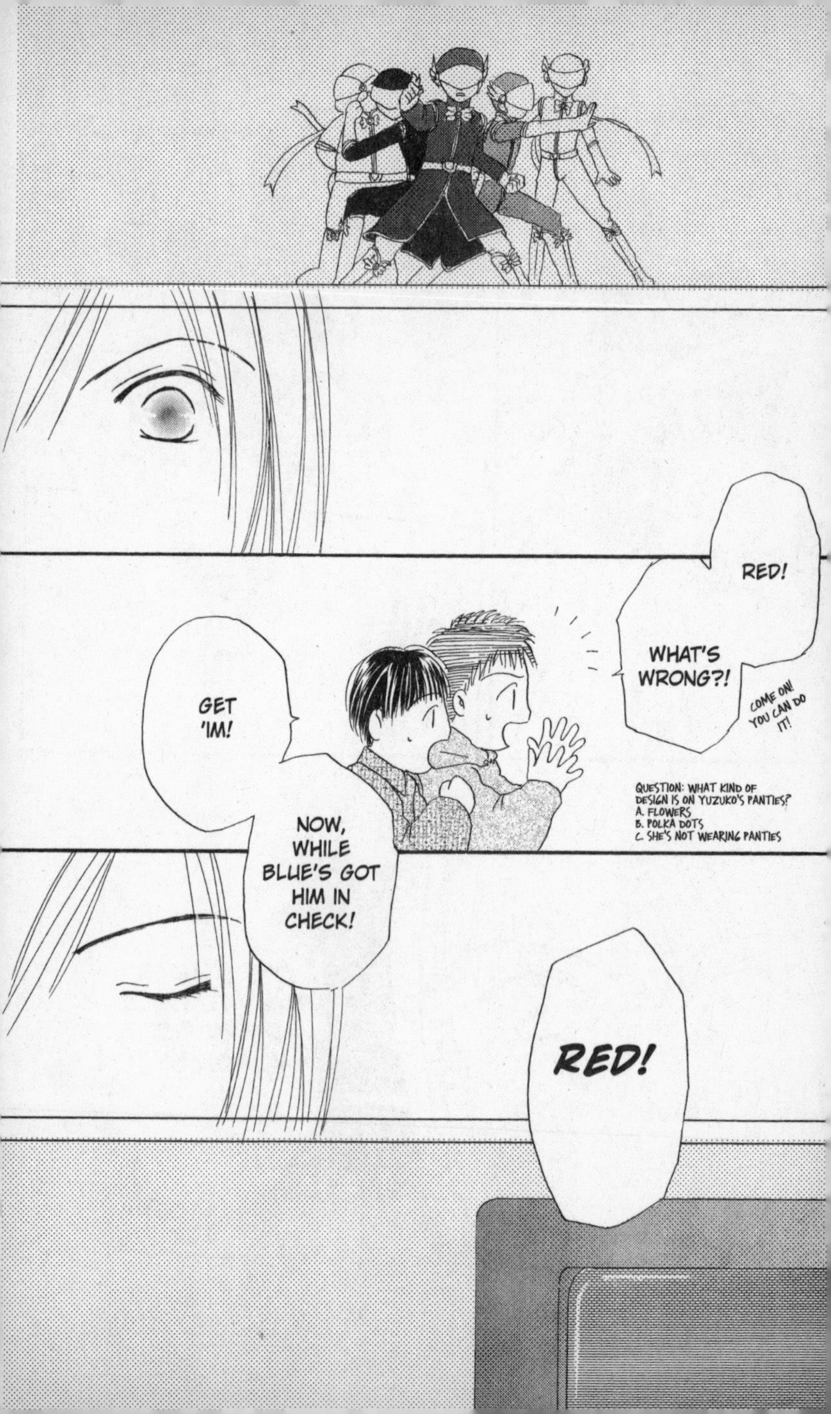
RED! WHAT'S WRONG?!
COME ON! YOU CAN DO IT!
GET 'IM!
NOW, WHILE BLUE'S GOT HIM IN CHECK!
QUESTION: WHAT KIND OF DESIGN IS ON YUZUKO'S PANTIES? A. FLOWERS B. POLKA DOTS C. SHE'S NOT WEARING PANTIES
RED!

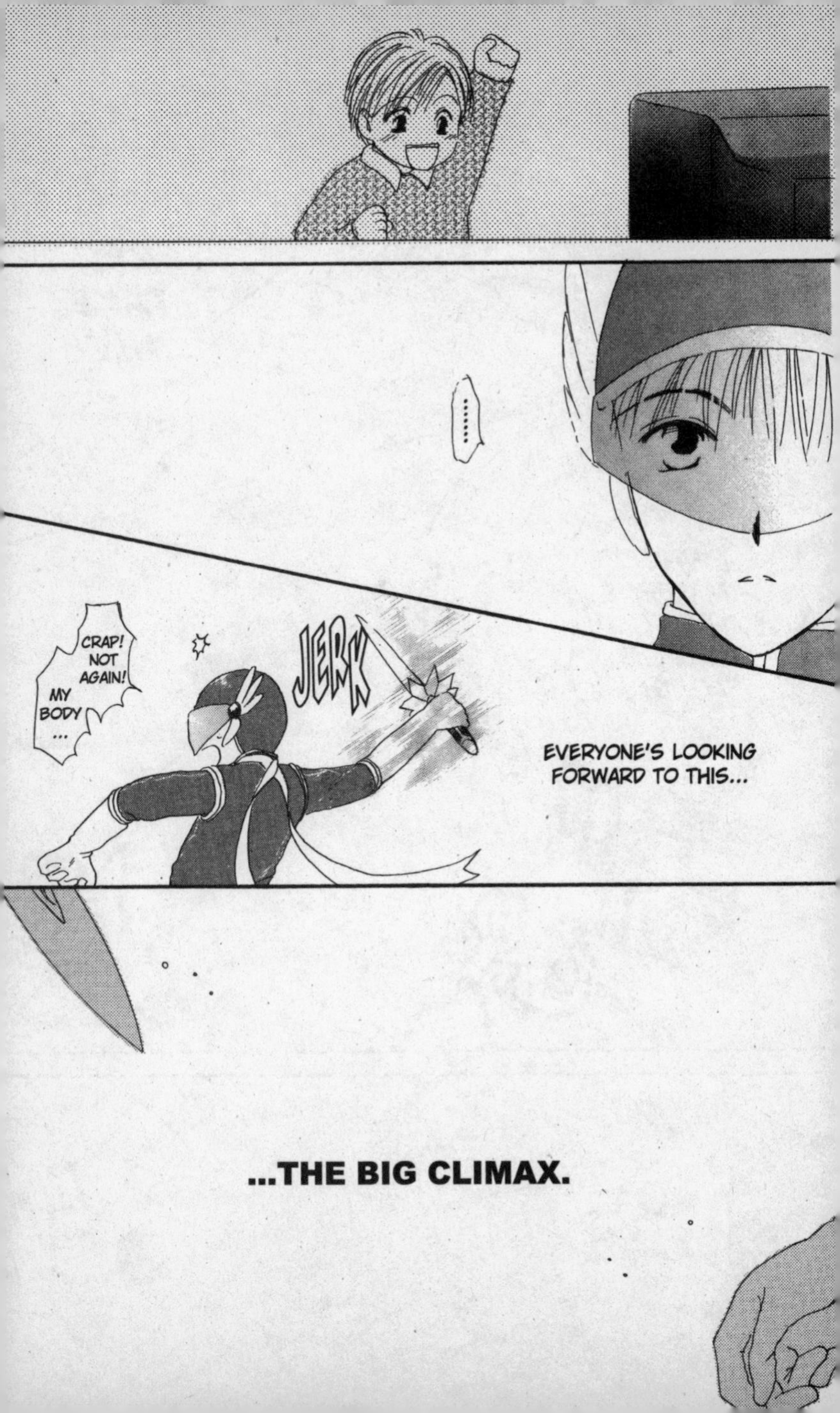
......
EVERYONE'S LOOKING FORWARD TO THIS...
JERK
CRAP! NOT AGAIN! MY BODY...
...THE BIG CLIMAX.

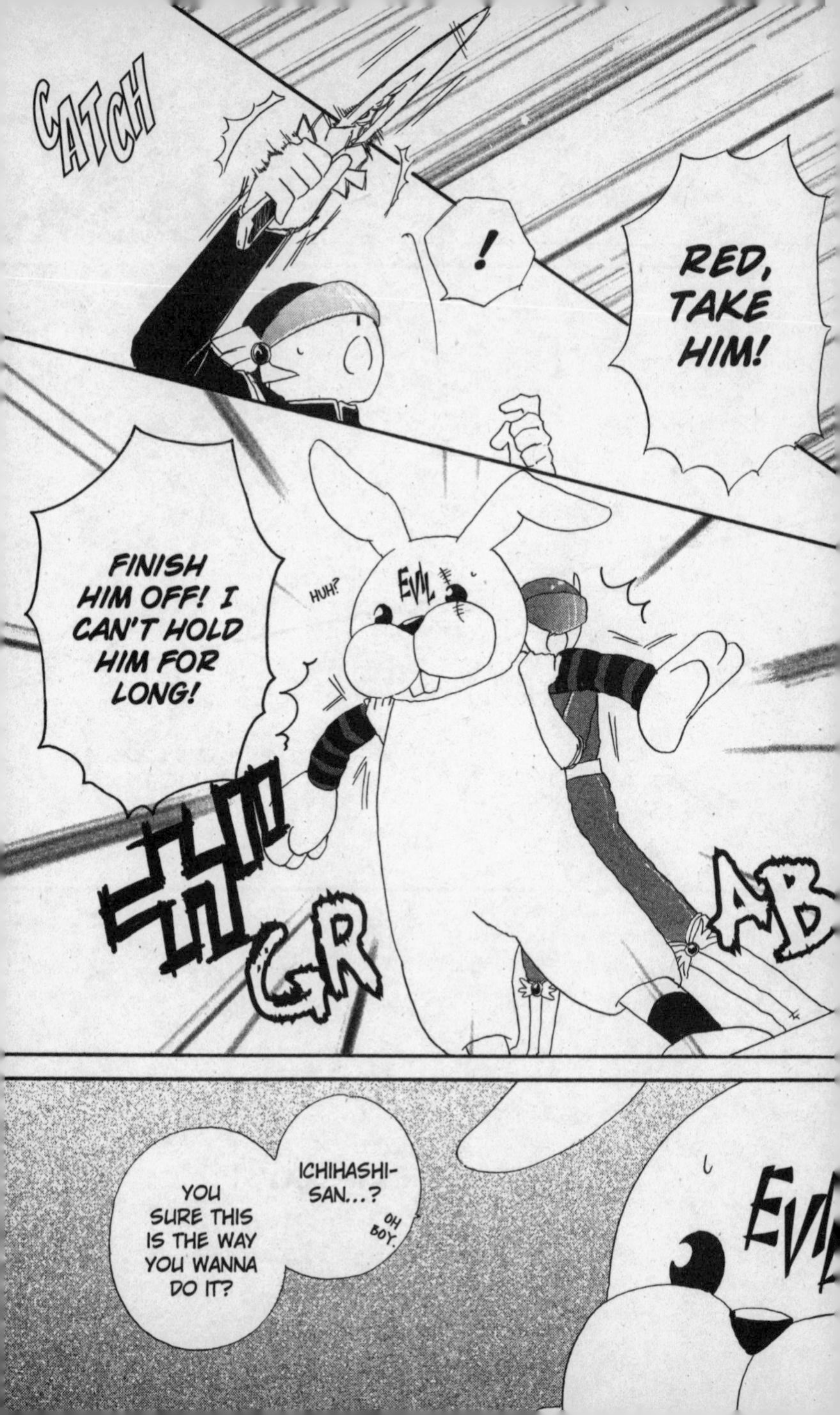
RED, TAKE HIM!
!
CATCH
EVIL
HUH?
FINISH HIM OFF! I CAN'T HOLD HIM FOR LONG!
AB
GR
ICHIHASHI-SAN...?
OH BOY.
YOU SURE THIS IS THE WAY YOU WANNA DO IT?
EVIL

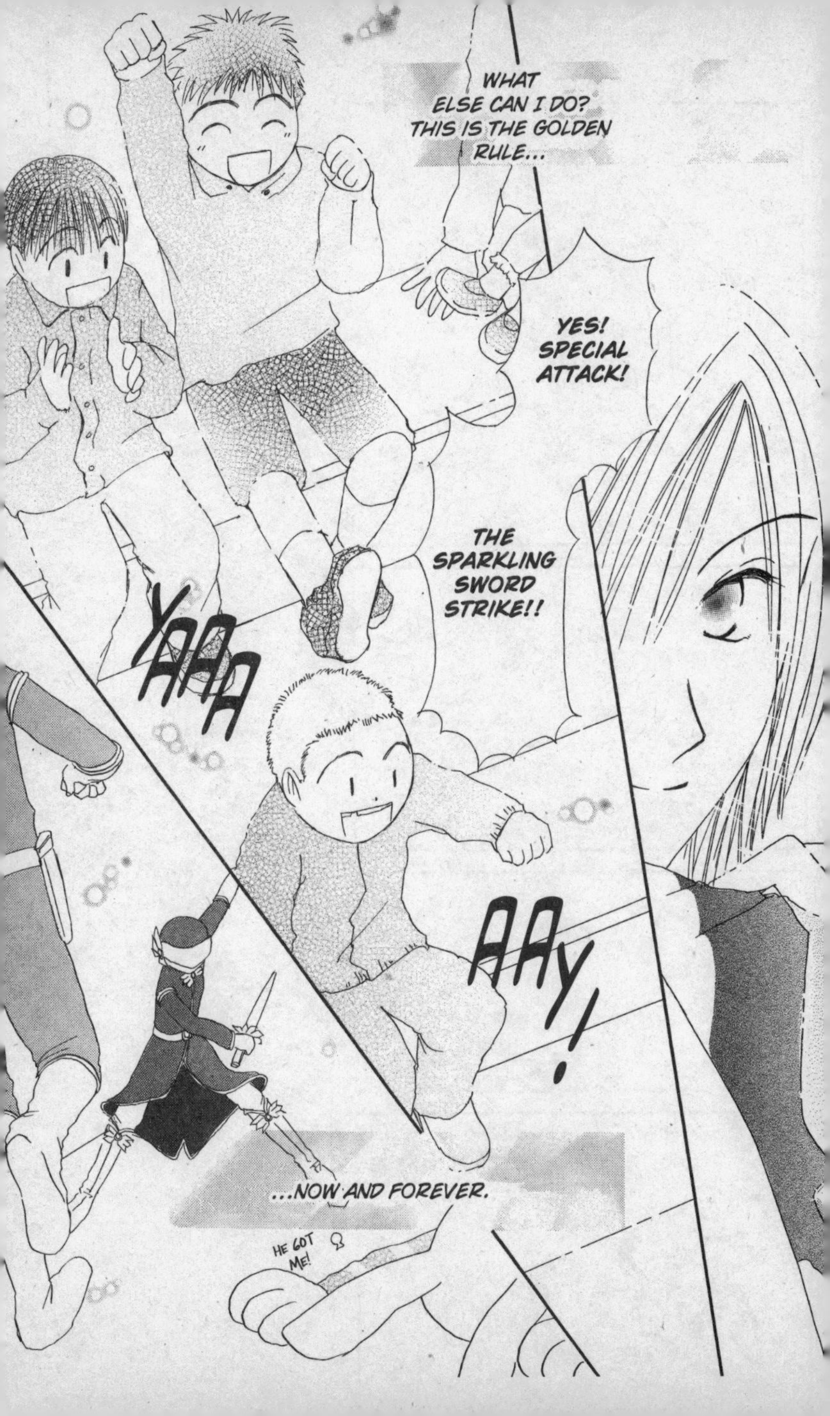
WHAT ELSE CAN I DO? THIS IS THE GOLDEN RULE...
YES! SPECIAL ATTACK!
THE SPARKLING SWORD STRIKE!!
YAAAA
AAY!
...NOW AND FOREVER.
HE GOT ME!

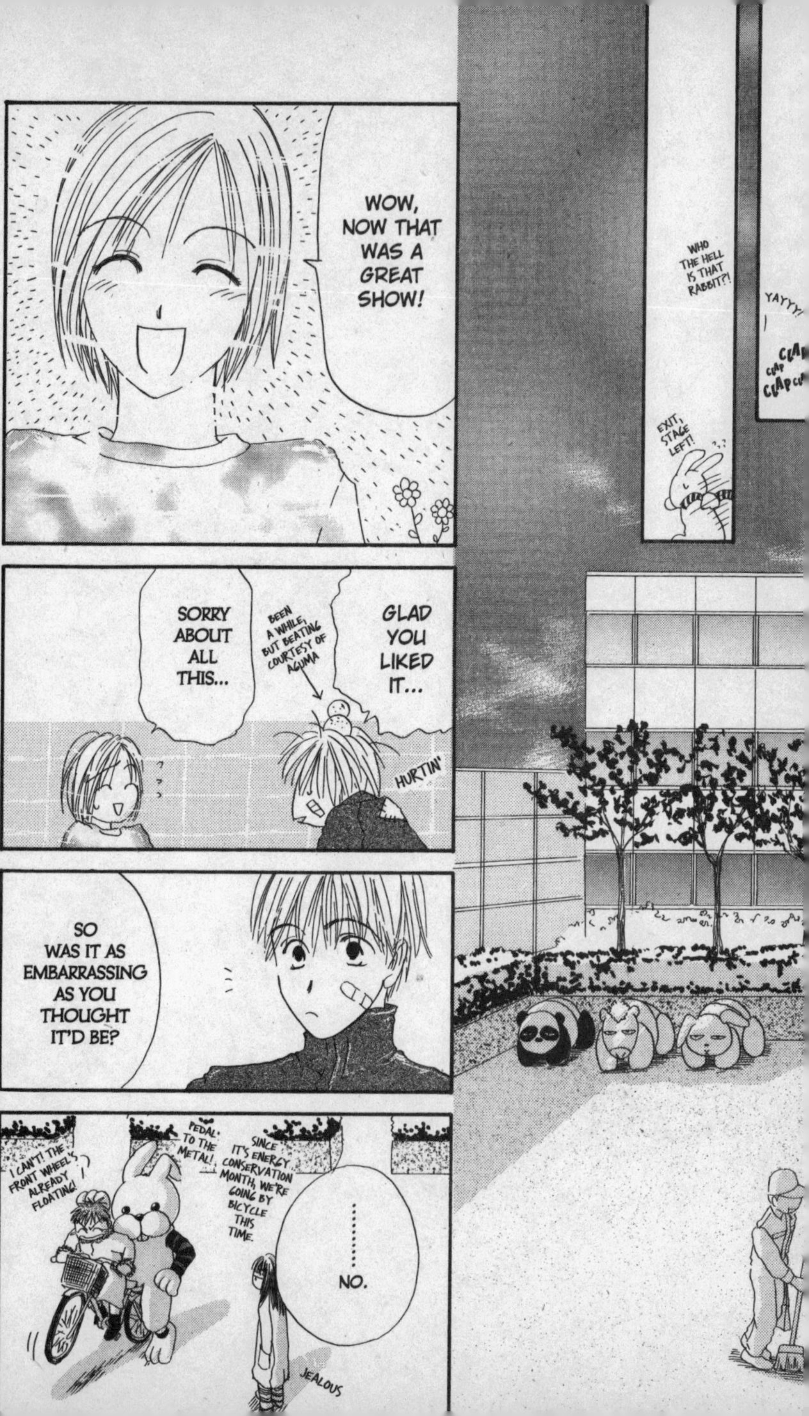
YAYYY!
CLAP CLAP CLAP CLAP
WHO THE HELL IS THAT RABBIT?!
EXIT, STAGE LEFT!
WOW, NOW THAT WAS A GREAT SHOW!
GLAD YOU LIKED IT...
BEEN A WHILE, BUT BEATING COURTESY OF AGUMA
HURTIN'
SORRY ABOUT ALL THIS...
SO WAS IT AS EMBARRASSING AS YOU THOUGHT IT'D BE?
......NO.
SINCE IT'S ENERGY CONSERVATION MONTH, WE'RE GOING BY BICYCLE THIS TIME.
PEDAL TO THE METAL!
I CAN'T! THE FRONT WHEEL'S ALREADY FLOATING!
JEALOUS

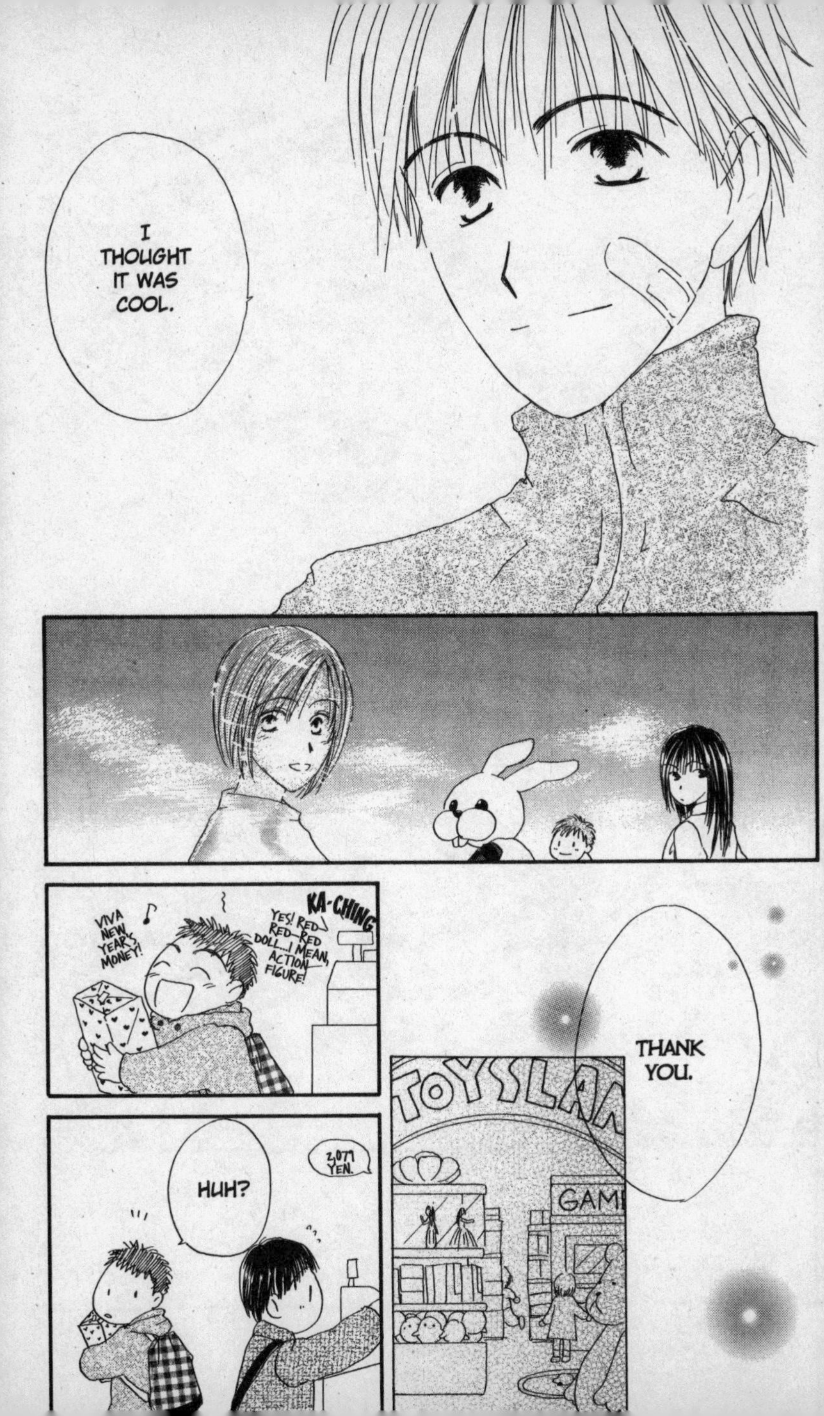
I THOUGHT IT WAS COOL.
THANK YOU.
TOYSLAN
GAM
KA-CHING
YES! RED-RED-RED DOLL...I MEAN, ACTION FIGURE!
VIVA NEW YEAR'S MONEY!
2,077 YEN.
HUH?

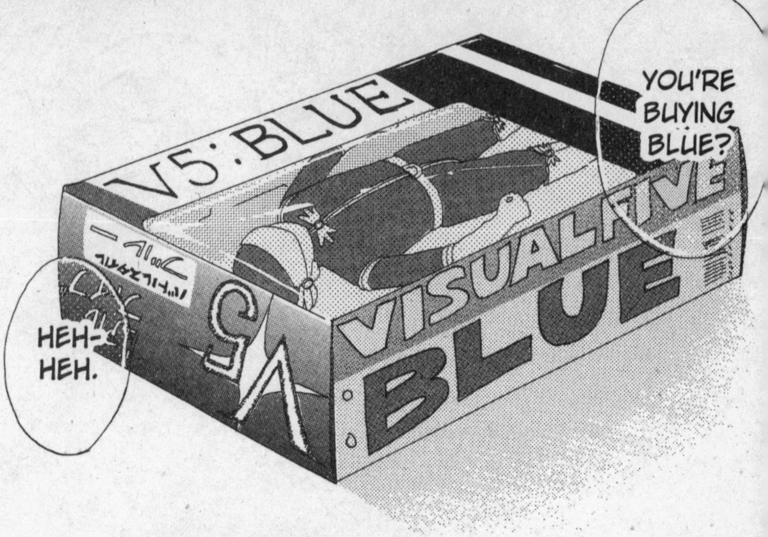
YOU'RE BUYING BLUE?
V5: BLUE
VISUALFIVE BLUE
V5
HEH-HEH.

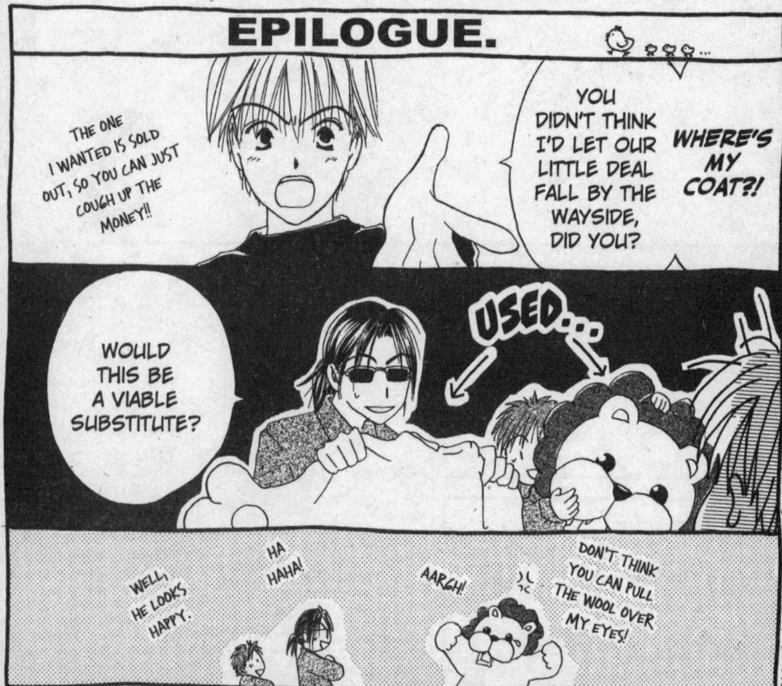
EPILOGUE.
YOU DIDN'T THINK I'D LET OUR LITTLE DEAL FALL BY THE WAYSIDE, DID YOU?
WHERE'S MY COAT?!
THE ONE I WANTED IS SOLD OUT, SO YOU CAN JUST COUGH UP THE MONEY!!
USED...
WOULD THIS BE A VIABLE SUBSTITUTE?
DON'T THINK YOU CAN PULL THE WOOL OVER MY EYES!
AARGH!
HA HAHA!
WELL, HE LOOKS HAPPY.

VERYVERY THANKS! → KAGAYA <BLACK> UZUKI, BISCO <PURPLE> HATORI, and JUNIOR HIGH SCHOOL YAMAMOTO

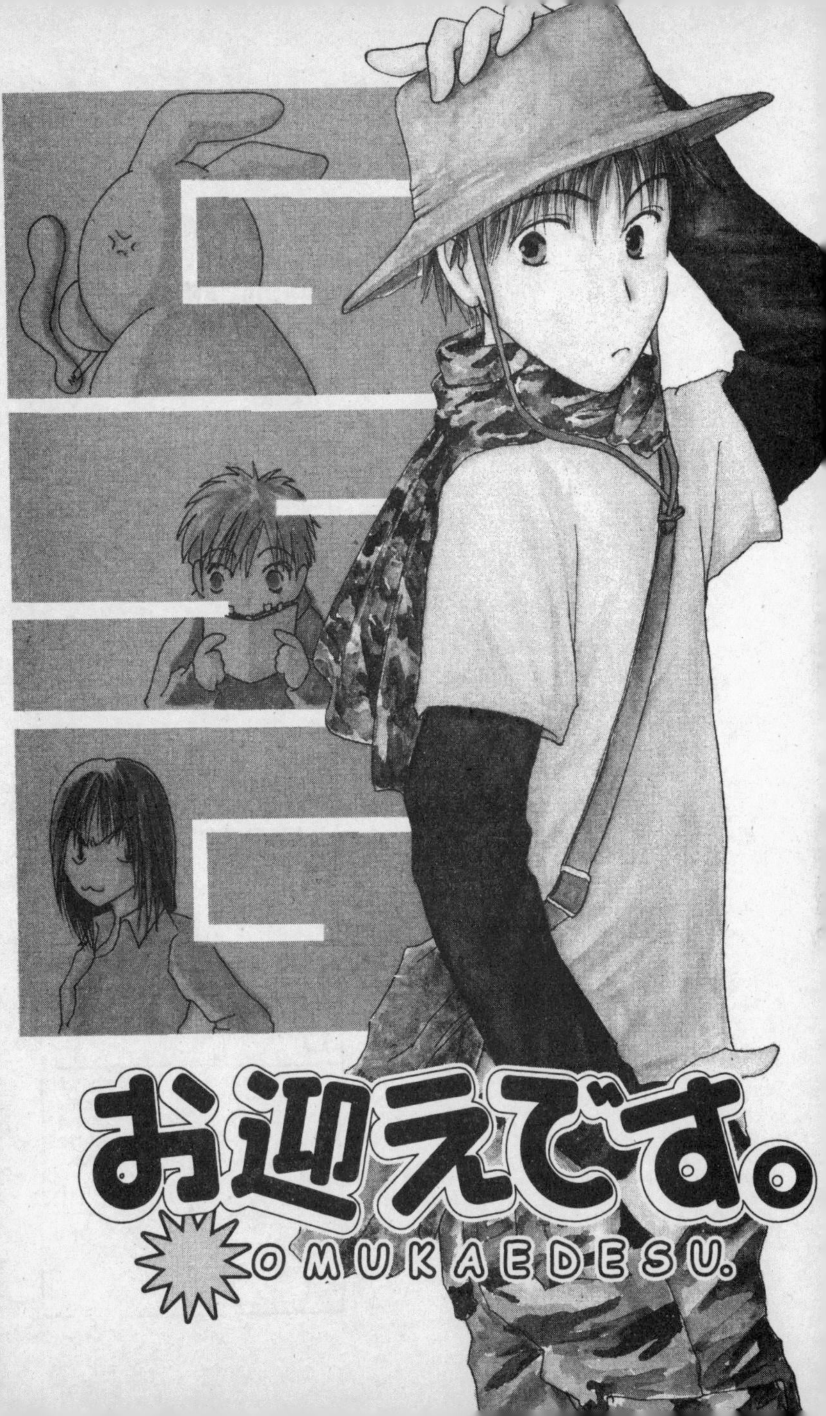
お迎えです。
OMUKAEDESU.

WANTED:
VARIOUS ANIMAL SUITS

"PIGEON"

AFTER SEEING SOMEONE'S REALISTIC DRAWINGS OF ONE OF THESE, IT LEFT A MAJOR IMPRESSION ON ME.

KON HACHIRO-SAN'S IDEA

SCARY

"SUMO MONTH"

THIS WOULD BE A REAL WINNER. CUTE! ♥

SAWADA RYOKO-SAN'S IDEA

MEATY

"MECA TANAKA"

• • • • • • •

NAGAHAMA NORIKO'S IDEA

YOU'RE NOT GONNA USE THIS ONE.

EH?! WHY NOT?

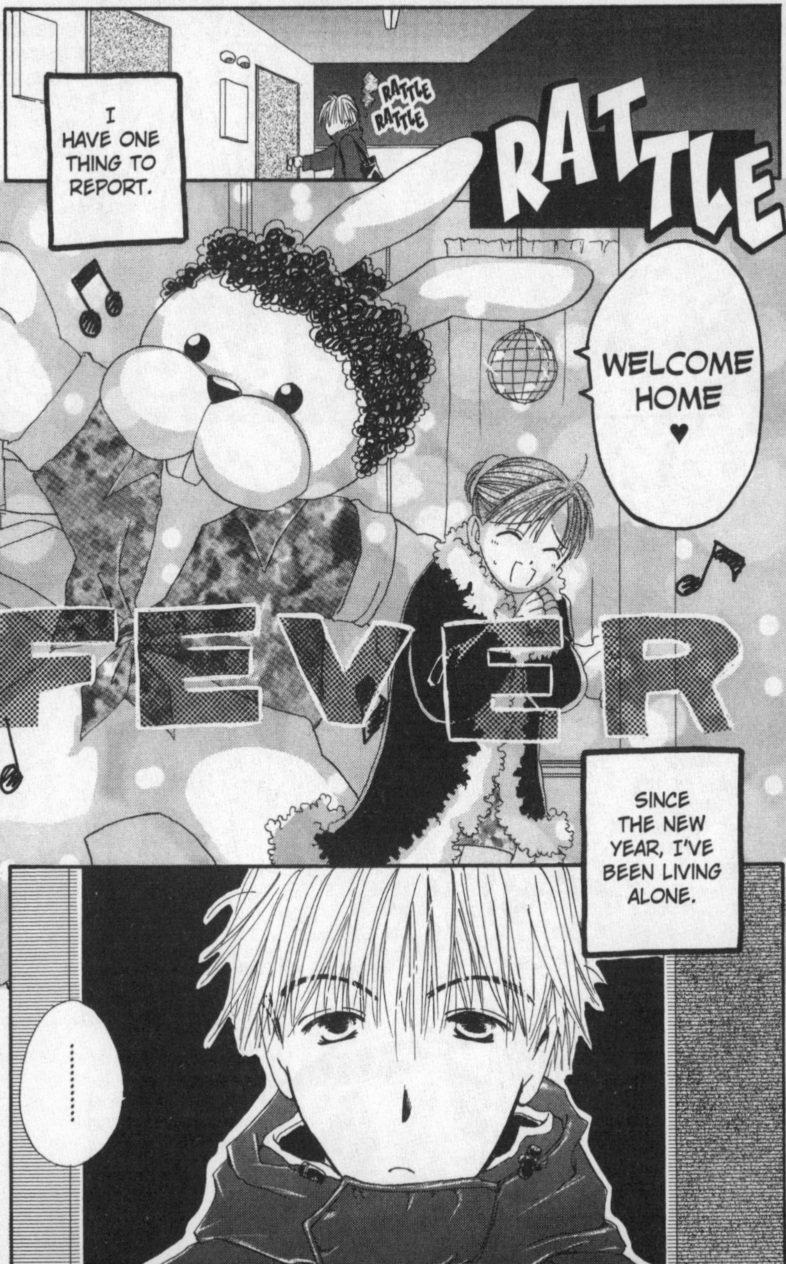
RATTLE RATTLE
I HAVE ONE THING TO REPORT.
RATTLE
WELCOME HOME ♥
FEVER
SINCE THE NEW YEAR, I'VE BEEN LIVING ALONE.
......

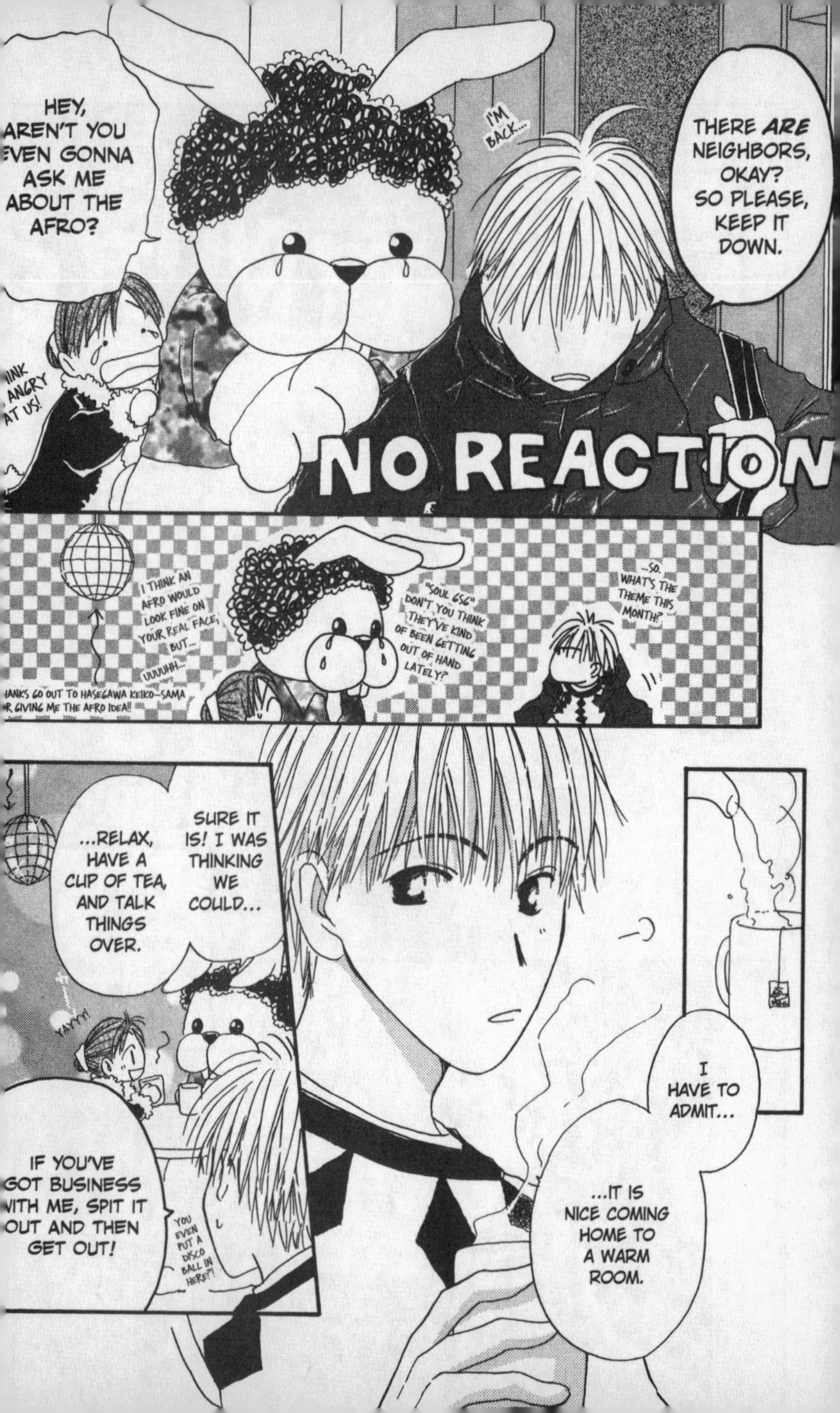
THERE ARE NEIGHBORS, OKAY? SO PLEASE, KEEP IT DOWN.
I'M BACK...
HEY, AREN'T YOU EVEN GONNA ASK ME ABOUT THE AFRO?
INK ANGRY AT US!
NO REACTION
...SO. WHAT'S THE THEME THIS MONTH?
"SOUL 656" DON'T YOU THINK THEY'VE KIND OF BEEN GETTING OUT OF HAND LATELY?
I THINK AN AFRO WOULD LOOK FINE ON YOUR REAL FACE, BUT...
UUUUHH...
HANKS GO OUT TO HASEGAWA KEIKO-SAMA OR GIVING ME THE AFRO IDEA!!
I HAVE TO ADMIT...
...IT IS NICE COMING HOME TO A WARM ROOM.
SURE IT IS! I WAS THINKING WE COULD...
...RELAX, HAVE A CUP OF TEA, AND TALK THINGS OVER.
YAYYY!
IF YOU'VE GOT BUSINESS WITH ME, SPIT IT OUT AND THEN GET OUT!
YOU EVEN PUT A DISCO BALL IN HERE?!

SUSPICIOUS

****

SINCE COMING OUT WITH THIS MANGA, I'VE BEEN DELUGED BY THE SAME QUESTION FROM READERS, NAMELY: "MECA TANAKA, ARE YOU A MAN OR A WOMAN?"

...CAN'T YOU TELL?...

LOOK AT THIS FACE.

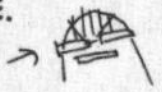

I GUESS I'D BETTER BE CLEAR ON THIS POINT... HEH-HEH-HEH... ACTUALLY, TANAKA MECA IS A...

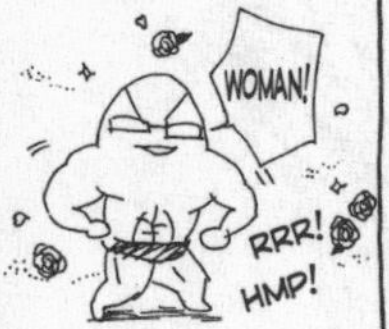
WOMAN!
RRR!
HMP!

I LOVE PRO WRESTLING AND SHOJO MANGA

...NO, REALLY, I AM A WOMAN.

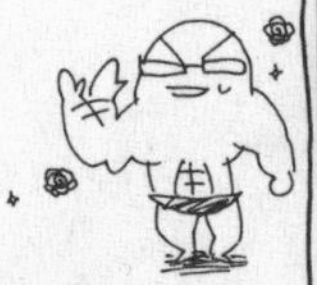

I'M NOT LYING!

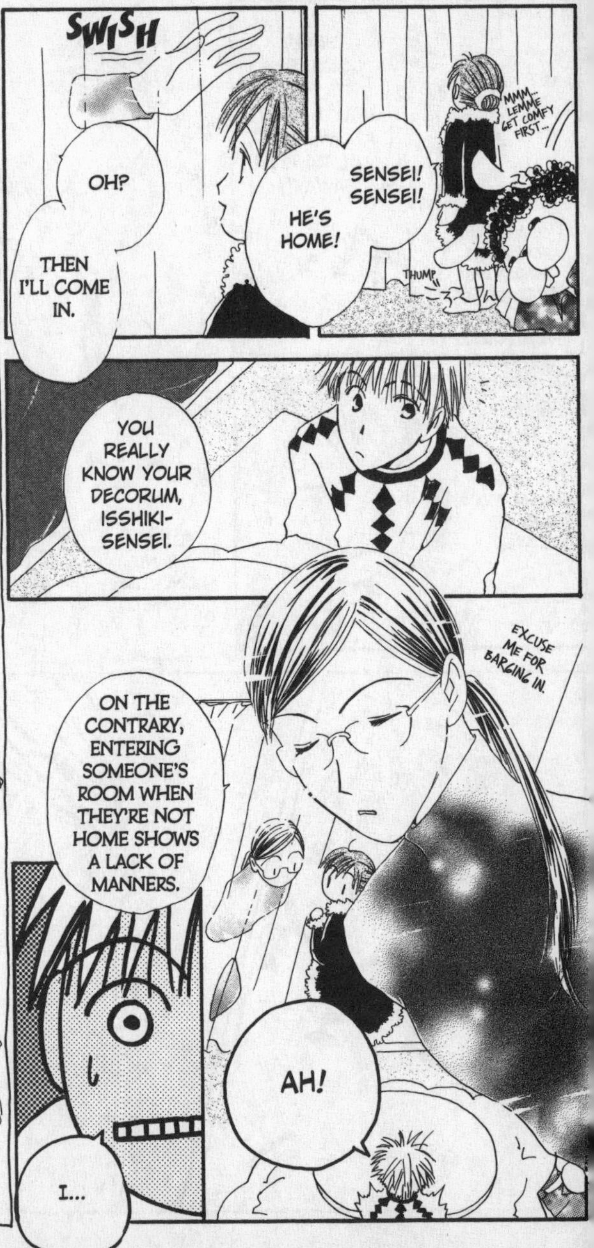
SENSEI! SENSEI!
HE'S HOME!
MMM... LEMME GET COMFY FIRST...
THUMP
SWISH
OH?
THEN I'LL COME IN.
YOU REALLY KNOW YOUR DECORUM, ISSHIKI-SENSEI.
EXCUSE ME FOR BARGING IN.
ON THE CONTRARY, ENTERING SOMEONE'S ROOM WHEN THEY'RE NOT HOME SHOWS A LACK OF MANNERS.
AH!
I...

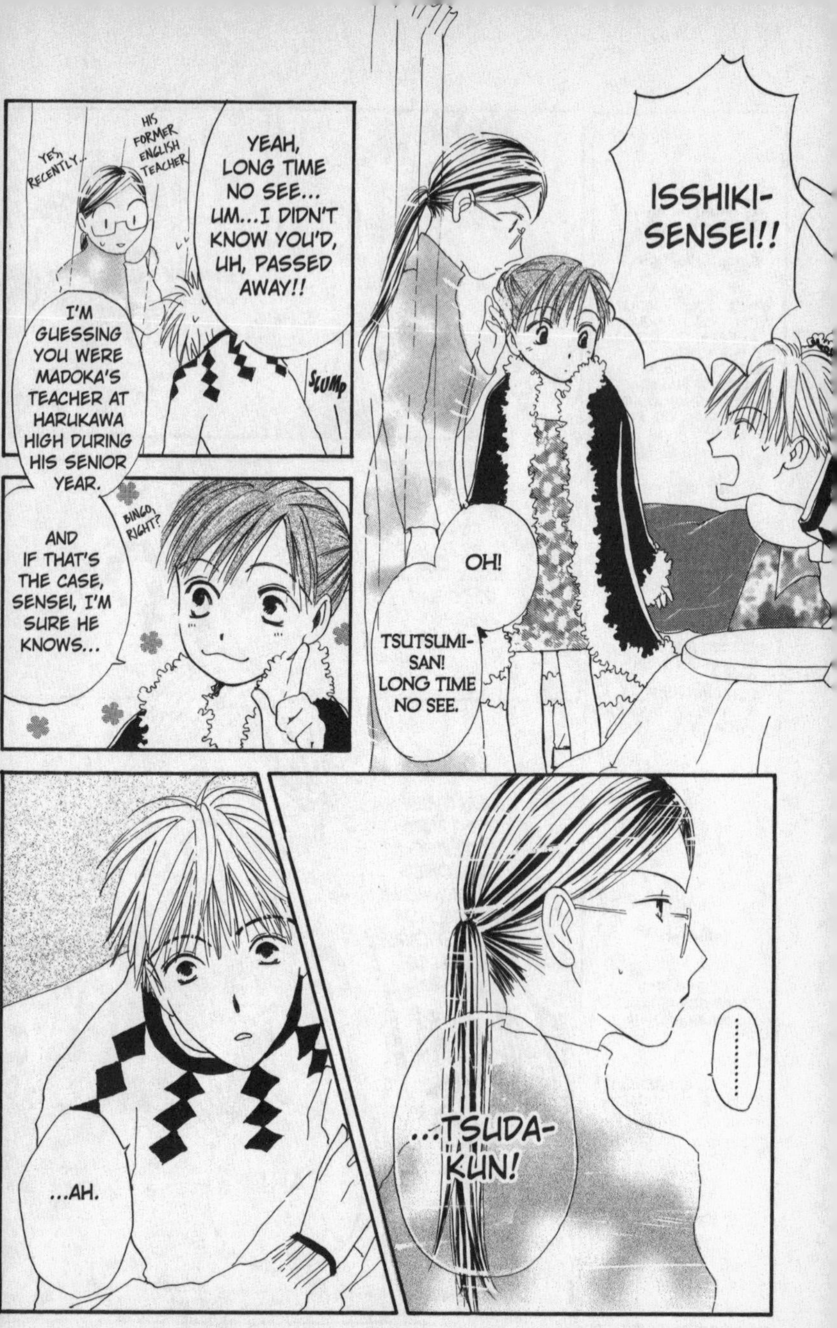
ISSHIKI-SENSEI!!
OH!
TSUTSUMI-SAN! LONG TIME NO SEE.
HIS FORMER ENGLISH TEACHER
YES, RECENTLY...
YEAH, LONG TIME NO SEE... UM...I DIDN'T KNOW YOU'D, UH, PASSED AWAY!!
SLUMP
I'M GUESSING YOU WERE MADOKA'S TEACHER AT HARUKAWA HIGH DURING HIS SENIOR YEAR.
BINGO, RIGHT?
AND IF THAT'S THE CASE, SENSEI, I'M SURE HE KNOWS...
......
...TSUDA-KUN!
...AH.

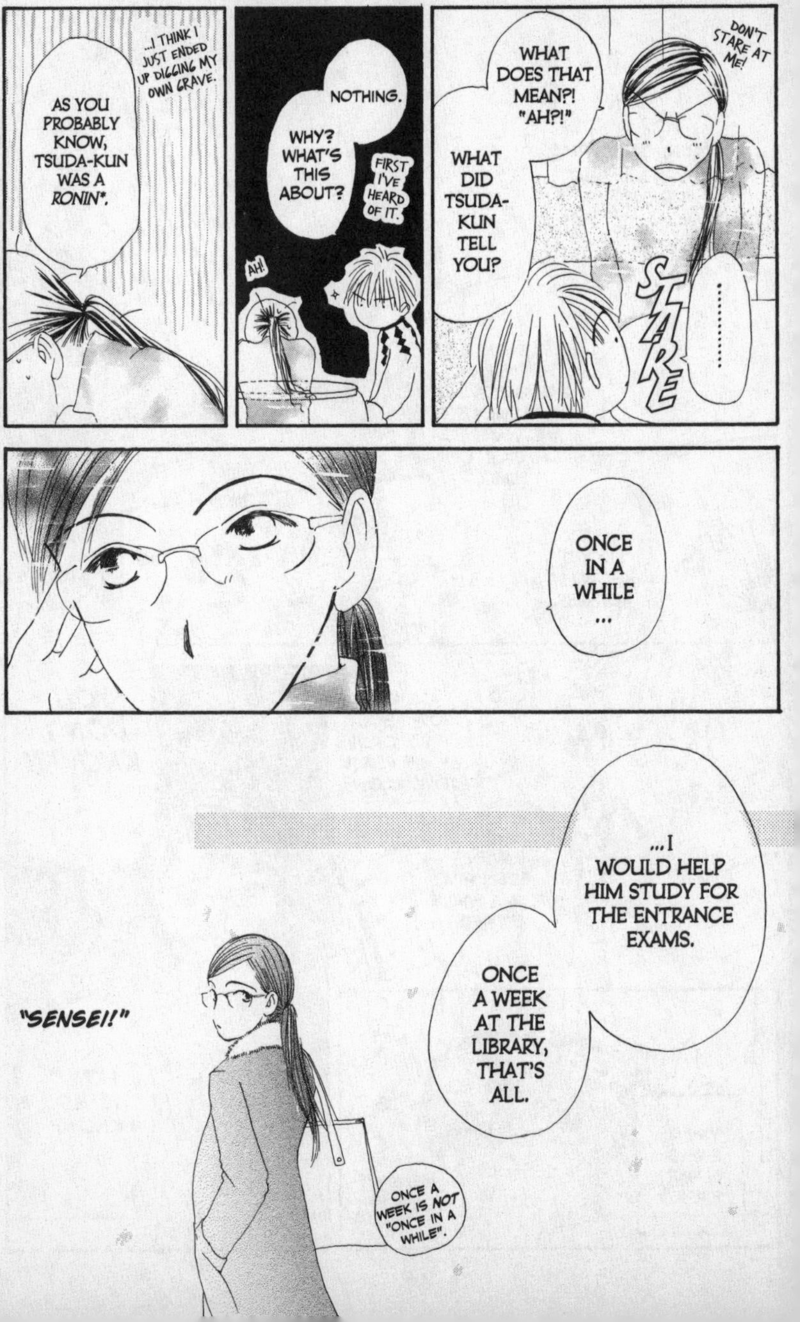
DON'T STARE AT ME!
WHAT DID TSUDA-KUN TELL YOU?
WHAT DOES THAT MEAN?! "AH?!"
STARE
......
FIRST I'VE HEARD OF IT.
WHY? WHAT'S THIS ABOUT?
NOTHING.
AH!
...I THINK I JUST ENDED UP DIGGING MY OWN GRAVE.
AS YOU PROBABLY KNOW, TSUDA-KUN WAS A *RONIN**.
ONCE IN A WHILE ...
...I WOULD HELP HIM STUDY FOR THE ENTRANCE EXAMS.
ONCE A WEEK AT THE LIBRARY, THAT'S ALL.
"SENSEI!"
ONCE A WEEK IS *NOT* "ONCE IN A WHILE".

* HIGH SCHOOL GRAD WHO'S FAILED TO ENTER COLLEGE AND IS STUDYING TO TRY ENTRANCE EXAMS AGAIN.

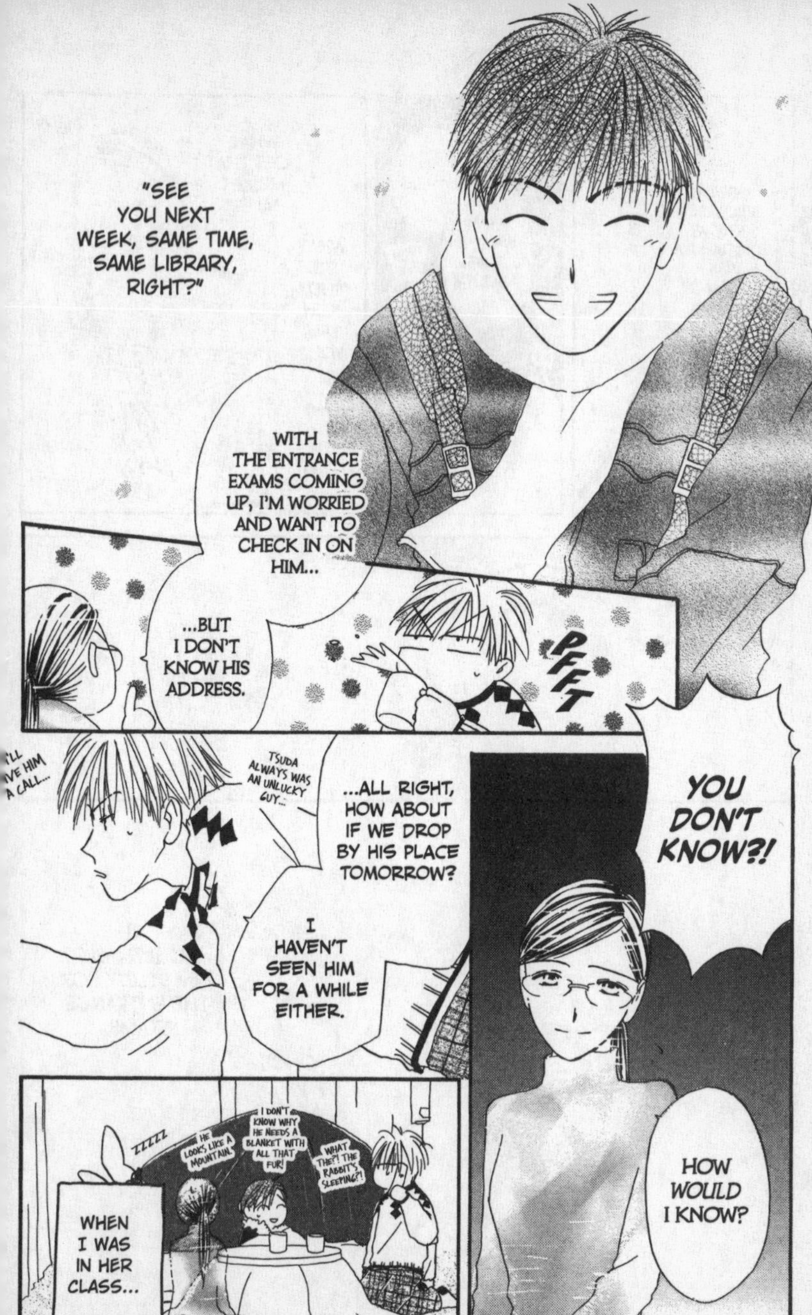
"SEE YOU NEXT WEEK, SAME TIME, SAME LIBRARY, RIGHT?"
WITH THE ENTRANCE EXAMS COMING UP, I'M WORRIED AND WANT TO CHECK IN ON HIM...
PFFT
...BUT I DON'T KNOW HIS ADDRESS.
YOU DON'T KNOW?!
HOW WOULD I KNOW?
...ALL RIGHT, HOW ABOUT IF WE DROP BY HIS PLACE TOMORROW?
I HAVEN'T SEEN HIM FOR A WHILE EITHER.
TSUDA ALWAYS WAS AN UNLUCKY GUY...
'LL VE HIM A CALL...
WHAT THE?! THE RABBIT'S SLEEPING?!
I DON'T KNOW WHY HE NEEDS A BLANKET WITH ALL THAT FUR!
HE LOOKS LIKE A MOUNTAIN.
ZZZZZ
WHEN I WAS IN HER CLASS...

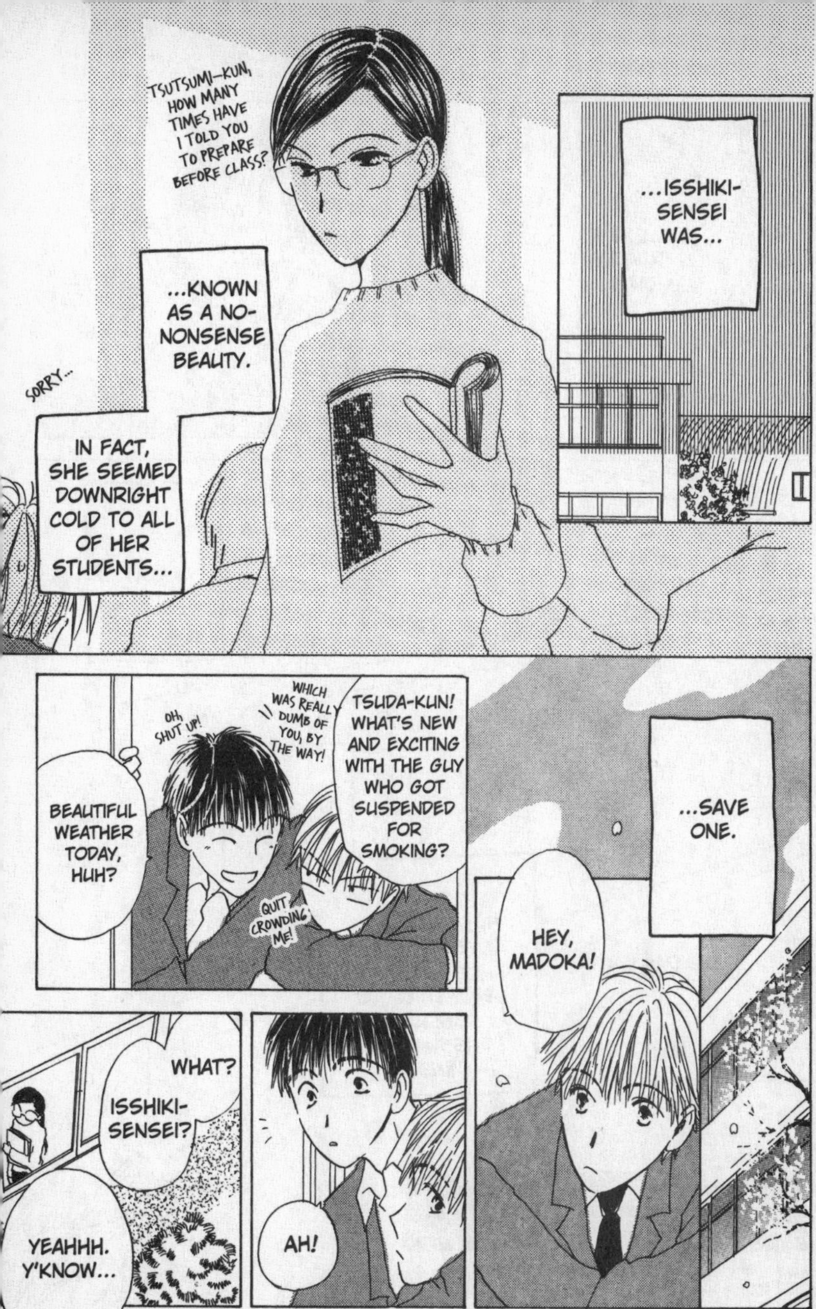
...ISSHIKI-SENSEI WAS...
TSUTSUMI-KUN, HOW MANY TIMES HAVE I TOLD YOU TO PREPARE BEFORE CLASS?
...KNOWN AS A NO-NONSENSE BEAUTY.
SORRY...
IN FACT, SHE SEEMED DOWNRIGHT COLD TO ALL OF HER STUDENTS...
...SAVE ONE.
HEY, MADOKA!
TSUDA-KUN! WHAT'S NEW AND EXCITING WITH THE GUY WHO GOT SUSPENDED FOR SMOKING?
WHICH WAS REALLY DUMB OF YOU, BY THE WAY!
OH, SHUT UP!
BEAUTIFUL WEATHER TODAY, HUH?
QUIT CROWDING ME!
AH!
WHAT?
ISSHIKI-SENSEI?
YEAHHH. Y'KNOW...

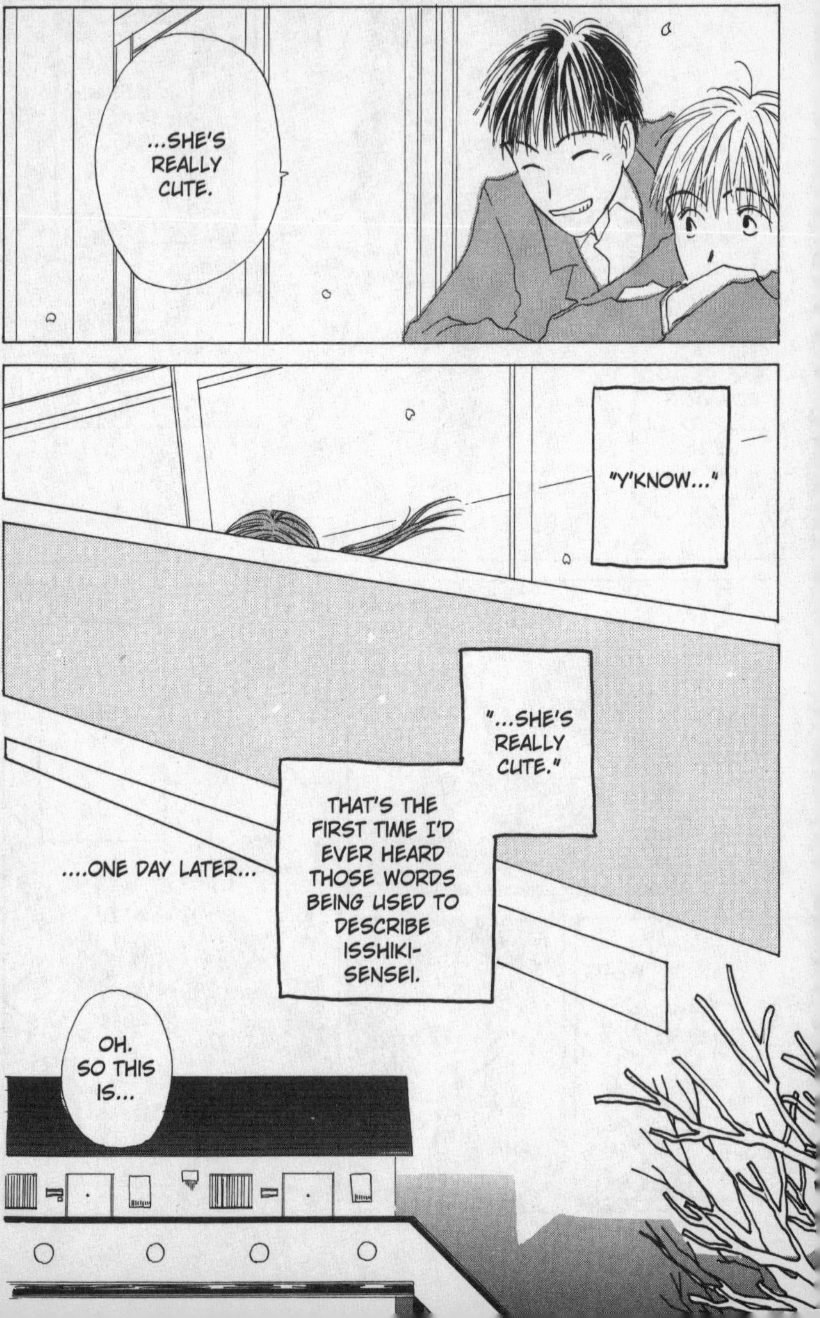
...SHE'S REALLY CUTE.
"Y'KNOW..."
"...SHE'S REALLY CUTE."
THAT'S THE FIRST TIME I'D EVER HEARD THOSE WORDS BEING USED TO DESCRIBE ISSHIKI-SENSEI.
....ONE DAY LATER...
OH. SO THIS IS...

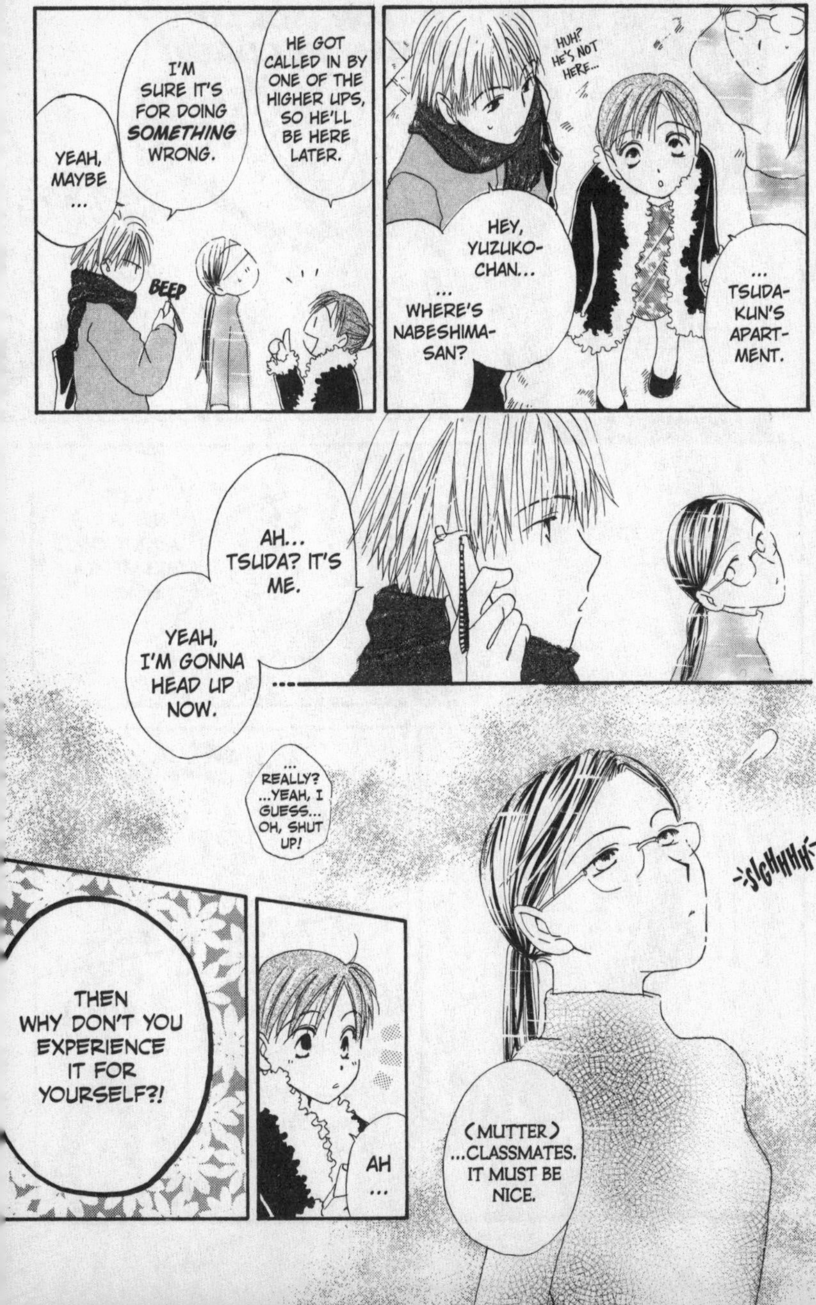
HUH? HE'S NOT HERE...
HEY, YUZUKO-CHAN... ...WHERE'S NABESHIMA-SAN?
...TSUDA-KUN'S APARTMENT.
HE GOT CALLED IN BY ONE OF THE HIGHER UPS, SO HE'LL BE HERE LATER.
I'M SURE IT'S FOR DOING SOMETHING WRONG.
YEAH, MAYBE...
BEEP
AH... TSUDA? IT'S ME.
YEAH, I'M GONNA HEAD UP NOW.
...REALLY? ...YEAH, I GUESS... OH, SHUT UP!
SIGHHHH
(MUTTER) ...CLASSMATES. IT MUST BE NICE.
AH...
THEN WHY DON'T YOU EXPERIENCE IT FOR YOURSELF?!

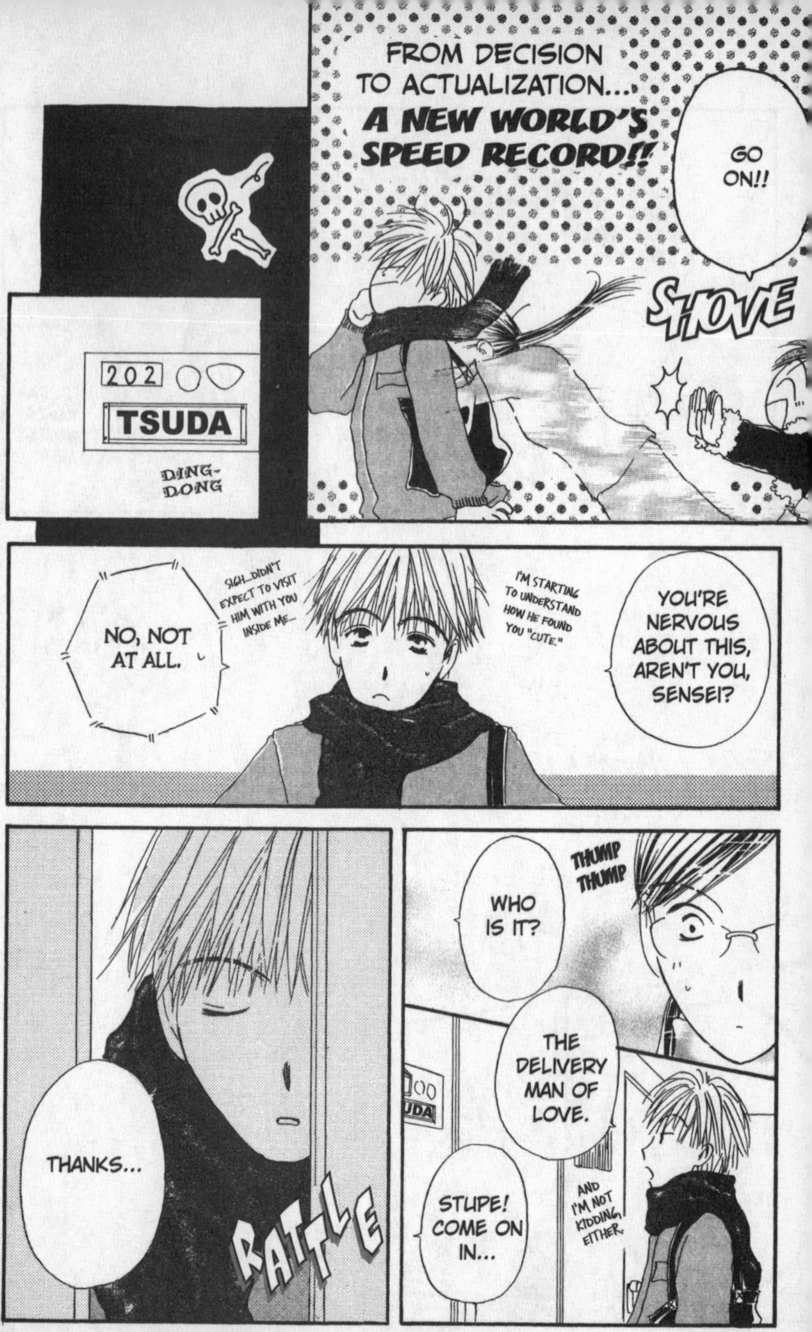
FROM DECISION TO ACTUALIZATION... A NEW WORLD'S SPEED RECORD!!
GO ON!!
SHOVE
202
TSUDA
DING-DONG
YOU'RE NERVOUS ABOUT THIS, AREN'T YOU, SENSEI?
I'M STARTING TO UNDERSTAND HOW HE FOUND YOU "CUTE."
SIGH...DIDN'T EXPECT TO VISIT HIM WITH YOU INSIDE ME...
NO, NOT AT ALL.
THUMP THUMP
WHO IS IT?
THE DELIVERY MAN OF LOVE.
AND I'M NOT KIDDING, EITHER.
STUPE! COME ON IN...
RATTLE
THANKS...

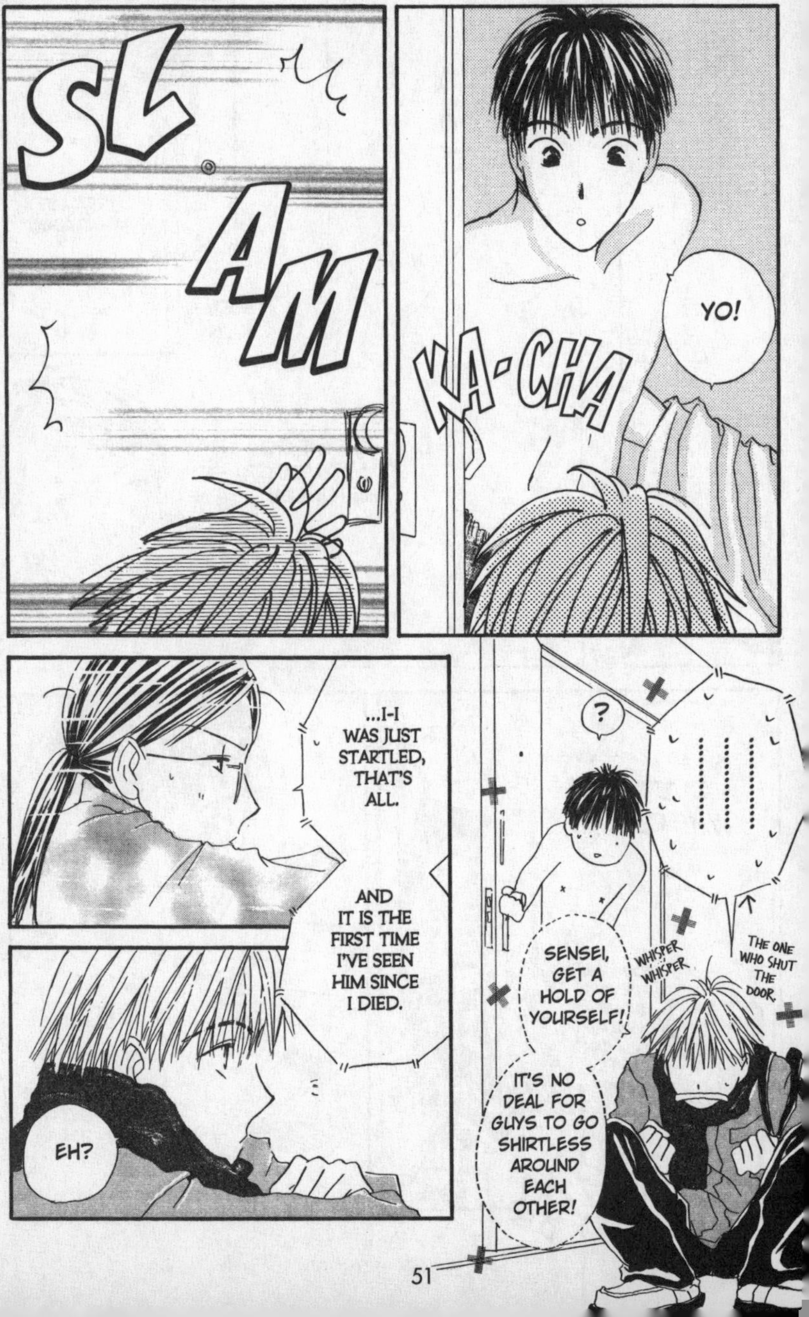
YO!
KA-CHA
SLAM
?
.....
THE ONE WHO SHUT THE DOOR.
WHISPER WHISPER
SENSEI, GET A HOLD OF YOURSELF!
IT'S NO DEAL FOR GUYS TO GO SHIRTLESS AROUND EACH OTHER!
...I-I WAS JUST STARTLED, THAT'S ALL.
AND IT IS THE FIRST TIME I'VE SEEN HIM SINCE I DIED.
EH?

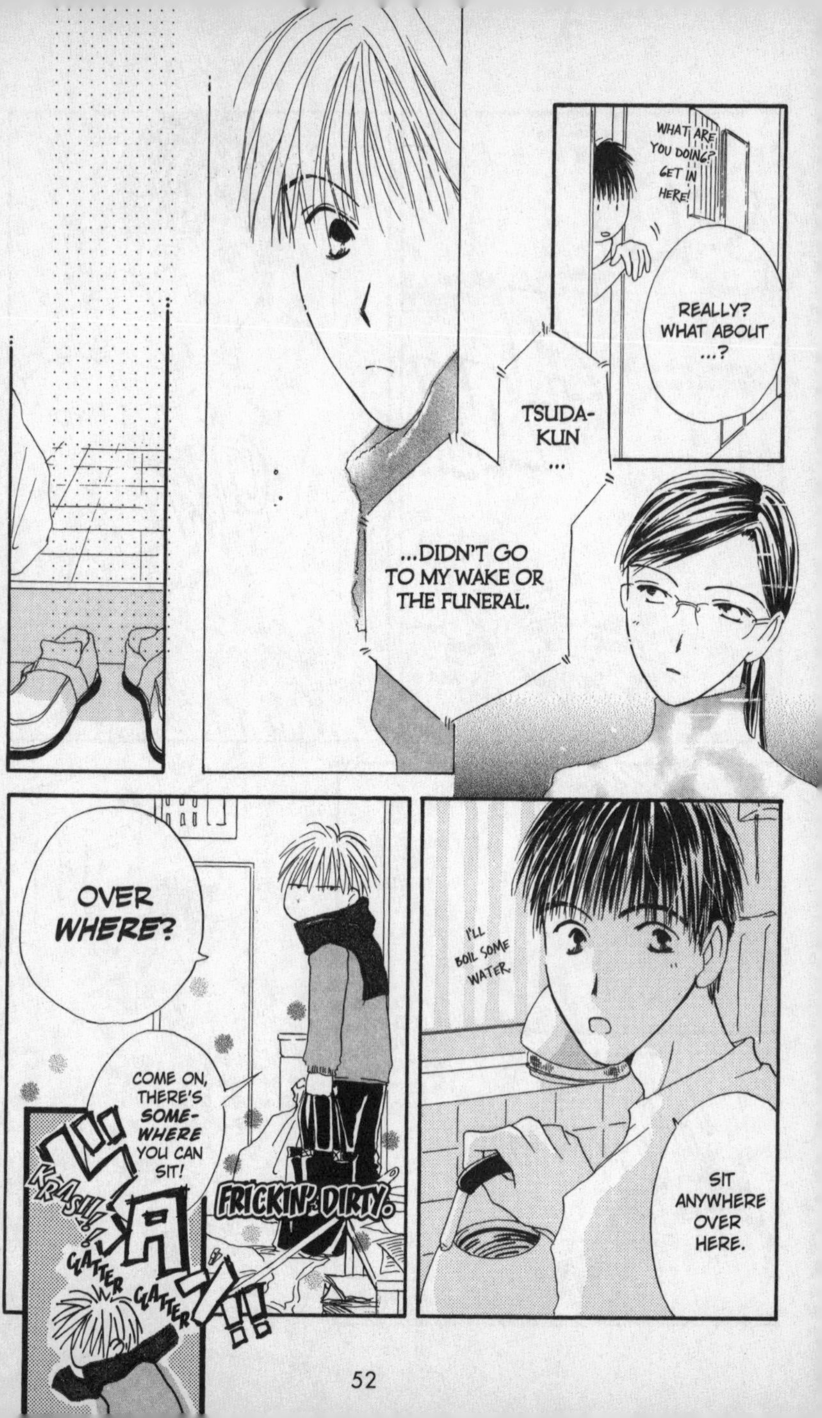
WHAT ARE YOU DOING? GET IN HERE!
REALLY? WHAT ABOUT ...?
TSUDA-KUN ...
...DIDN'T GO TO MY WAKE OR THE FUNERAL.
I'LL BOIL SOME WATER.
SIT ANYWHERE OVER HERE.
OVER WHERE?
COME ON, THERE'S SOME-WHERE YOU CAN SIT!
FRICKIN' DIRTY.
KRASH!!
CLATTER CLATTER

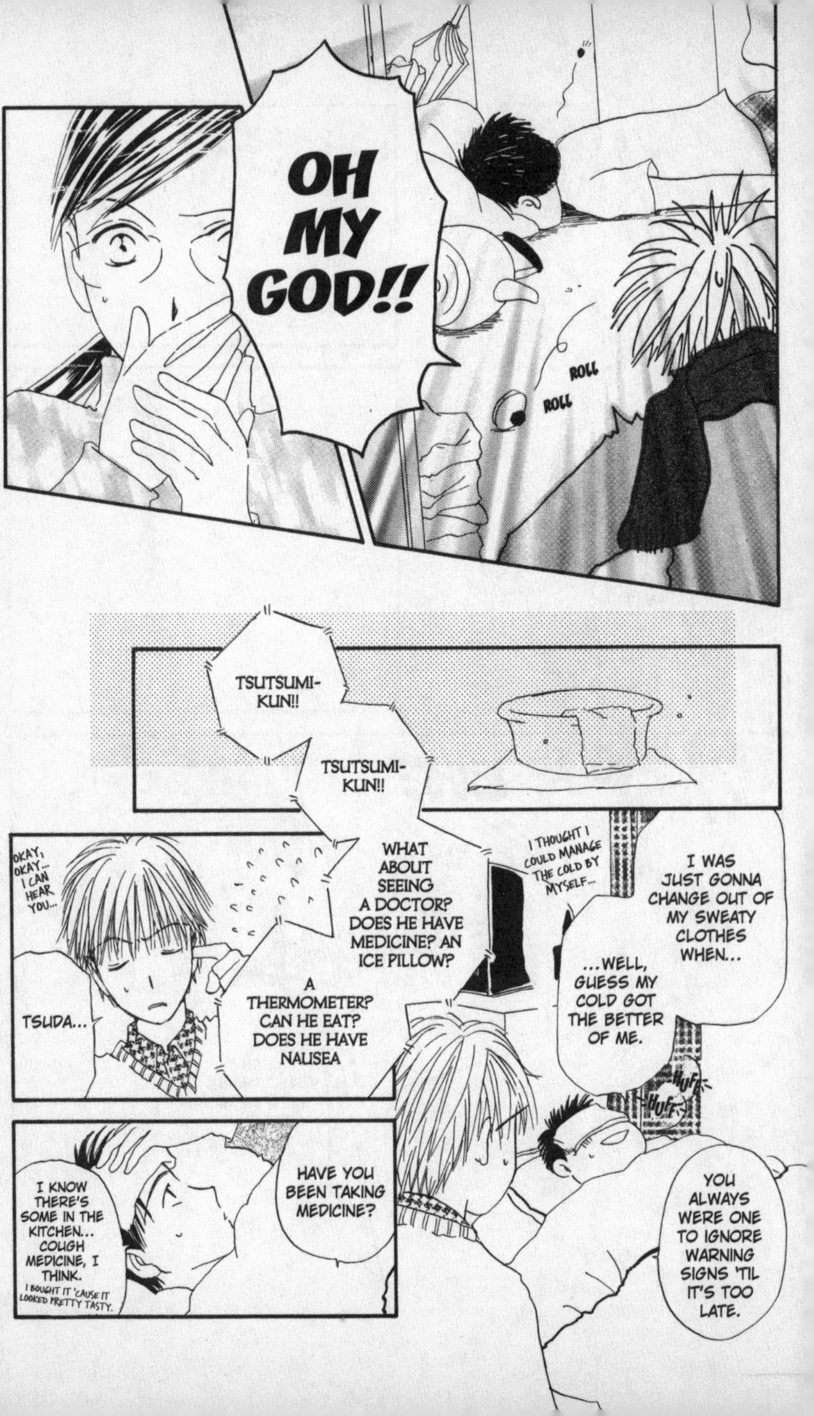
OH MY GOD!!
ROLL
ROLL
TSUTSUMI-KUN!!
TSUTSUMI-KUN!!
I WAS JUST GONNA CHANGE OUT OF MY SWEATY CLOTHES WHEN...
...WELL, GUESS MY COLD GOT THE BETTER OF ME.
I THOUGHT I COULD MANAGE THE COLD BY MYSELF...
HUFF
HUFF
WHAT ABOUT SEEING A DOCTOR? DOES HE HAVE MEDICINE? AN ICE PILLOW?
A THERMOMETER? CAN HE EAT? DOES HE HAVE NAUSEA
OKAY, OKAY... I CAN HEAR YOU...
TSUDA...
YOU ALWAYS WERE ONE TO IGNORE WARNING SIGNS 'TIL IT'S TOO LATE.
HAVE YOU BEEN TAKING MEDICINE?
I KNOW THERE'S SOME IN THE KITCHEN... COUGH MEDICINE, I THINK.
I BOUGHT IT 'CAUSE IT LOOKED PRETTY TASTY.

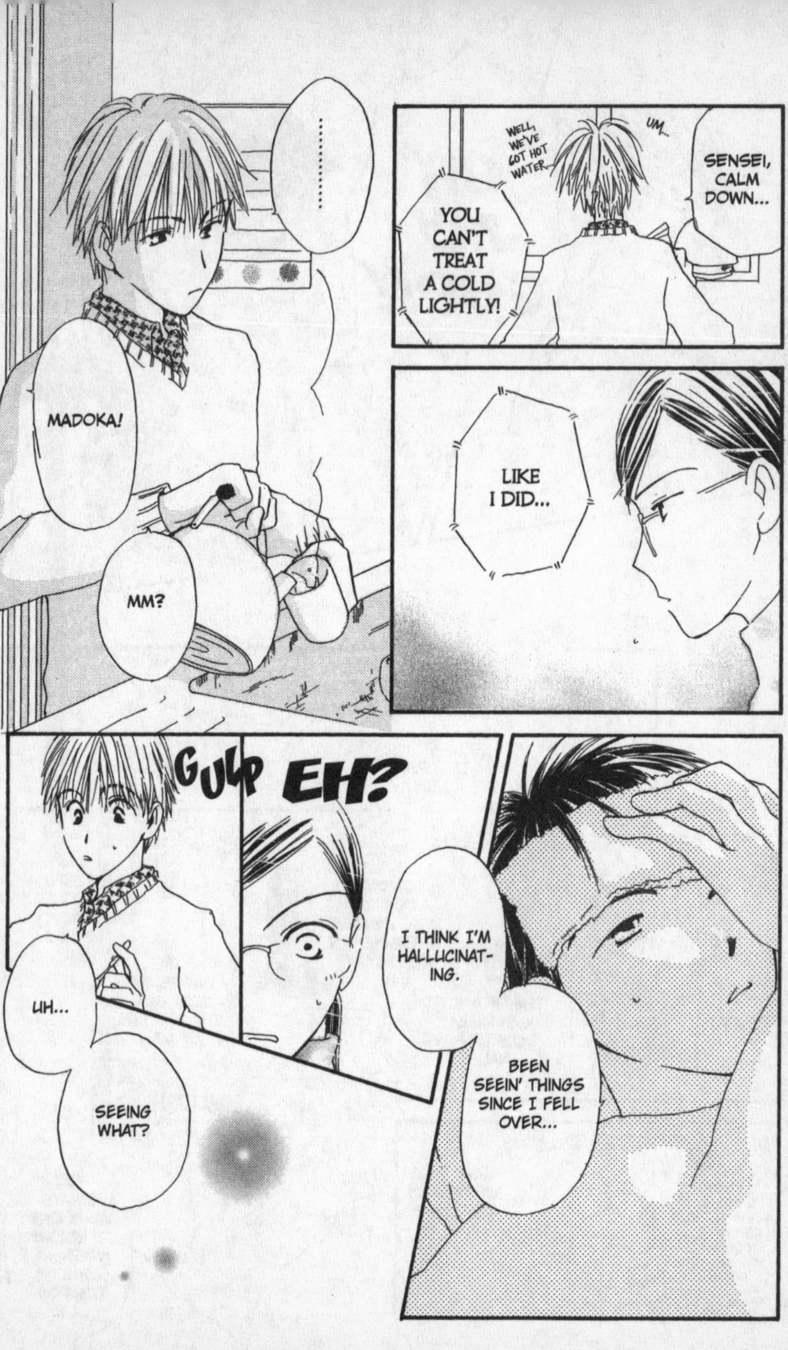
SENSEI, CALM DOWN...
UM...
WELL, WE'VE GOT HOT WATER...
YOU CAN'T TREAT A COLD LIGHTLY!
LIKE I DID...
......
MADOKA!
MM?
I THINK I'M HALLUCINAT-ING.
BEEN SEEIN' THINGS SINCE I FELL OVER...
EH?
GULP
UH...
SEEING WHAT?

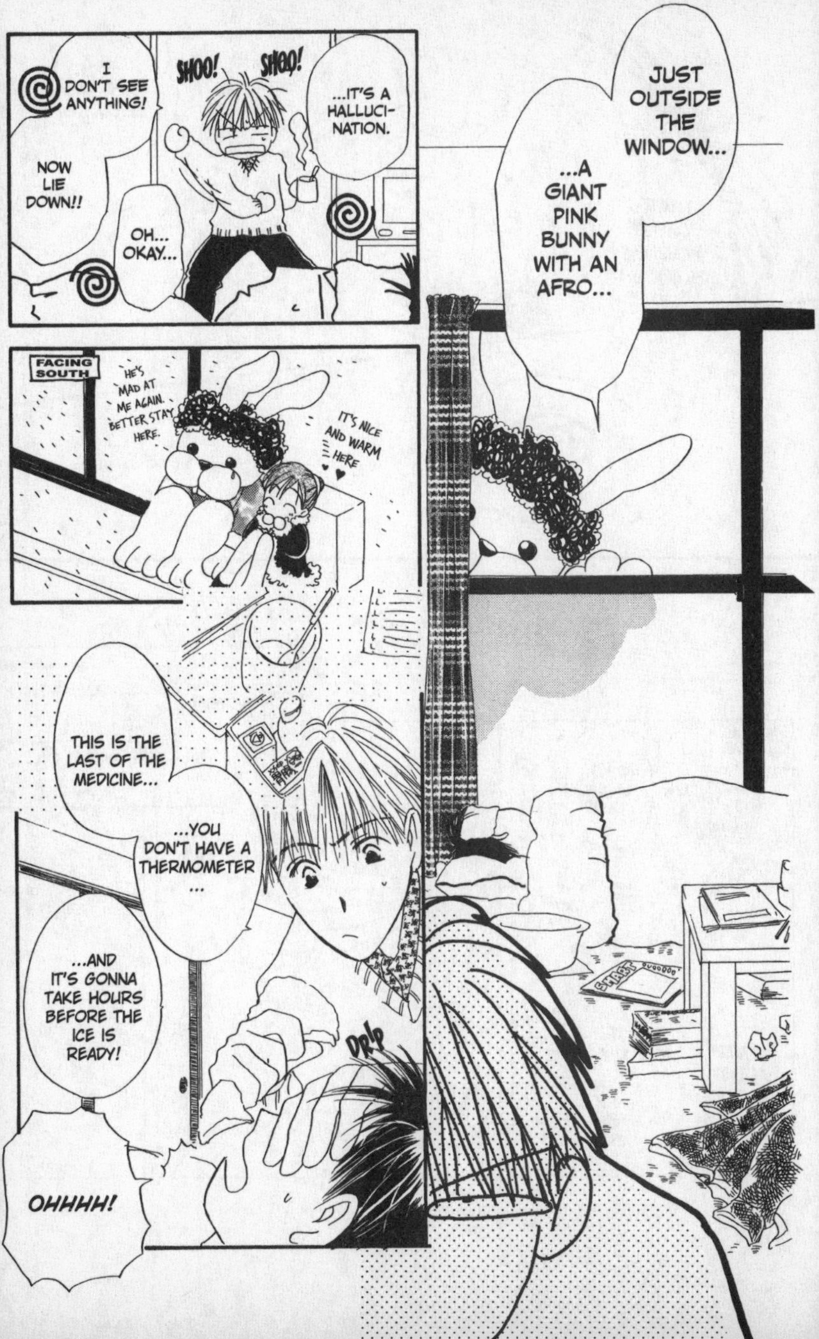
JUST OUTSIDE THE WINDOW...
...A GIANT PINK BUNNY WITH AN AFRO...
SHOO! SHOO!
...IT'S A HALLUCINATION.
I DON'T SEE ANYTHING!
NOW LIE DOWN!!
OH... OKAY...
FACING SOUTH
IT'S NICE AND WARM HERE
HE'S MAD AT ME AGAIN. BETTER STAY HERE.
THIS IS THE LAST OF THE MEDICINE...
...YOU DON'T HAVE A THERMOMETER ...
...AND IT'S GONNA TAKE HOURS BEFORE THE ICE IS READY!
DRIP
OHHHH!

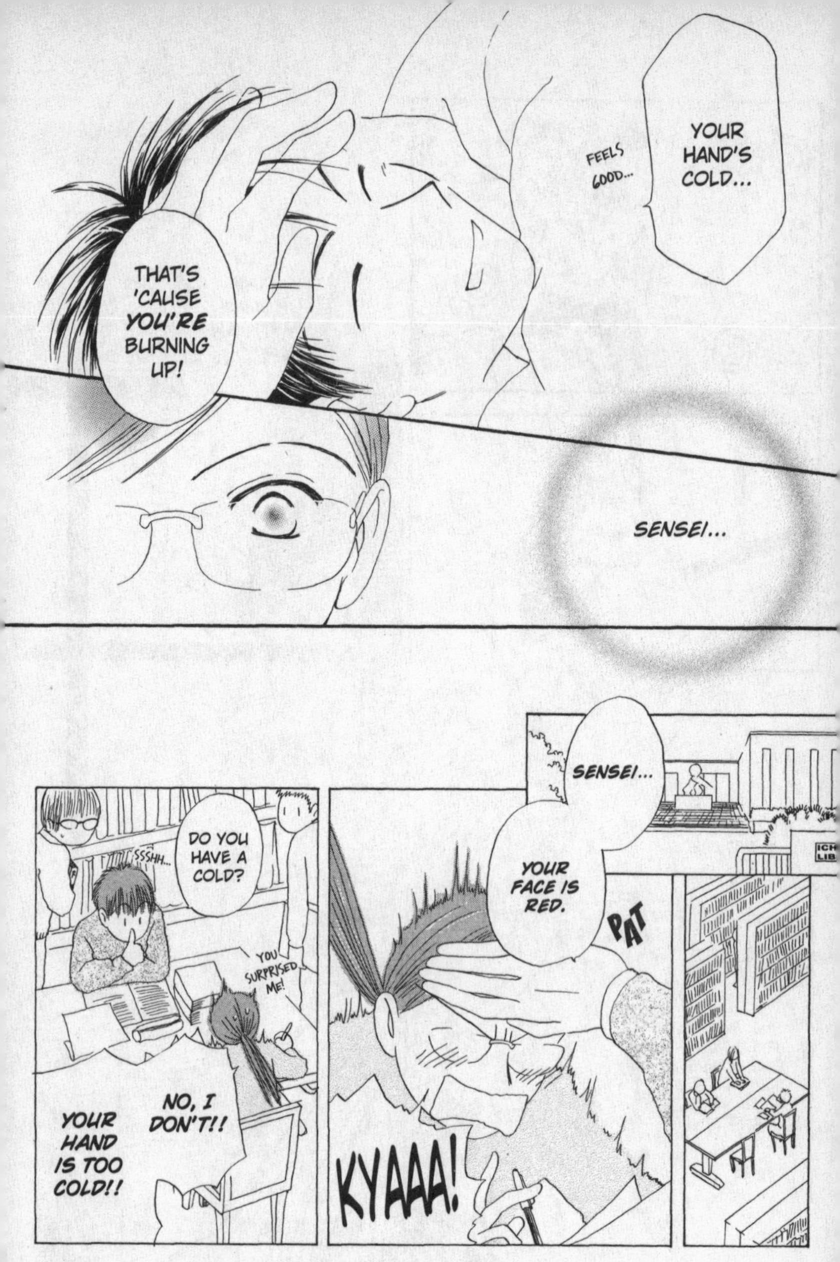
YOUR HAND'S COLD...
FEELS GOOD...
THAT'S 'CAUSE YOU'RE BURNING UP!
SENSEI...
SENSEI...
YOUR FACE IS RED.
PAT
KYAAA!
DO YOU HAVE A COLD?
SSSHH...
YOU SURPRISED ME!
NO, I DON'T!!
YOUR HAND IS TOO COLD!!

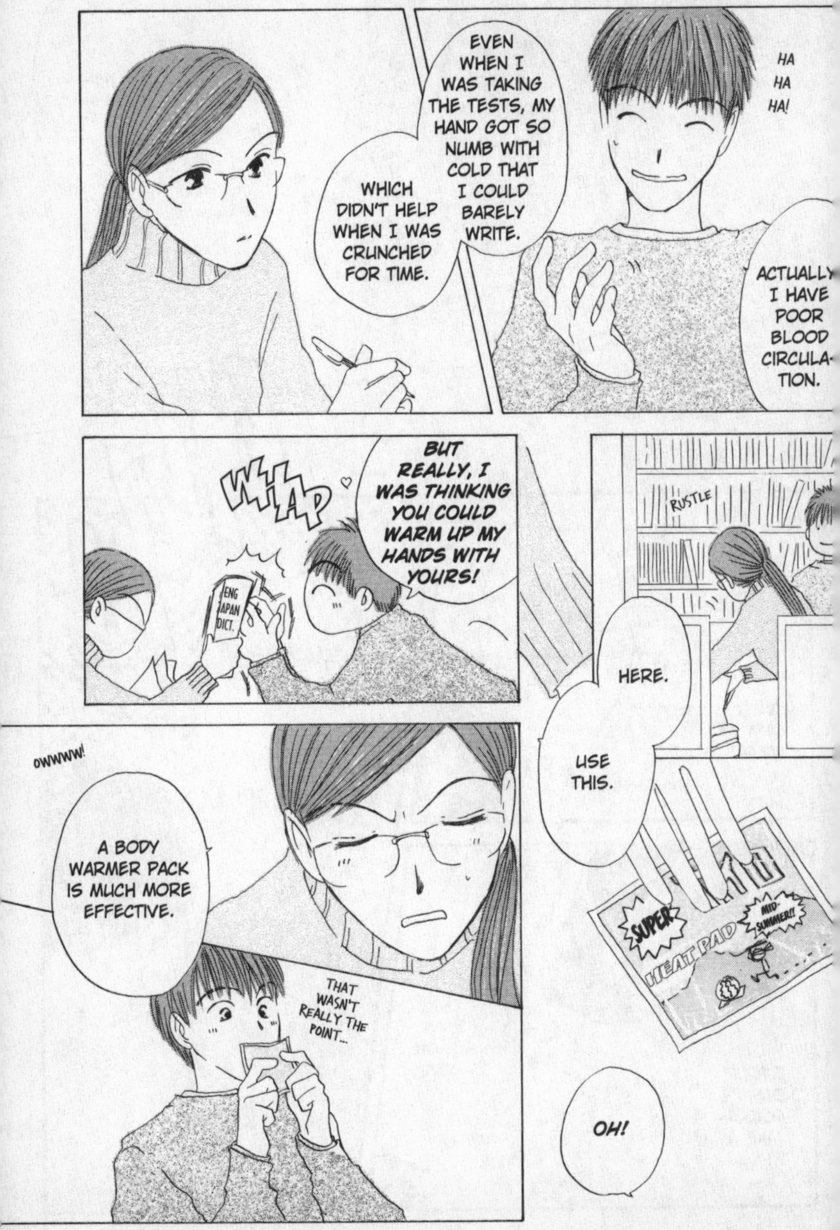
HA HA HA!
ACTUALLY I HAVE POOR BLOOD CIRCULATION.
EVEN WHEN I WAS TAKING THE TESTS, MY HAND GOT SO NUMB WITH COLD THAT I COULD BARELY WRITE.
WHICH DIDN'T HELP WHEN I WAS CRUNCHED FOR TIME.
BUT REALLY, I WAS THINKING YOU COULD WARM UP MY HANDS WITH YOURS!
WHAP
ENG JAPAN DICT.
OWWWW!
A BODY WARMER PACK IS MUCH MORE EFFECTIVE.
RUSTLE
HERE.
USE THIS.
SUPER
HEAT PAD
MID-SUMMER!!
OH!
THAT WASN'T REALLY THE POINT...

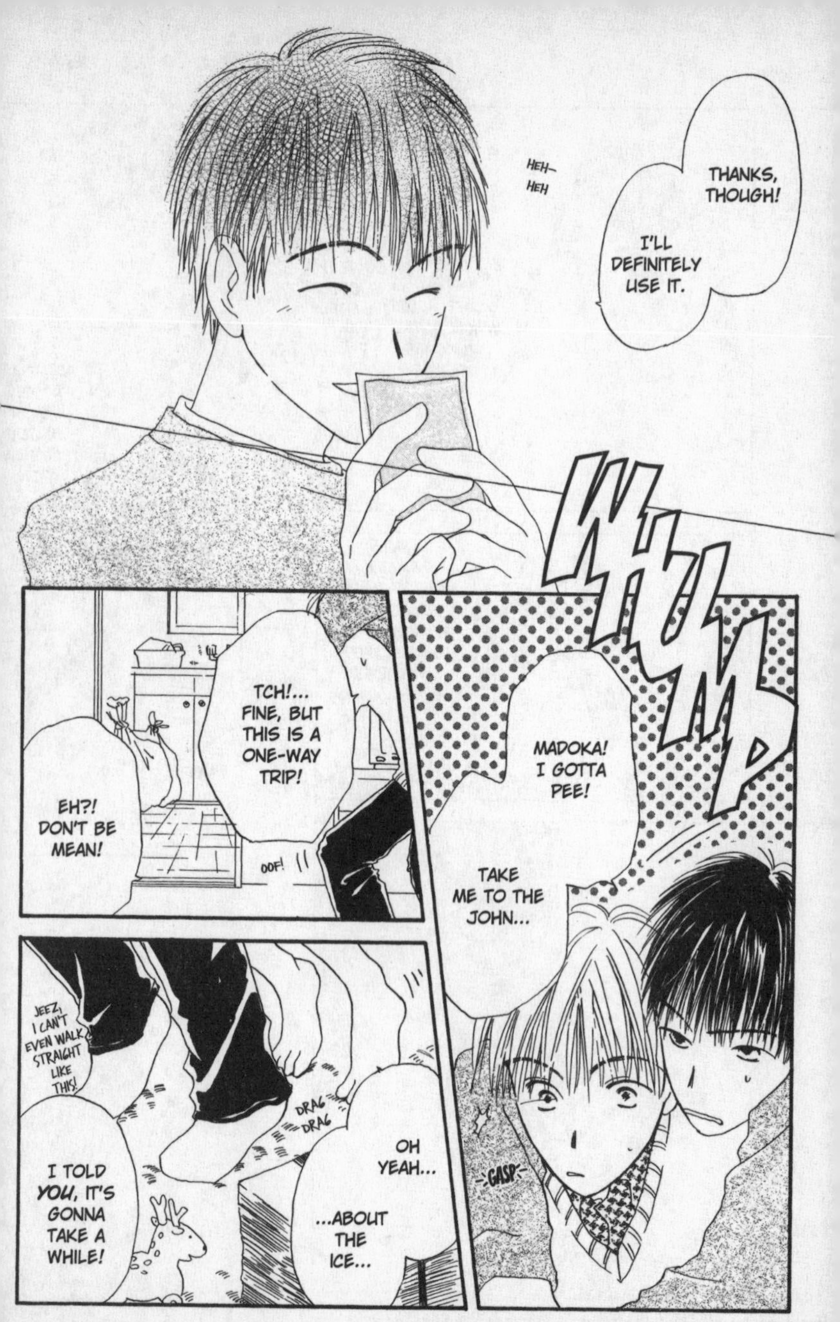
THANKS, THOUGH!
I'LL DEFINITELY USE IT.
HEH-HEH
WHUMP
MADOKA! I GOTTA PEE!
TAKE ME TO THE JOHN...
GASP
TCH!... FINE, BUT THIS IS A ONE-WAY TRIP!
EH?! DON'T BE MEAN!
OOF!
OH YEAH...
...ABOUT THE ICE...
DRAG DRAG
JEEZ, I CAN'T EVEN WALK STRAIGHT LIKE THIS!
I TOLD *YOU*, IT'S GONNA TAKE A WHILE!

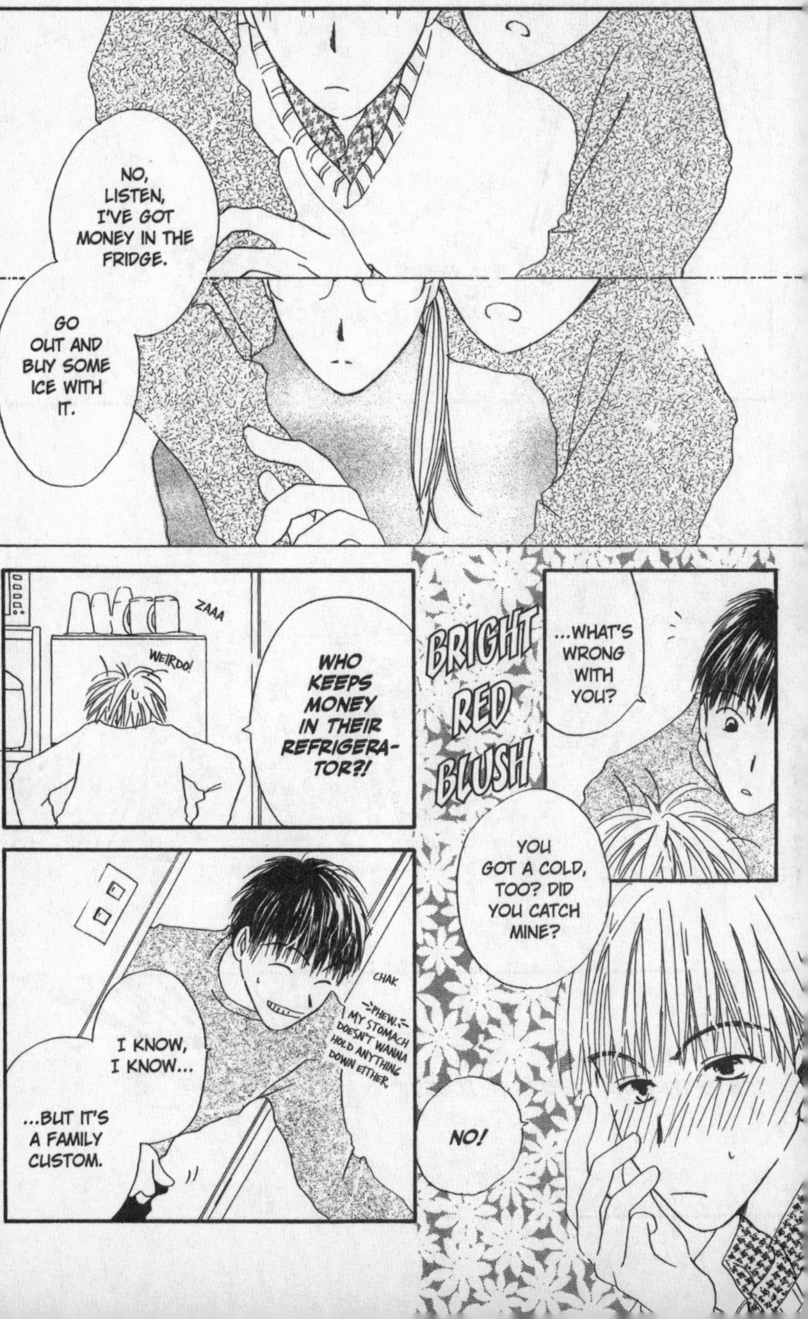
NO, LISTEN, I'VE GOT MONEY IN THE FRIDGE.
GO OUT AND BUY SOME ICE WITH IT.
...WHAT'S WRONG WITH YOU?
BRIGHT RED BLUSH
YOU GOT A COLD, TOO? DID YOU CATCH MINE?
NO!
ZAAA
WEIRDO!
WHO KEEPS MONEY IN THEIR REFRIGERA-TOR?!
CHAK
PHEW. MY STOMACH DOESN'T WANNA HOLD ANYTHING DOWN EITHER.
I KNOW, I KNOW...
...BUT IT'S A FAMILY CUSTOM.

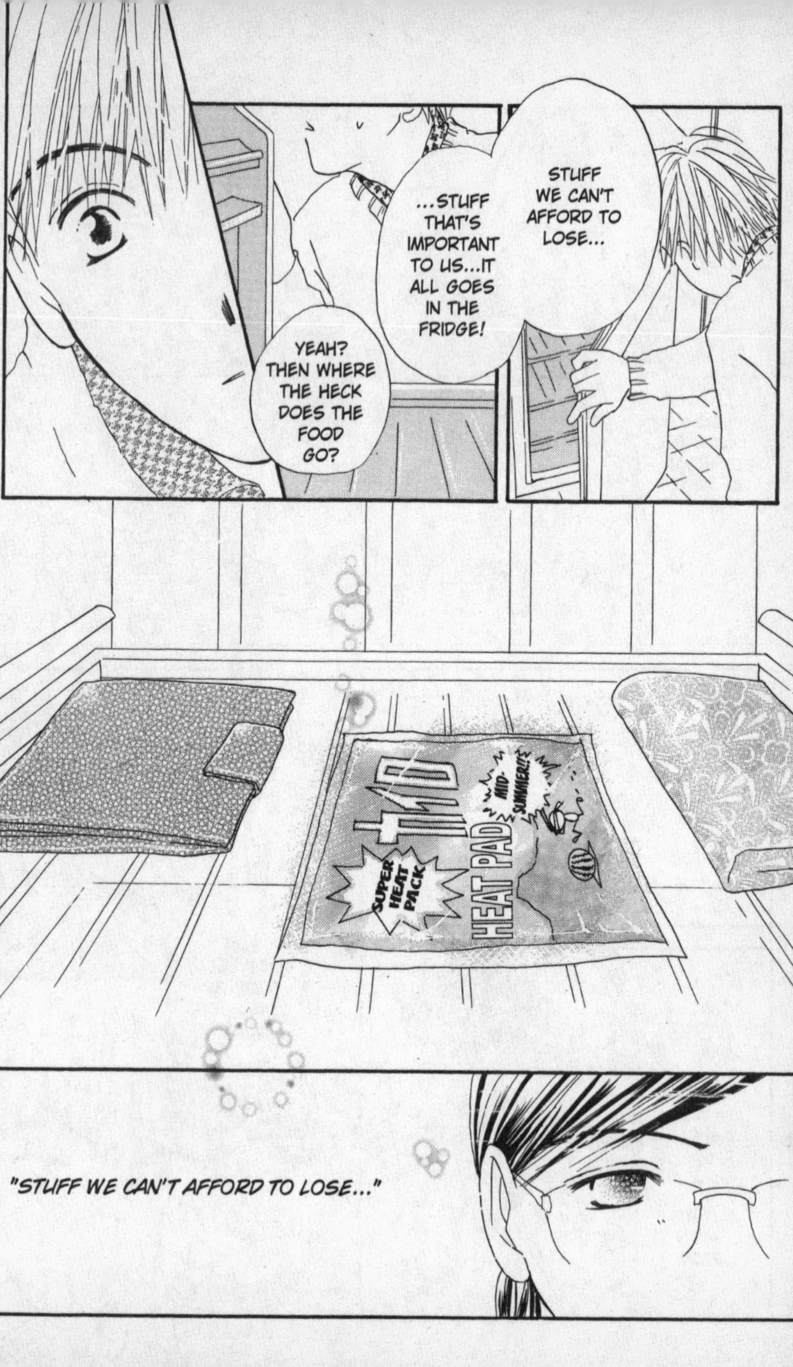
STUFF WE CAN'T AFFORD TO LOSE...
...STUFF THAT'S IMPORTANT TO US...IT ALL GOES IN THE FRIDGE!
YEAH? THEN WHERE THE HECK DOES THE FOOD GO?
MID-SUMMER!!
HEAT PAD
SUPER HEAT PACK
"STUFF WE CAN'T AFFORD TO LOSE..."

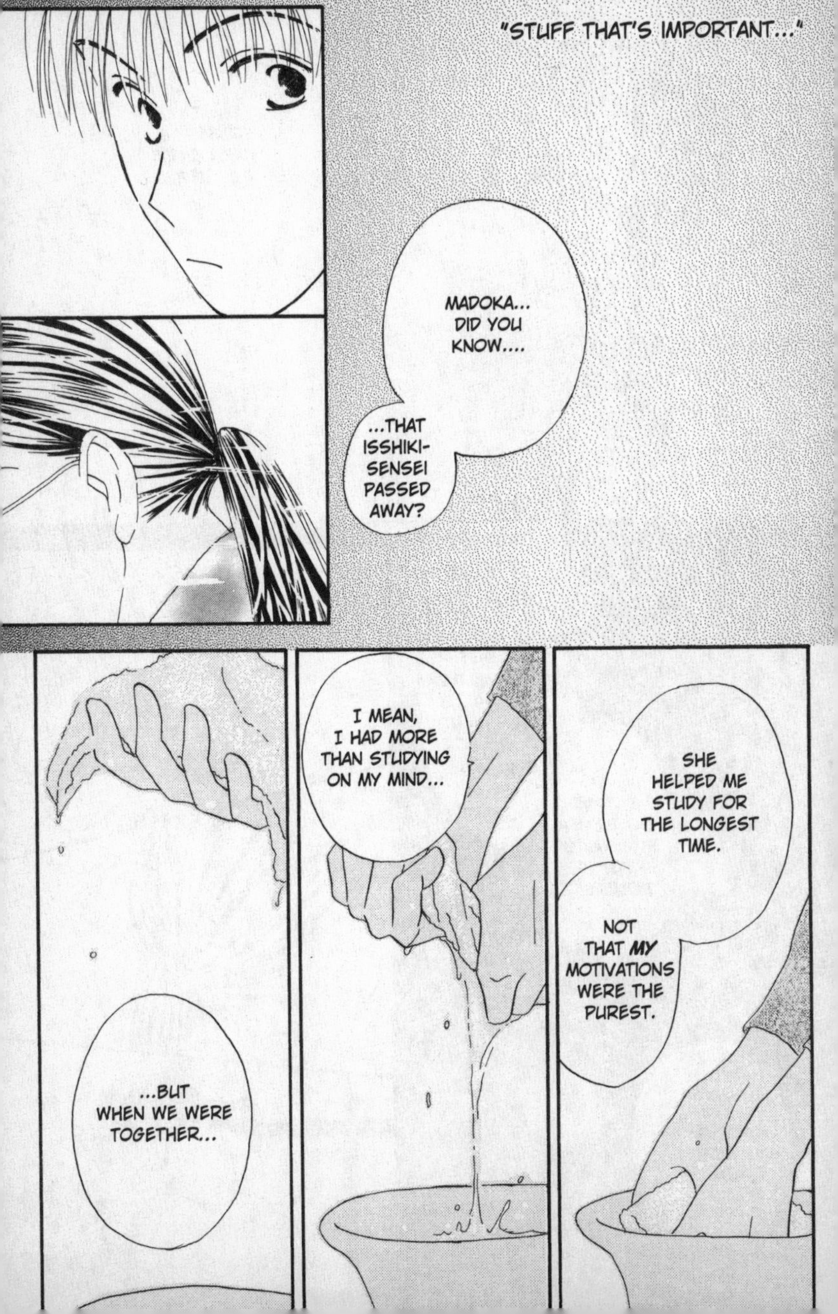
"STUFF THAT'S IMPORTANT..."
MADOKA... DID YOU KNOW....
...THAT ISSHIKI-SENSEI PASSED AWAY?
SHE HELPED ME STUDY FOR THE LONGEST TIME.
NOT THAT *MY* MOTIVATIONS WERE THE PUREST.
I MEAN, I HAD MORE THAN STUDYING ON MY MIND...
...BUT WHEN WE WERE TOGETHER...

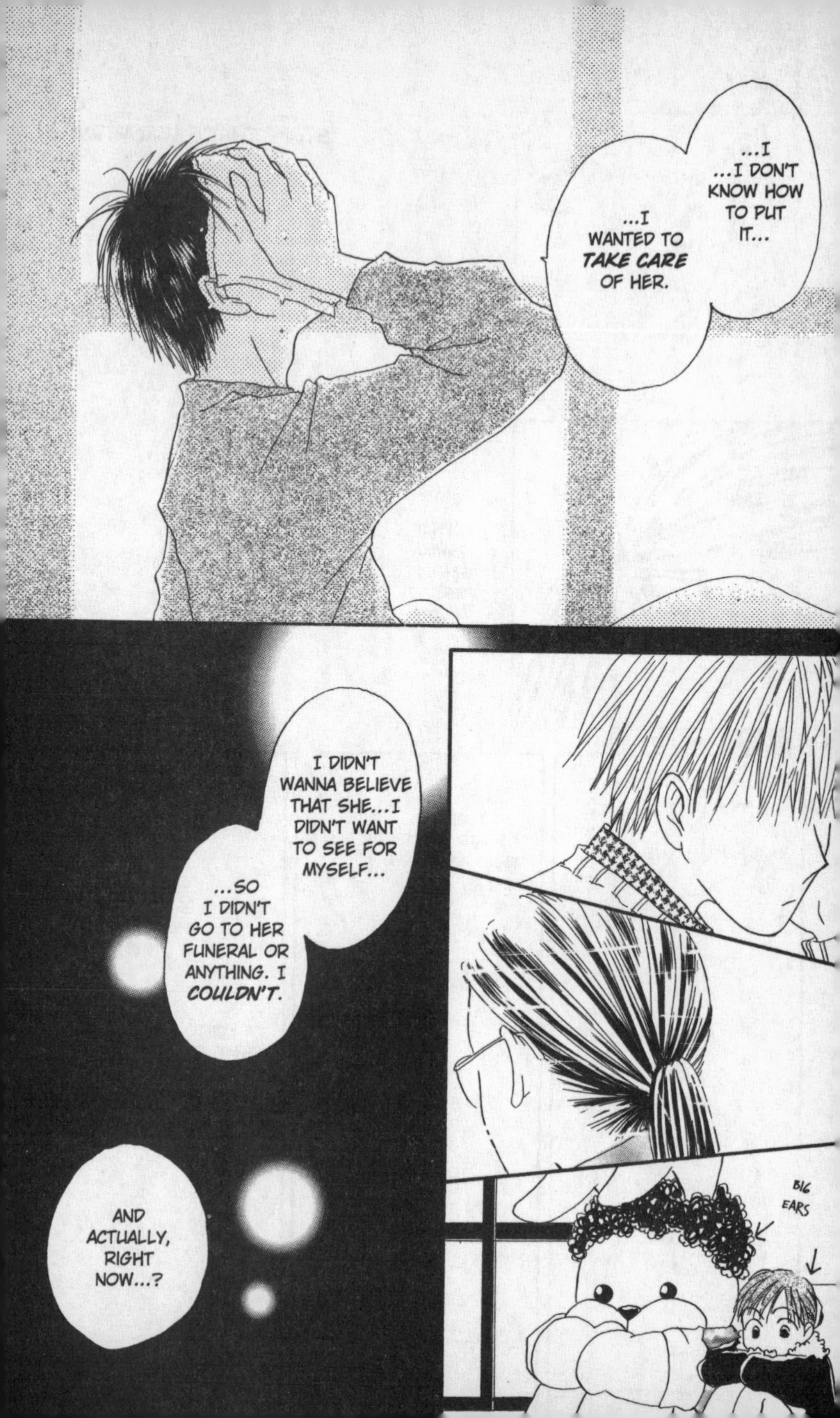
...I ...I DON'T KNOW HOW TO PUT IT...
...I WANTED TO *TAKE CARE* OF HER.
BIG EARS
I DIDN'T WANNA BELIEVE THAT SHE...I DIDN'T WANT TO SEE FOR MYSELF...
...SO I DIDN'T GO TO HER FUNERAL OR ANYTHING. I *COULDN'T*.
AND ACTUALLY, RIGHT NOW...?

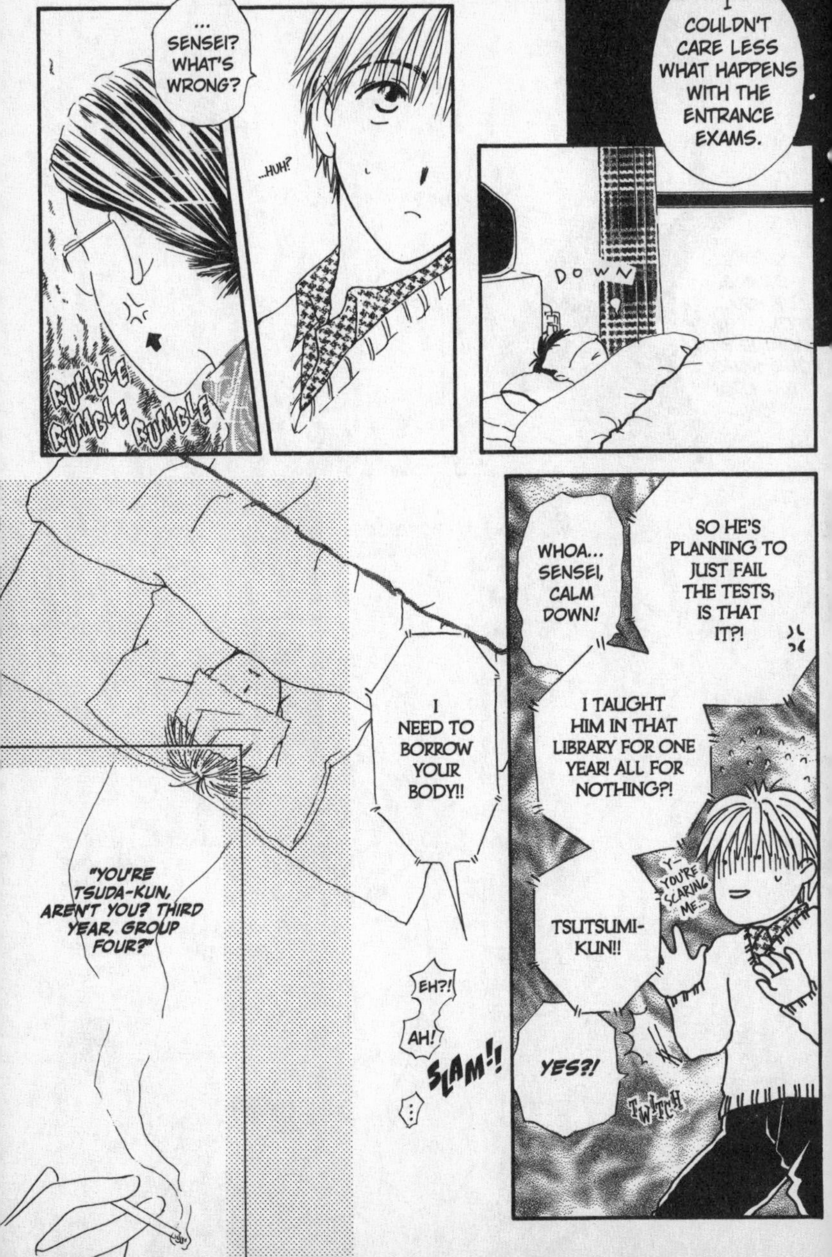
I COULDN'T CARE LESS WHAT HAPPENS WITH THE ENTRANCE EXAMS.
DOWN
... SENSEI? WHAT'S WRONG?
...HUH?
RUMBLE RUMBLE RUMBLE
SO HE'S PLANNING TO JUST FAIL THE TESTS, IS THAT IT?!
WHOA... SENSEI, CALM DOWN!
I TAUGHT HIM IN THAT LIBRARY FOR ONE YEAR! ALL FOR NOTHING?!
Y-YOU'RE SCARING ME...
TSUTSUMI-KUN!!
YES?!
TWITCH
I NEED TO BORROW YOUR BODY!!
EH?!
AH!
SLAM!!
...
"YOU'RE TSUDA-KUN, AREN'T YOU? THIRD YEAR, GROUP FOUR?"

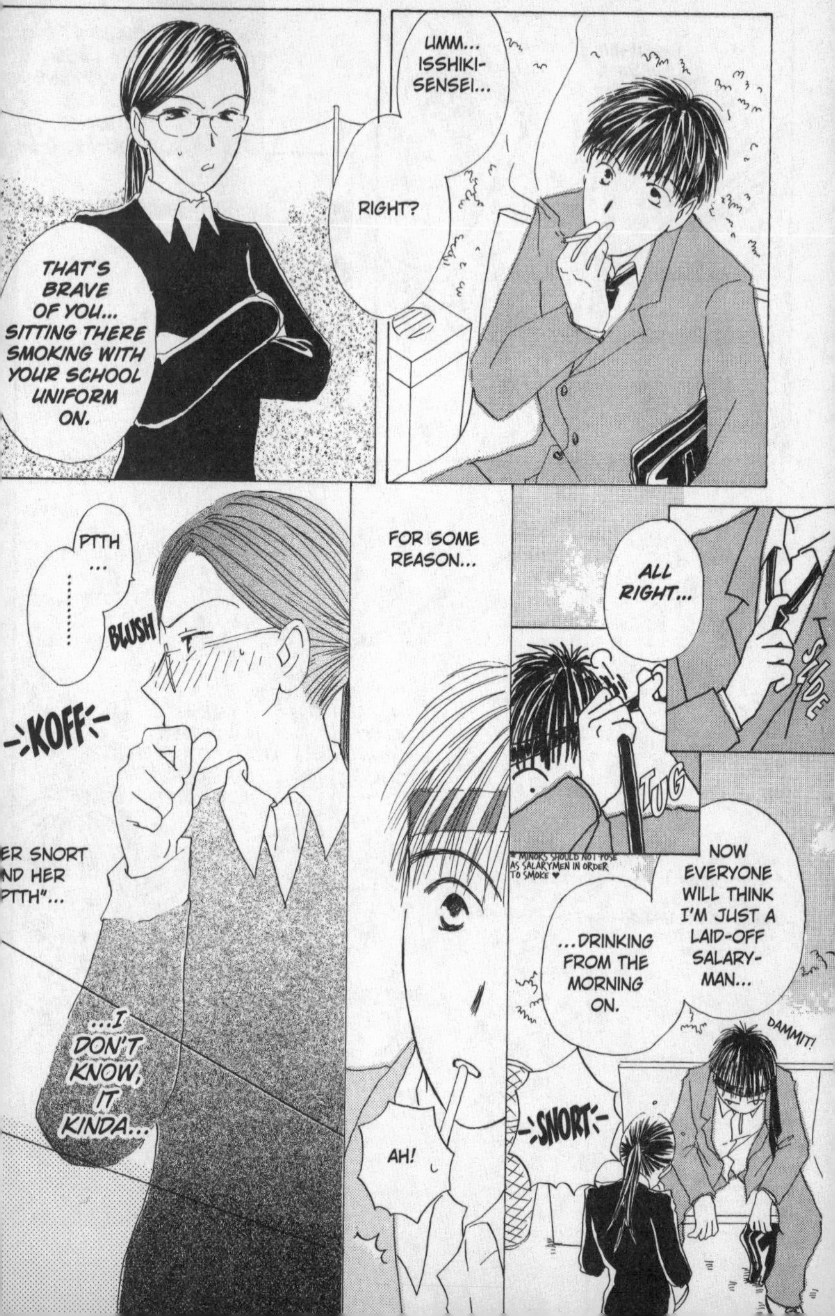
UMM... ISSHIKI-SENSEI...
RIGHT?
THAT'S BRAVE OF YOU... SITTING THERE SMOKING WITH YOUR SCHOOL UNIFORM ON.
ALL RIGHT...
SLIDE
TUG
* MINORS SHOULD NOT POSE AS SALARYMEN IN ORDER TO SMOKE ♥
NOW EVERYONE WILL THINK I'M JUST A LAID-OFF SALARY-MAN...
...DRINKING FROM THE MORNING ON.
DAMMIT!
SNORT
FOR SOME REASON...
AH!
PTTH ... .
BLUSH
KOFF
ER SNORT
ND HER
PTTH"...
...I DON'T KNOW, IT KINDA...

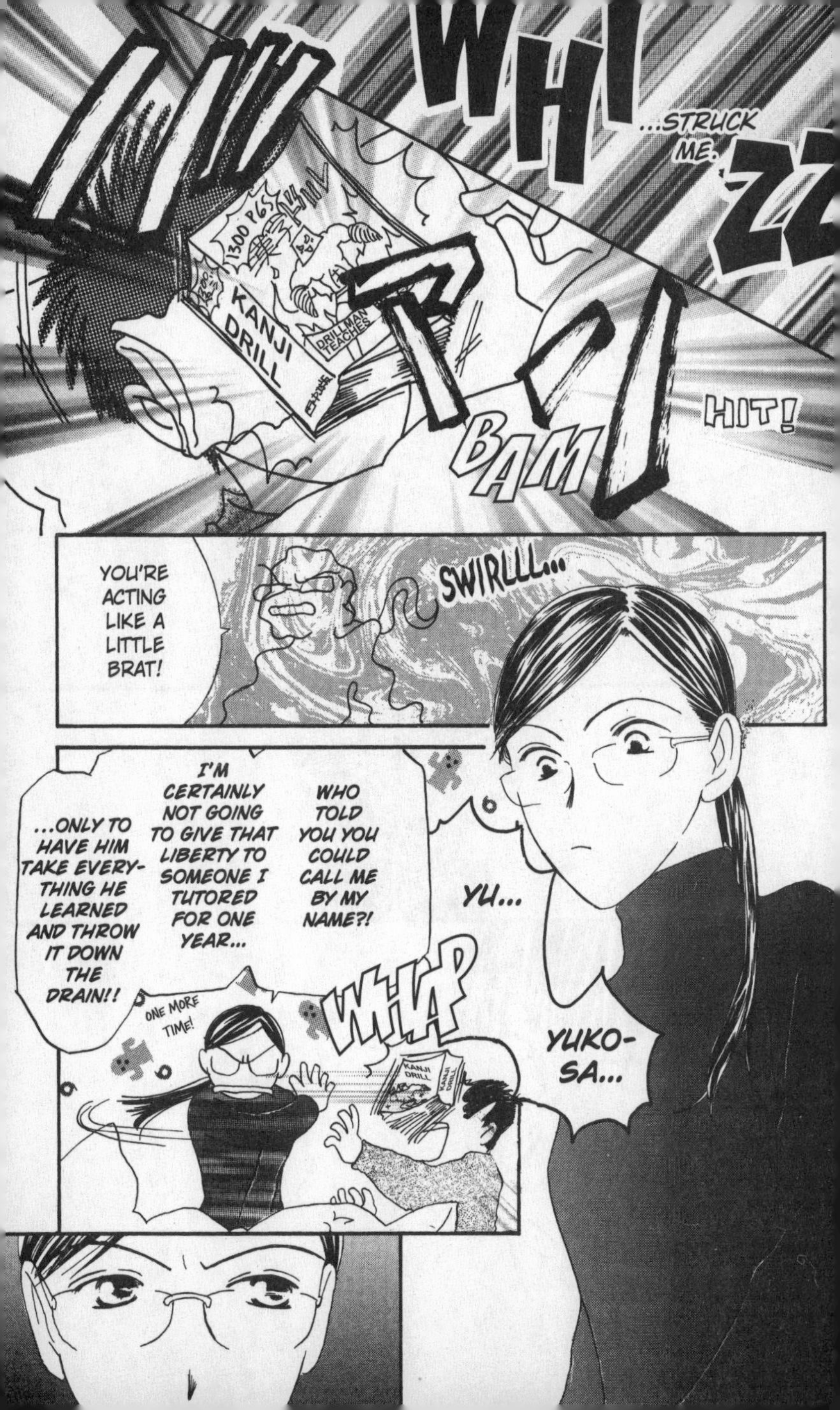
WHI
...STRUCK ME.
ZZ
1300 PGS
KANJI DRILL
DRILLMAN TEACHES
BAM
HIT!
SWIRLLL...
YOU'RE ACTING LIKE A LITTLE BRAT!
YU...
YUKO-SA...
WHO TOLD YOU YOU COULD CALL ME BY MY NAME?!
I'M CERTAINLY NOT GOING TO GIVE THAT LIBERTY TO SOMEONE I TUTORED FOR ONE YEAR...
...ONLY TO HAVE HIM TAKE EVERY-THING HE LEARNED AND THROW IT DOWN THE DRAIN!!
WHAP
ONE MORE TIME!
KANJI DRILL

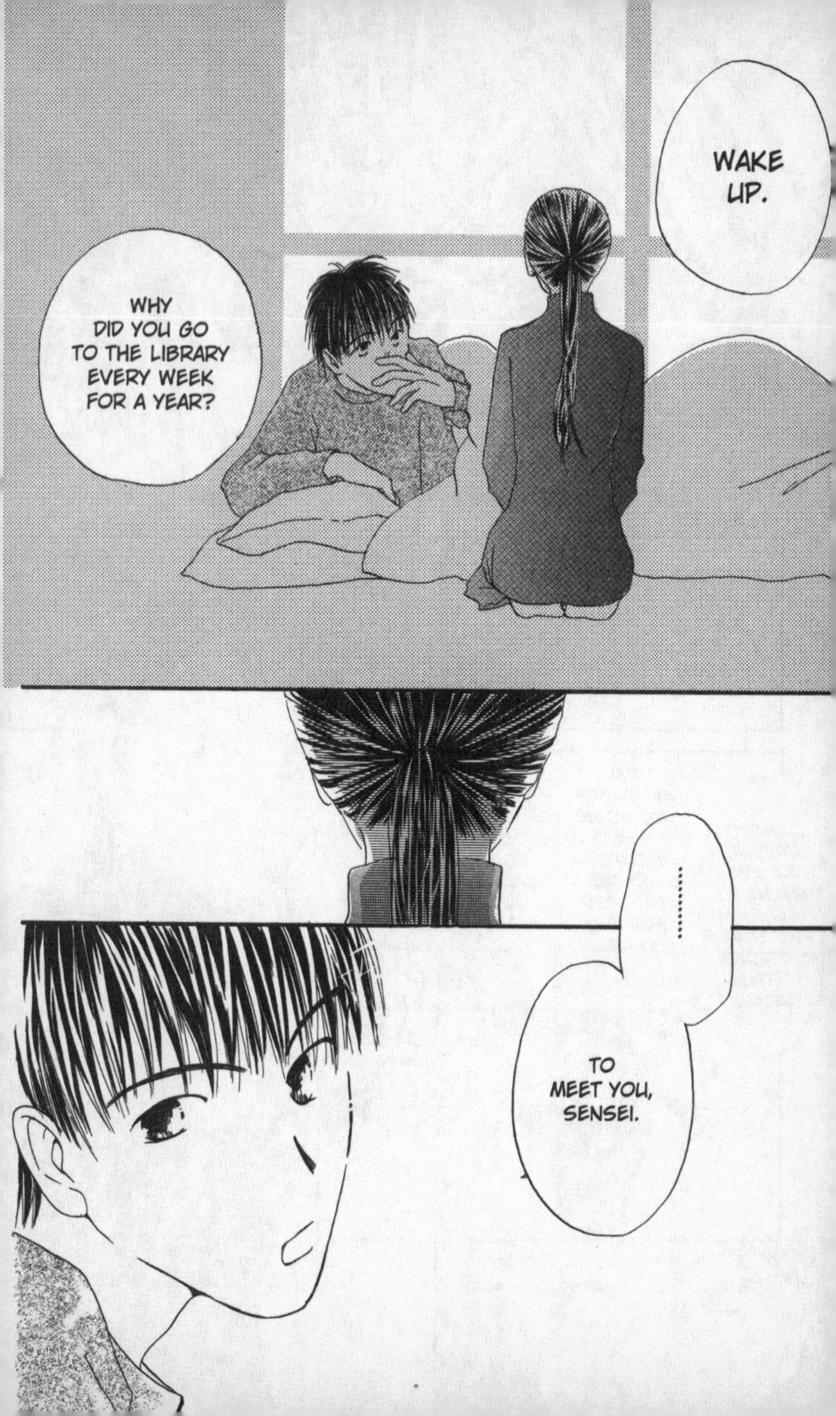
WAKE UP.
WHY DID YOU GO TO THE LIBRARY EVERY WEEK FOR A YEAR?
......
TO MEET YOU, SENSEI.

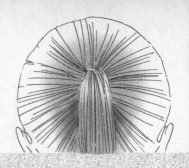

THOSE WEEKENDS AT THE LIBRARY...

SO YOU'RE SAYING, WHEN I DIED...

...YOU STOPPED CARING ABOUT THE ENTRANCE EXAMS? YOU STOPPED CARING ABOUT GOING TO COLLEGE?

I KEPT MY PROMISE AND WENT EVERY TIME...

DO YOU KNOW HOW MUCH TROUBLE YOU PUT ME THROUGH?

YOU CAN'T BE SERIOUS!

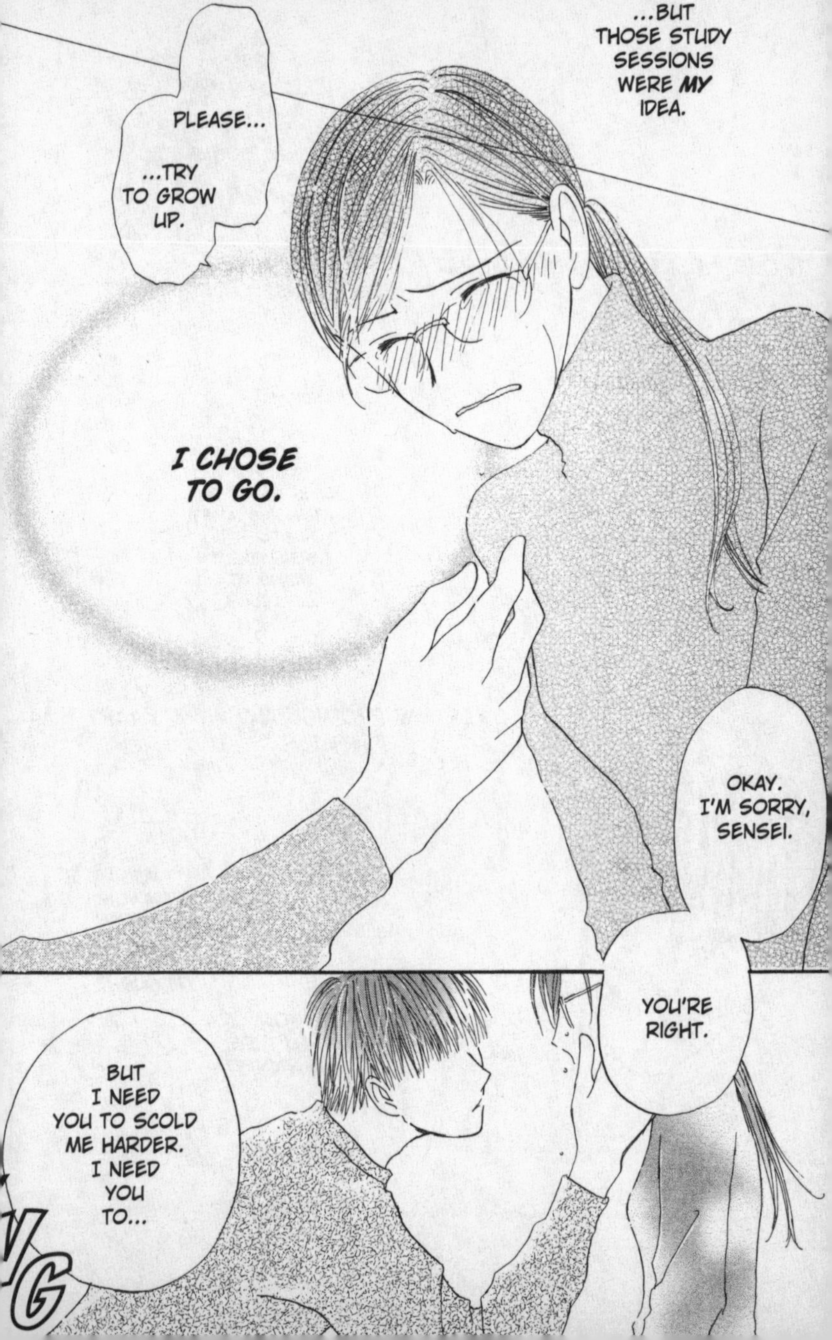
...BUT THOSE STUDY SESSIONS WERE MY IDEA.
PLEASE...
...TRY TO GROW UP.
I CHOSE TO GO.
OKAY. I'M SORRY, SENSEI.
YOU'RE RIGHT.
BUT I NEED YOU TO SCOLD ME HARDER. I NEED YOU TO...

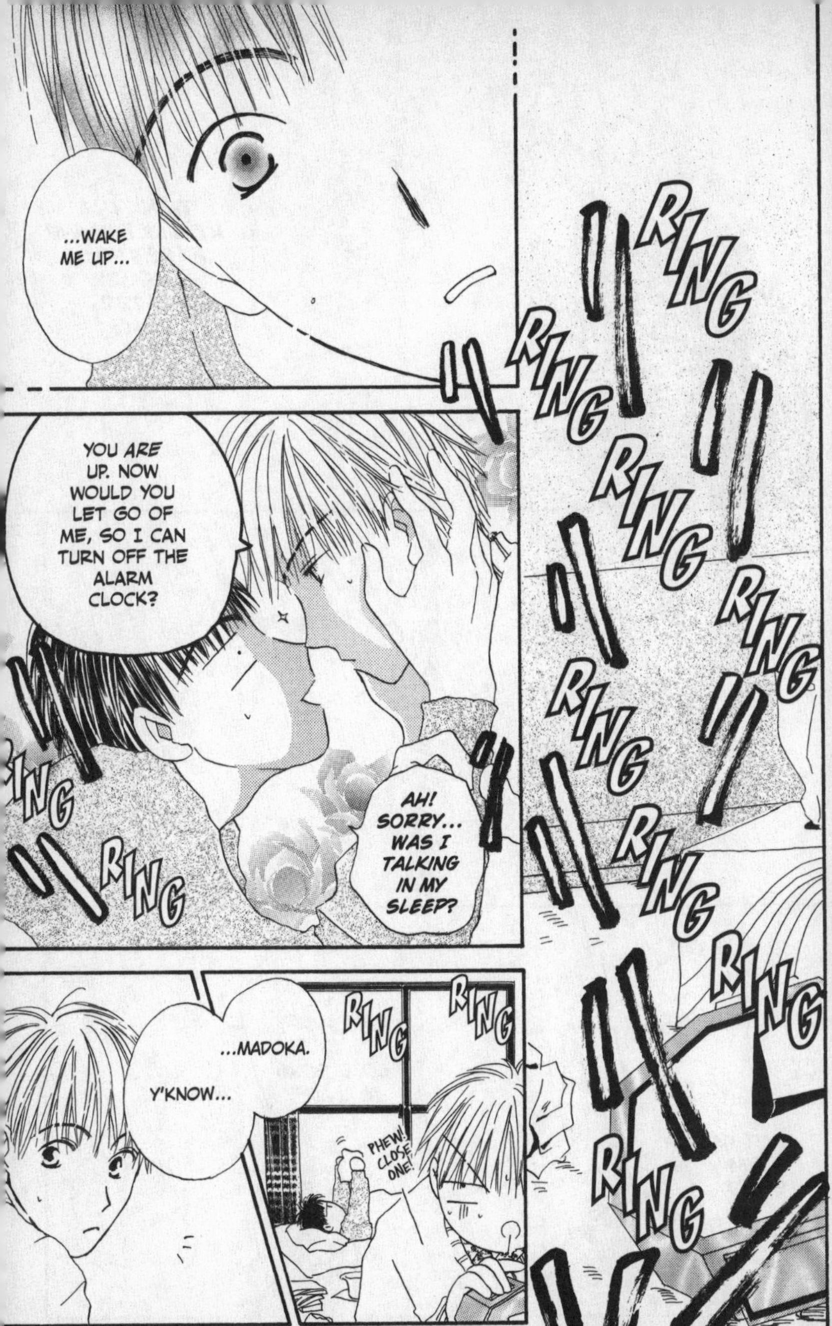
RING RING RING RING RING RING RING RING
...WAKE ME UP...
YOU ARE UP. NOW WOULD YOU LET GO OF ME, SO I CAN TURN OFF THE ALARM CLOCK?
AH! SORRY... WAS I TALKING IN MY SLEEP?
RING
RING RING
PHEW! CLOSE ONE!
...MADOKA.
Y'KNOW...

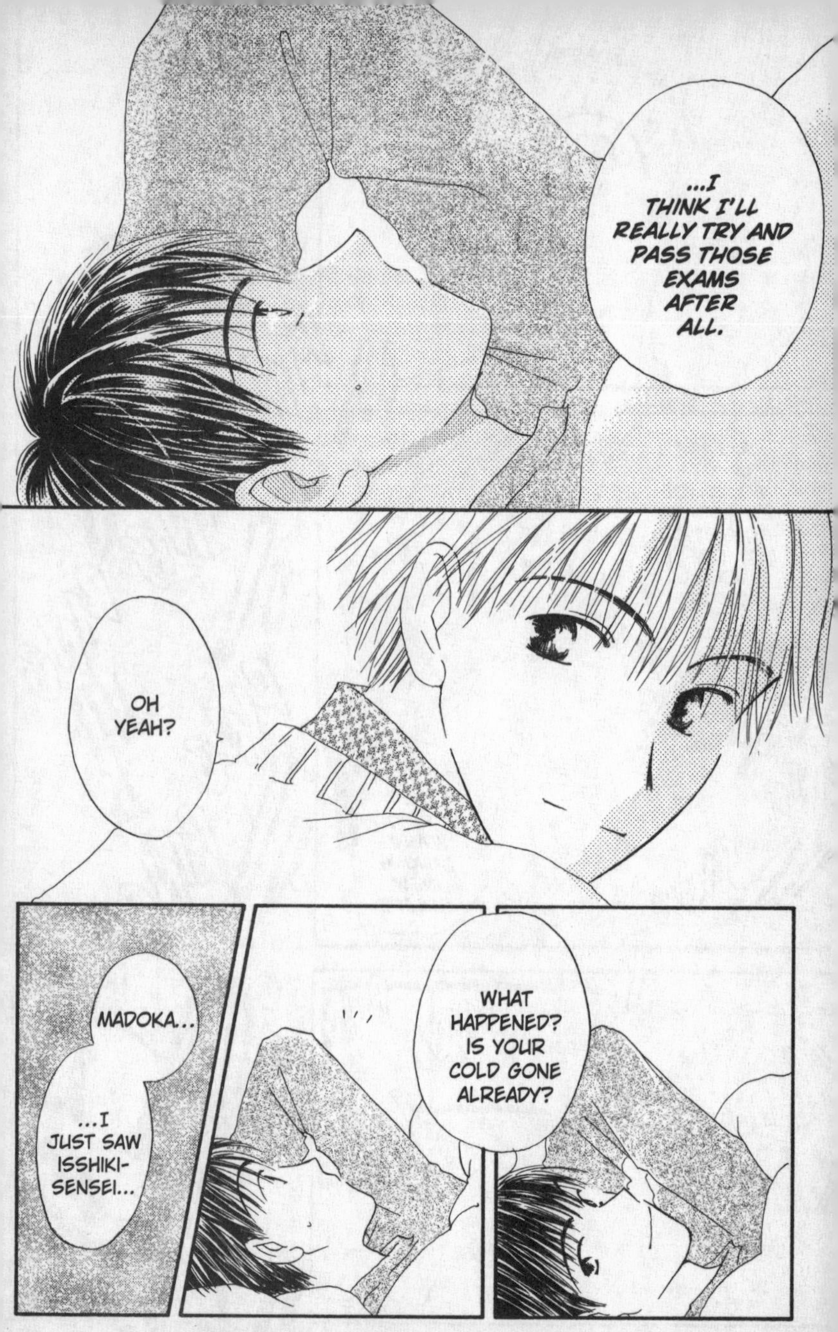
...I THINK I'LL REALLY TRY AND PASS THOSE EXAMS AFTER ALL.
OH YEAH?
WHAT HAPPENED? IS YOUR COLD GONE ALREADY?
MADOKA...
...I JUST SAW ISSHIKI-SENSEI...

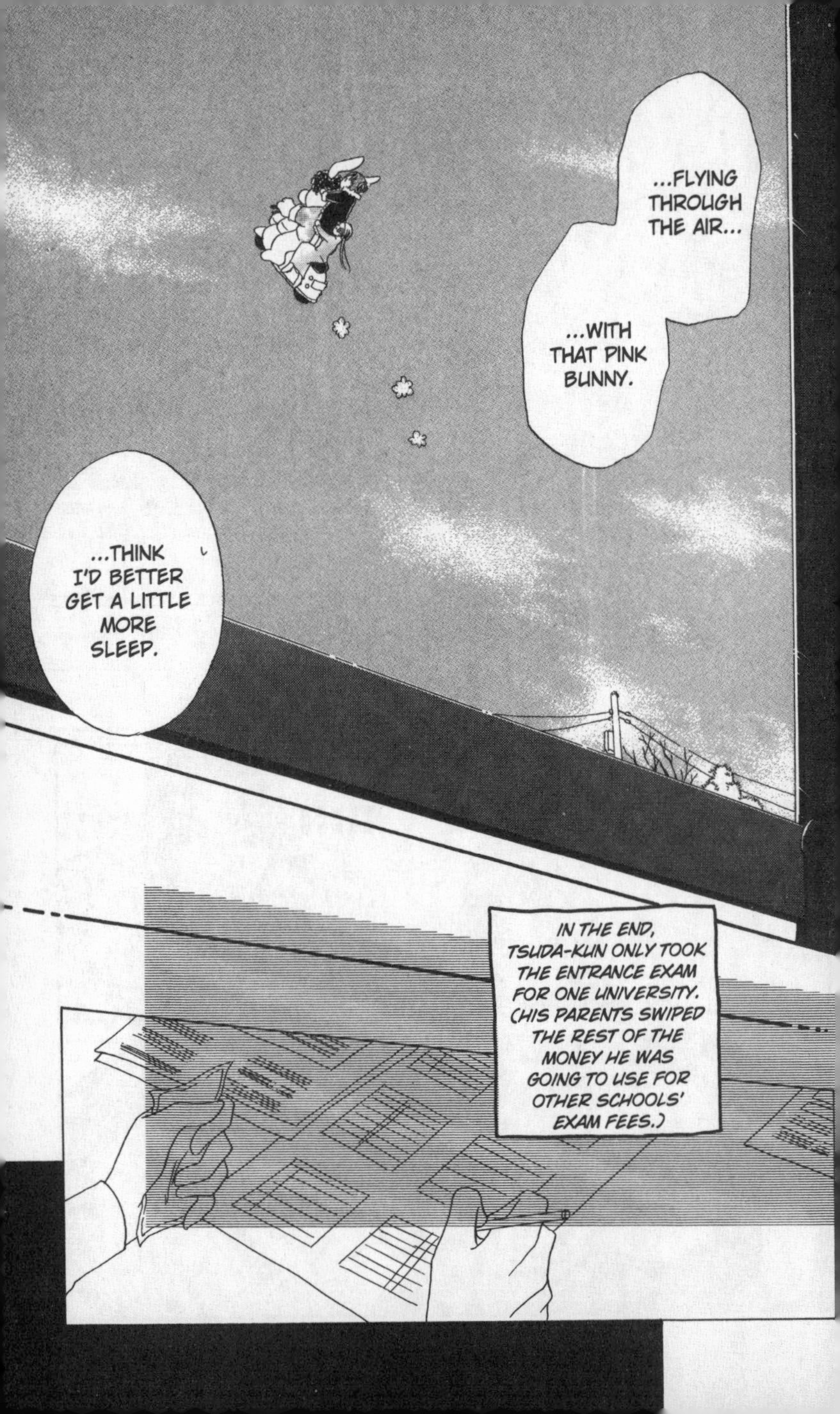
...FLYING THROUGH THE AIR...
...WITH THAT PINK BUNNY.
...THINK I'D BETTER GET A LITTLE MORE SLEEP.
IN THE END, TSUDA-KUN ONLY TOOK THE ENTRANCE EXAM FOR ONE UNIVERSITY. (HIS PARENTS SWIPED THE REST OF THE MONEY HE WAS GOING TO USE FOR OTHER SCHOOLS' EXAM FEES.)

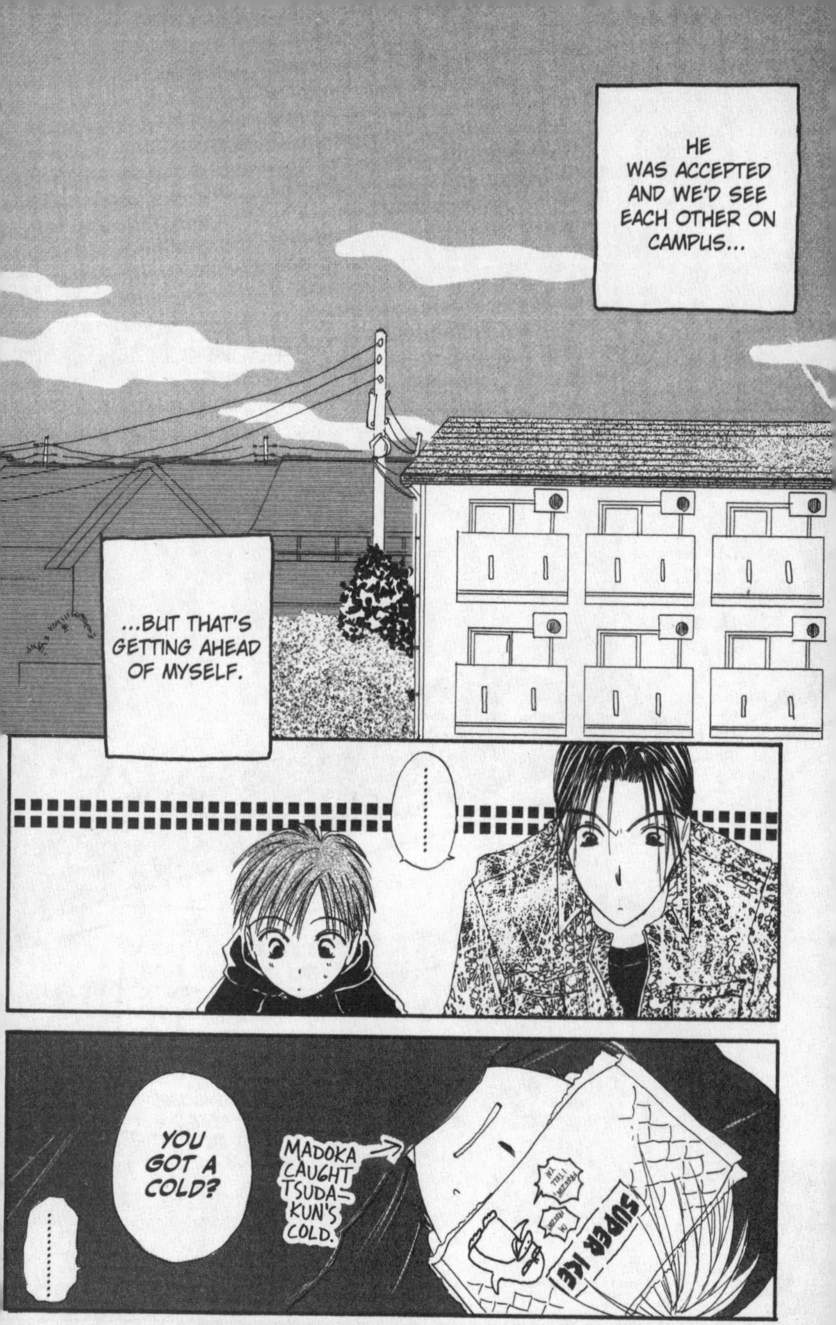
HE WAS ACCEPTED AND WE'D SEE EACH OTHER ON CAMPUS...
...BUT THAT'S GETTING AHEAD OF MYSELF.
......
SUPER ICE
MADOKA CAUGHT TSUDA-KUN'S COLD.
YOU GOT A COLD?
......

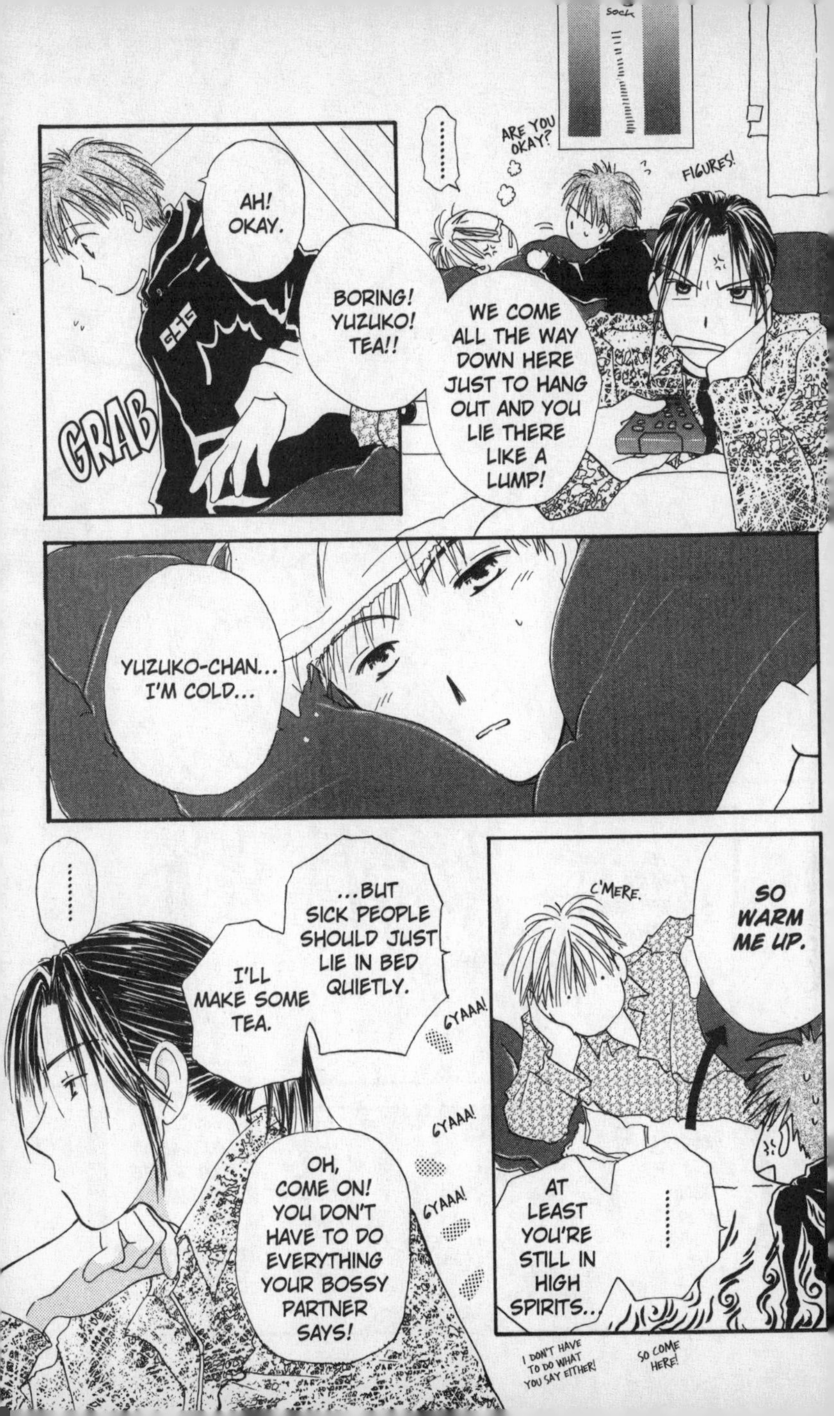

SOCK
ARE YOU OKAY?
FIGURES!
WE COME ALL THE WAY DOWN HERE JUST TO HANG OUT AND YOU LIE THERE LIKE A LUMP!
BORING! YUZUKO! TEA!!
......
AH! OKAY.
GRAB
YUZUKO-CHAN... I'M COLD...
SO WARM ME UP.
C'MERE.
......
AT LEAST YOU'RE STILL IN HIGH SPIRITS...
I DON'T HAVE TO DO WHAT YOU SAY EITHER!
SO COME HERE!
......
...BUT SICK PEOPLE SHOULD JUST LIE IN BED QUIETLY.
I'LL MAKE SOME TEA.
GYAAA!
GYAAA!
GYAAA!
OH, COME ON! YOU DON'T HAVE TO DO EVERYTHING YOUR BOSSY PARTNER SAYS!

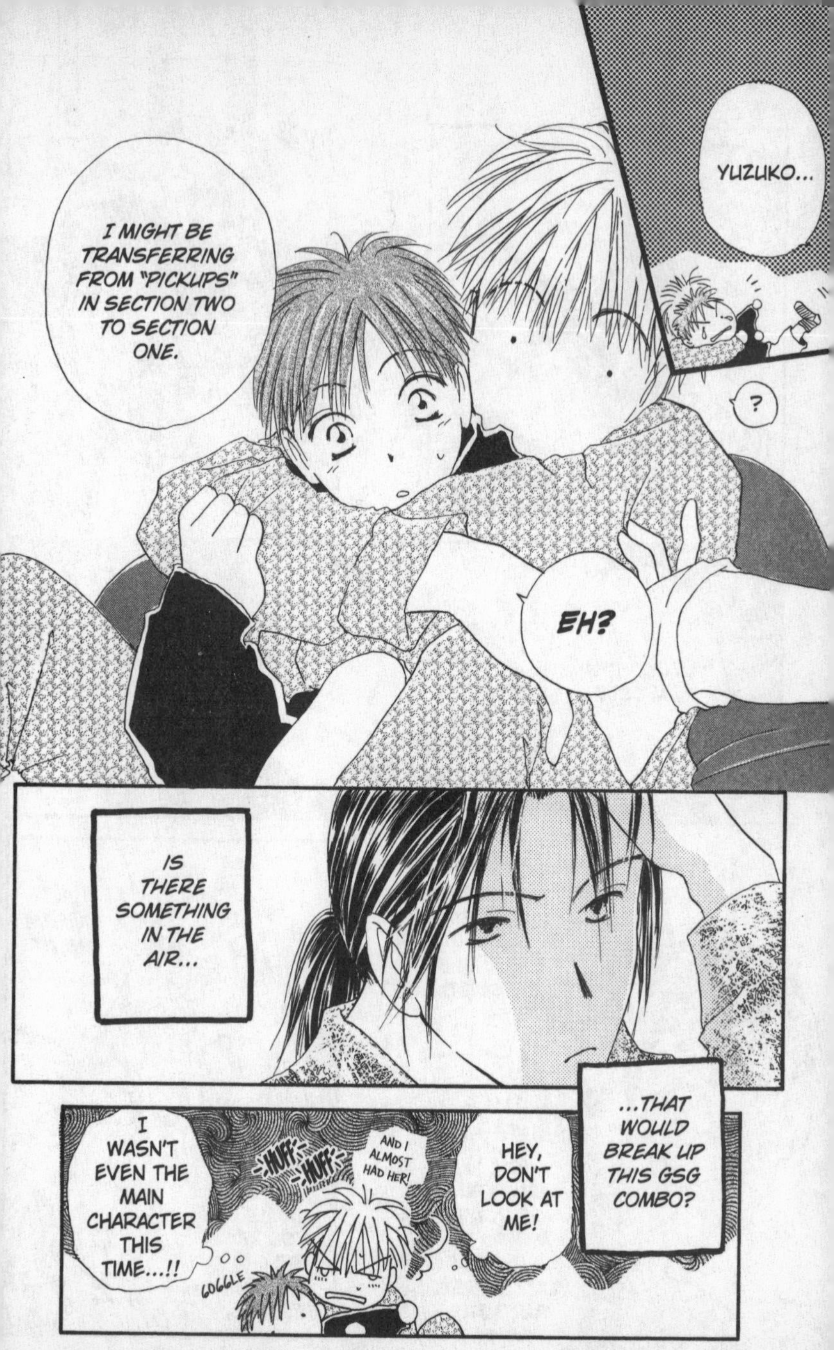
YUZUKO...
?
I MIGHT BE TRANSFERRING FROM "PICKUPS" IN SECTION TWO TO SECTION ONE.
EH?
IS THERE SOMETHING IN THE AIR...
...THAT WOULD BREAK UP THIS GSG COMBO?
HEY, DON'T LOOK AT ME!
AND I ALMOST HAD HER!
HUFF HUFF
I WASN'T EVEN THE MAIN CHARACTER THIS TIME...!!
GOGGLE

お迎えです。

OMUKAEDESU.

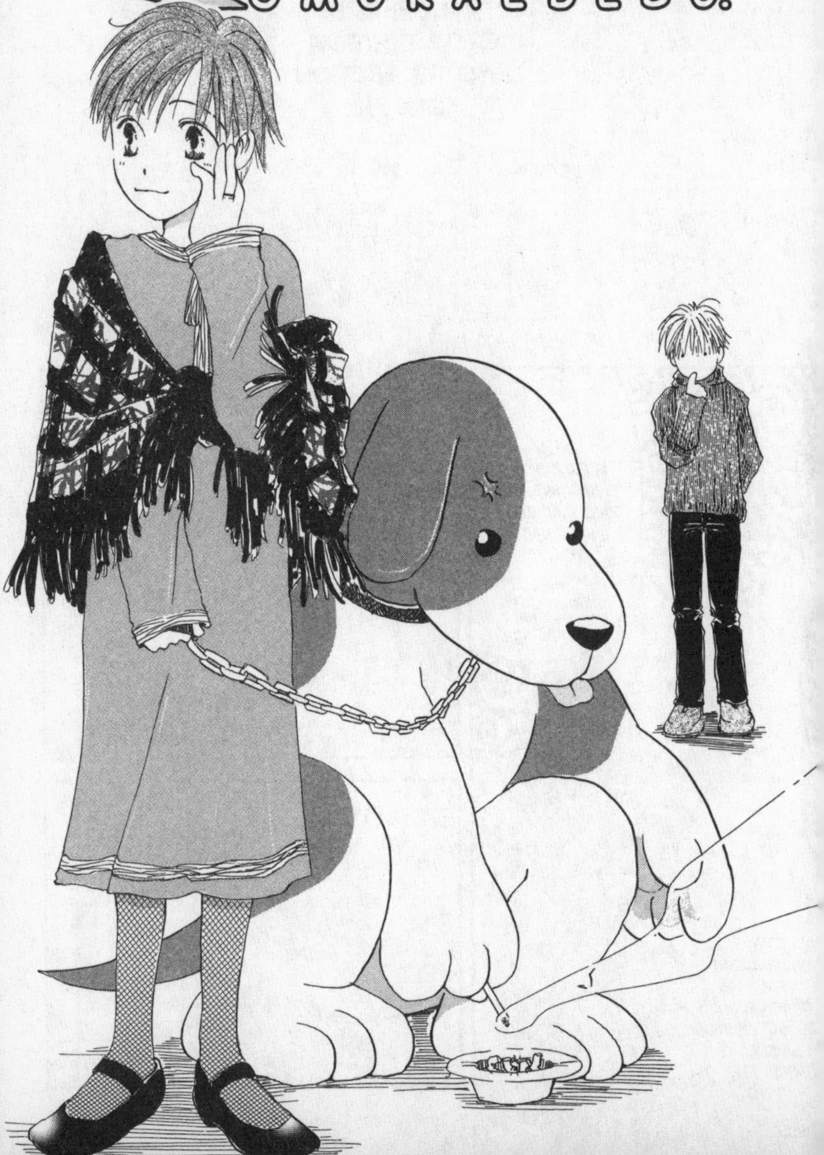

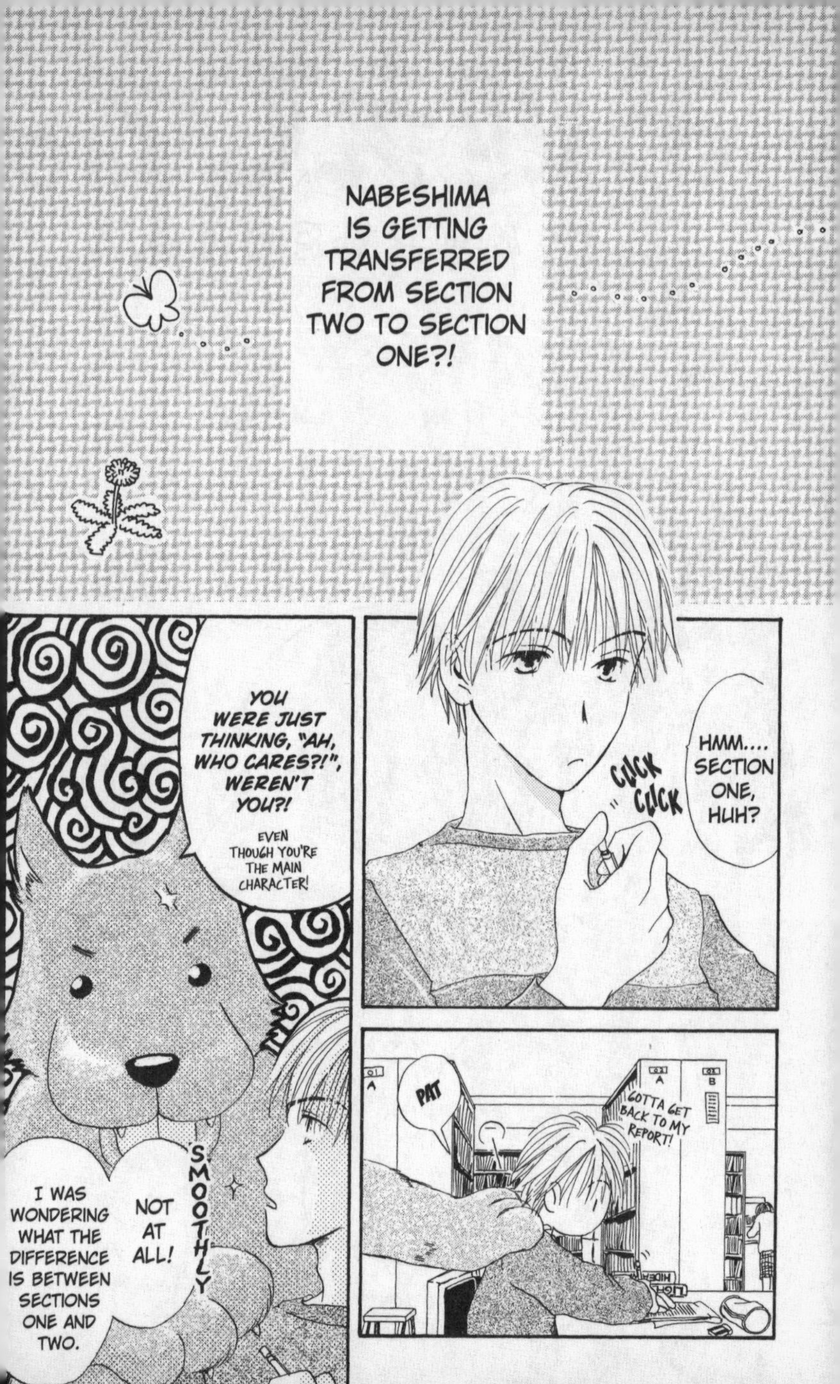
NABESHIMA IS GETTING TRANSFERRED FROM SECTION TWO TO SECTION ONE?!
CLICK CLICK
HMM.... SECTION ONE, HUH?
PAT
GOTTA GET BACK TO MY REPORT!
YOU WERE JUST THINKING, "AH, WHO CARES?!", WEREN'T YOU?!
EVEN THOUGH YOU'RE THE MAIN CHARACTER!
SMOOTHLY
NOT AT ALL!
I WAS WONDERING WHAT THE DIFFERENCE IS BETWEEN SECTIONS ONE AND TWO.

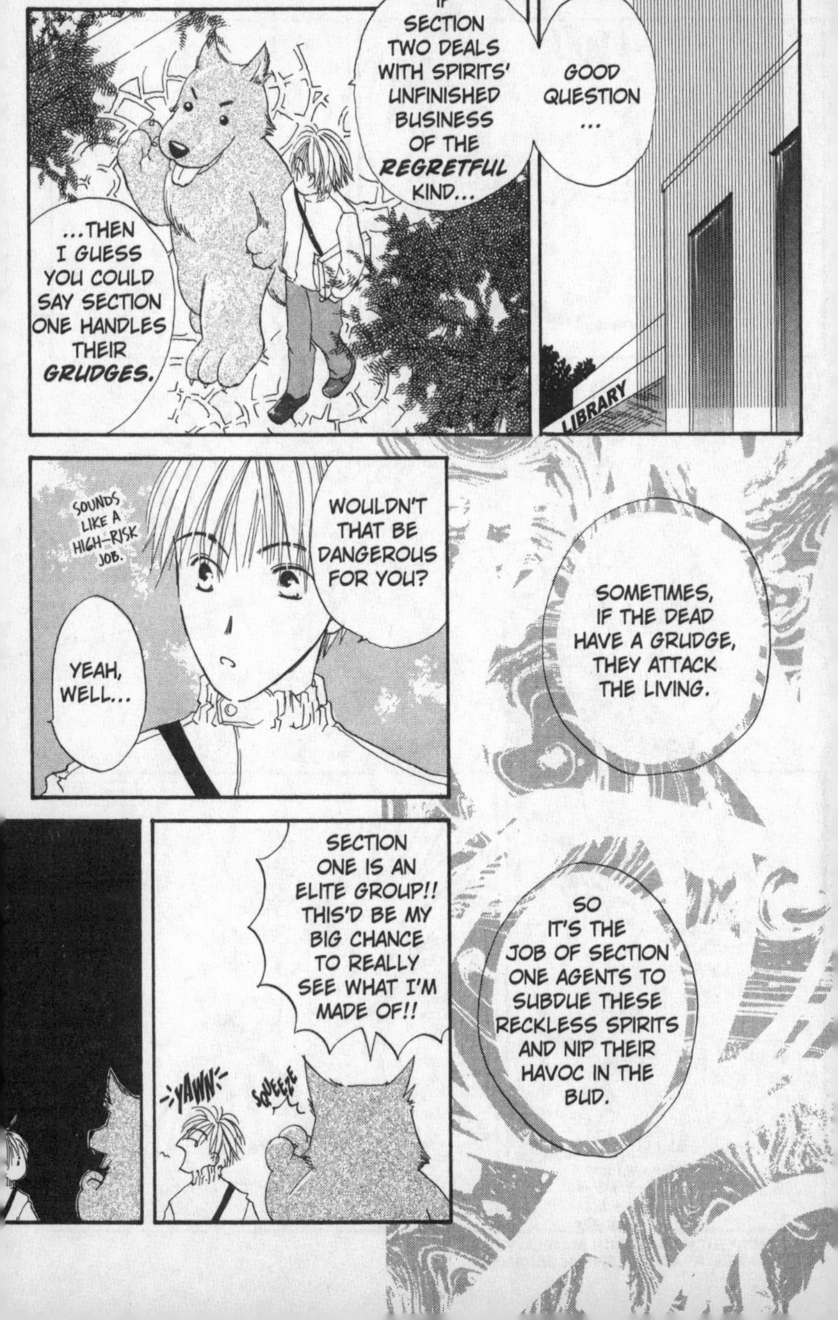
GOOD QUESTION ...
IF SECTION TWO DEALS WITH SPIRITS' UNFINISHED BUSINESS OF THE REGRETFUL KIND...
...THEN I GUESS YOU COULD SAY SECTION ONE HANDLES THEIR GRUDGES.
LIBRARY
SOMETIMES, IF THE DEAD HAVE A GRUDGE, THEY ATTACK THE LIVING.
SO IT'S THE JOB OF SECTION ONE AGENTS TO SUBDUE THESE RECKLESS SPIRITS AND NIP THEIR HAVOC IN THE BUD.
WOULDN'T THAT BE DANGEROUS FOR YOU?
SOUNDS LIKE A HIGH-RISK JOB.
YEAH, WELL...
SECTION ONE IS AN ELITE GROUP!! THIS'D BE MY BIG CHANCE TO REALLY SEE WHAT I'M MADE OF!!
SQUEEZE
YAWN

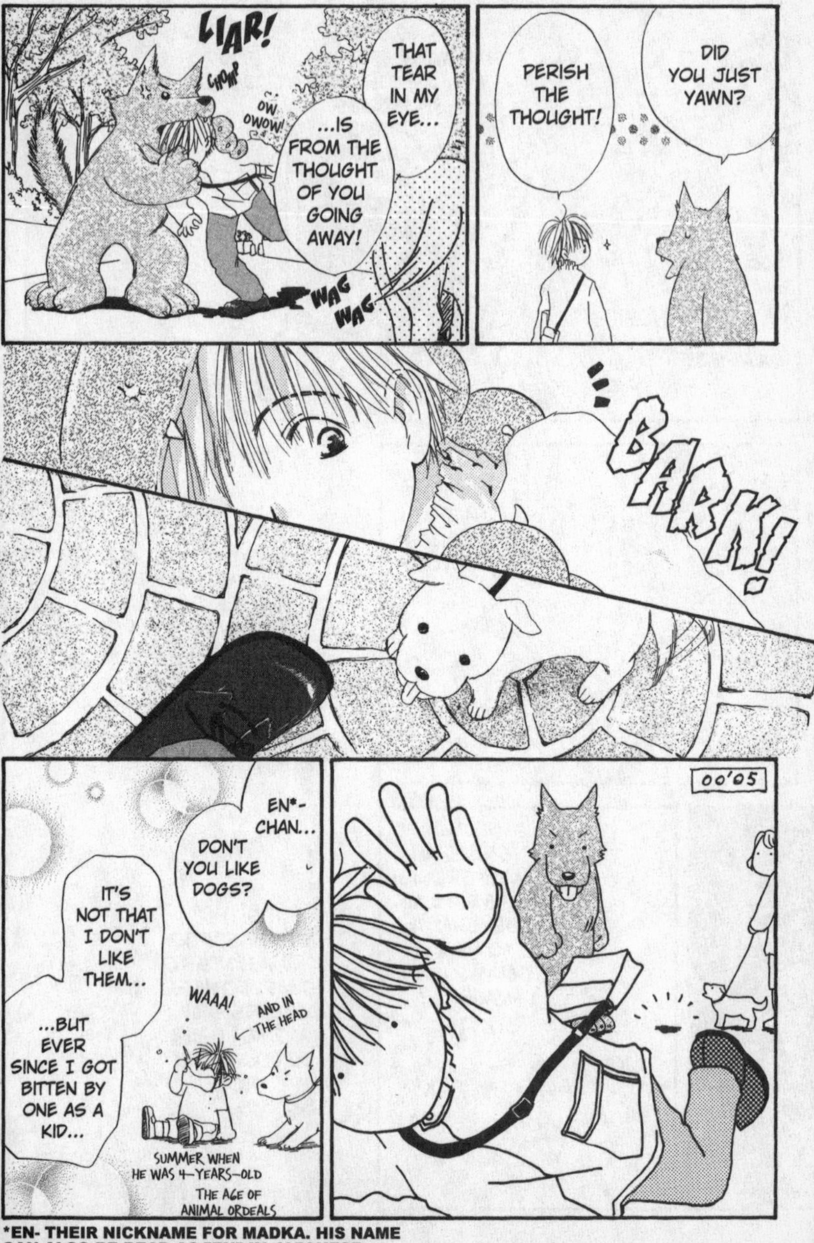
DID YOU JUST YAWN?
PERISH THE THOUGHT!
THAT TEAR IN MY EYE...
...IS FROM THE THOUGHT OF YOU GOING AWAY!
LIAR!
CHOMP
OW OWOW!
WAG WAG
BARK!
00'05
EN*-CHAN... DON'T YOU LIKE DOGS?
IT'S NOT THAT I DON'T LIKE THEM...
...BUT EVER SINCE I GOT BITTEN BY ONE AS A KID...
AND IN THE HEAD
WAAA!
SUMMER WHEN HE WAS 4-YEARS-OLD
THE AGE OF ANIMAL ORDEALS

*EN- THEIR NICKNAME FOR MADKA. HIS NAME CAN ALSO BE READ AS "EN" IN JAPANESE.

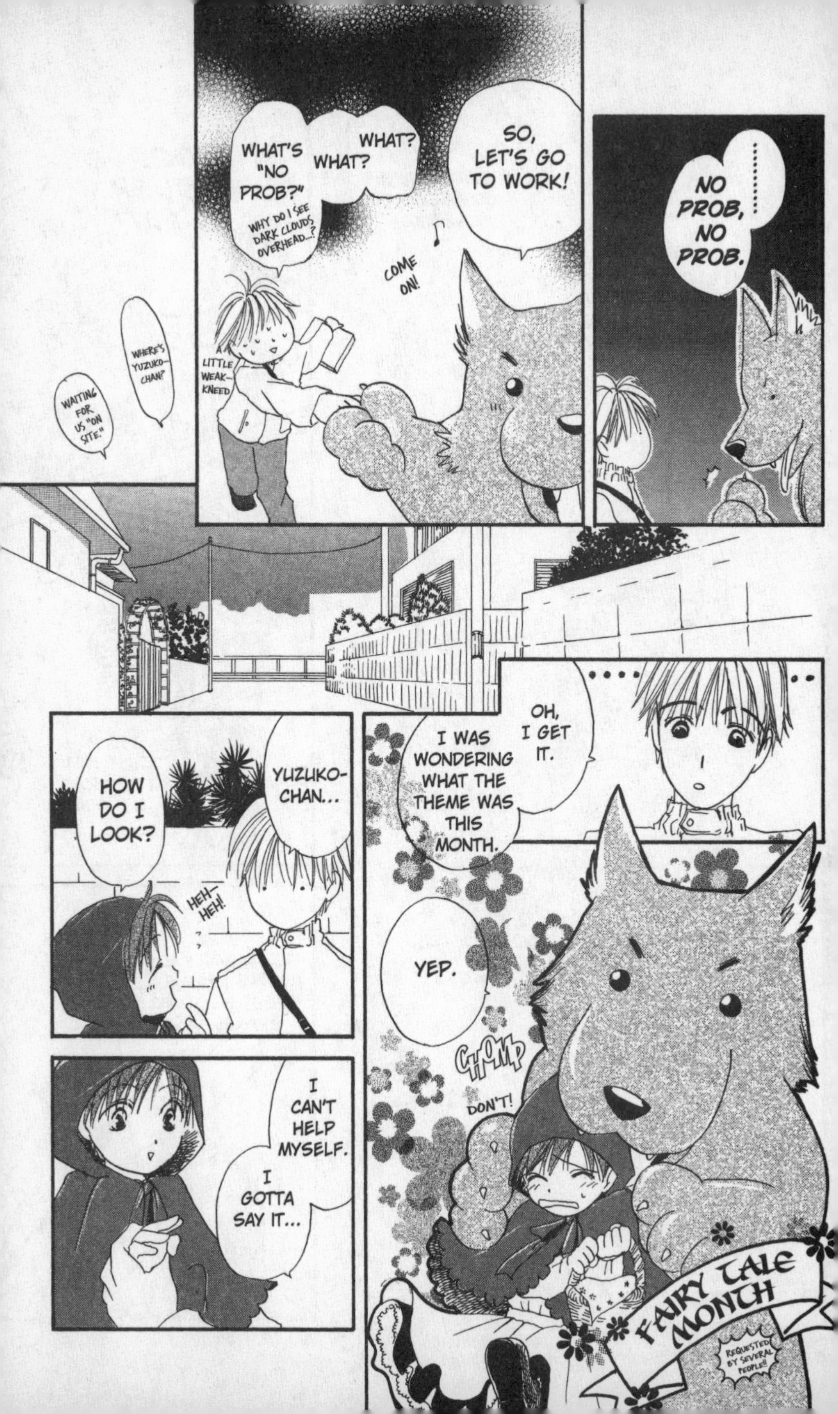
......
NO PROB, NO PROB.
SO, LET'S GO TO WORK!
WHAT? WHAT?
WHAT'S "NO PROB?"
WHY DO I SEE DARK CLOUDS OVERHEAD...?
COME ON!
A LITTLE WEAK-KNEED
WHERE'S YUZUKO-CHAN?
WAITING FOR US "ON SITE."
YUZUKO-CHAN...
HOW DO I LOOK?
HEH-HEH!
I CAN'T HELP MYSELF.
I GOTTA SAY IT...
....
OH, I GET IT.
I WAS WONDERING WHAT THE THEME WAS THIS MONTH.
YEP.
CHOMP
DON'T!
FAIRY TALE MONTH
REQUESTED BY SEVERAL PEOPLE!!

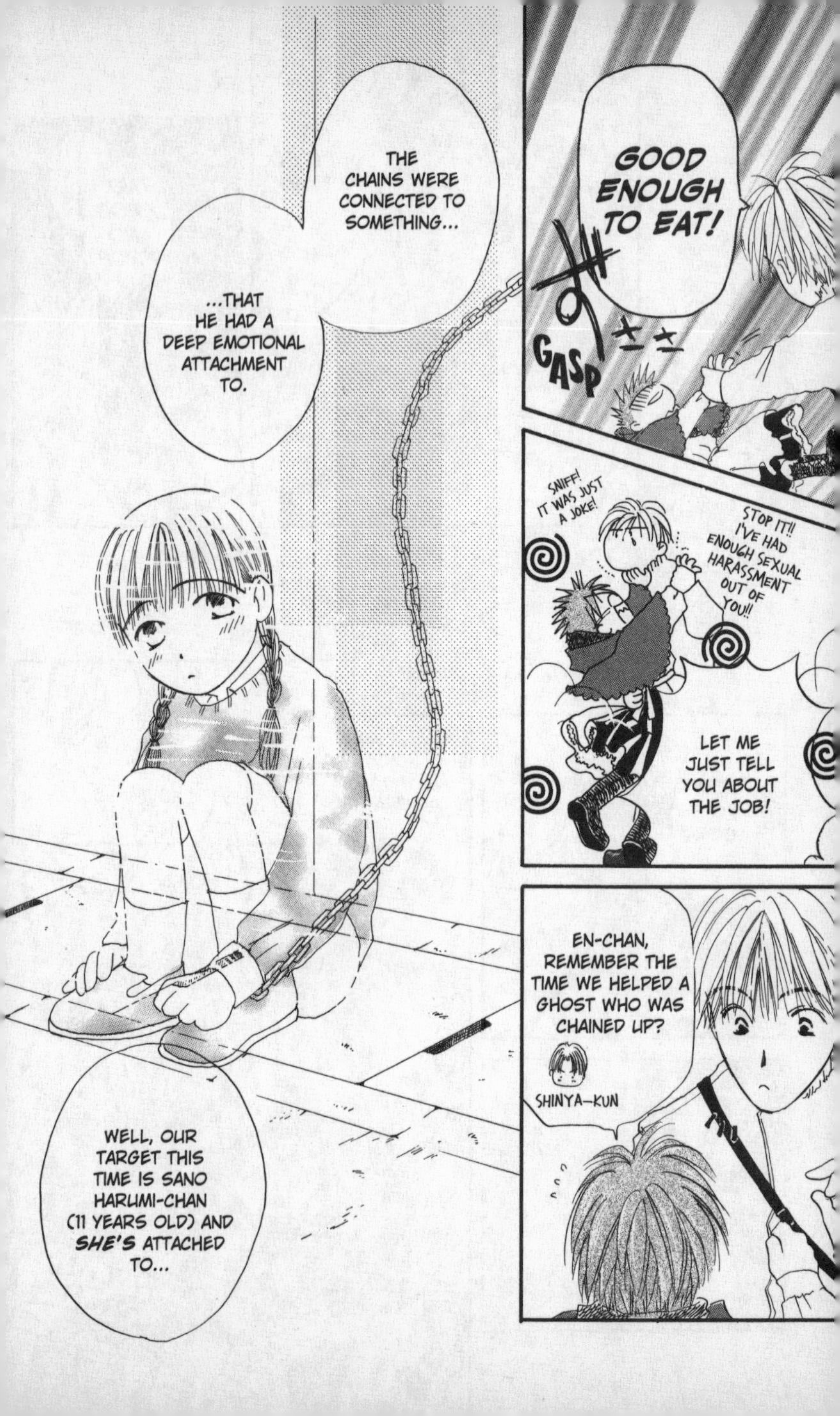
GOOD ENOUGH TO EAT!
GASP
STOP IT!! I'VE HAD ENOUGH SEXUAL HARASSMENT OUT OF YOU!!
SNIFF! IT WAS JUST A JOKE!
LET ME JUST TELL YOU ABOUT THE JOB!
EN-CHAN, REMEMBER THE TIME WE HELPED A GHOST WHO WAS CHAINED UP?
SHINYA-KUN
THE CHAINS WERE CONNECTED TO SOMETHING...
...THAT HE HAD A DEEP EMOTIONAL ATTACHMENT TO.
WELL, OUR TARGET THIS TIME IS SANO HARUMI-CHAN (11 YEARS OLD) AND SHE'S ATTACHED TO...

BEWARE OF DOG

BEWARE
OF
DOG
THUD
THUD
HEY, WAIT! WAIT!
THAT SIGN IS JUST A BLUFF!
I'M OUTTA HERE.
RIGHT, HARUMI-CHAN?!
THUD
I CAN'T DO THIS, I CAN'T DO THIS, I CAN'T DO THIS!
UH... UM...

I BITE, BABY. ♥

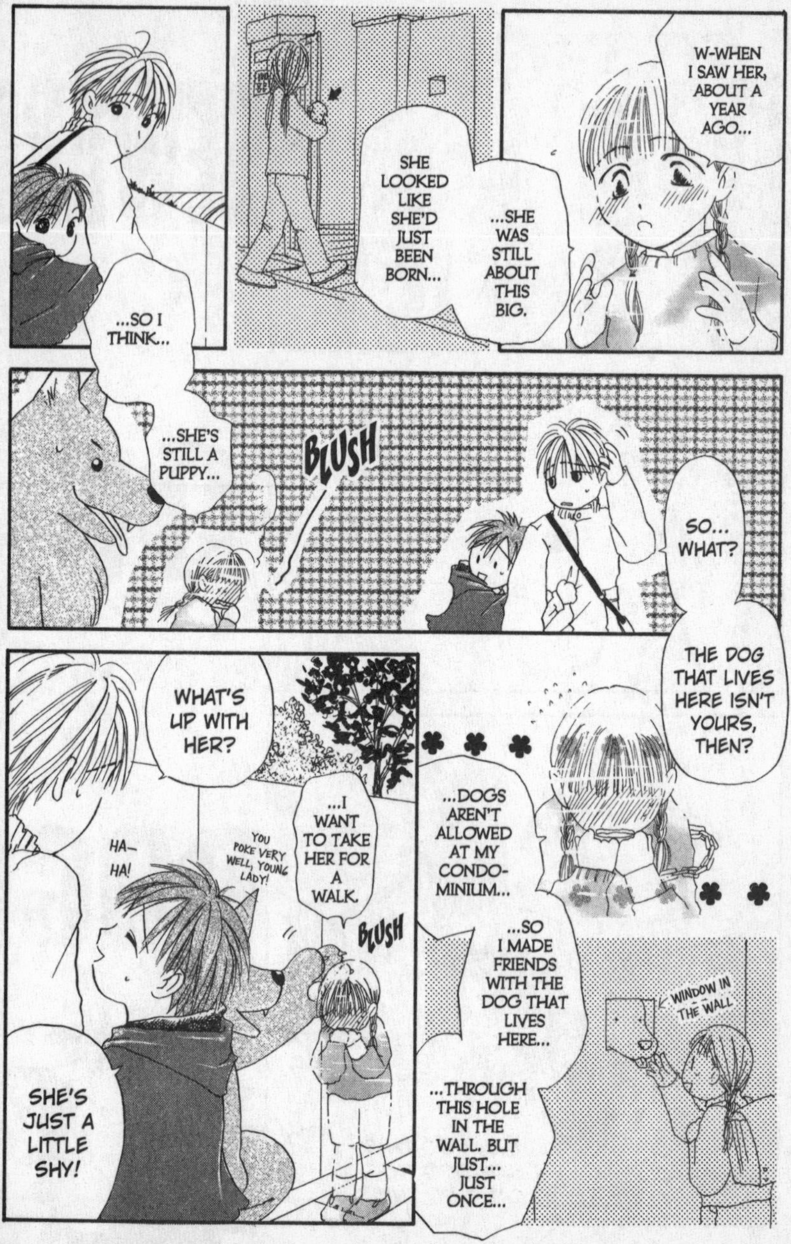
W-WHEN I SAW HER, ABOUT A YEAR AGO...
...SHE WAS STILL ABOUT THIS BIG.
SHE LOOKED LIKE SHE'D JUST BEEN BORN...
...SO I THINK...
...SHE'S STILL A PUPPY...
BLUSH
SO... WHAT?
THE DOG THAT LIVES HERE ISN'T YOURS, THEN?
...DOGS AREN'T ALLOWED AT MY CONDO-MINIUM...
...SO I MADE FRIENDS WITH THE DOG THAT LIVES HERE...
WINDOW IN THE WALL
...THROUGH THIS HOLE IN THE WALL. BUT JUST... JUST ONCE...
...I WANT TO TAKE HER FOR A WALK.
BLUSH
WHAT'S UP WITH HER?
YOU POKE VERY WELL, YOUNG LADY!
HA-HA!
SHE'S JUST A LITTLE SHY!

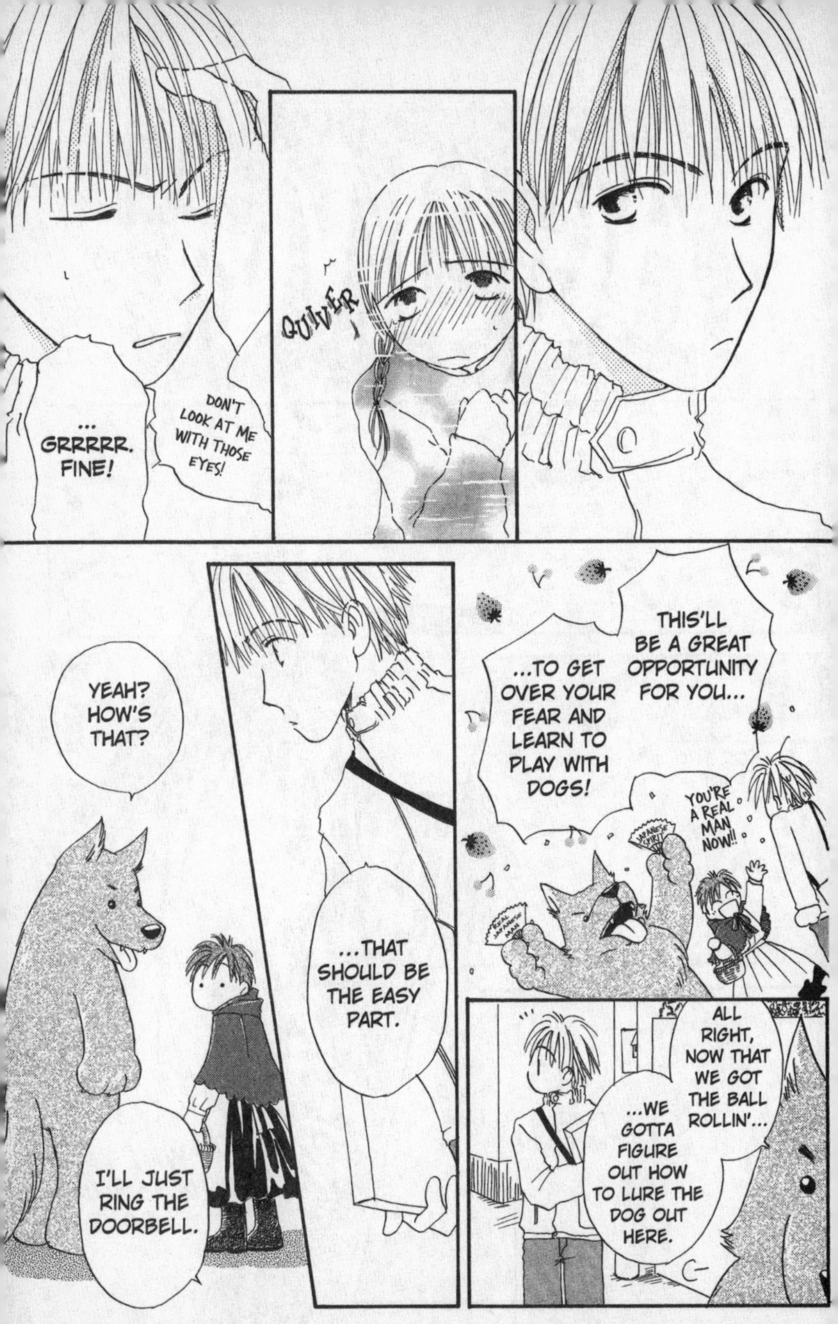
QUIVER
DON'T LOOK AT ME WITH THOSE EYES!
... GRRRRR. FINE!
THIS'LL BE A GREAT OPPORTUNITY FOR YOU...
...TO GET OVER YOUR FEAR AND LEARN TO PLAY WITH DOGS!
YOU'RE A REAL MAN NOW!!
JAPANESE SPIRIT
REAL JAPANESE MAN
ALL RIGHT, NOW THAT WE GOT THE BALL ROLLIN'...
...WE GOTTA FIGURE OUT HOW TO LURE THE DOG OUT HERE.
...THAT SHOULD BE THE EASY PART.
YEAH? HOW'S THAT?
I'LL JUST RING THE DOORBELL.

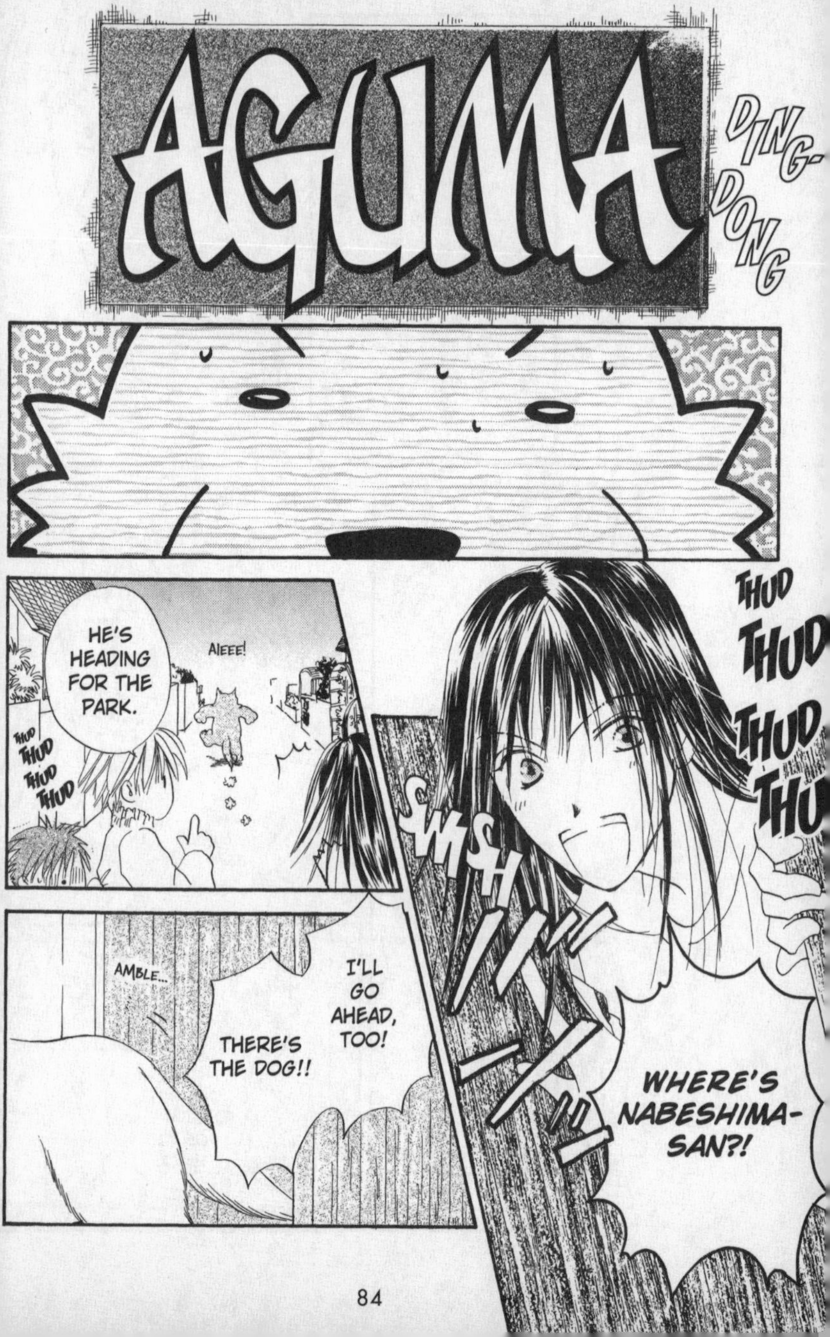
AGUMA
DING-DONG
THUD THUD THUD THU
HE'S HEADING FOR THE PARK.
AIEEE!
THUD THUD THUD THUD
SWSH
I'LL GO AHEAD, TOO!
THERE'S THE DOG!!
AMBLE...
WHERE'S NABESHIMA-SAN?!

HER NAME IS BESSIE.

SHE'S REALLY GENTLE, SO DON'T WORRY!

PYRENE'S DOG

TCH. I'LL CATCH UP TO HIM!

WHAT A CUTIE!

BESSIE... I WONDER IF SHE TOOK THE NAME FROM NABESHIMA-SAN?

BUT SHE IS REALLY GENTLE...

SHE'S A LITTLE TOO BIG FOR MY TASTE...

I'M SORRY, HARUMI-CHAN...

HE'LL LEND YOU HIS BODY AFTER HE GETS A LITTLE MORE USED TO BEING AROUND THE DOG.

FLASH

85

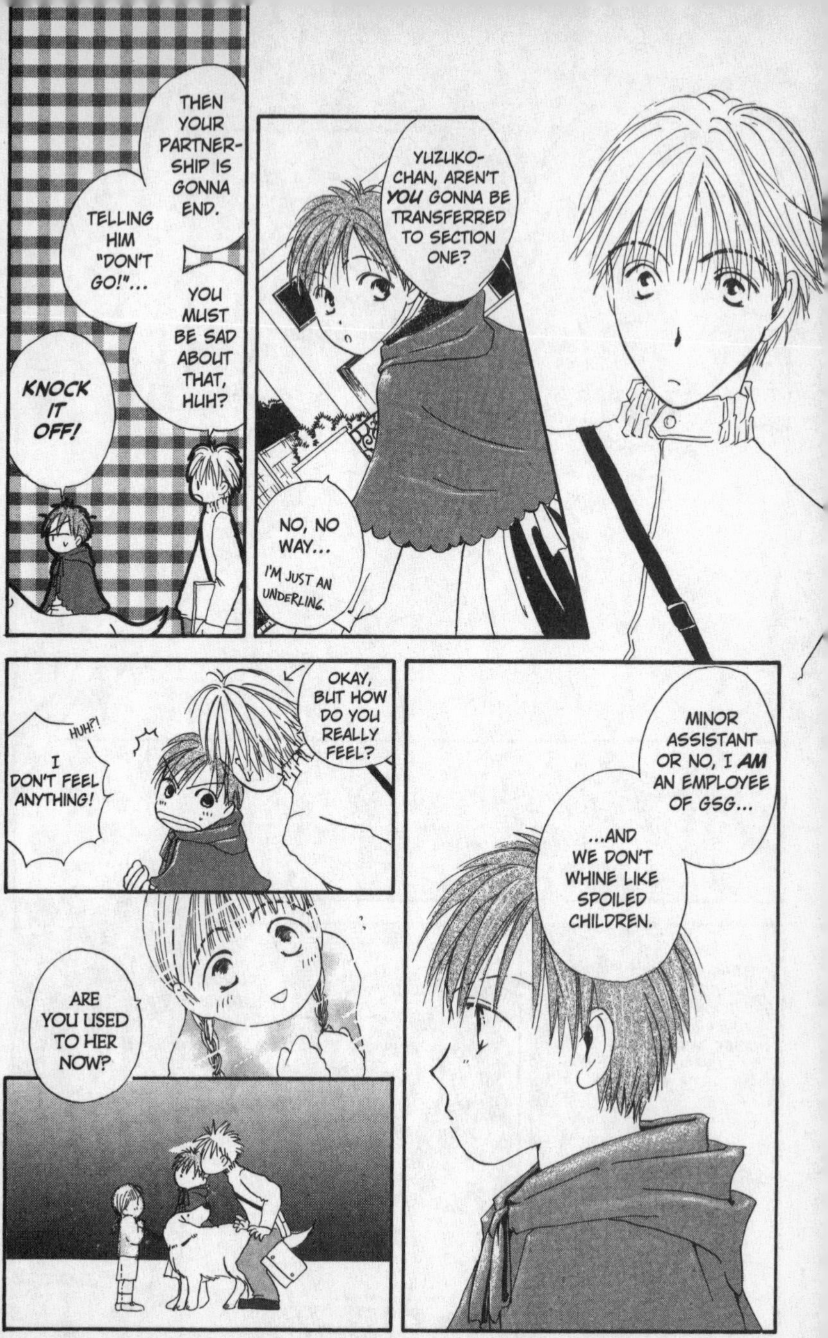
YUZUKO-CHAN, AREN'T *YOU* GONNA BE TRANSFERRED TO SECTION ONE?
NO, NO WAY...
I'M JUST AN UNDERLING.
THEN YOUR PARTNERSHIP IS GONNA END.
TELLING HIM "DON'T GO!"...
YOU MUST BE SAD ABOUT THAT, HUH?
KNOCK IT OFF!
MINOR ASSISTANT OR NO, I *AM* AN EMPLOYEE OF GSG...
...AND WE DON'T WHINE LIKE SPOILED CHILDREN.
OKAY, BUT HOW DO YOU REALLY FEEL?
HUH?!
I DON'T FEEL ANYTHING!
ARE YOU USED TO HER NOW?

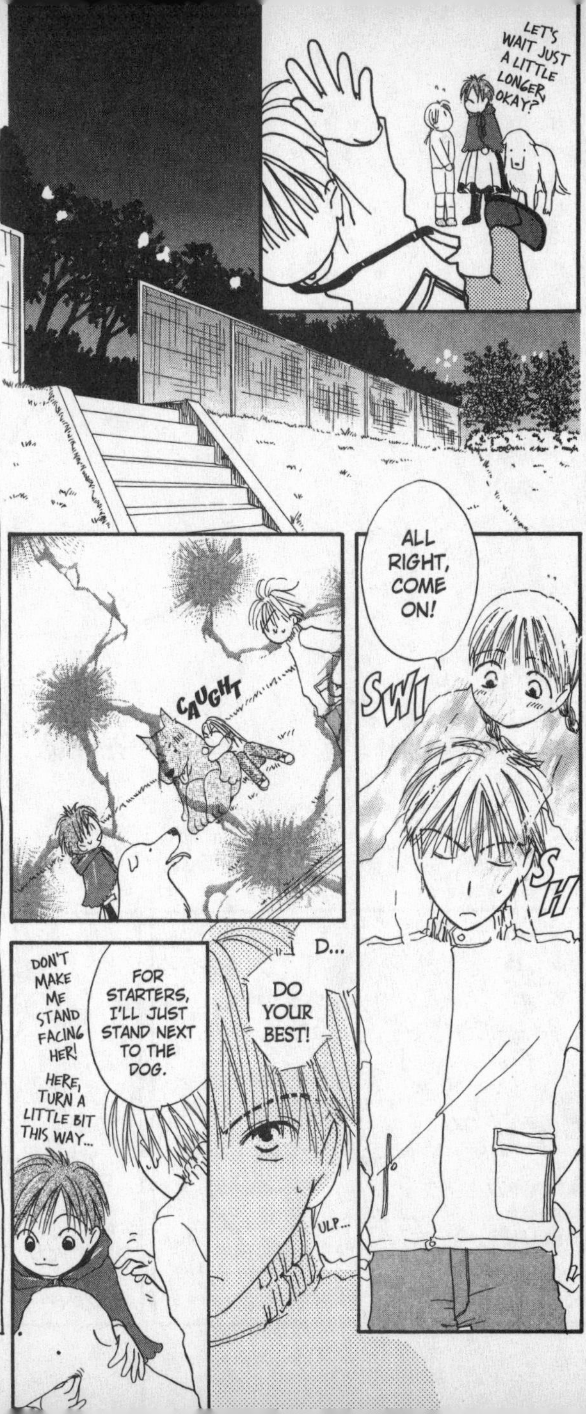
LET'S WAIT JUST A LITTLE LONGER, OKAY?
ALL RIGHT, COME ON!
SWI
SH
CAUGHT
D...
DO YOUR BEST!
FOR STARTERS, I'LL JUST STAND NEXT TO THE DOG.
DON'T MAKE ME STAND FACING HER!
HERE, TURN A LITTLE BIT THIS WAY...
ULP...

SERIALIZATION.

****

WHEN I STARTED THIS SERIES, IT WAS THE FIRST TIME I'D DONE A THREE-PART STORY. AND IN THOSE THREE MONTHS, I REALIZED HOW TOUGH IT WAS TO DO A CONTINUING STORY.

UNTIL THEN, I'D JUST DONE "DONE-IN-ONE PART" STORIES AND EACH TIME I HAD SOMEONE TO HELP ME WORK ON IT, BUT FOR SOME REASON, THE INSTANT I DECIDED TO GO WITH A CONTINUING STORY, IT ALL FELL ON MY SHOULDERS ALONE.

EVEN SO, IT'S ONE OF THOSE THINGS THAT IF YOU JUST APPLY YOURSELF, IT'LL WORK OUT...

I GOT A CALL FROM MY EDITOR, ASKING ME IF I NEEDED ANY HELP, BUT...

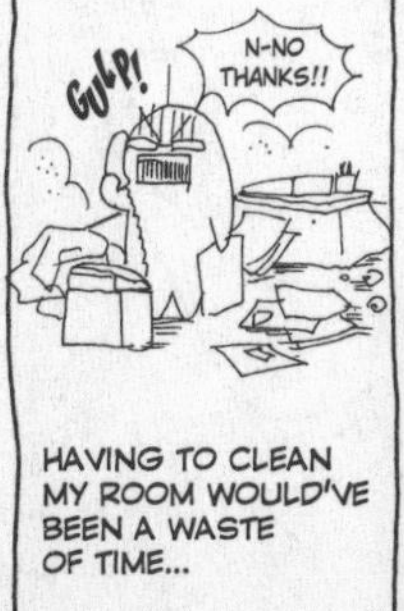
GULP!
N-NO THANKS!!

HAVING TO CLEAN MY ROOM WOULD'VE BEEN A WASTE OF TIME...

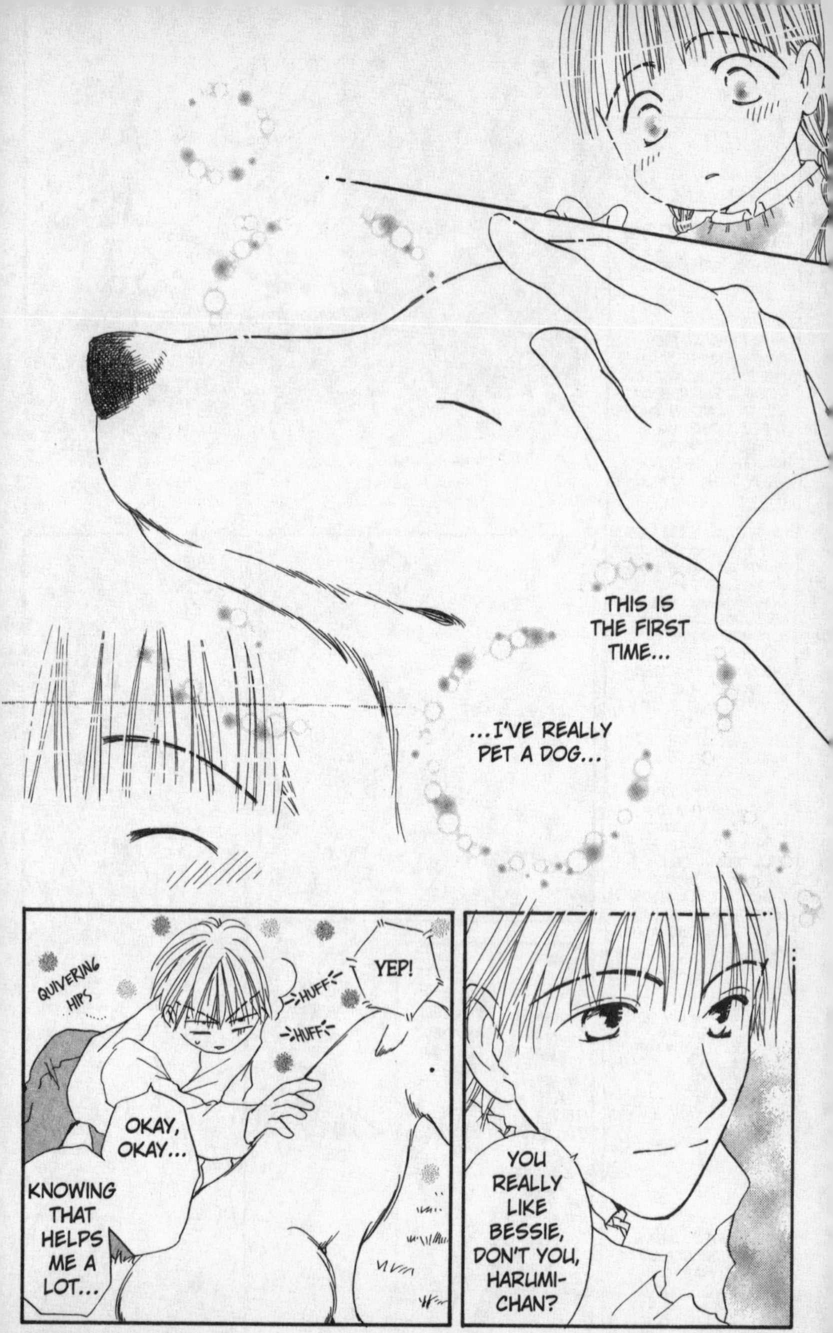
THIS IS THE FIRST TIME...
...I'VE REALLY PET A DOG...
YOU REALLY LIKE BESSIE, DON'T YOU, HARUMI-CHAN?
YEP!
HUFF
HUFF
QUIVERING HIPS
OKAY, OKAY...
KNOWING THAT HELPS ME A LOT...

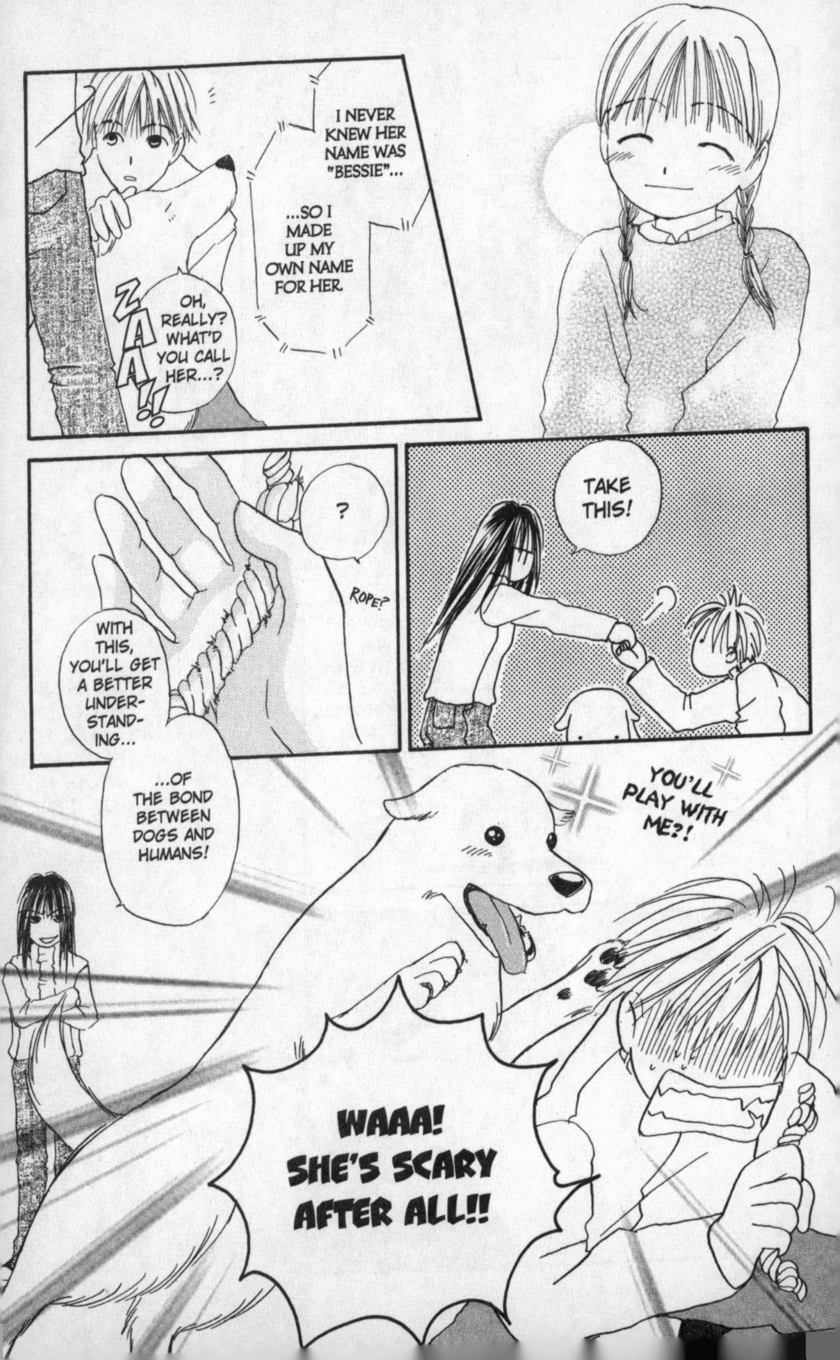
I NEVER KNEW HER NAME WAS "BESSIE"...
...SO I MADE UP MY OWN NAME FOR HER.
OH, REALLY? WHAT'D YOU CALL HER...?
ZAA!!
TAKE THIS!
?
ROPE?
WITH THIS, YOU'LL GET A BETTER UNDER-STANDING-ING...
...OF THE BOND BETWEEN DOGS AND HUMANS!
YOU'LL PLAY WITH ME?!
WAAA! SHE'S SCARY AFTER ALL!!

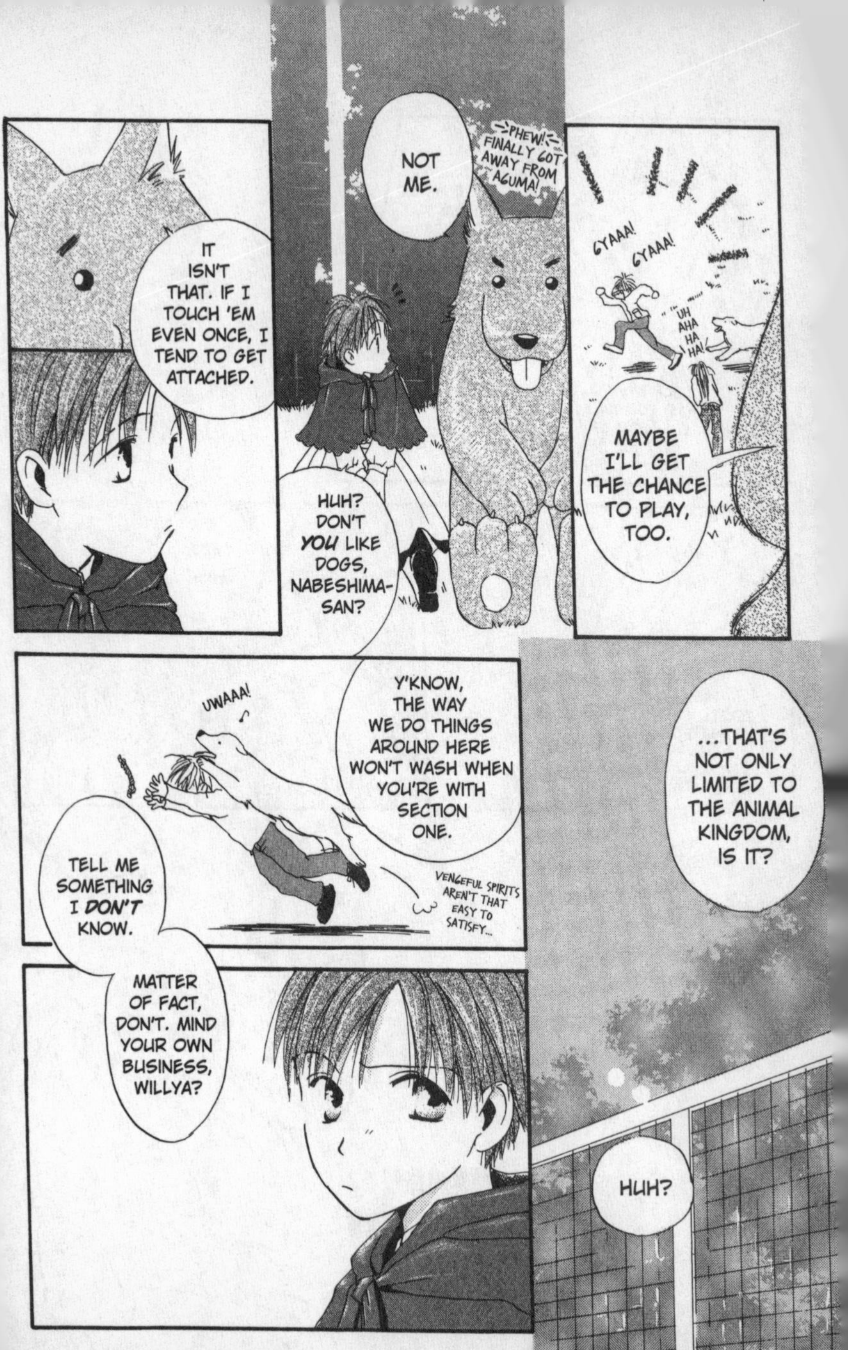
GYAAA!
GYAAA!
UH AHA HA HA!
MAYBE I'LL GET THE CHANCE TO PLAY, TOO.
PHEW! FINALLY GOT AWAY FROM AGUMA!
HUH? DON'T *YOU* LIKE DOGS, NABESHIMA-SAN?
NOT ME.
IT ISN'T THAT. IF I TOUCH 'EM EVEN ONCE, I TEND TO GET ATTACHED.
Y'KNOW, THE WAY WE DO THINGS AROUND HERE WON'T WASH WHEN YOU'RE WITH SECTION ONE.
UWAAA!
VENGEFUL SPIRITS AREN'T THAT EASY TO SATISFY...
TELL ME SOMETHING I *DON'T* KNOW.
...THAT'S NOT ONLY LIMITED TO THE ANIMAL KINGDOM, IS IT?
HUH?
MATTER OF FACT, DON'T. MIND YOUR OWN BUSINESS, WILLYA?

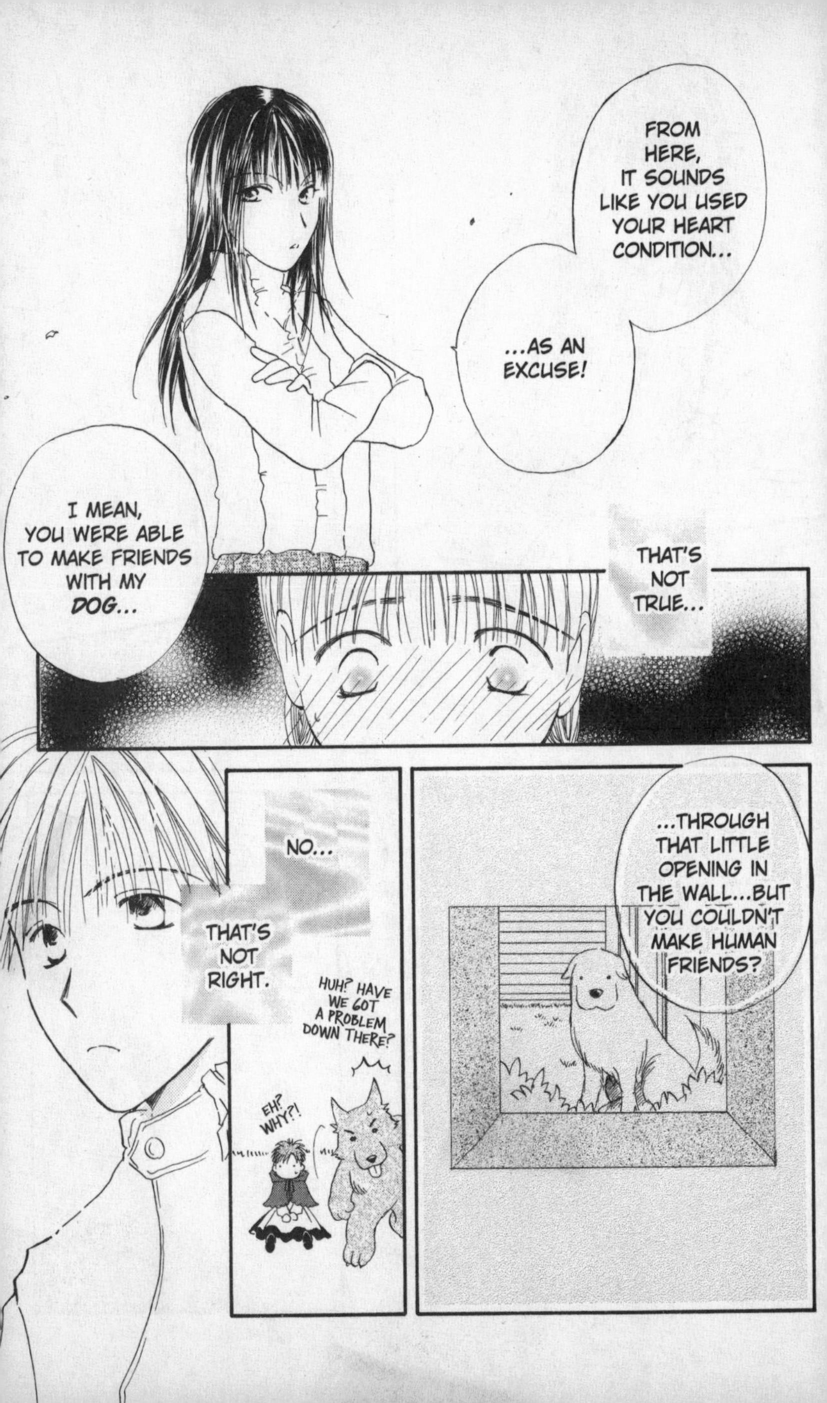
FROM HERE, IT SOUNDS LIKE YOU USED YOUR HEART CONDITION...
...AS AN EXCUSE!
I MEAN, YOU WERE ABLE TO MAKE FRIENDS WITH MY *DOG*...
THAT'S NOT TRUE...
...THROUGH THAT LITTLE OPENING IN THE WALL...BUT YOU COULDN'T MAKE HUMAN FRIENDS?
NO...
THAT'S NOT RIGHT.
HUH? HAVE WE GOT A PROBLEM DOWN THERE?
EH? WHY?!

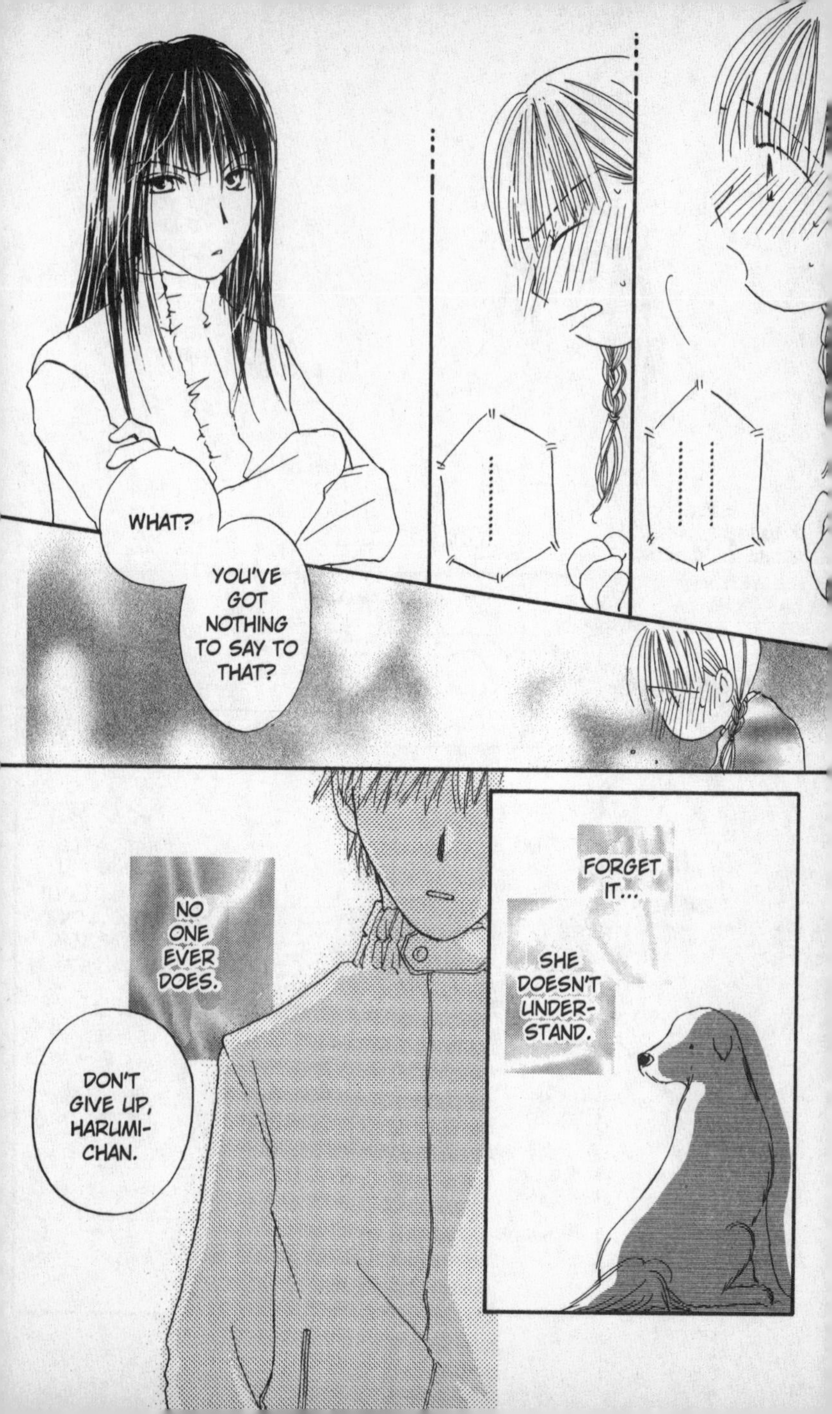
WHAT?
YOU'VE GOT NOTHING TO SAY TO THAT?
FORGET IT...
SHE DOESN'T UNDER-STAND.
NO ONE EVER DOES.
DON'T GIVE UP, HARUMI-CHAN.

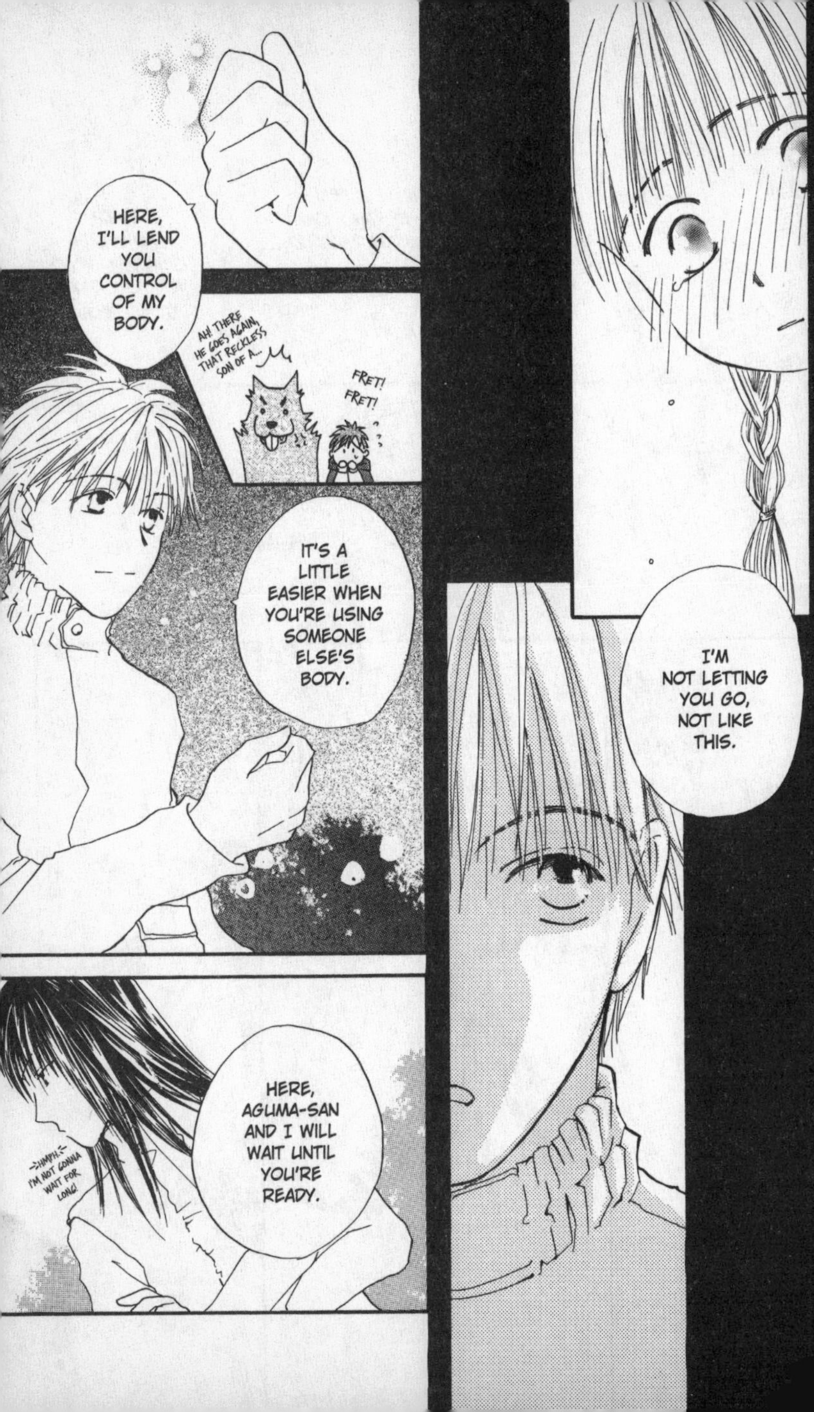
I'M NOT LETTING YOU GO, NOT LIKE THIS.
HERE, I'LL LEND YOU CONTROL OF MY BODY.
AH! THERE HE GOES AGAIN, THAT RECKLESS SON OF A...
FRET! FRET!
IT'S A LITTLE EASIER WHEN YOU'RE USING SOMEONE ELSE'S BODY.
HERE, AGUMA-SAN AND I WILL WAIT UNTIL YOU'RE READY.
HMPH. I'M NOT GONNA WAIT FOR LONG!

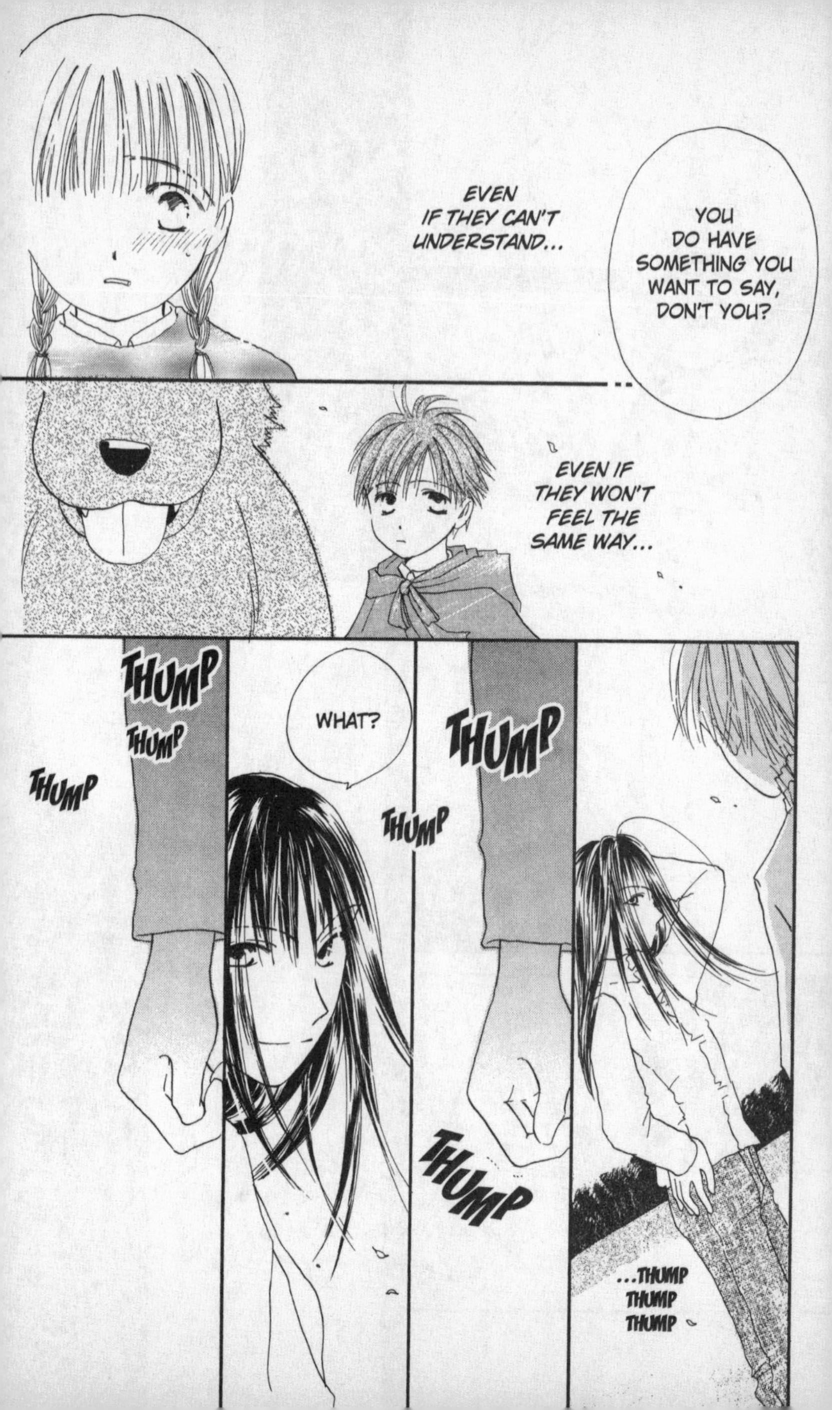
YOU DO HAVE SOMETHING YOU WANT TO SAY, DON'T YOU?
EVEN IF THEY CAN'T UNDERSTAND...
EVEN IF THEY WON'T FEEL THE SAME WAY...
...THUMP THUMP THUMP
THUMP
THUMP
WHAT?
THUMP
THUMP
THUMP
THUMP

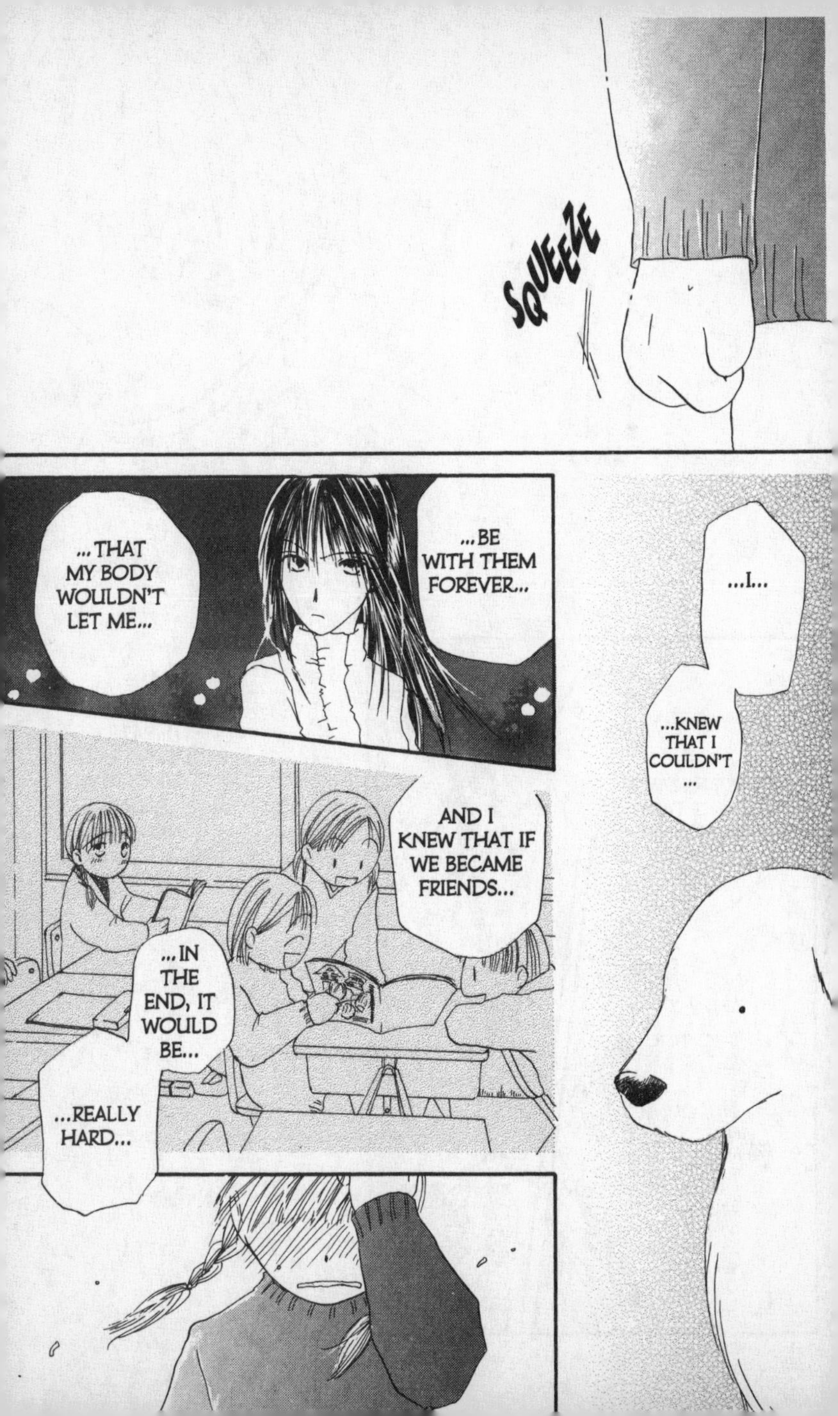
SQUEEZE
...I...
...KNEW THAT I COULDN'T ...
...BE WITH THEM FOREVER...
...THAT MY BODY WOULDN'T LET ME...
AND I KNEW THAT IF WE BECAME FRIENDS...
...IN THE END, IT WOULD BE...
...REALLY HARD...

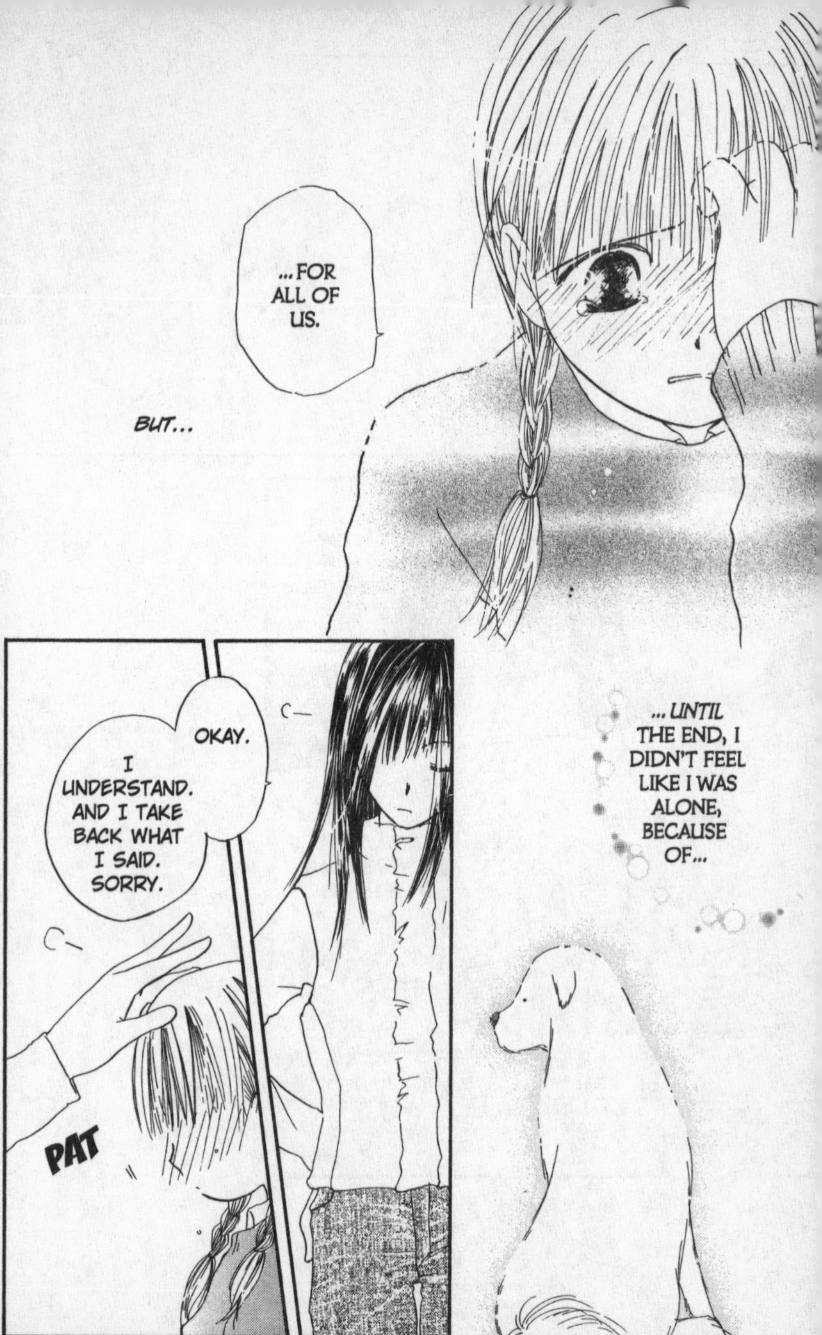
...FOR ALL OF US.
BUT...
...UNTIL THE END, I DIDN'T FEEL LIKE I WAS ALONE, BECAUSE OF...
OKAY.
I UNDERSTAND. AND I TAKE BACK WHAT I SAID. SORRY.
PAT

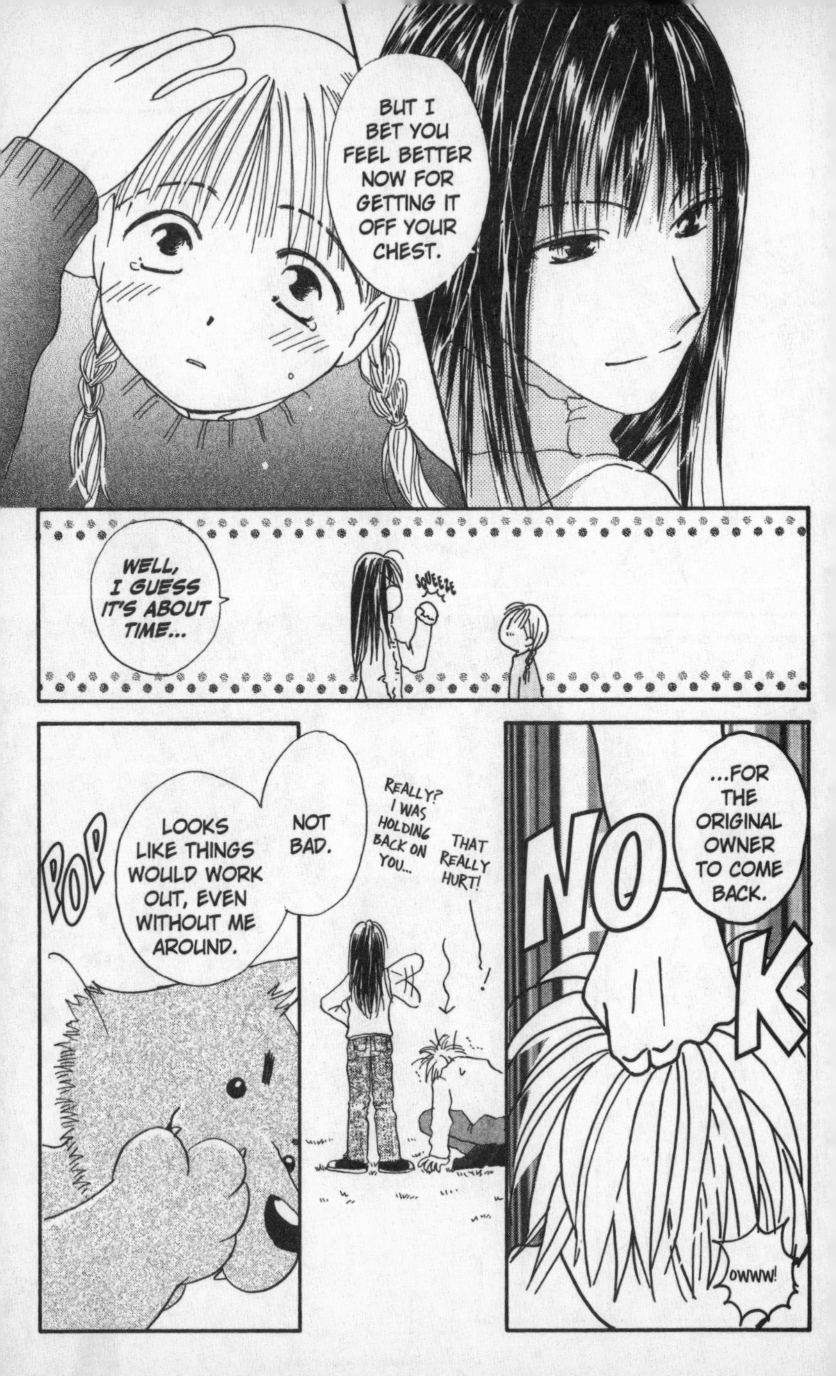
BUT I BET YOU FEEL BETTER NOW FOR GETTING IT OFF YOUR CHEST.
SQUEEZE
WELL, I GUESS IT'S ABOUT TIME...
...FOR THE ORIGINAL OWNER TO COME BACK.
NOK
OWWW!
THAT REALLY HURT!
REALLY? I WAS HOLDING BACK ON YOU...
NOT BAD.
LOOKS LIKE THINGS WOULD WORK OUT, EVEN WITHOUT ME AROUND.
POP

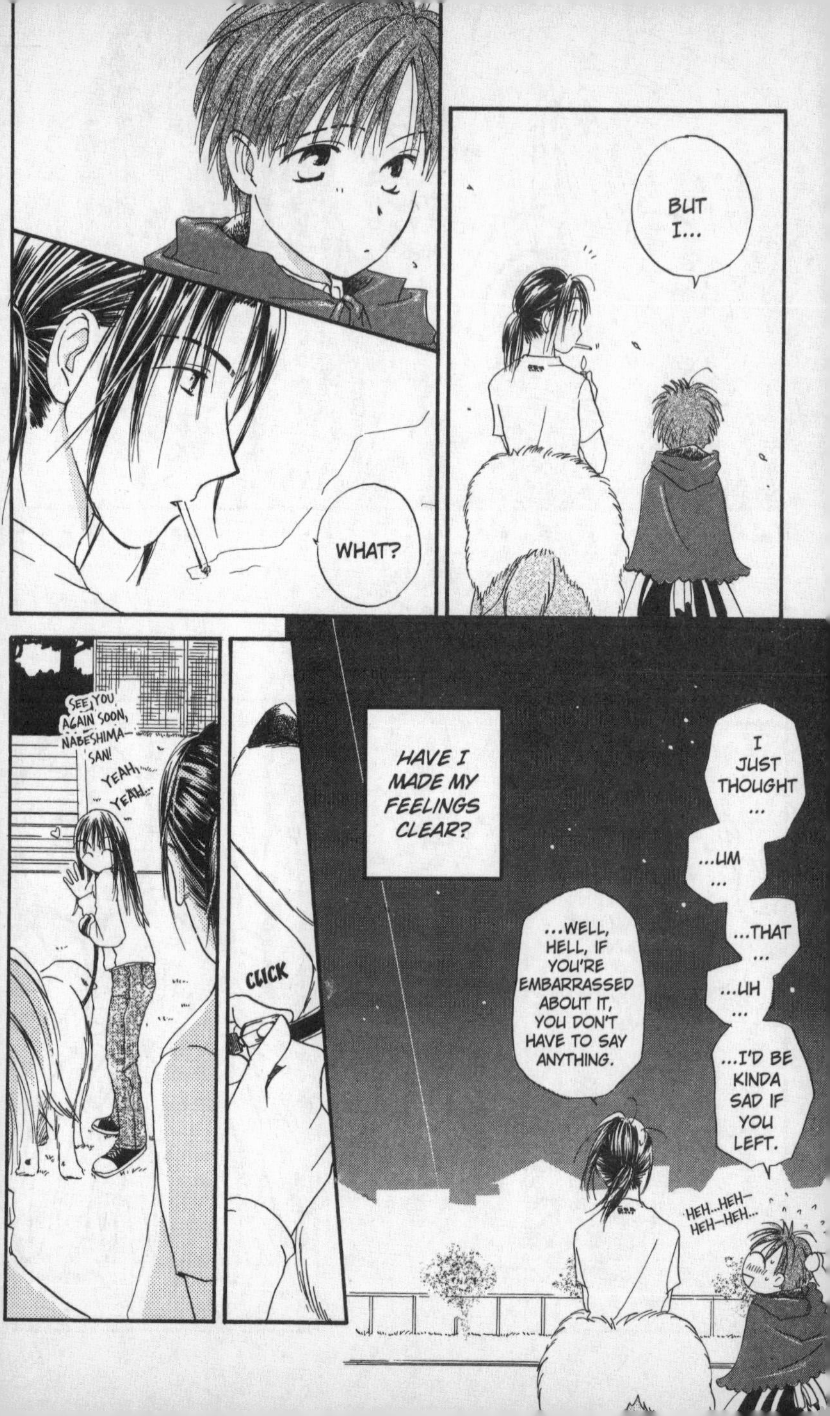
BUT I...
WHAT?
I JUST THOUGHT ... ...UM ... ...THAT ... ...UH ... ...I'D BE KINDA SAD IF YOU LEFT.
HEH...HEH-HEH-HEH...
...WELL, HELL, IF YOU'RE EMBARRASSED ABOUT IT, YOU DON'T HAVE TO SAY ANYTHING.
HAVE I MADE MY FEELINGS CLEAR?
CLICK
SEE YOU AGAIN SOON, NABESHIMA-SAN!
YEAH... YEAH...

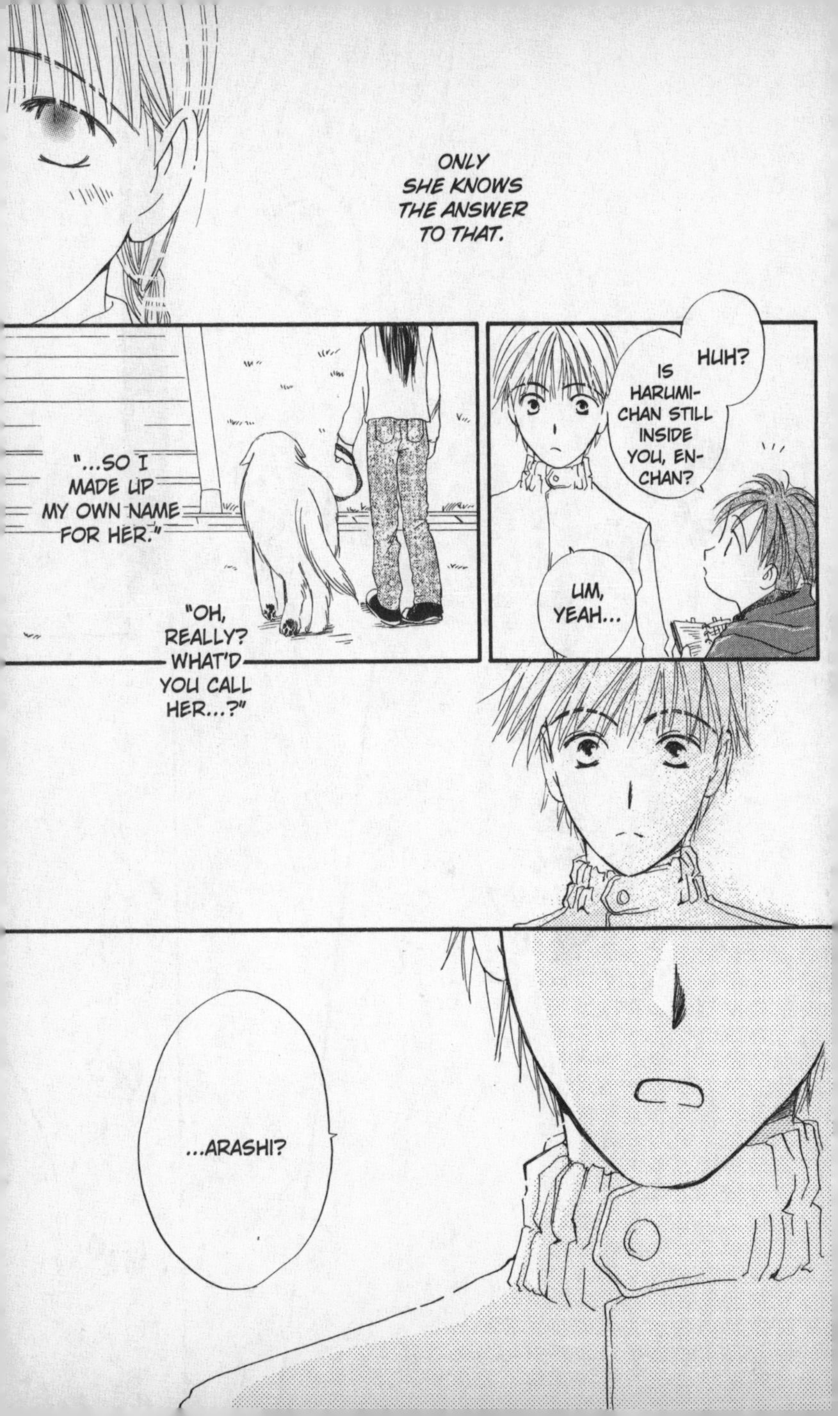
ONLY SHE KNOWS THE ANSWER TO THAT.
HUH?
IS HARUMI-CHAN STILL INSIDE YOU, EN-CHAN?
UM, YEAH...
"...SO I MADE UP MY OWN NAME FOR HER."
"OH, REALLY? WHAT'D YOU CALL HER...?"
...ARASHI?

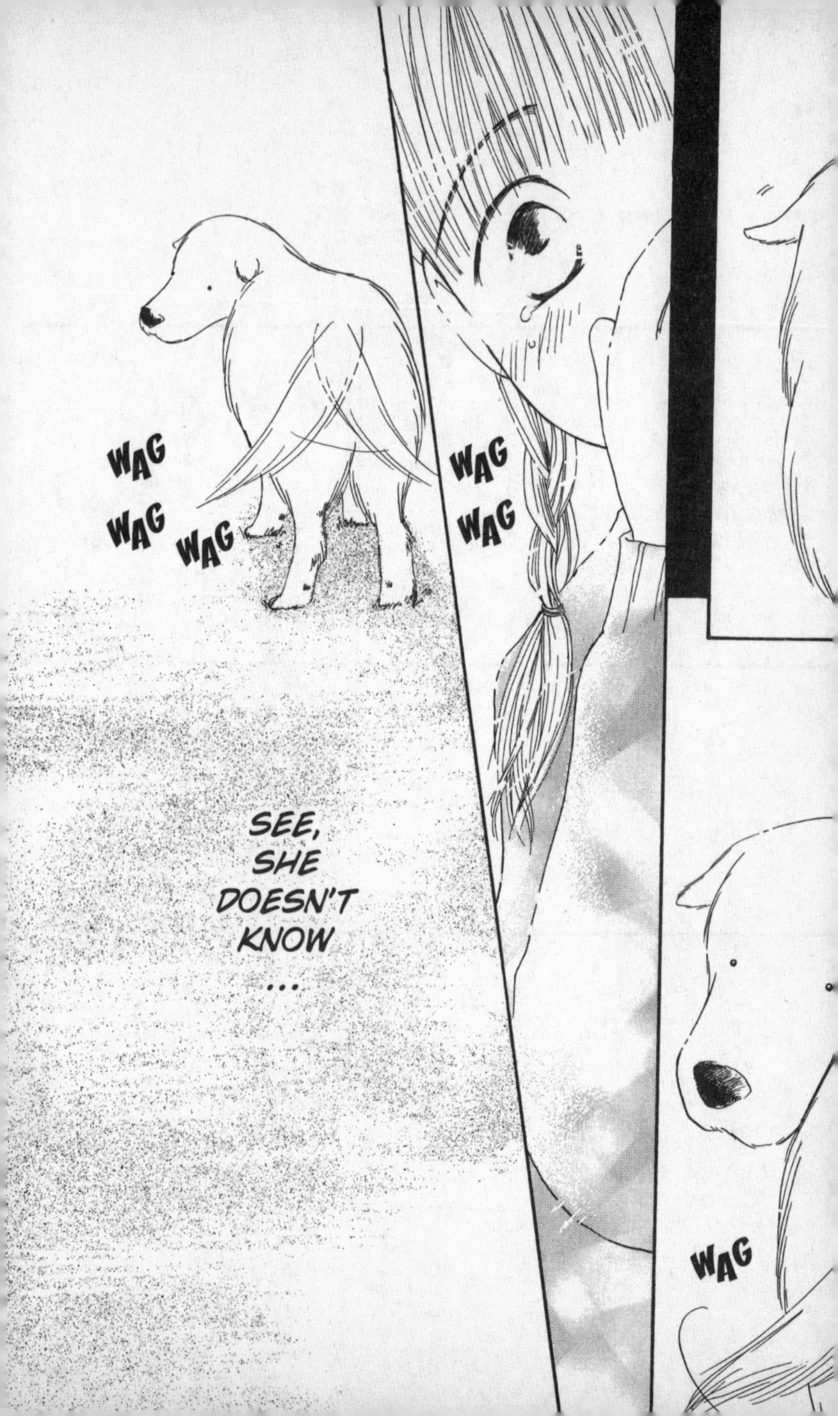
WAG
WAG
WAG
WAG
WAG
WAG
SEE, SHE DOESN'T KNOW ...

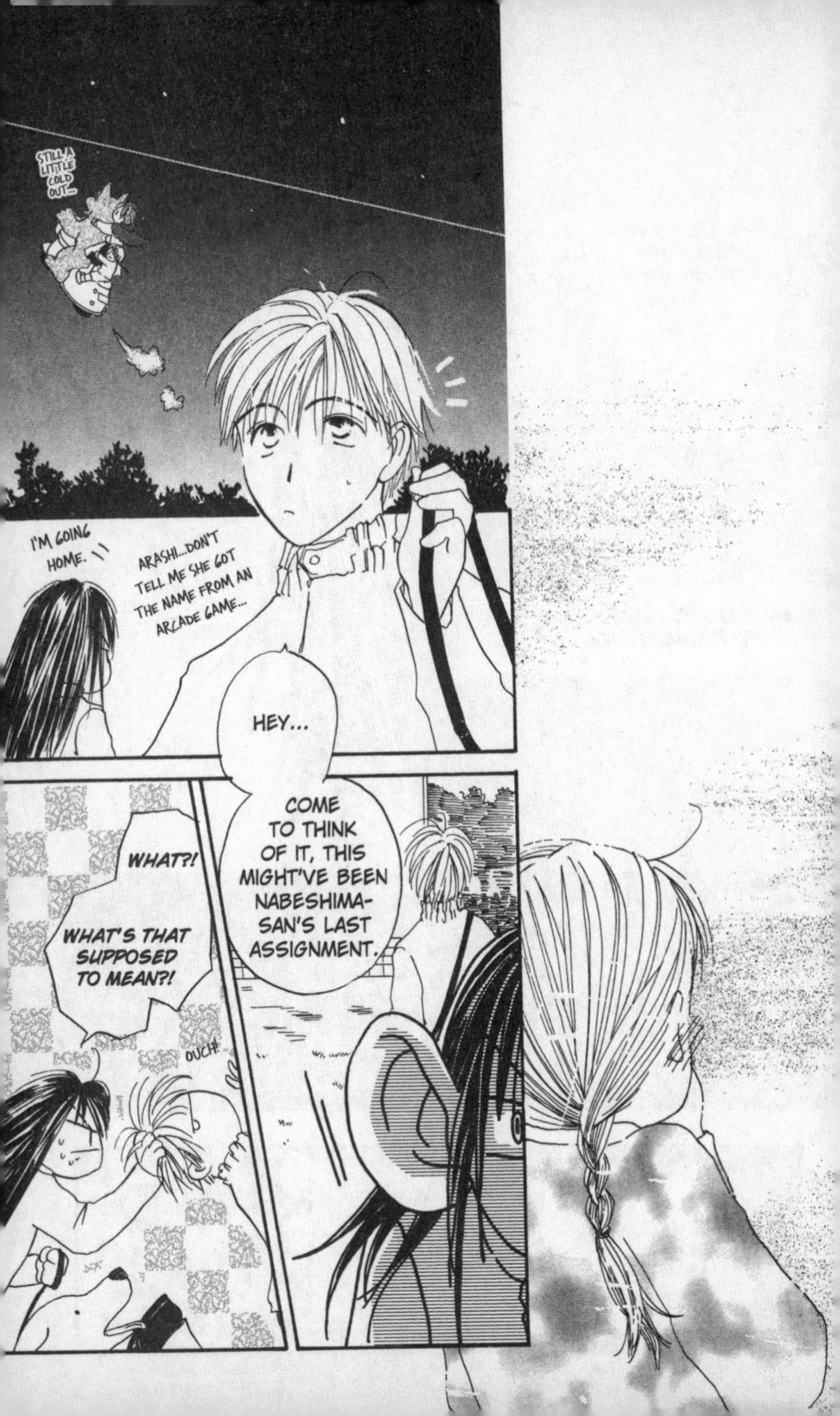
STILL A LITTLE COLD OUT...
ARASHI...DON'T TELL ME SHE GOT THE NAME FROM AN ARCADE GAME...
I'M GOING HOME.
HEY...
COME TO THINK OF IT, THIS MIGHT'VE BEEN NABESHIMA-SAN'S LAST ASSIGNMENT.
WHAT?!
WHAT'S THAT SUPPOSED TO MEAN?!
OUCH!

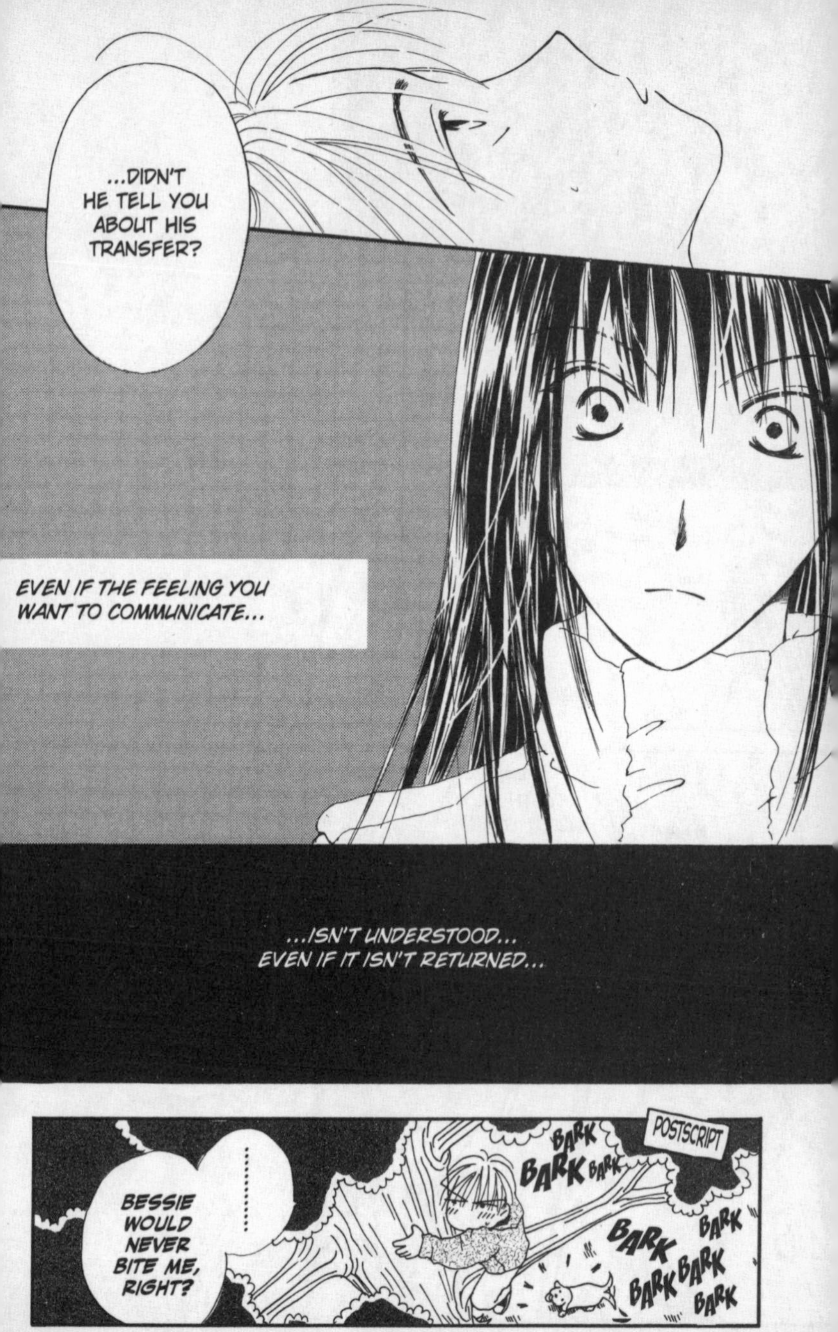
...DIDN'T HE TELL YOU ABOUT HIS TRANSFER?
EVEN IF THE FEELING YOU WANT TO COMMUNICATE...
...ISN'T UNDERSTOOD... EVEN IF IT ISN'T RETURNED...
POSTSCRIPT
BARK BARK BARK
BARK BARK BARK BARK BARK
......
BESSIE WOULD NEVER BITE ME, RIGHT?

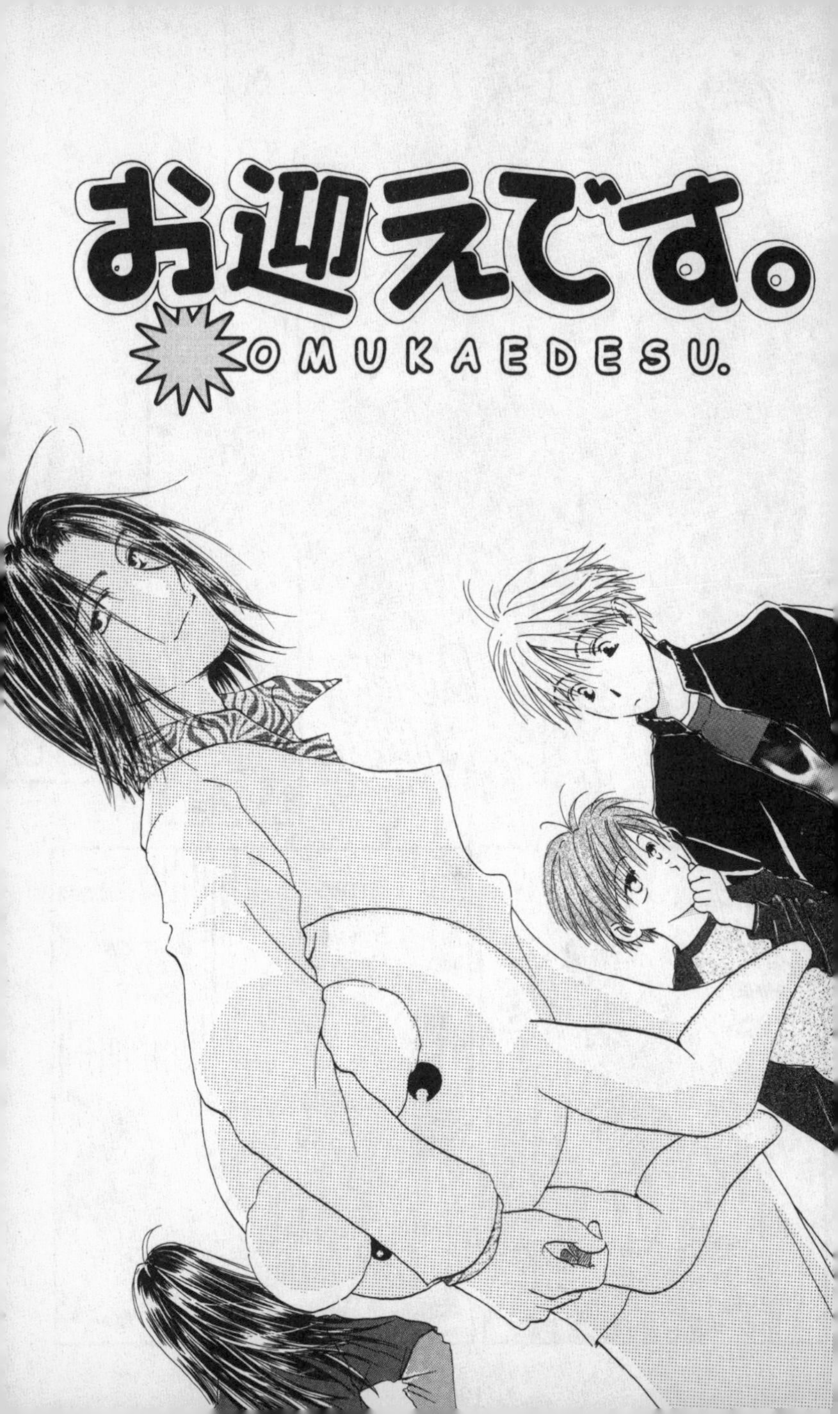
お迎えです。
OMUKAEDESU.

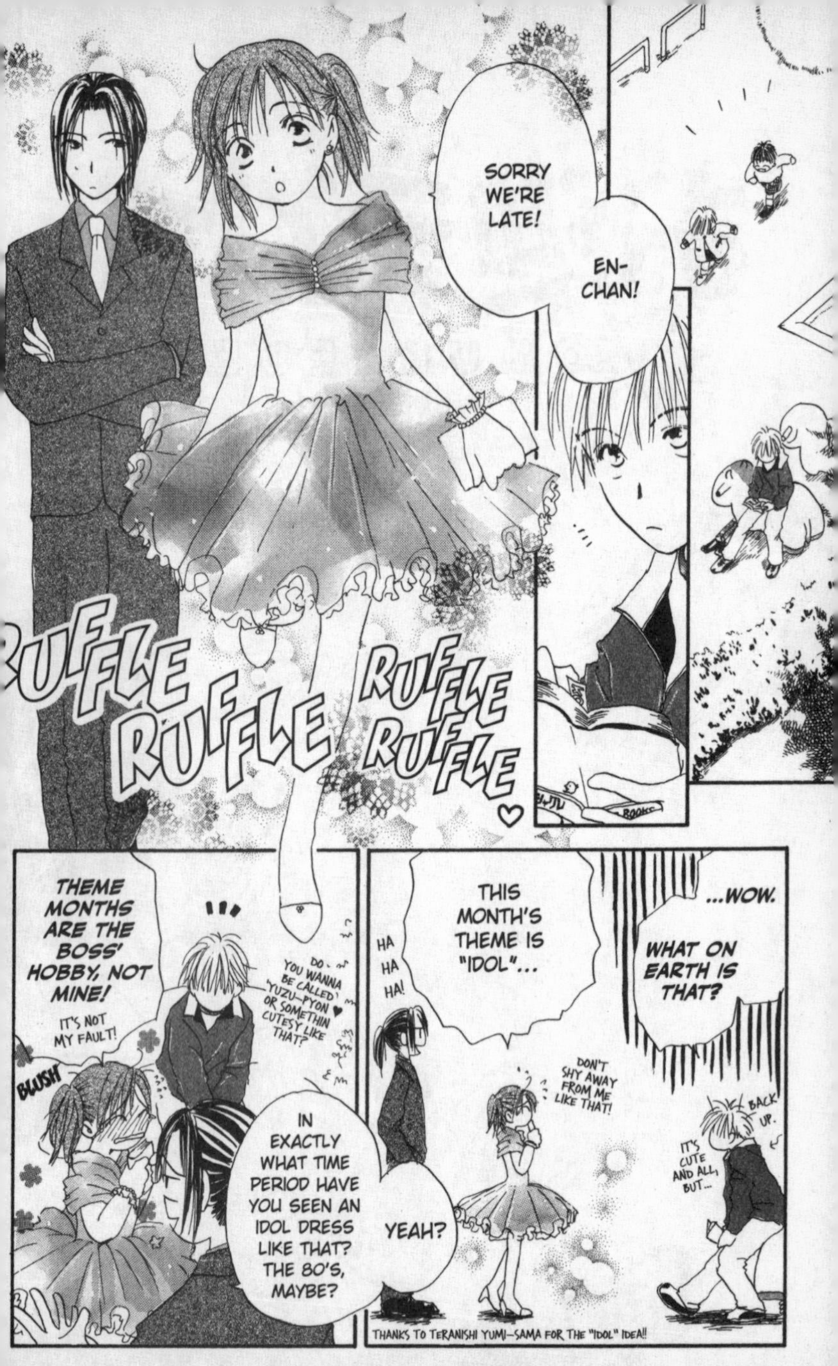
EN-CHAN!
SORRY WE'RE LATE!
RUFFLE RUFFLE RUFFLE RUFFLE ♡
...WOW.
WHAT ON EARTH IS THAT?
THIS MONTH'S THEME IS "IDOL"...
HA HA HA!
BACK UP.
IT'S CUTE AND ALL, BUT...
DON'T SHY AWAY FROM ME LIKE THAT!
THANKS TO TERANISHI YUMI-SAMA FOR THE "IDOL" IDEA!!
DO YOU WANNA BE CALLED 'YUZU-PYON' ♥ OR SOMETHIN CUTESY LIKE THAT?
THEME MONTHS ARE THE BOSS' HOBBY, NOT MINE!
IT'S NOT MY FAULT!
BLUSH
IN EXACTLY WHAT TIME PERIOD HAVE YOU SEEN AN IDOL DRESS LIKE THAT? THE 80'S, MAYBE?
YEAH?

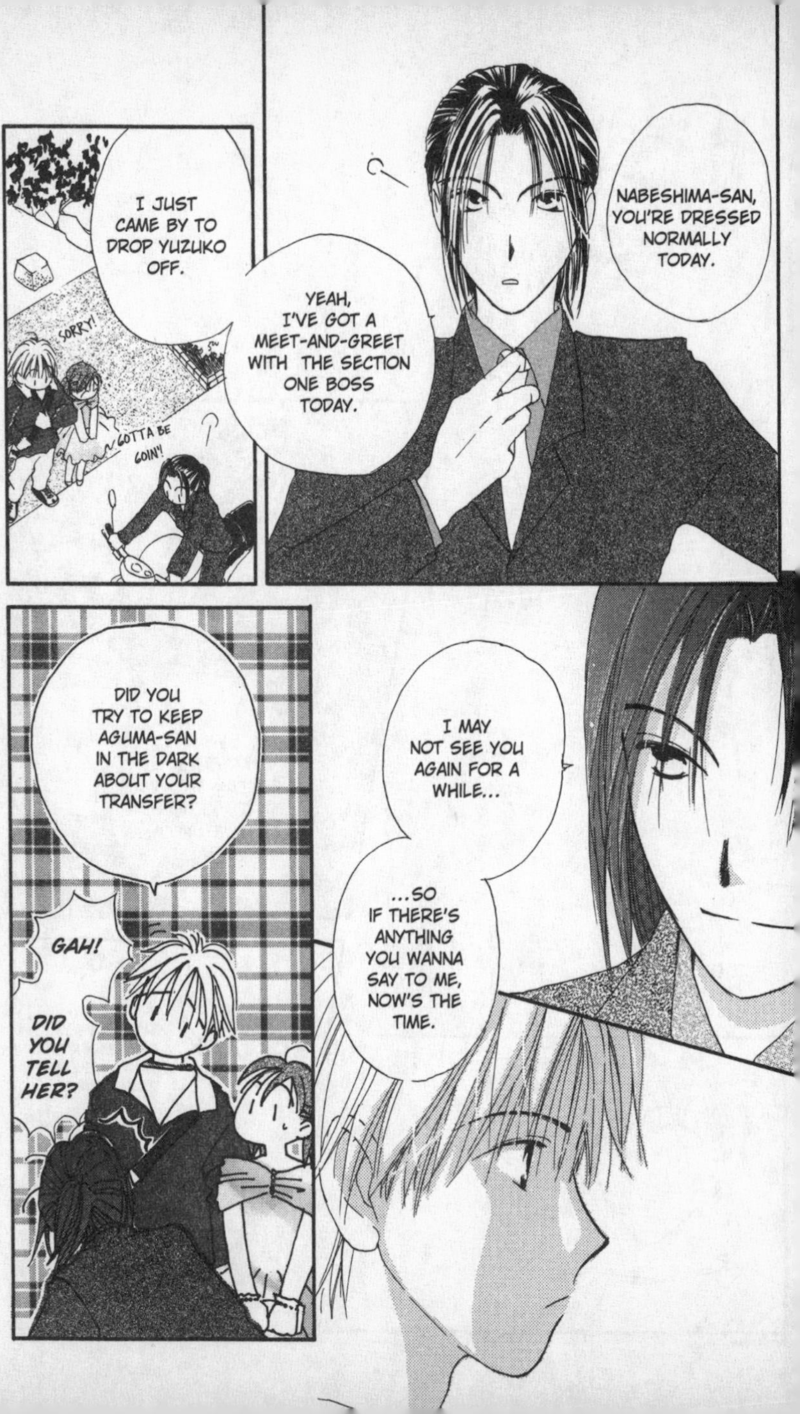
NABESHIMA-SAN, YOU'RE DRESSED NORMALLY TODAY.
YEAH, I'VE GOT A MEET-AND-GREET WITH THE SECTION ONE BOSS TODAY.
I JUST CAME BY TO DROP YUZUKO OFF.
SORRY!
GOTTA BE GOIN'!
I MAY NOT SEE YOU AGAIN FOR A WHILE...
...SO IF THERE'S ANYTHING YOU WANNA SAY TO ME, NOW'S THE TIME.
DID YOU TRY TO KEEP AGUMA-SAN IN THE DARK ABOUT YOUR TRANSFER?
GAH!
DID YOU TELL HER?

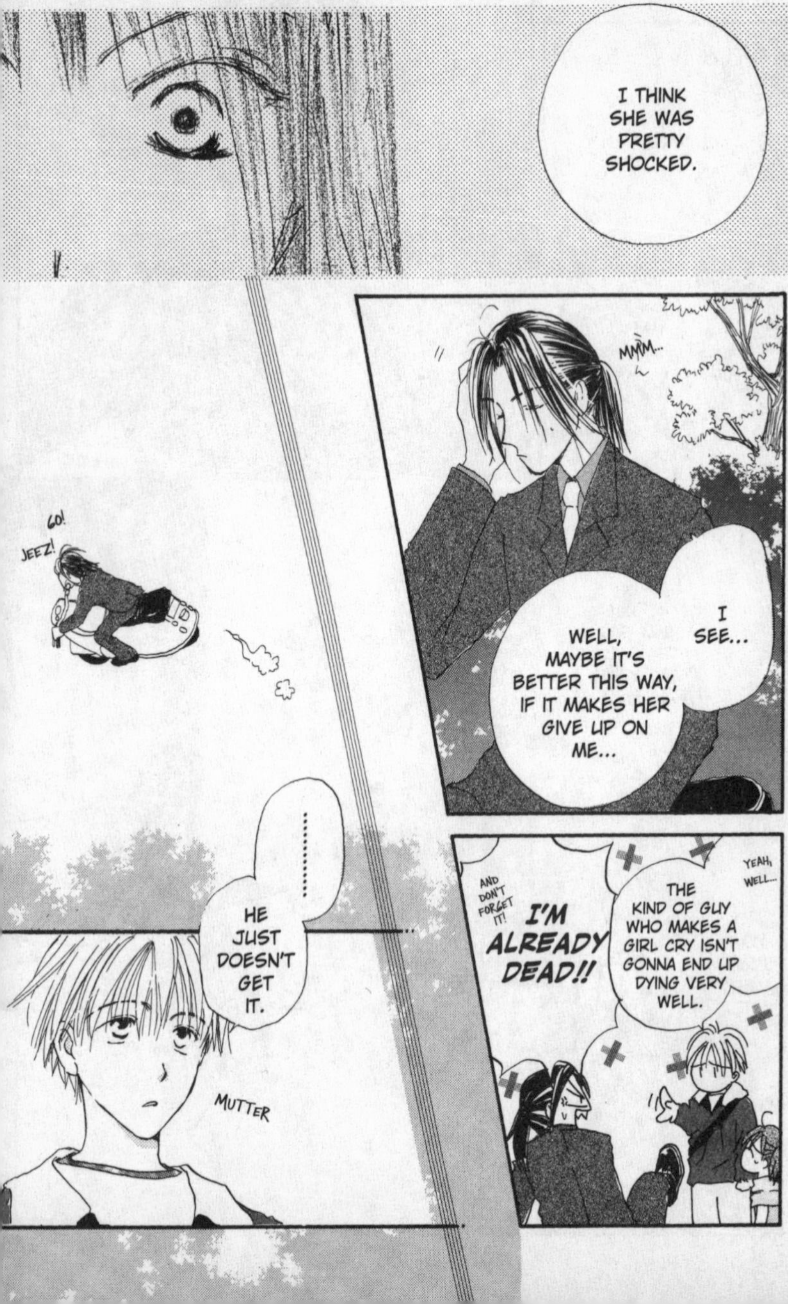
I THINK SHE WAS PRETTY SHOCKED.
MMM...
I SEE...
WELL, MAYBE IT'S BETTER THIS WAY, IF IT MAKES HER GIVE UP ON ME...
GO!
JEEZ!
YEAH, WELL...
THE KIND OF GUY WHO MAKES A GIRL CRY ISN'T GONNA END UP DYING VERY WELL.
I'M ALREADY DEAD!!
AND DON'T FORGET IT!
......
HE JUST DOESN'T GET IT.
MUTTER

DEMANDS

****

I'VE GOTTEN A LOT OF LETTERS SAYING "GIVE US CHARACTER PROFILES!", SO I THOUGHT I'D USE THIS SPACE FOR A FEW SIMPLE PROFILES.

MADOKA TSUTSUMI

BIRTHDAY: JULY 19
BLOOD TYPE: B
5 FT. 8 IN

NABESHIMA

BIRTHDAY: JUNE 4
DAY OF DEATH: APRIL 10
BLOOD TYPE: O
6 FT. 0 IN

YUZUKO

BIRTHDAY: MARCH 3
DAY OF DEATH: 8/27
BLOOD TYPE: O
4 FT. 9 IN

AGUMA

BIRTHDAY: 11/29
BLOOD TYPE: A
5 FT. 5 IN

I BET YOU DIDN'T THINK THE PROFILES WOULD BE THIS SIMPLE! SORRY...

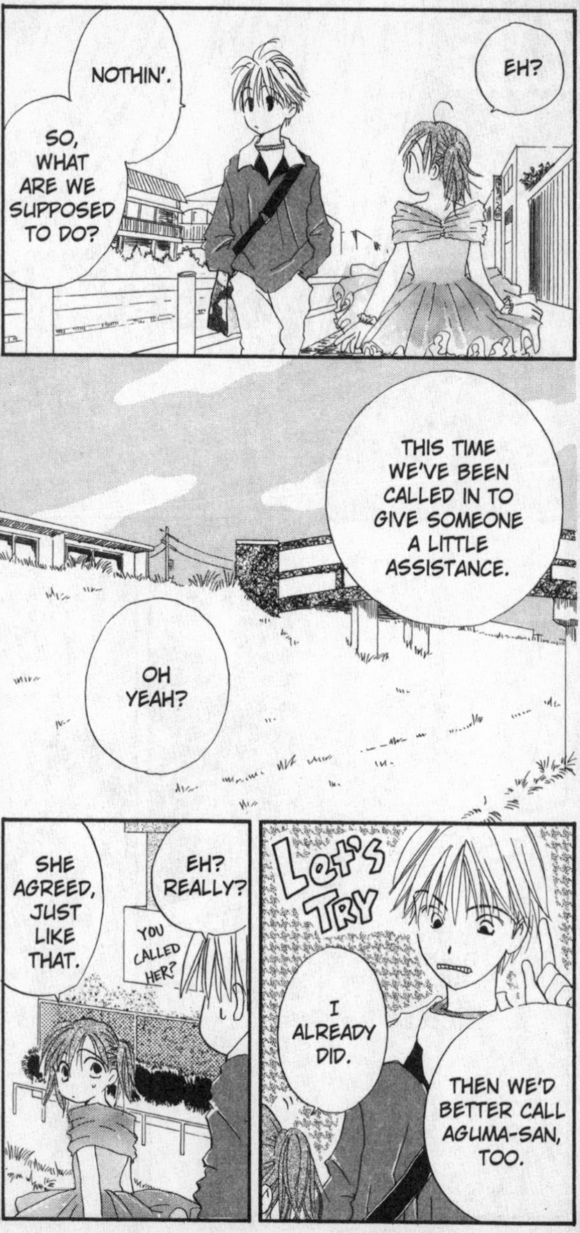
EH?
NOTHIN'.
SO, WHAT ARE WE SUPPOSED TO DO?
THIS TIME WE'VE BEEN CALLED IN TO GIVE SOMEONE A LITTLE ASSISTANCE.
OH YEAH?
Let's TRY
THEN WE'D BETTER CALL AGUMA-SAN, TOO.
I ALREADY DID.
EH? REALLY?
YOU CALLED HER?
SHE AGREED, JUST LIKE THAT.

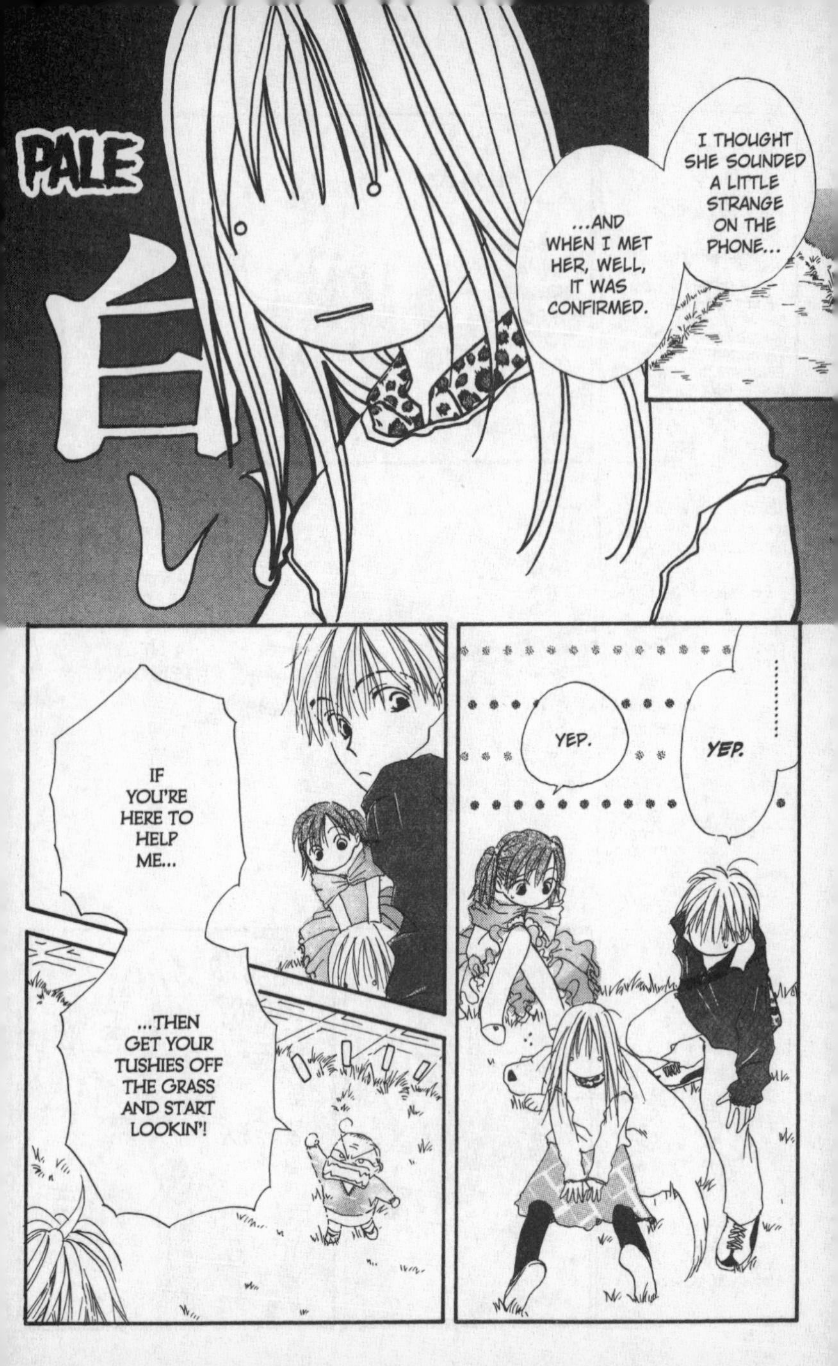
I THOUGHT SHE SOUNDED A LITTLE STRANGE ON THE PHONE...
...AND WHEN I MET HER, WELL, IT WAS CONFIRMED.
PALE
YEP.
YEP.
IF YOU'RE HERE TO HELP ME...
...THEN GET YOUR TUSHIES OFF THE GRASS AND START LOOKIN'!

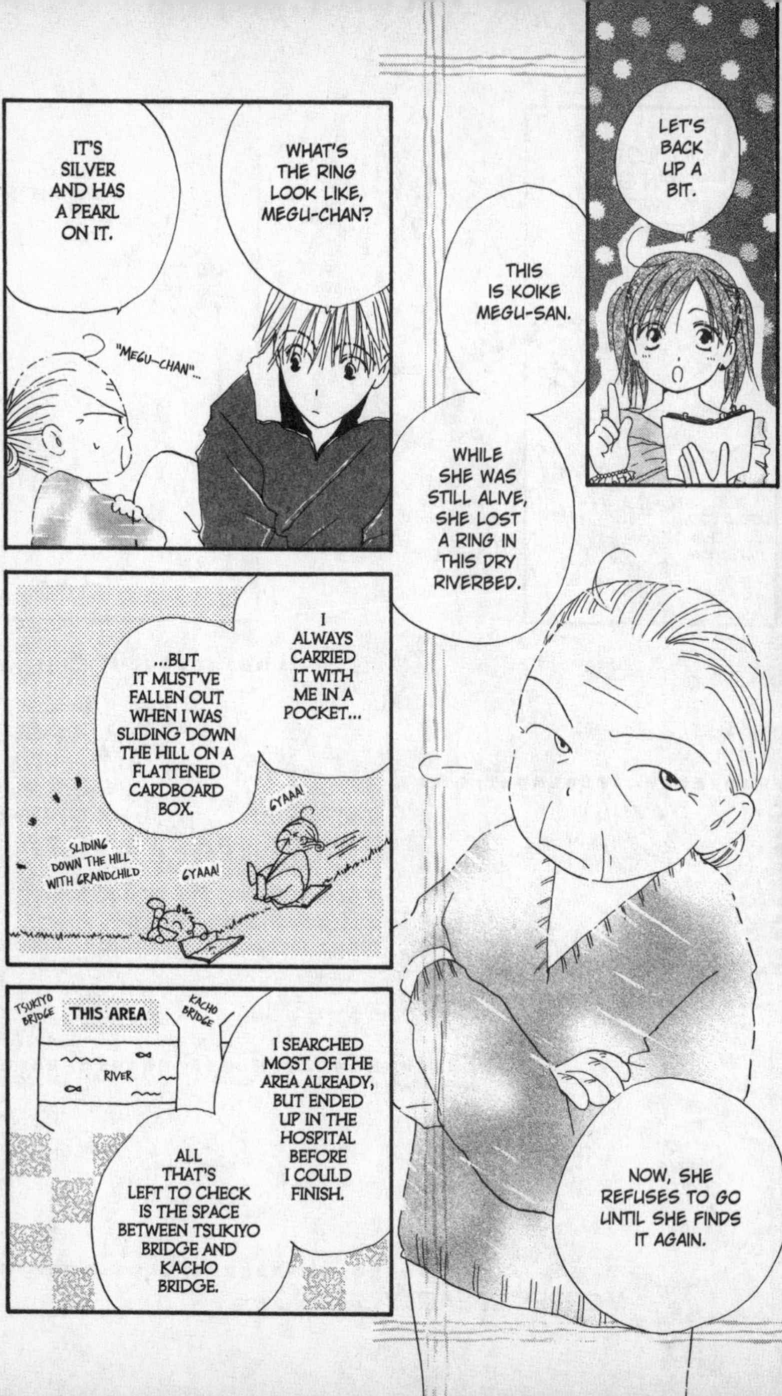
LET'S BACK UP A BIT.
THIS IS KOIKE MEGU-SAN.
WHILE SHE WAS STILL ALIVE, SHE LOST A RING IN THIS DRY RIVERBED.
NOW, SHE REFUSES TO GO UNTIL SHE FINDS IT AGAIN.
WHAT'S THE RING LOOK LIKE, MEGU-CHAN?
IT'S SILVER AND HAS A PEARL ON IT.
"MEGU-CHAN"...
I ALWAYS CARRIED IT WITH ME IN A POCKET...
...BUT IT MUST'VE FALLEN OUT WHEN I WAS SLIDING DOWN THE HILL ON A FLATTENED CARDBOARD BOX.
GYAAA!
SLIDING DOWN THE HILL WITH GRANDCHILD
GYAAA!
KACHO BRIDGE
THIS AREA
TSUKIYO BRIDGE
RIVER
I SEARCHED MOST OF THE AREA ALREADY, BUT ENDED UP IN THE HOSPITAL BEFORE I COULD FINISH.
ALL THAT'S LEFT TO CHECK IS THE SPACE BETWEEN TSUKIYO BRIDGE AND KACHO BRIDGE.

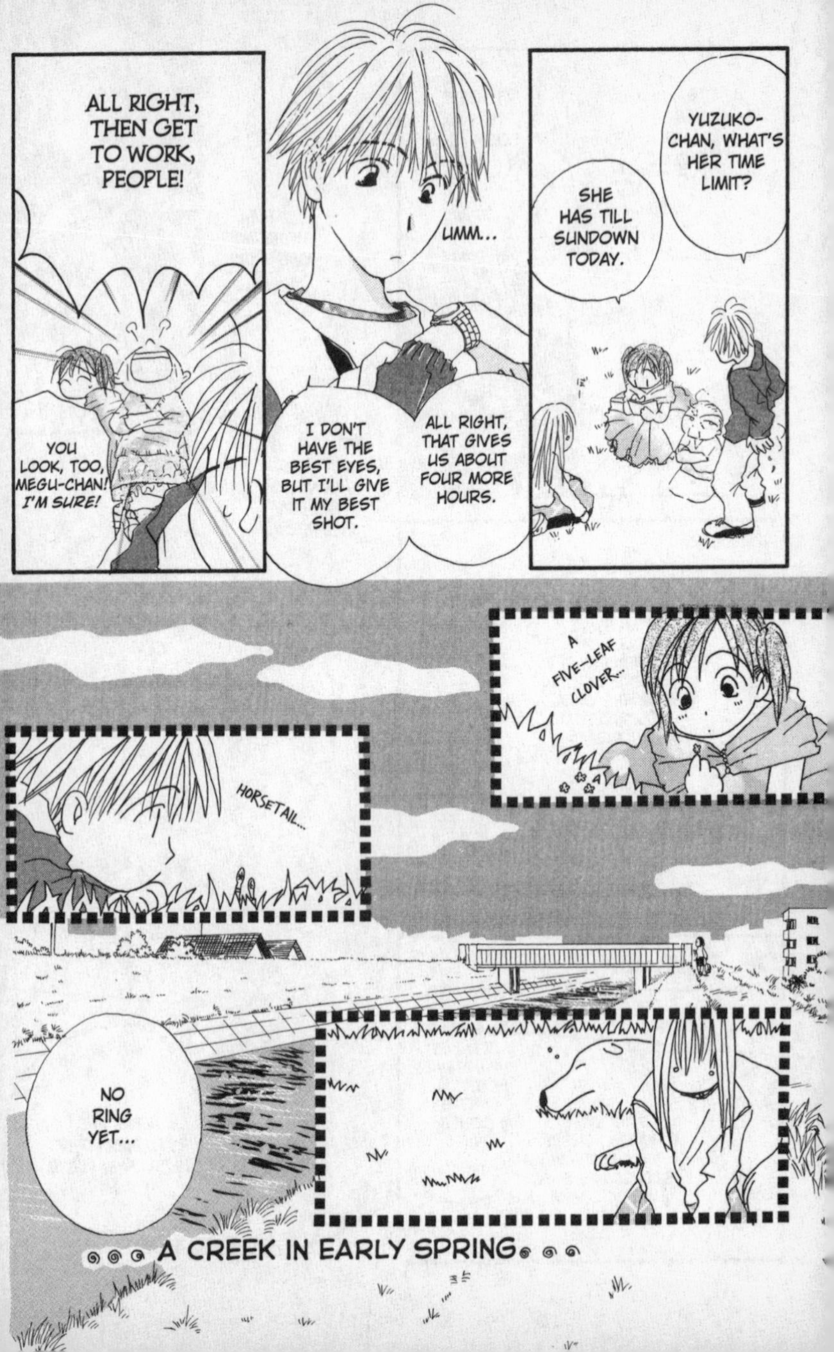

YUZUKO-CHAN, WHAT'S HER TIME LIMIT?
SHE HAS TILL SUNDOWN TODAY.
UMM...
ALL RIGHT, THAT GIVES US ABOUT FOUR MORE HOURS.
I DON'T HAVE THE BEST EYES, BUT I'LL GIVE IT MY BEST SHOT.
ALL RIGHT, THEN GET TO WORK, PEOPLE!
YOU LOOK, TOO, MEGU-CHAN! I'M SURE!
A FIVE-LEAF CLOVER...
HORSETAIL...
NO RING YET...
A CREEK IN EARLY SPRING

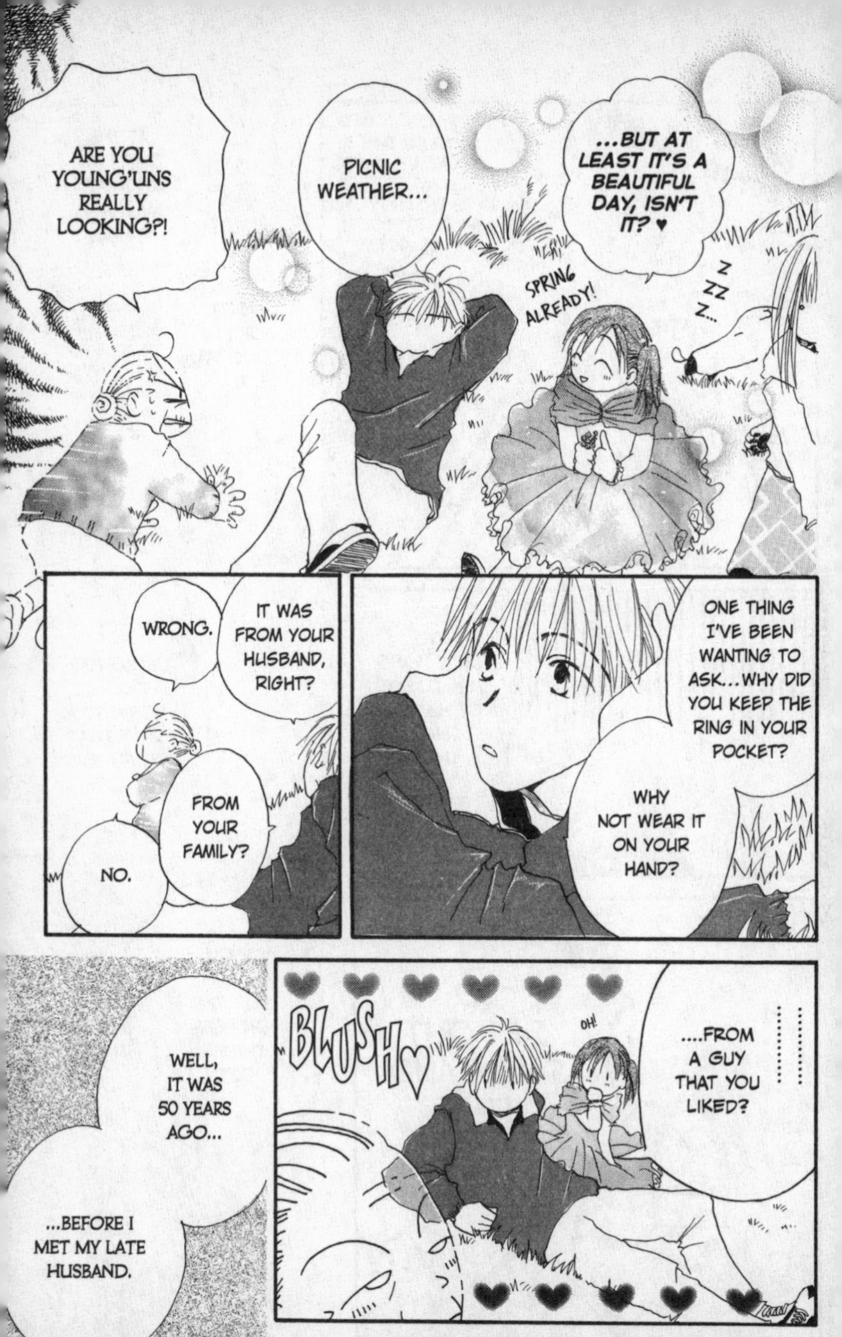

...BUT AT LEAST IT'S A BEAUTIFUL DAY, ISN'T IT? ♥
Z ZZ Z...
SPRING ALREADY!
PICNIC WEATHER...
ARE YOU YOUNG'UNS REALLY LOOKING?!
ONE THING I'VE BEEN WANTING TO ASK...WHY DID YOU KEEP THE RING IN YOUR POCKET?
WHY NOT WEAR IT ON YOUR HAND?
IT WAS FROM YOUR HUSBAND, RIGHT?
WRONG.
FROM YOUR FAMILY?
NO.
....FROM A GUY THAT YOU LIKED?
....
OH!
BLUSH♥
WELL, IT WAS 50 YEARS AGO...
...BEFORE I MET MY LATE HUSBAND.

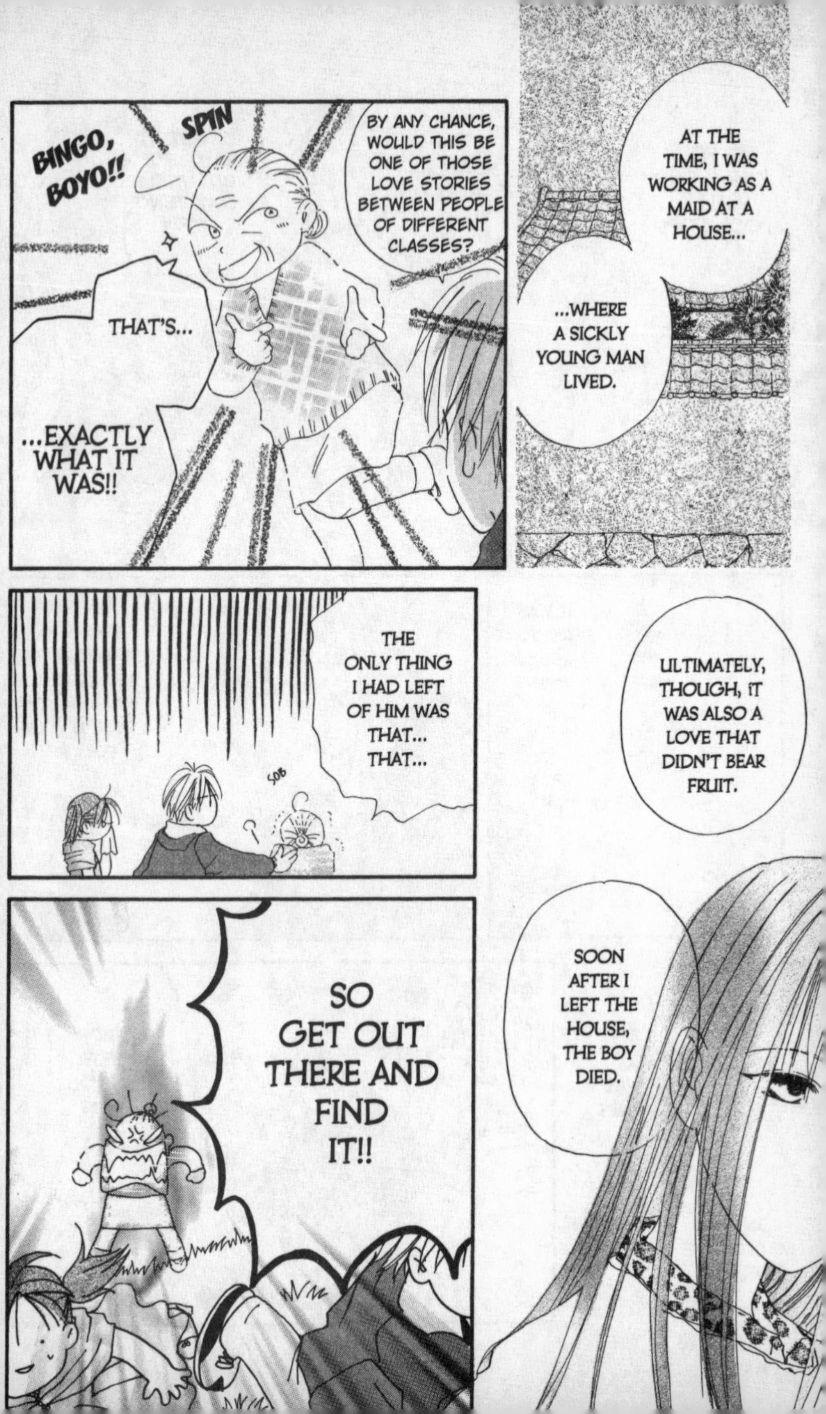
AT THE TIME, I WAS WORKING AS A MAID AT A HOUSE...
...WHERE A SICKLY YOUNG MAN LIVED.
BY ANY CHANCE, WOULD THIS BE ONE OF THOSE LOVE STORIES BETWEEN PEOPLE OF DIFFERENT CLASSES?
SPIN
BINGO, BOYO!!
THAT'S...
...EXACTLY WHAT IT WAS!!
ULTIMATELY, THOUGH, IT WAS ALSO A LOVE THAT DIDN'T BEAR FRUIT.
SOON AFTER I LEFT THE HOUSE, THE BOY DIED.
THE ONLY THING I HAD LEFT OF HIM WAS THAT... THAT...
SOB
SO GET OUT THERE AND FIND IT!!

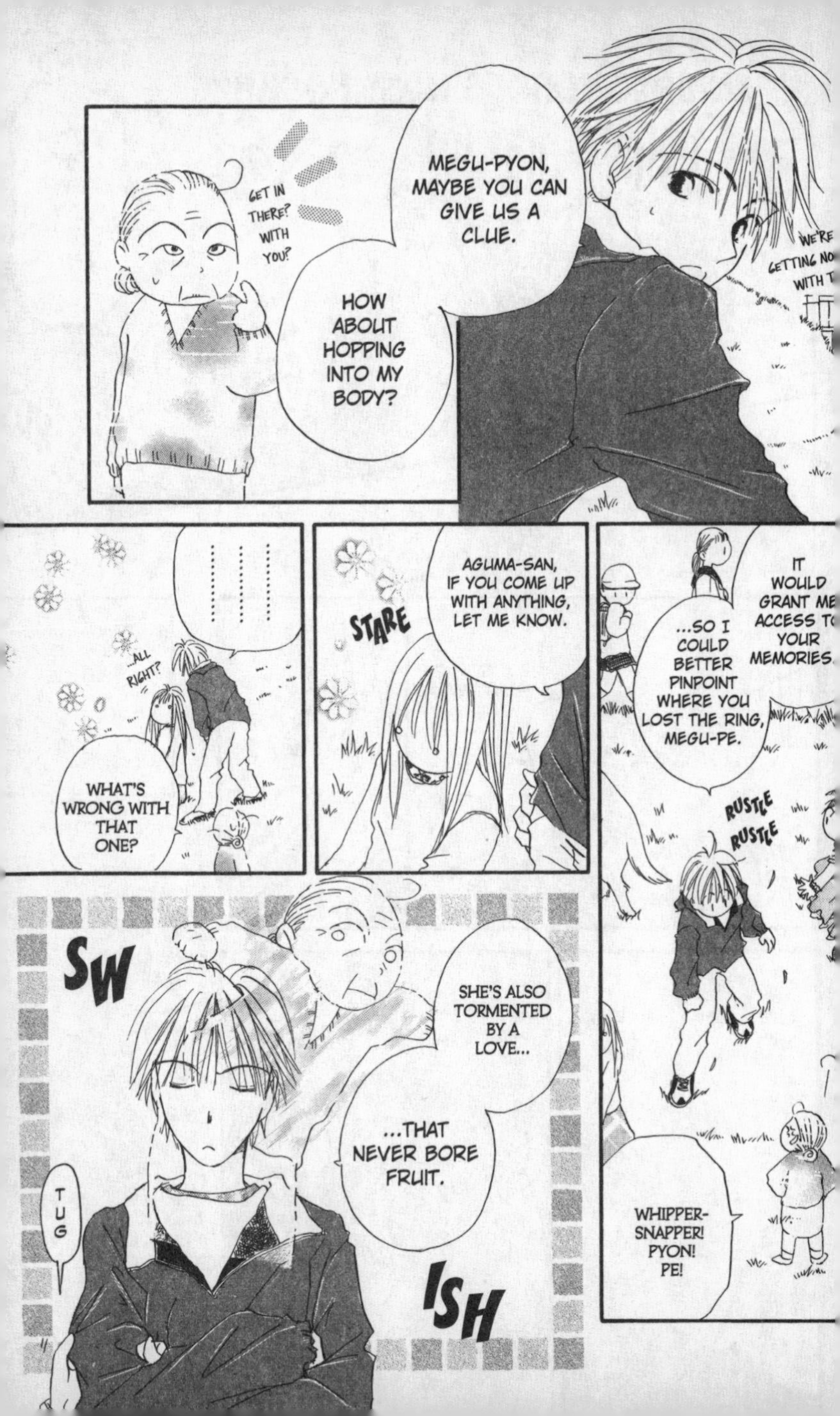
MEGU-PYON, MAYBE YOU CAN GIVE US A CLUE.
HOW ABOUT HOPPING INTO MY BODY?
GET IN THERE? WITH YOU?
IT WOULD GRANT ME ACCESS TO YOUR MEMORIES.
...SO I COULD BETTER PINPOINT WHERE YOU LOST THE RING, MEGU-PE.
RUSTLE RUSTLE
WHIPPER-SNAPPER! PYON! PE!
AGUMA-SAN, IF YOU COME UP WITH ANYTHING, LET ME KNOW.
STARE
......
...ALL RIGHT?
WHAT'S WRONG WITH THAT ONE?
SW
SHE'S ALSO TORMENTED BY A LOVE...
...THAT NEVER BORE FRUIT.
ISH
TUG

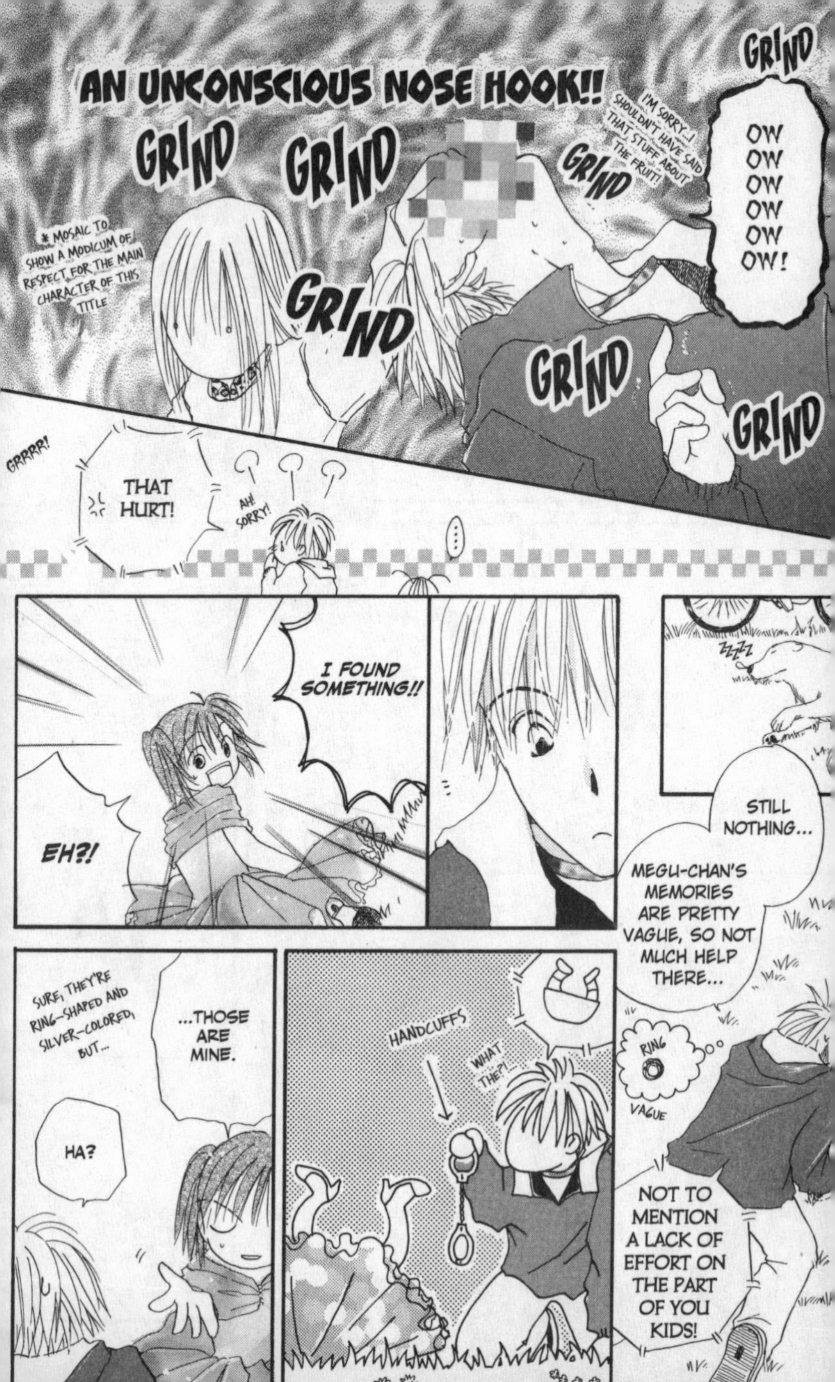
GRIND
OW OW OW OW OW OW!
I'M SORRY...I SHOULDN'T HAVE SAID THAT STUFF ABOUT THE FRUIT!
GRIND
AN UNCONSCIOUS NOSE HOOK!!
GRIND
GRIND
* MOSAIC TO SHOW A MODICUM OF RESPECT FOR THE MAIN CHARACTER OF THIS TITLE
GRIND
GRIND
GRIND
AH! SORRY!
THAT HURT!
GRRRR!
ZZZZ
STILL NOTHING...
MEGU-CHAN'S MEMORIES ARE PRETTY VAGUE, SO NOT MUCH HELP THERE...
RING
VAGUE
NOT TO MENTION A LACK OF EFFORT ON THE PART OF YOU KIDS!
I FOUND SOMETHING!!
EH?!
HANDCUFFS
WHAT THE?!
...THOSE ARE MINE.
SURE, THEY'RE RING-SHAPED AND SILVER-COLORED, BUT...
HA?

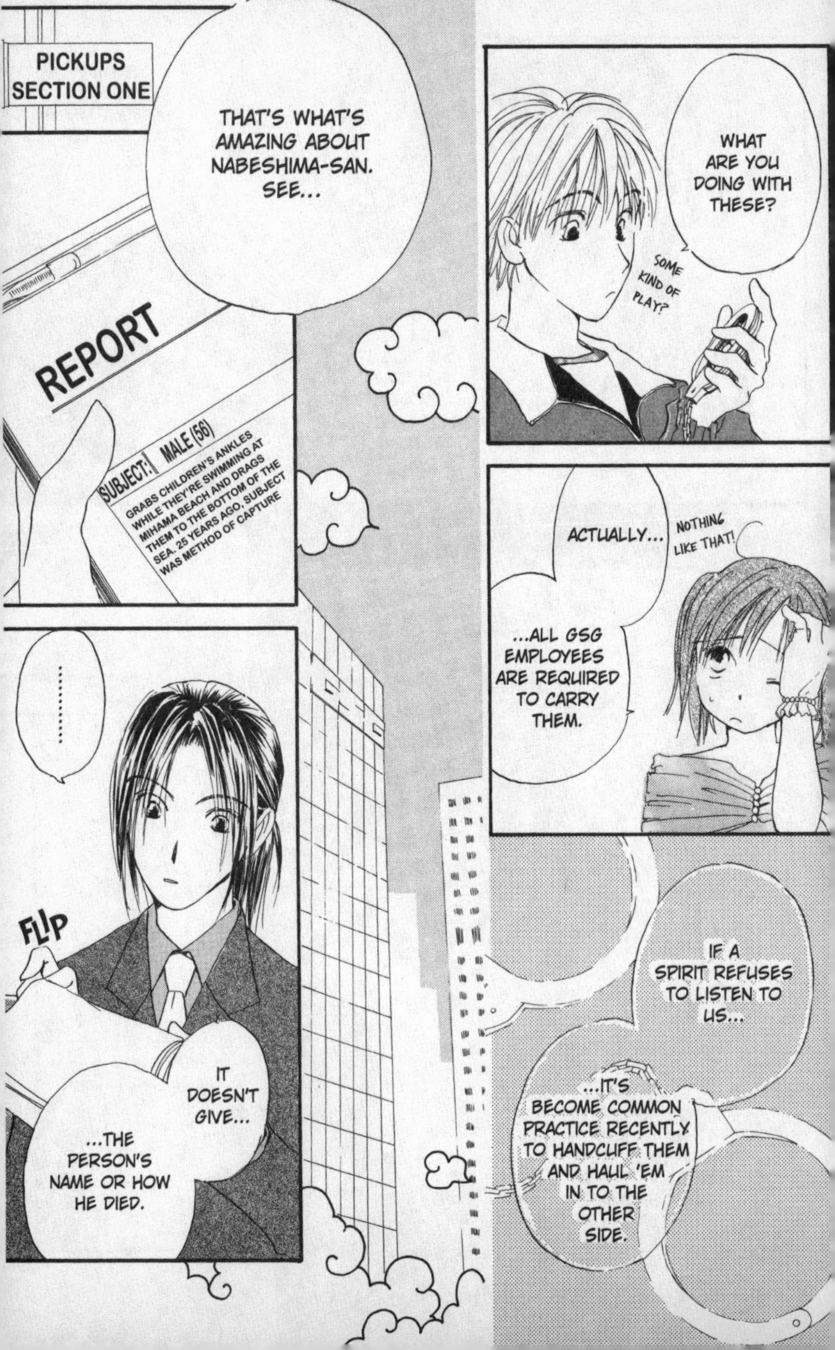
WHAT ARE YOU DOING WITH THESE?
SOME KIND OF PLAY?
NOTHING LIKE THAT!
ACTUALLY...
...ALL GSG EMPLOYEES ARE REQUIRED TO CARRY THEM.
IF A SPIRIT REFUSES TO LISTEN TO US...
...IT'S BECOME COMMON PRACTICE RECENTLY TO HANDCUFF THEM AND HAUL 'EM IN TO THE OTHER SIDE.
PICKUPS SECTION ONE
THAT'S WHAT'S AMAZING ABOUT NABESHIMA-SAN. SEE...
REPORT
SUBJECT: MALE (56)
GRABS CHILDREN'S ANKLES WHILE THEY'RE SWIMMING AT MIHAMA BEACH AND DRAGS THEM TO THE BOTTOM OF THE SEA. 25 YEARS AGO, SUBJECT WAS METHOD OF CAPTURE
....
FLIP
IT DOESN'T GIVE...
...THE PERSON'S NAME OR HOW HE DIED.

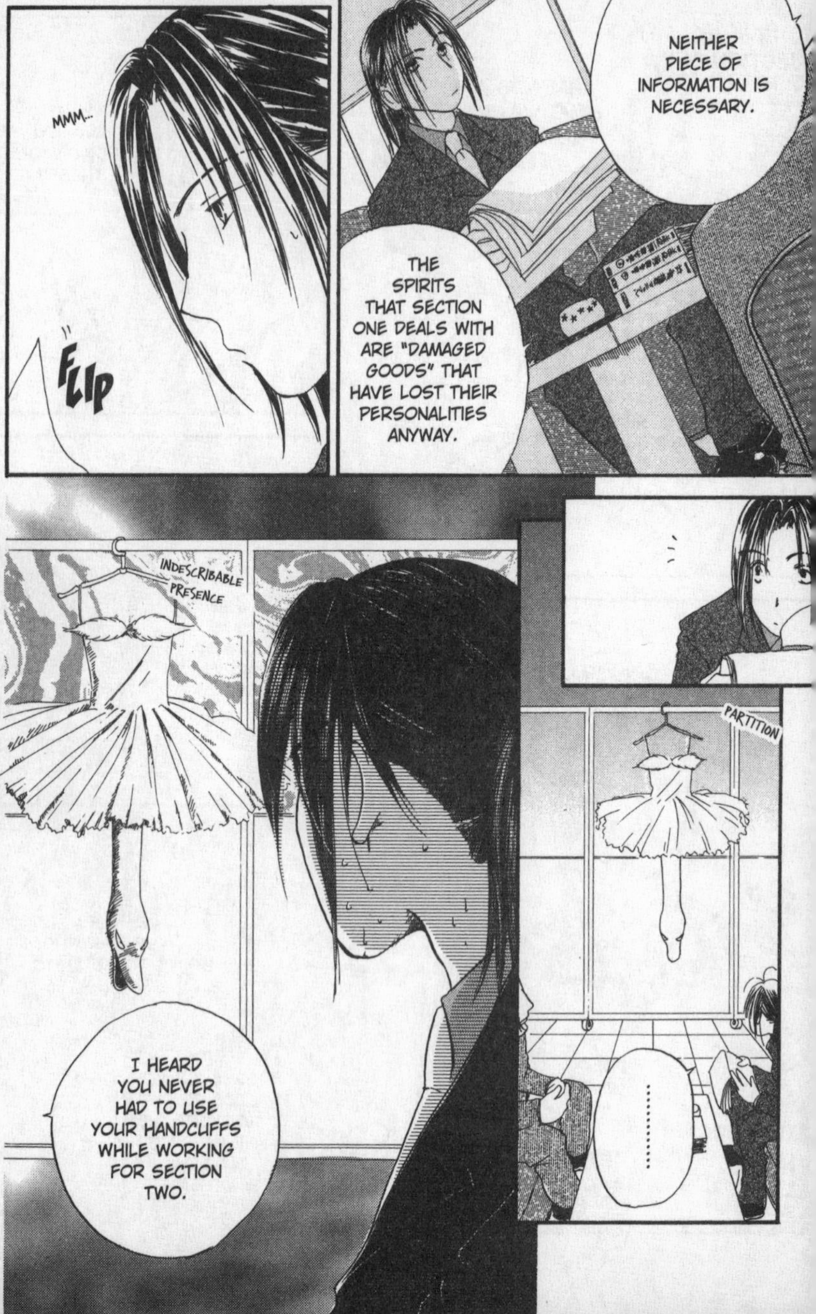
HA HA HA HA
NEITHER PIECE OF INFORMATION IS NECESSARY.
THE SPIRITS THAT SECTION ONE DEALS WITH ARE "DAMAGED GOODS" THAT HAVE LOST THEIR PERSONALITIES ANYWAY.
MMM...
FLIP
PARTITION
......
INDESCRIBABLE PRESENCE
I HEARD YOU NEVER HAD TO USE YOUR HANDCUFFS WHILE WORKING FOR SECTION TWO.

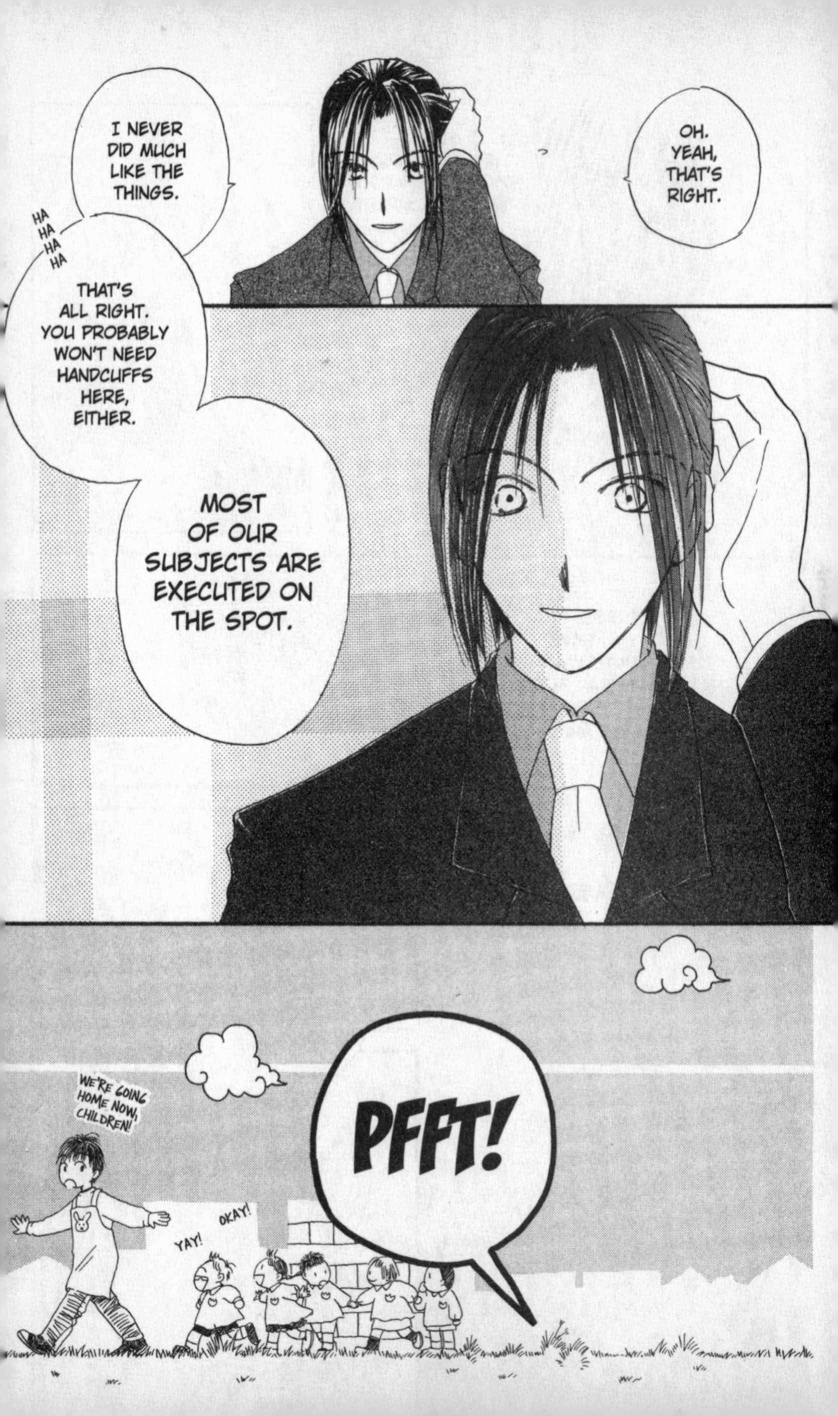
OH. YEAH, THAT'S RIGHT.
I NEVER DID MUCH LIKE THE THINGS.
HA HA HA HA
THAT'S ALL RIGHT. YOU PROBABLY WON'T NEED HANDCUFFS HERE, EITHER.
MOST OF OUR SUBJECTS ARE EXECUTED ON THE SPOT.
PFFT!
WE'RE GOING HOME NOW, CHILDREN!
OKAY!
YAY!

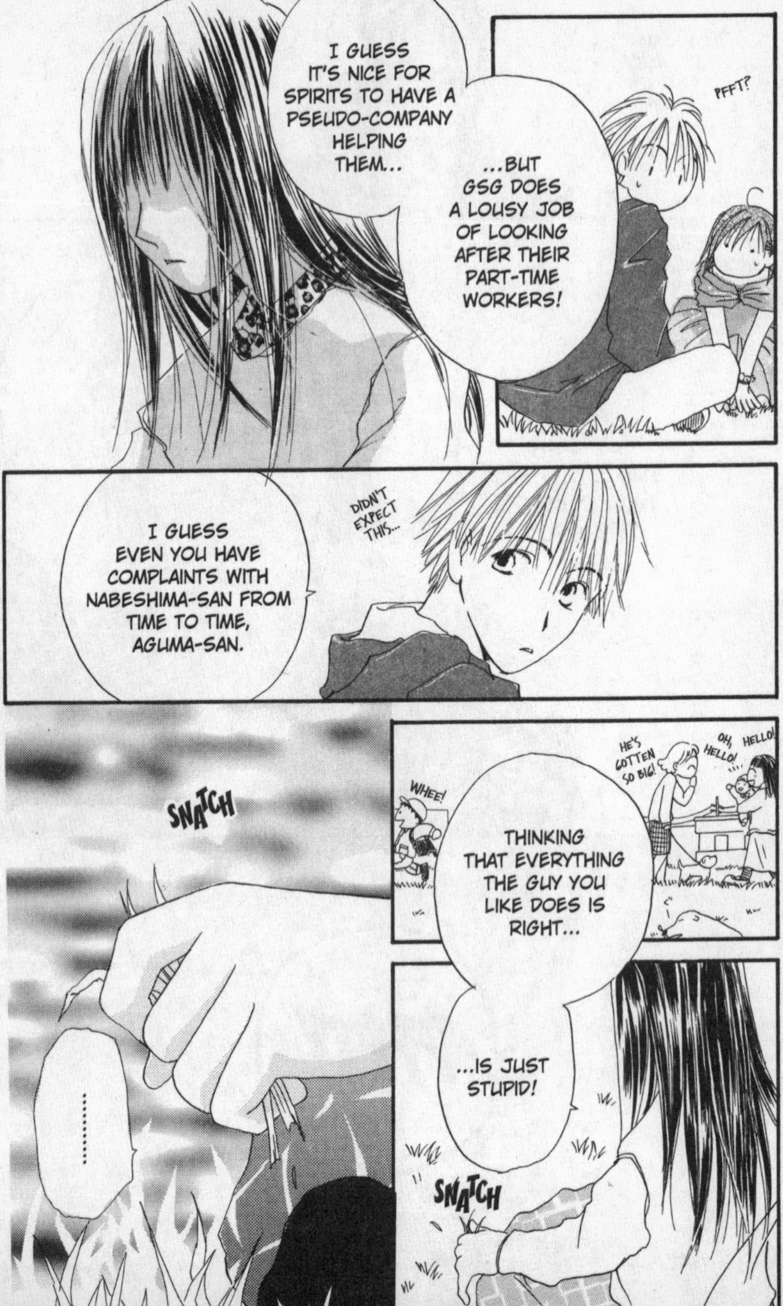
PFFT?
I GUESS IT'S NICE FOR SPIRITS TO HAVE A PSEUDO-COMPANY HELPING THEM...
...BUT GSG DOES A LOUSY JOB OF LOOKING AFTER THEIR PART-TIME WORKERS!
DIDN'T EXPECT THIS...
I GUESS EVEN YOU HAVE COMPLAINTS WITH NABESHIMA-SAN FROM TIME TO TIME, AGUMA-SAN.
OH, HELLO!
HELLO!
HE'S GOTTEN SO BIG!
WHEE!
THINKING THAT EVERYTHING THE GUY YOU LIKE DOES IS RIGHT...
...IS JUST STUPID!
SNATCH
SNATCH
....

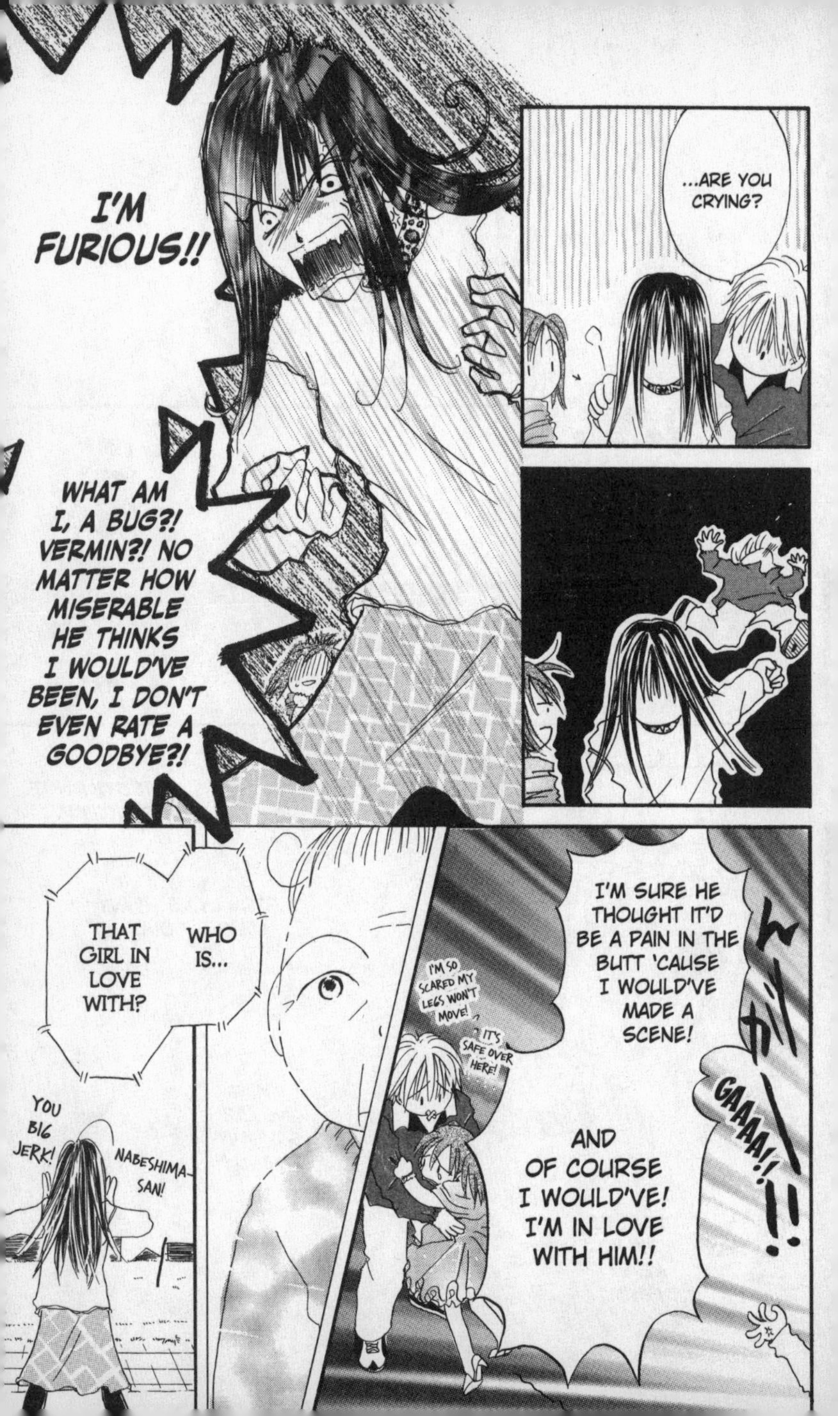
...ARE YOU CRYING?
I'M FURIOUS!!
WHAT AM I, A BUG?! VERMIN?! NO MATTER HOW MISERABLE HE THINKS I WOULD'VE BEEN, I DON'T EVEN RATE A GOODBYE?!
I'M SURE HE THOUGHT IT'D BE A PAIN IN THE BUTT 'CAUSE I WOULD'VE MADE A SCENE!
GAAAA!!
I'M SO SCARED MY LEGS WON'T MOVE!
IT'S SAFE OVER HERE!
AND OF COURSE I WOULD'VE! I'M IN LOVE WITH HIM!!
WHO IS...
THAT GIRL IN LOVE WITH?
YOU BIG JERK!
NABESHIMA-SAN!

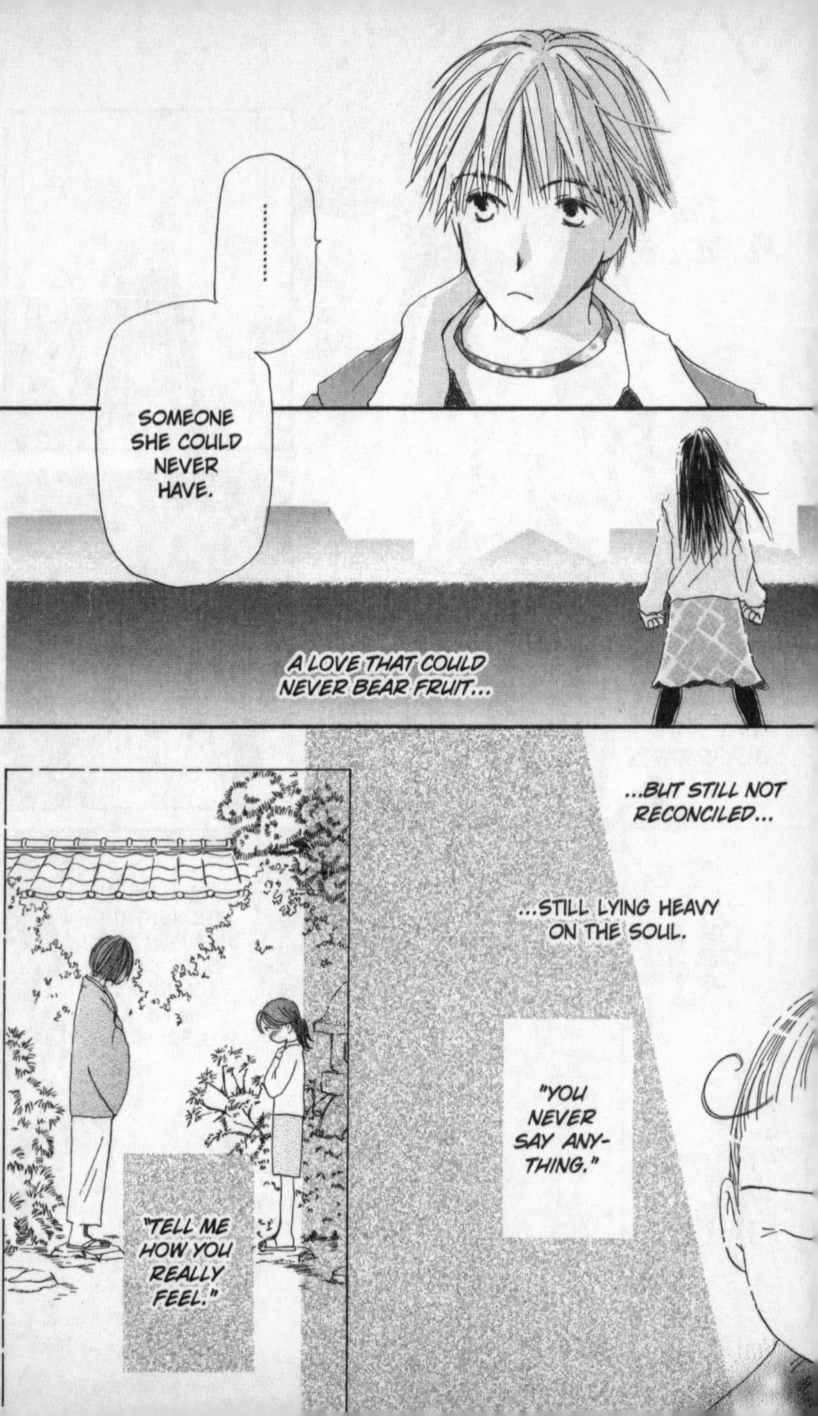
......
SOMEONE SHE COULD NEVER HAVE.
A LOVE THAT COULD NEVER BEAR FRUIT...
...BUT STILL NOT RECONCILED...
...STILL LYING HEAVY ON THE SOUL.
"YOU NEVER SAY ANY-THING."
"TELL ME HOW YOU REALLY FEEL."

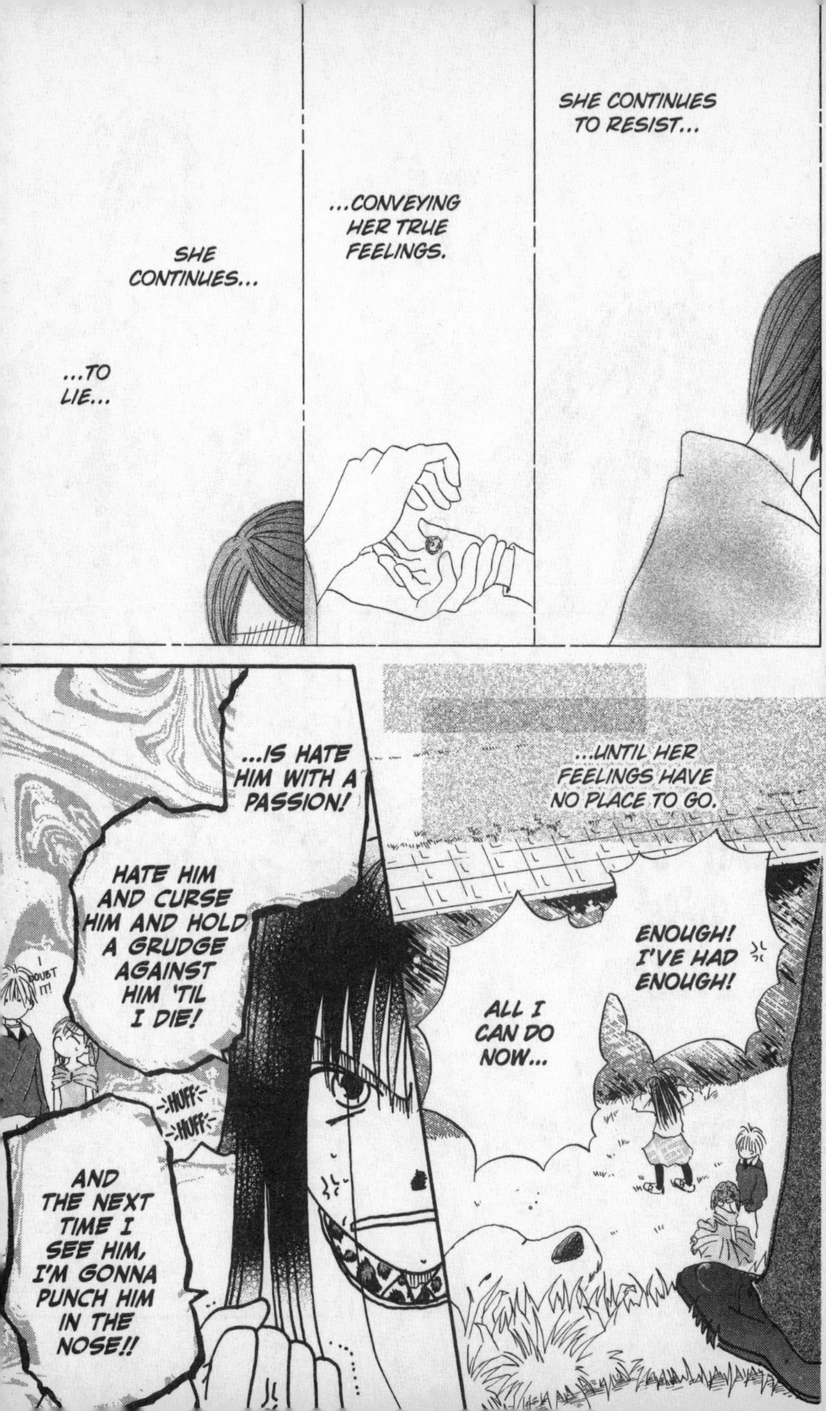
SHE CONTINUES TO RESIST...
...CONVEYING HER TRUE FEELINGS.
SHE CONTINUES...
...TO LIE...
...UNTIL HER FEELINGS HAVE NO PLACE TO GO.
ENOUGH! I'VE HAD ENOUGH!
ALL I CAN DO NOW...
...IS HATE HIM WITH A PASSION!
HATE HIM AND CURSE HIM AND HOLD A GRUDGE AGAINST HIM 'TIL I DIE!
I DOUBT IT!
HUFF
HUFF
AND THE NEXT TIME I SEE HIM, I'M GONNA PUNCH HIM IN THE NOSE!!

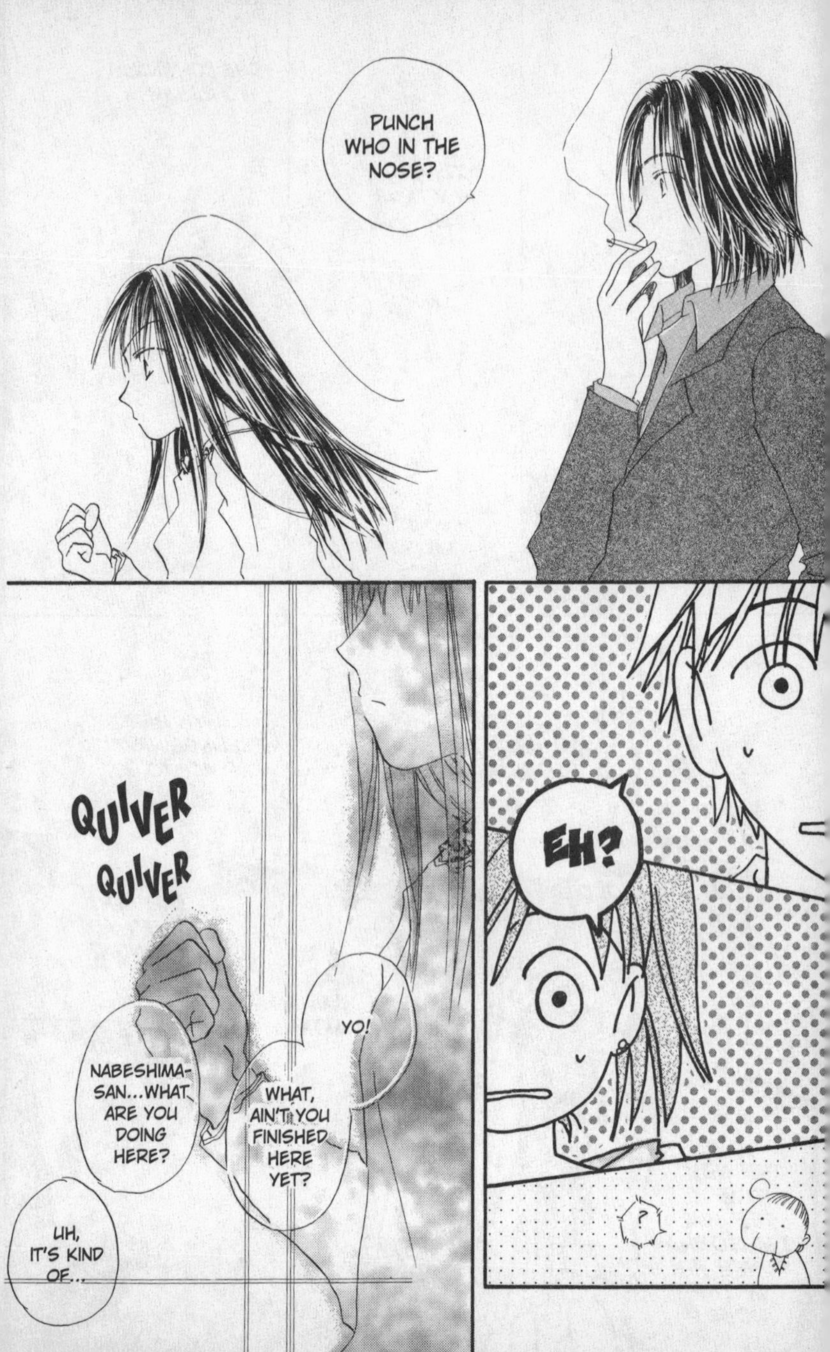
PUNCH WHO IN THE NOSE?
EH?
?
QUIVER QUIVER
YO!
WHAT, AIN'T YOU FINISHED HERE YET?
NABESHIMA-SAN...WHAT ARE YOU DOING HERE?
UH, IT'S KIND OF..

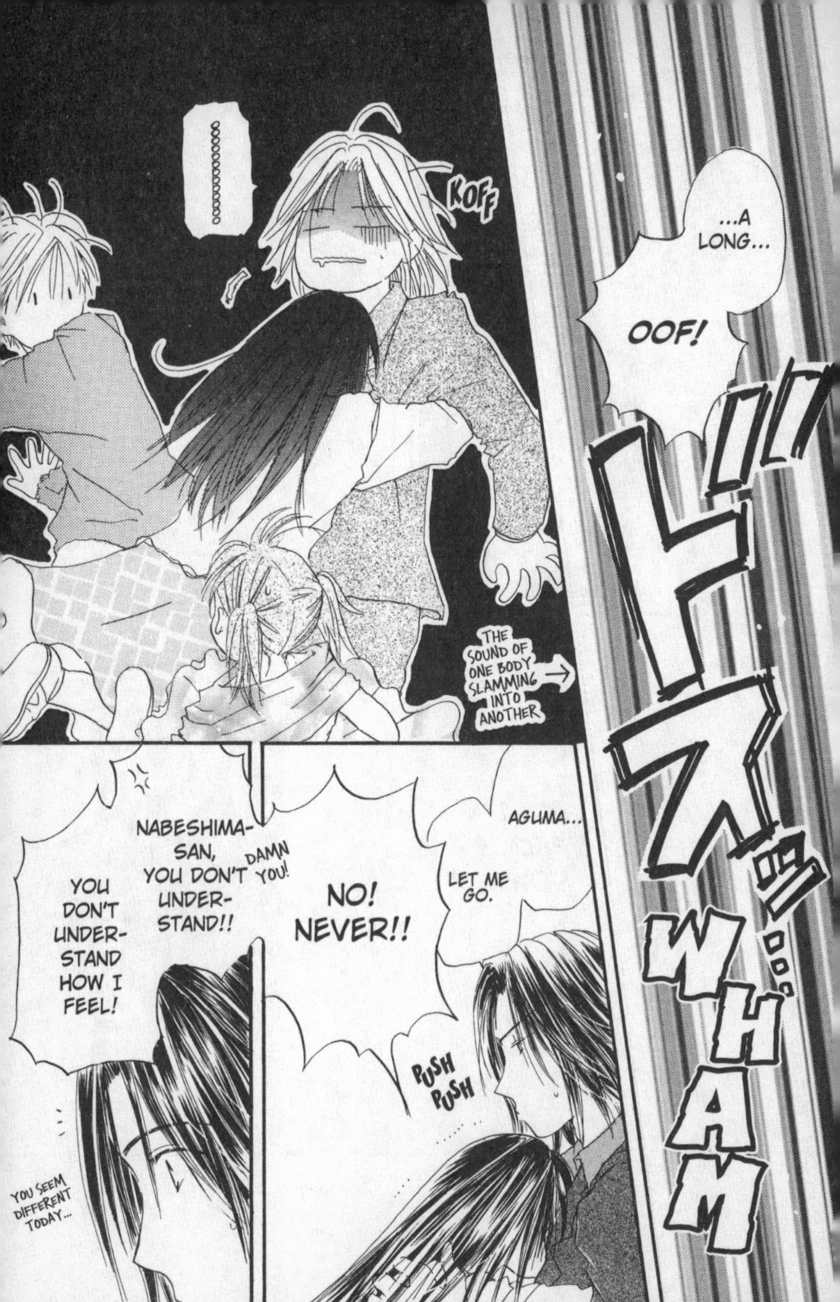

...A LONG...
OOF!
WHAM
OOOOOOOOOOOOO...
KOFF
THE SOUND OF ONE BODY SLAMMING INTO ANOTHER
AGUMA...
LET ME GO.
NO! NEVER!!
PUSH PUSH
NABESHIMA-SAN, YOU DON'T UNDER-STAND!!
DAMN YOU!
YOU DON'T UNDER-STAND HOW I FEEL!
YOU SEEM DIFFERENT TODAY...

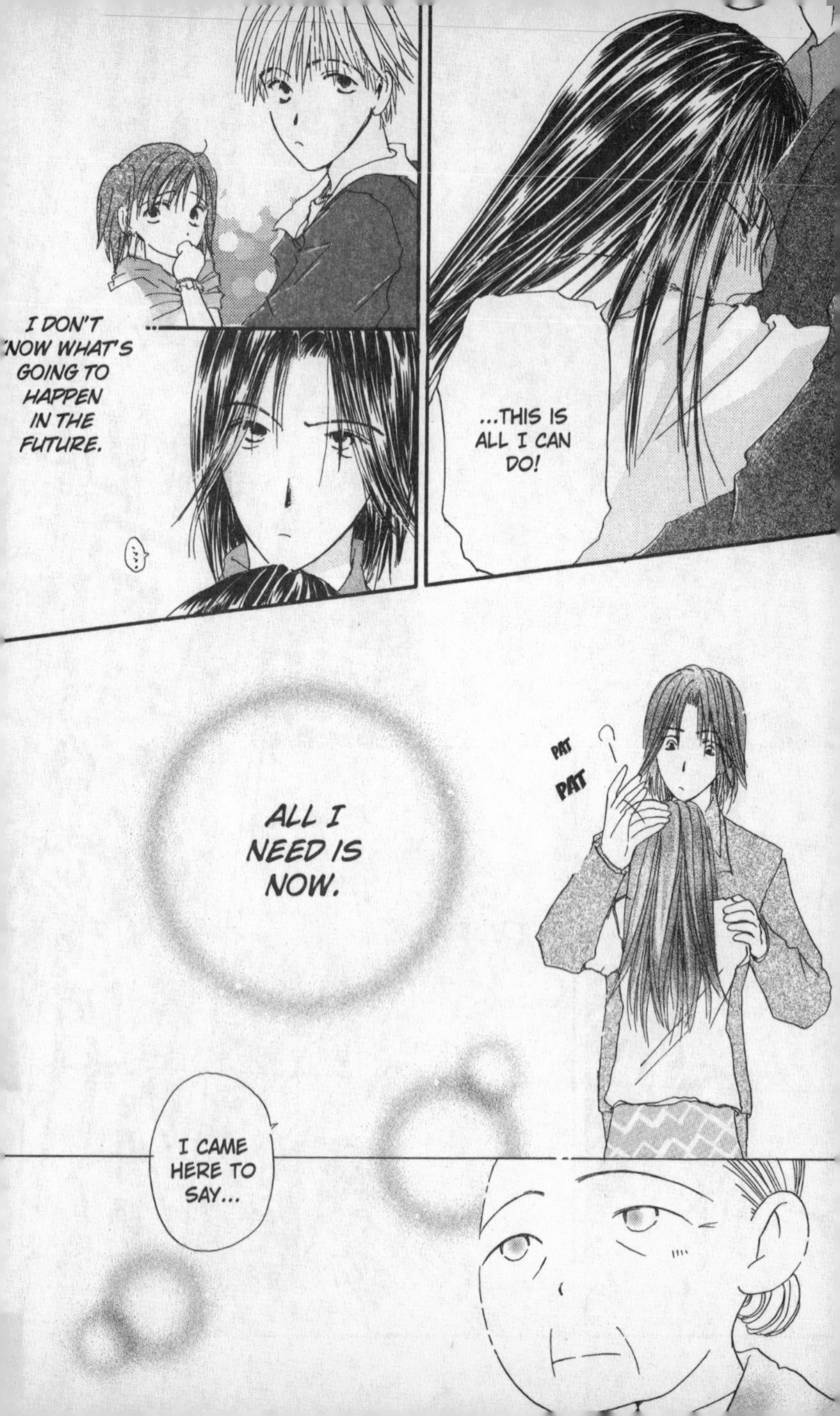
...THIS IS ALL I CAN DO!
I DON'T KNOW WHAT'S GOING TO HAPPEN IN THE FUTURE.
...
PAT PAT
ALL I NEED IS NOW.
I CAME HERE TO SAY...

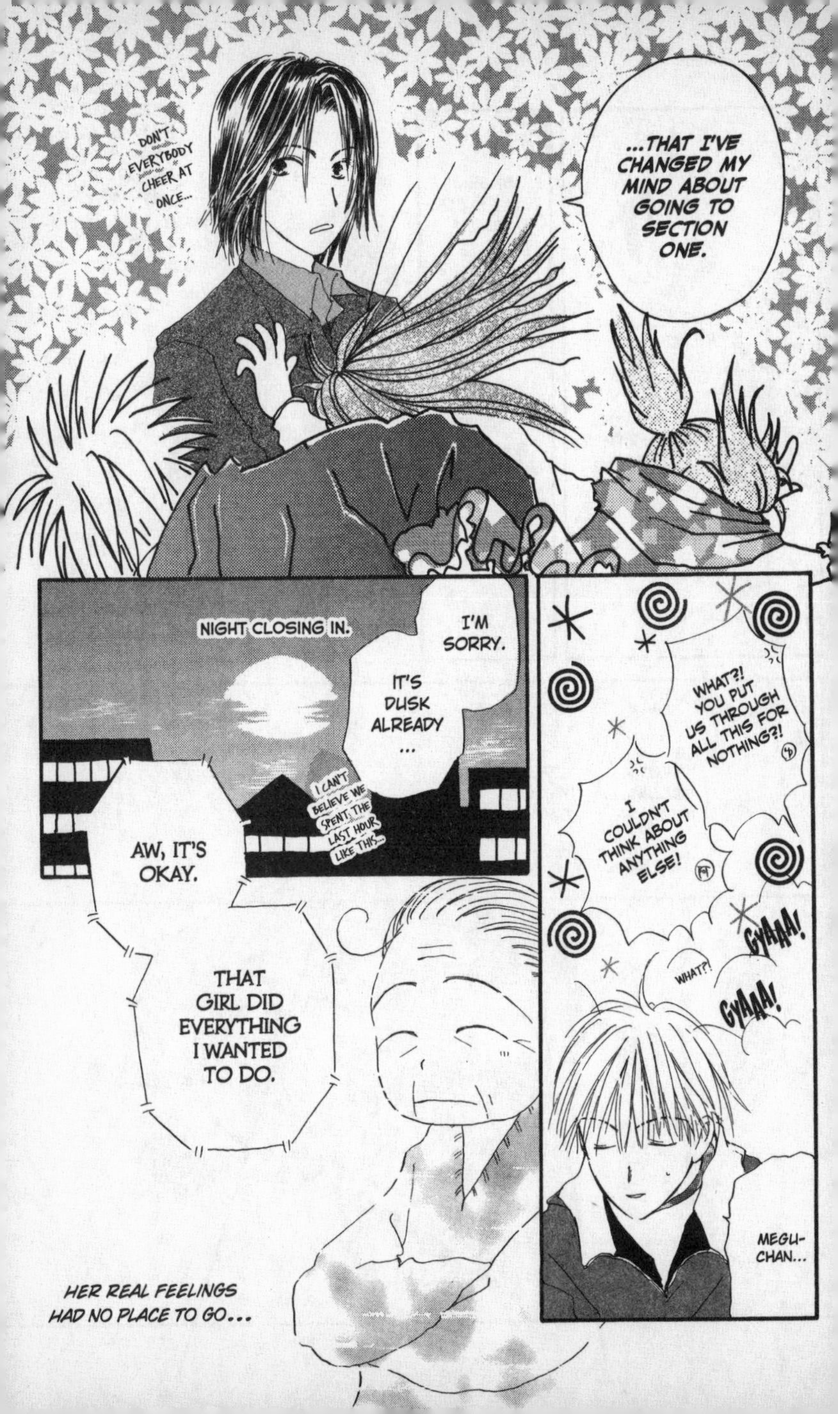
...THAT I'VE CHANGED MY MIND ABOUT GOING TO SECTION ONE.
DON'T EVERYBODY CHEER AT ONCE...
WHAT?! YOU PUT US THROUGH ALL THIS FOR NOTHING?!
I COULDN'T THINK ABOUT ANYTHING ELSE!
GYAAA!
GYAAA!
WHAT?
MEGU-CHAN...
NIGHT CLOSING IN.
I'M SORRY.
IT'S DUSK ALREADY...
I CAN'T BELIEVE WE SPENT THE LAST HOUR LIKE THIS...
AW, IT'S OKAY.
THAT GIRL DID EVERYTHING I WANTED TO DO.
HER REAL FEELINGS HAD NO PLACE TO GO...

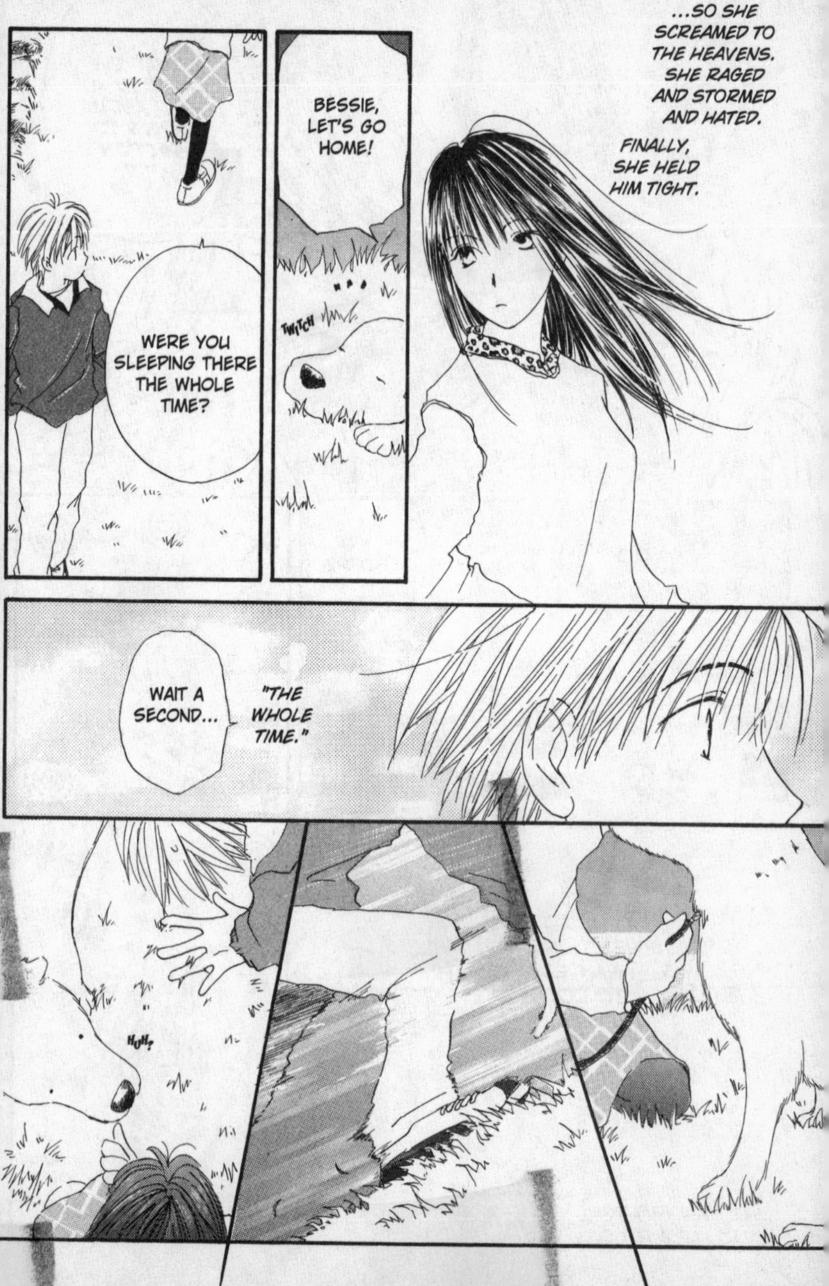
...SO SHE SCREAMED TO THE HEAVENS. SHE RAGED AND STORMED AND HATED.
FINALLY, SHE HELD HIM TIGHT.
BESSIE, LET'S GO HOME!
TWITCH
WERE YOU SLEEPING THERE THE WHOLE TIME?
WAIT A SECOND...
"THE WHOLE TIME."
HUH?

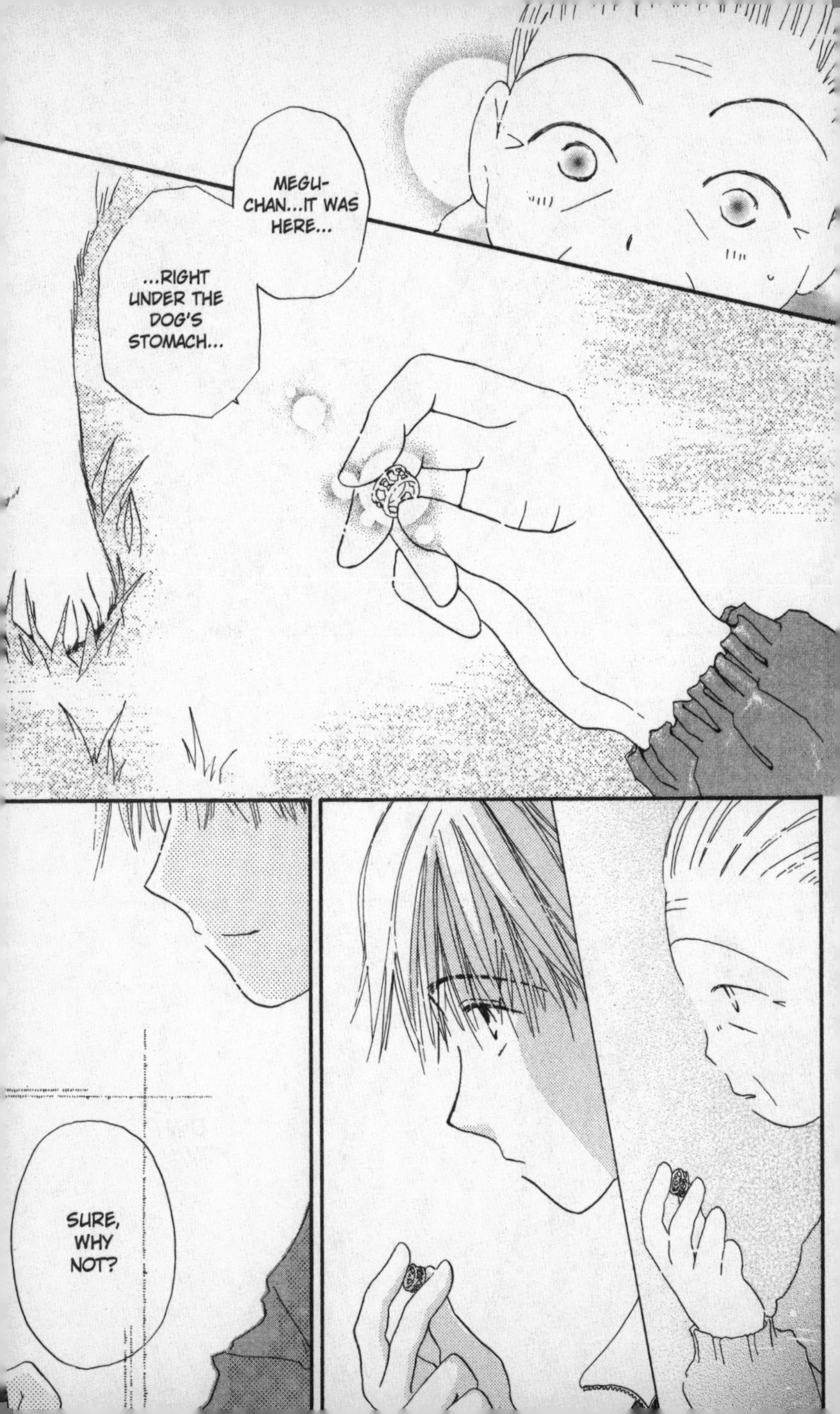
MEGU-CHAN...IT WAS HERE...
...RIGHT UNDER THE DOG'S STOMACH...
SURE, WHY NOT?

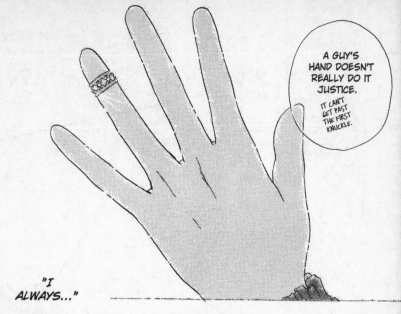

A GUY'S HAND DOESN'T REALLY DO IT JUSTICE.

IT CAN'T GET PAST THE FIRST KNUCKLE.

"I ALWAYS..."

"...LOVED YOU."

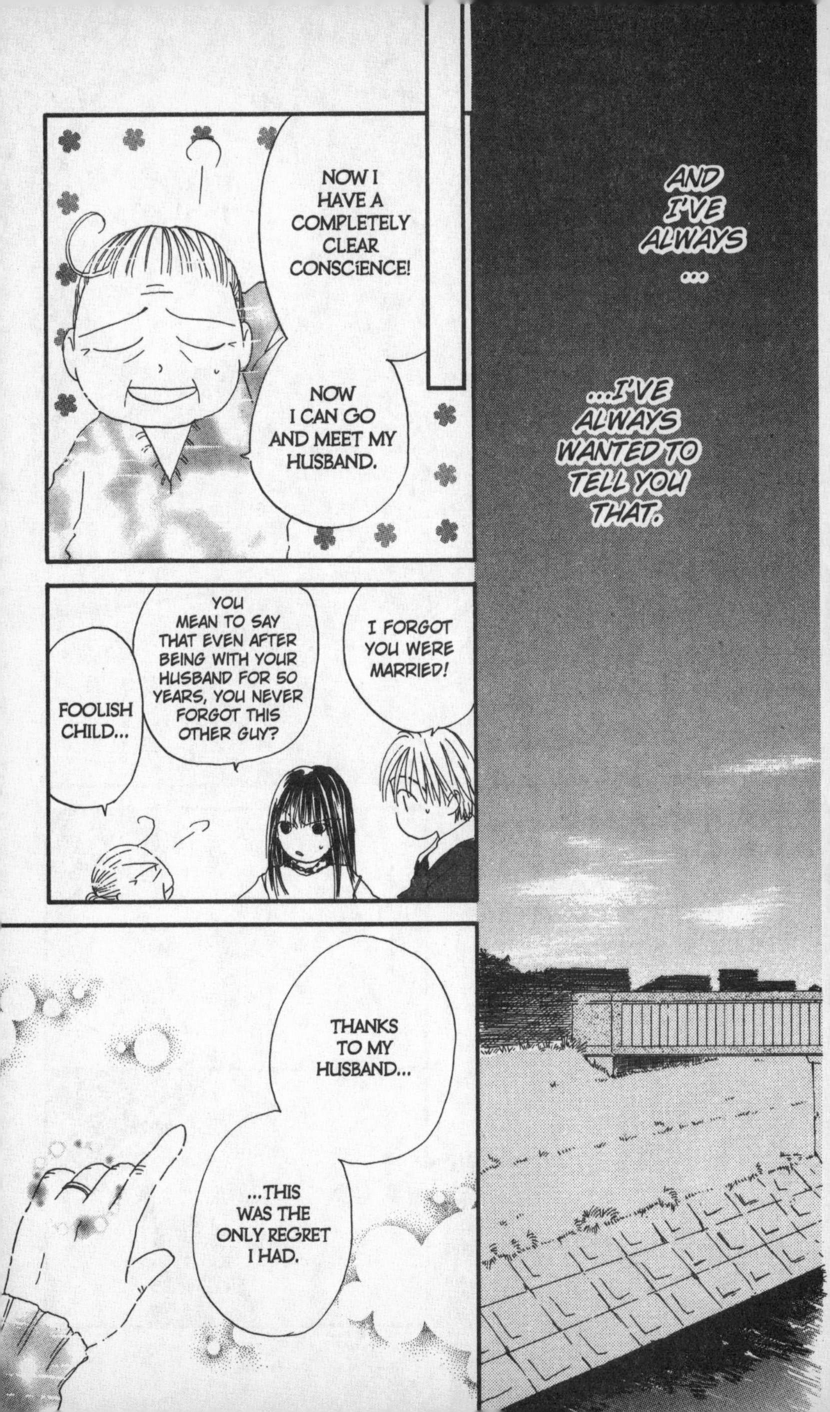

AND I'VE ALWAYS ...
...I'VE ALWAYS WANTED TO TELL YOU THAT.
NOW I HAVE A COMPLETELY CLEAR CONSCIENCE!
NOW I CAN GO AND MEET MY HUSBAND.
I FORGOT YOU WERE MARRIED!
YOU MEAN TO SAY THAT EVEN AFTER BEING WITH YOUR HUSBAND FOR 50 YEARS, YOU NEVER FORGOT THIS OTHER GUY?
FOOLISH CHILD...
THANKS TO MY HUSBAND...
...THIS WAS THE ONLY REGRET I HAD.

SORRY!

HEY!

HE KEPT ME HAPPY FOR 50 YEARS.

WHAT MADE YOU DECIDE NOT TO TRANSFER TO SECTION ONE?

I DIDN'T WANNA MISS OUT ON SECTION TWO'S IDOL MONTH!

AH...

RUFFLE

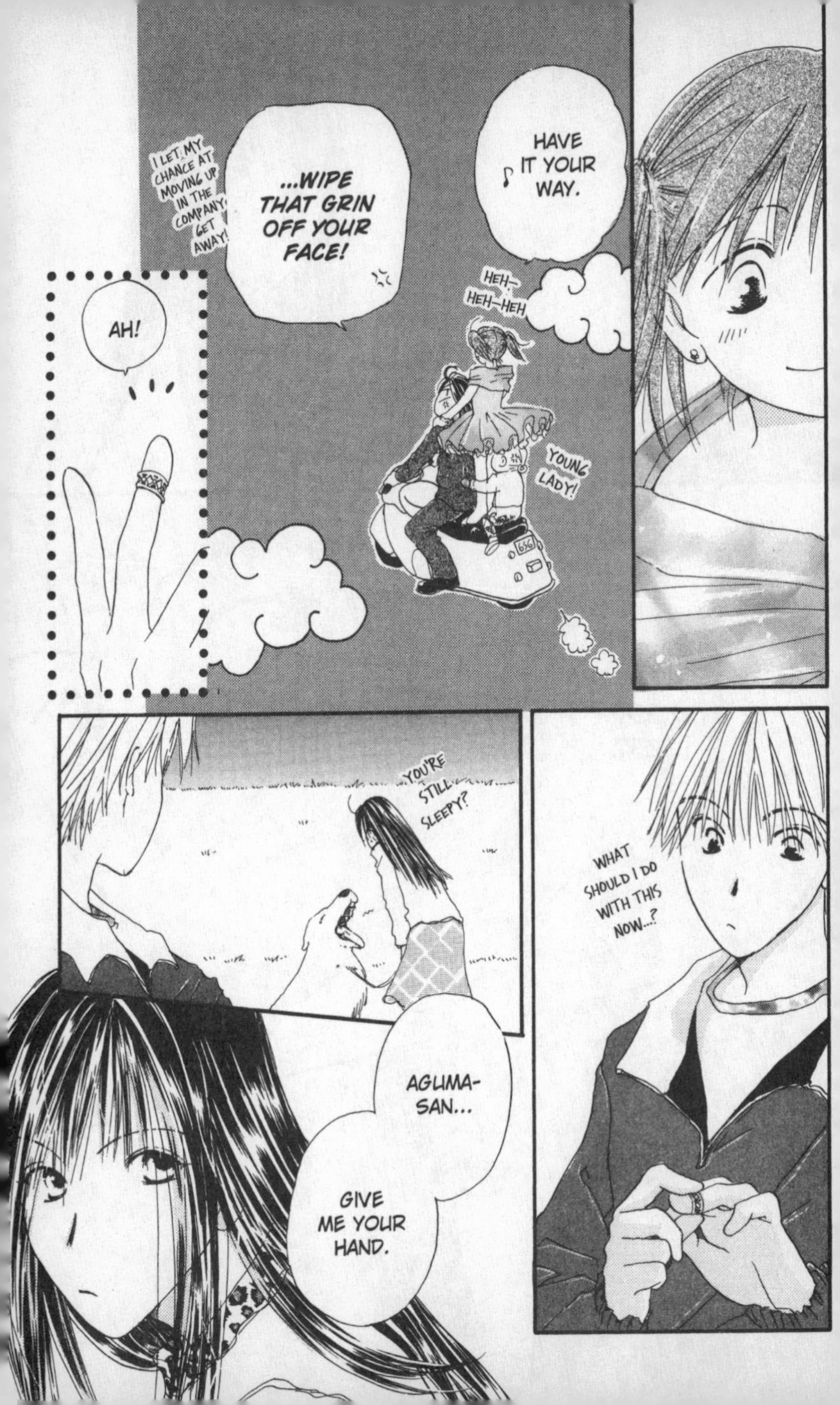
HAVE IT YOUR WAY.
HEH-HEH-HEH
...WIPE THAT GRIN OFF YOUR FACE!
I LET MY CHANCE AT MOVING UP IN THE COMPANY GET AWAY!
YOUNG LADY!
AH!
WHAT SHOULD I DO WITH THIS NOW...?
YOU'RE STILL SLEEPY?
AGUMA-SAN...
GIVE ME YOUR HAND.

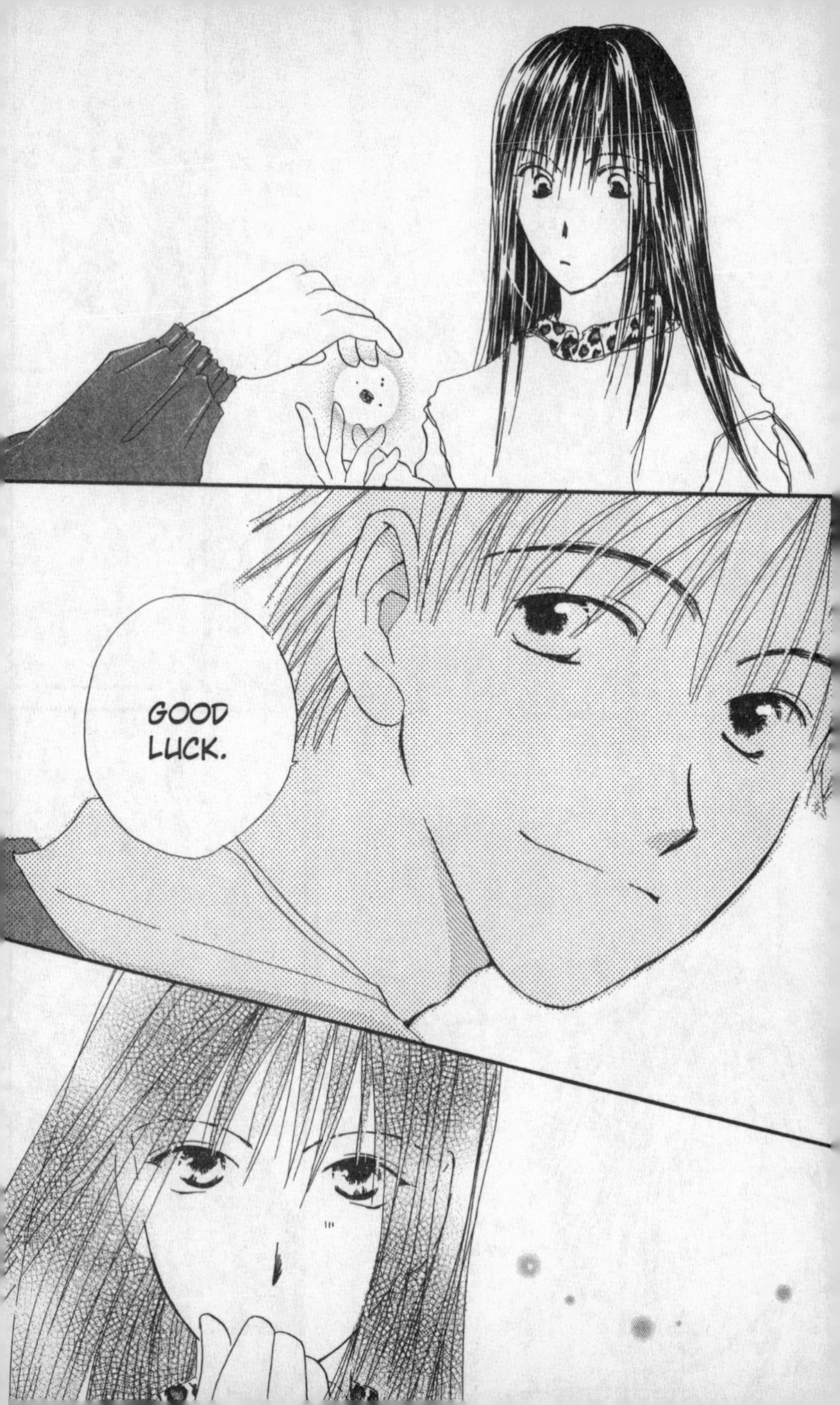
GOOD LUCK.

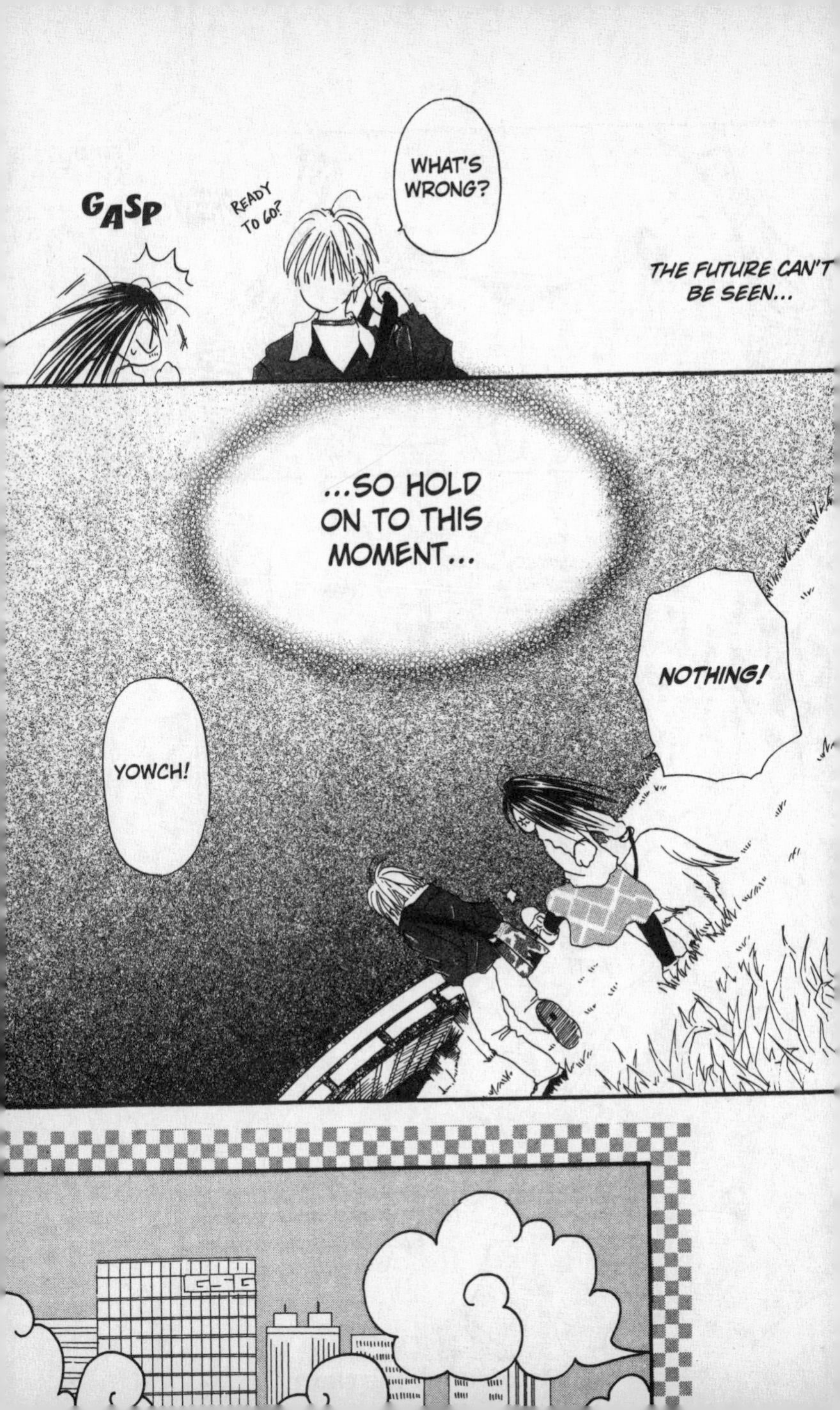
THE FUTURE CAN'T BE SEEN...
WHAT'S WRONG?
READY TO GO?
GASP
...SO HOLD ON TO THIS MOMENT...
NOTHING!
YOWCH!

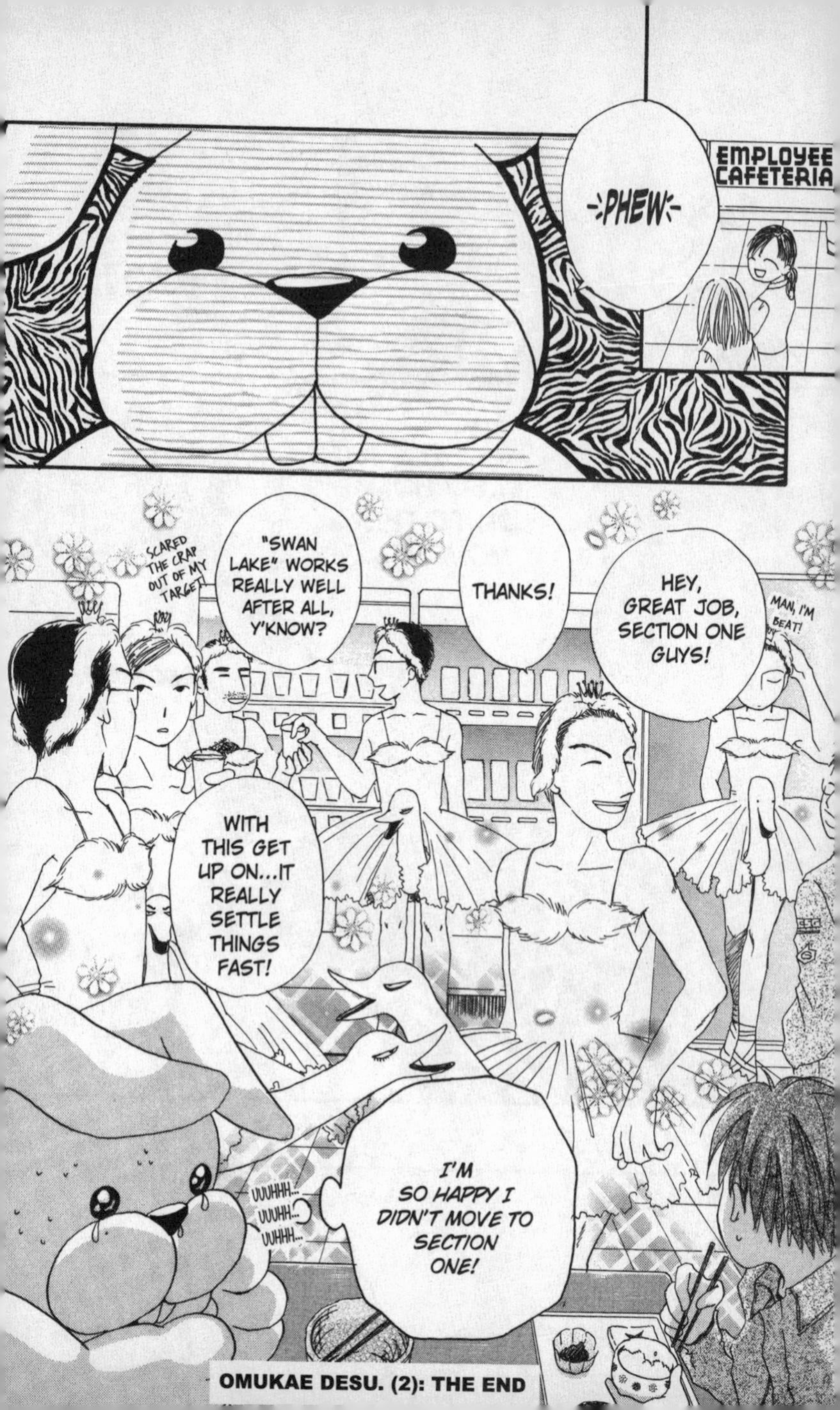
EMPLOYEE CAFETERIA
-PHEW-
MAN, I'M BEAT!
HEY, GREAT JOB, SECTION ONE GUYS!
THANKS!
"SWAN LAKE" WORKS REALLY WELL AFTER ALL, Y'KNOW?
SCARED THE CRAP OUT OF MY TARGET
WITH THIS GET UP ON...IT REALLY SETTLE THINGS FAST!
I'M SO HAPPY I DIDN'T MOVE TO SECTION ONE!
UUUHHH... UUUHH... UUHHH...
OMUKAE DESU. (2): THE END

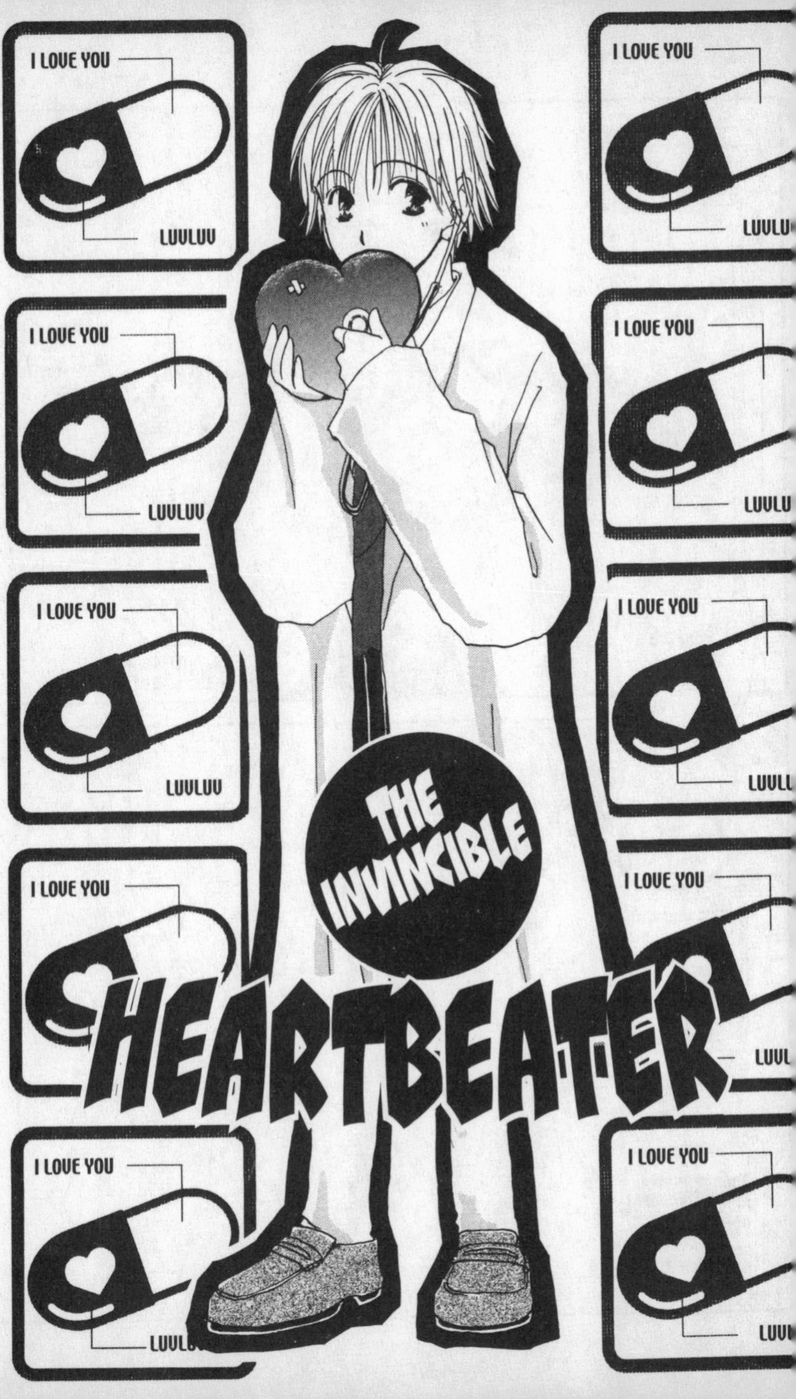
THE INVINCIBLE
HEARTBEATER
I LOVE YOU
LUVLUV

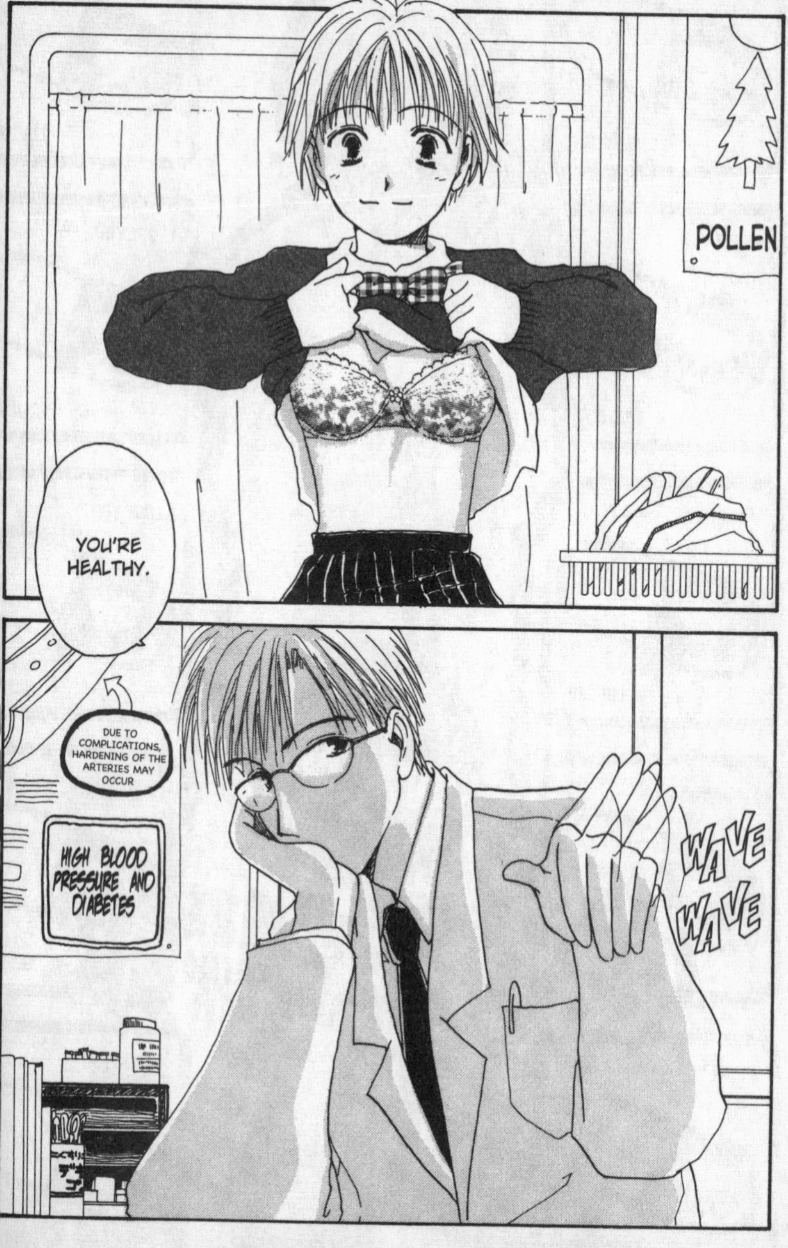
POLLEN
YOU'RE HEALTHY.
WAVE WAVE
DUE TO COMPLICATIONS, HARDENING OF THE ARTERIES MAY OCCUR
HIGH BLOOD PRESSURE AND DIABETES

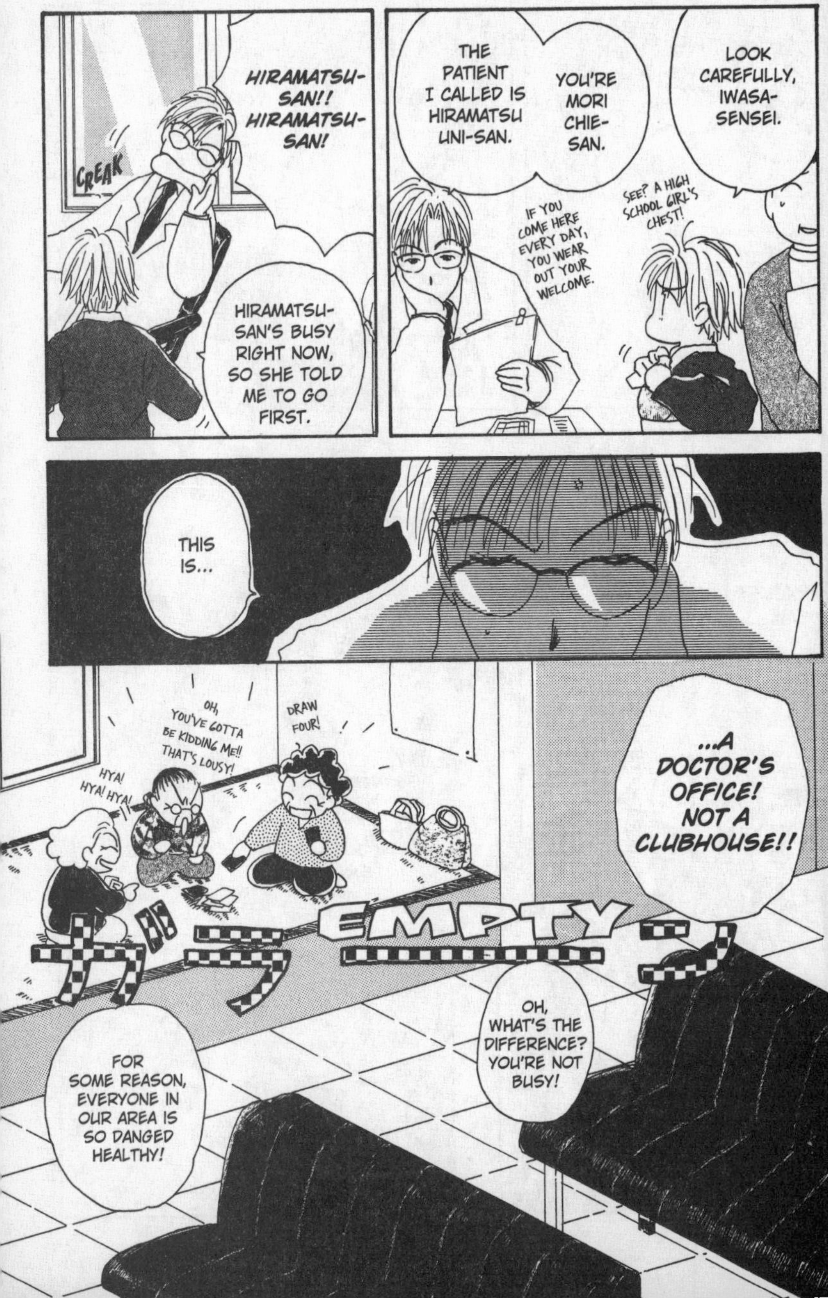
LOOK CAREFULLY, IWASA-SENSEI.
SEE? A HIGH SCHOOL GIRL'S CHEST!
YOU'RE MORI CHIE-SAN.
THE PATIENT I CALLED IS HIRAMATSU UNI-SAN.
IF YOU COME HERE EVERY DAY, YOU WEAR OUT YOUR WELCOME.
HIRAMATSU-SAN!! HIRAMATSU-SAN!
CREAK
HIRAMATSU-SAN'S BUSY RIGHT NOW, SO SHE TOLD ME TO GO FIRST.
THIS IS...
...A DOCTOR'S OFFICE! NOT A CLUBHOUSE!!
DRAW FOUR!
OH, YOU'VE GOTTA BE KIDDING ME!! THAT'S LOUSY!
HYA! HYA! HYA!
EMPTY
OH, WHAT'S THE DIFFERENCE? YOU'RE NOT BUSY!
FOR SOME REASON, EVERYONE IN OUR AREA IS SO DANGED HEALTHY!

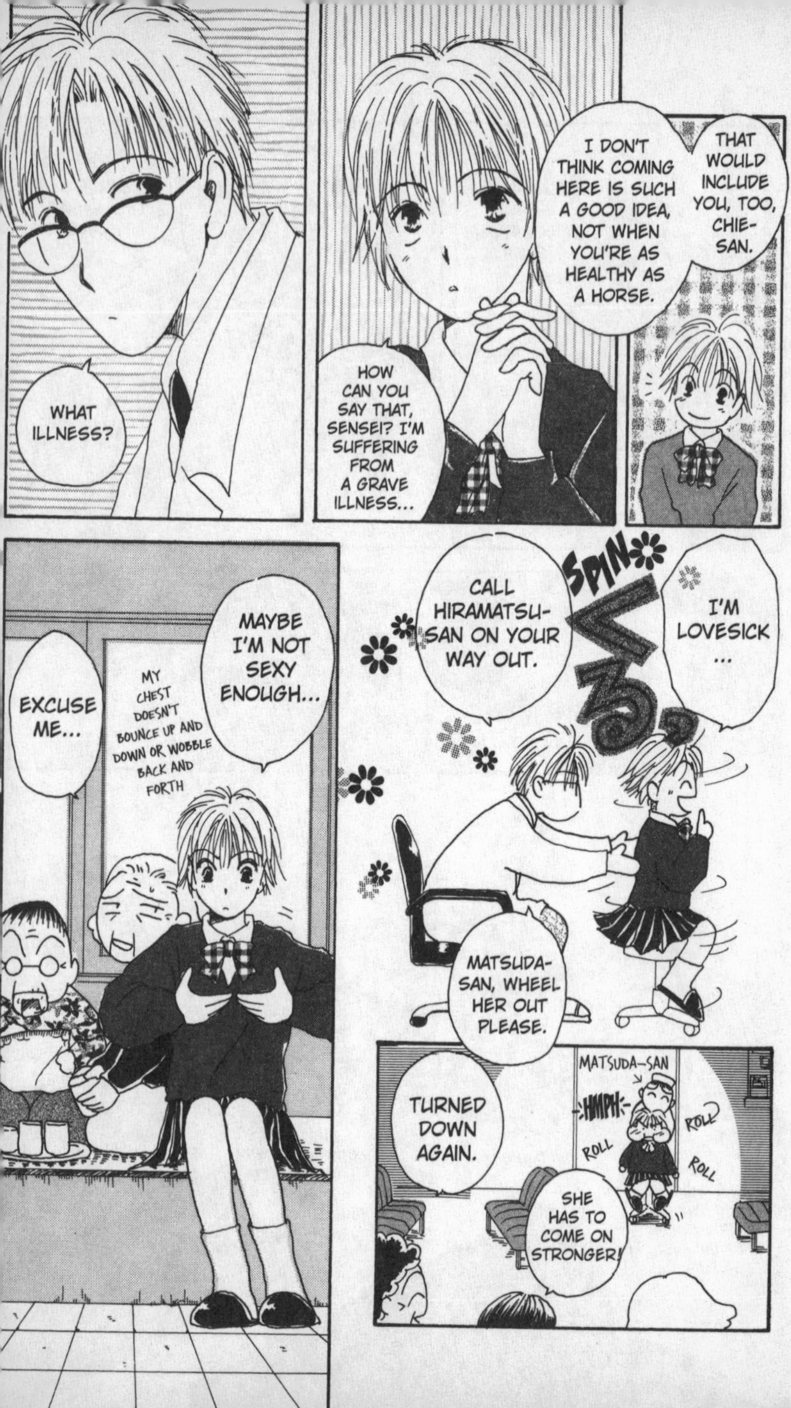
I DON'T THINK COMING HERE IS SUCH A GOOD IDEA, NOT WHEN YOU'RE AS HEALTHY AS A HORSE.
THAT WOULD INCLUDE YOU, TOO, CHIE-SAN.
HOW CAN YOU SAY THAT, SENSEI? I'M SUFFERING FROM A GRAVE ILLNESS...
WHAT ILLNESS?
I'M LOVESICK ...
SPIN
くるっ
CALL HIRAMATSU-SAN ON YOUR WAY OUT.
MATSUDA-SAN, WHEEL HER OUT PLEASE.
MATSUDA-SAN
HMPH
ROLL
ROLL
ROLL
TURNED DOWN AGAIN.
SHE HAS TO COME ON STRONGER!
MAYBE I'M NOT SEXY ENOUGH...
MY CHEST DOESN'T BOUNCE UP AND DOWN OR WOBBLE BACK AND FORTH
EXCUSE ME...

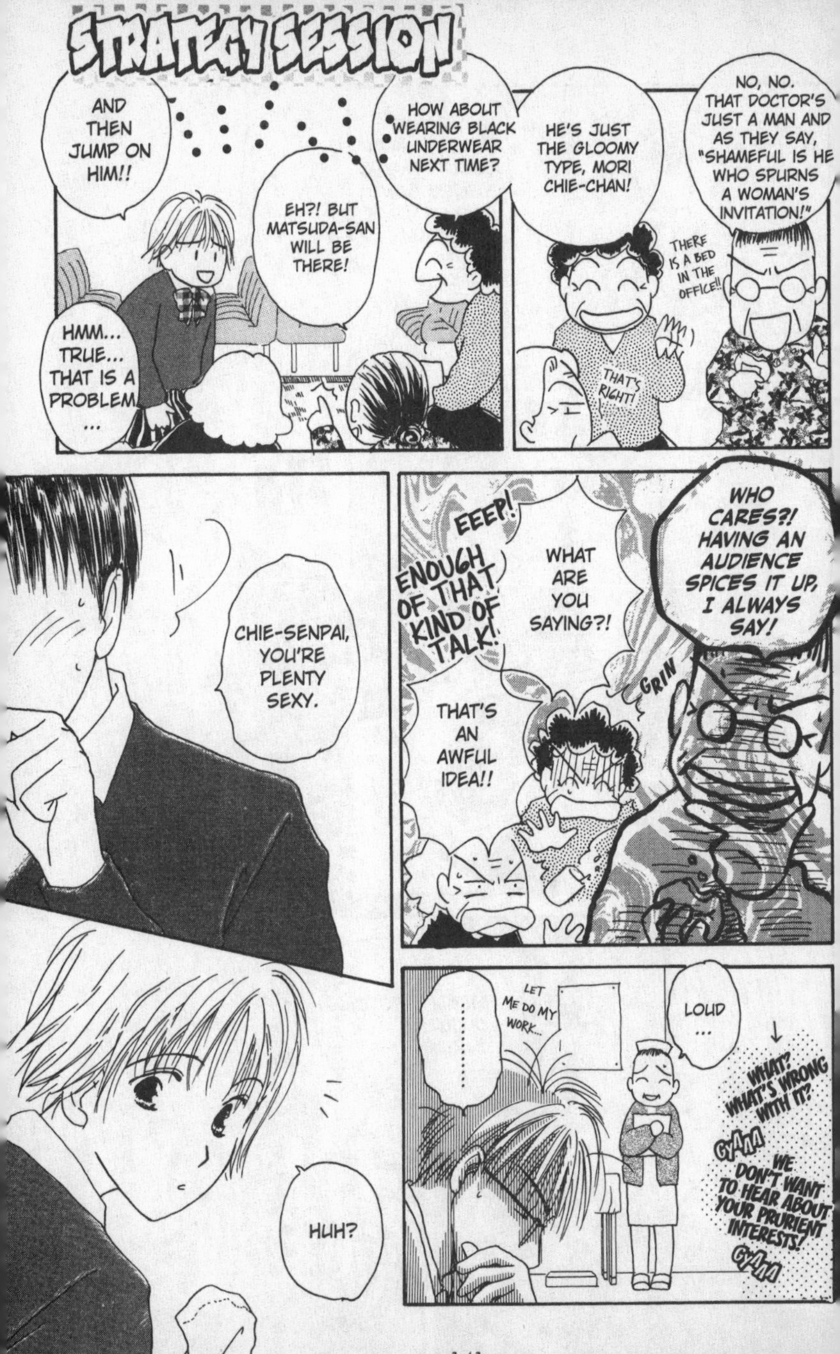
STRATEGY SESSION
NO, NO. THAT DOCTOR'S JUST A MAN AND AS THEY SAY, "SHAMEFUL IS HE WHO SPURNS A WOMAN'S INVITATION!"
HE'S JUST THE GLOOMY TYPE, MORI CHIE-CHAN!
THERE IS A BED IN THE OFFICE!!
THAT'S RIGHT!
HOW ABOUT WEARING BLACK UNDERWEAR NEXT TIME?
EH?! BUT MATSUDA-SAN WILL BE THERE!
AND THEN JUMP ON HIM!!
HMM... TRUE... THAT IS A PROBLEM ...
WHO CARES?! HAVING AN AUDIENCE SPICES IT UP, I ALWAYS SAY!
WHAT ARE YOU SAYING?!
EEEP!
ENOUGH OF THAT KIND OF TALK!
GRIN
THAT'S AN AWFUL IDEA!!
WHAT? WHAT'S WRONG WITH IT?
GYAAA
WE DON'T WANT TO HEAR ABOUT YOUR PRURIENT INTERESTS!
GYAAA
LOUD ...
LET ME DO MY WORK...
......
CHIE-SENPAI, YOU'RE PLENTY SEXY.
HUH?

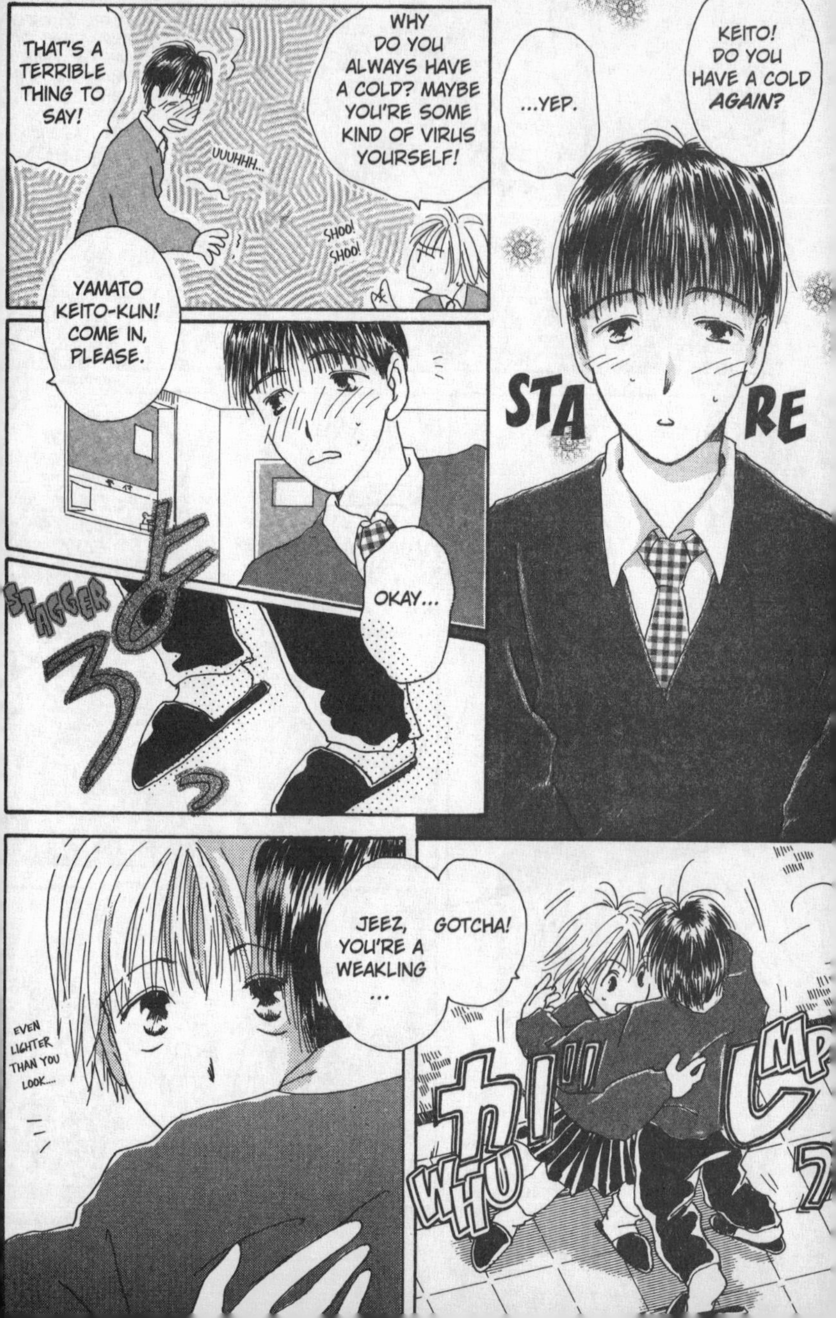
KEITO! DO YOU HAVE A COLD AGAIN?
...YEP.
STARE
WHY DO YOU ALWAYS HAVE A COLD? MAYBE YOU'RE SOME KIND OF VIRUS YOURSELF!
SHOO! SHOO!
UUUHHH...
THAT'S A TERRIBLE THING TO SAY!
YAMATO KEITO-KUN! COME IN, PLEASE.
OKAY...
STAGGER
GOTCHA!
JEEZ, YOU'RE A WEAKLING ...
EVEN LIGHTER THAN YOU LOOK...

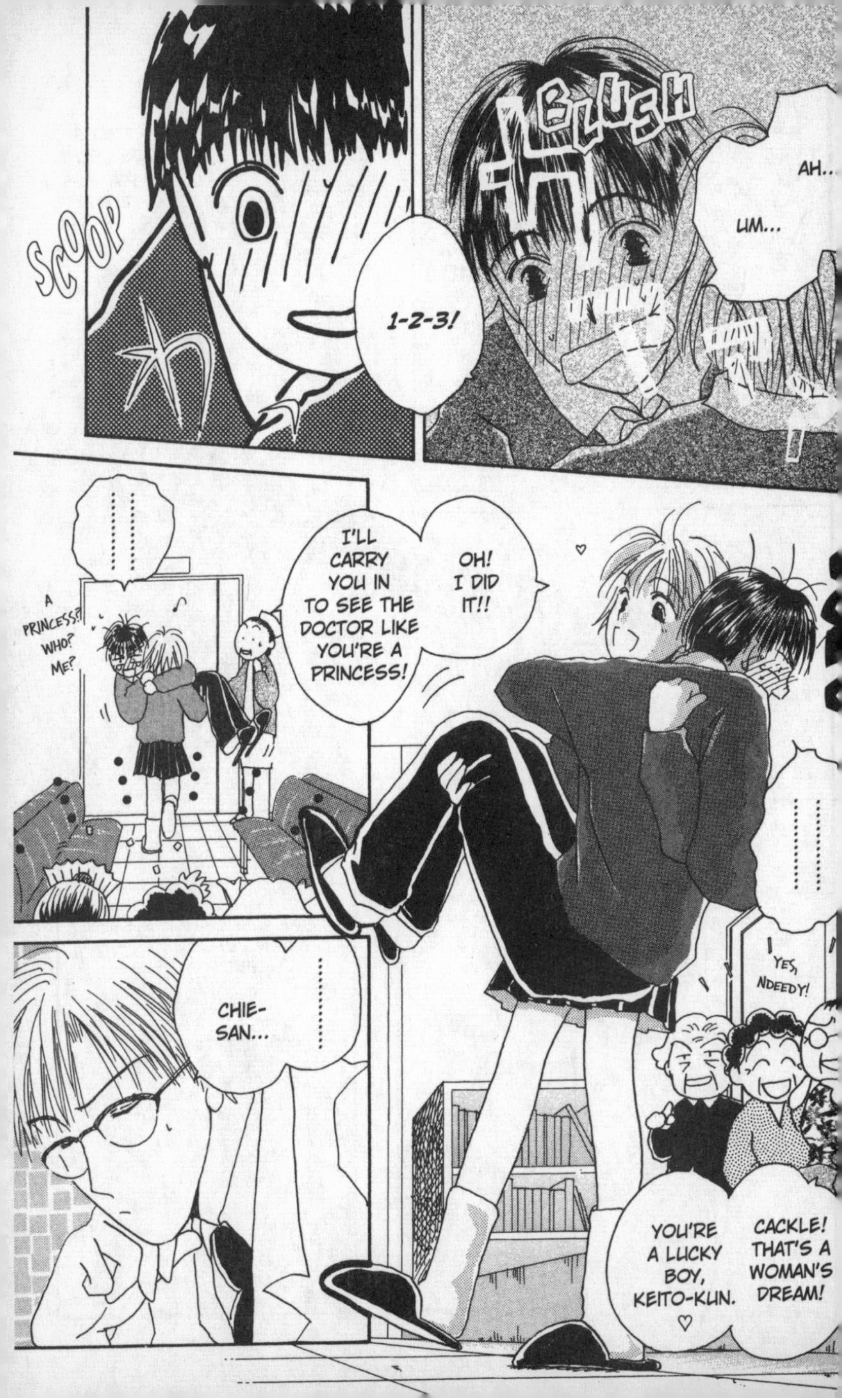
BLUSH
AH...
UM...
1-2-3!
SCOOP
I'LL CARRY YOU IN TO SEE THE DOCTOR LIKE YOU'RE A PRINCESS!
OH! I DID IT!!
......
YES, NDEEDY!
CACKLE! THAT'S A WOMAN'S DREAM!
YOU'RE A LUCKY BOY, KEITO-KUN. ♡
......
A PRINCESS?? WHO? ME?
......
CHIE-SAN...

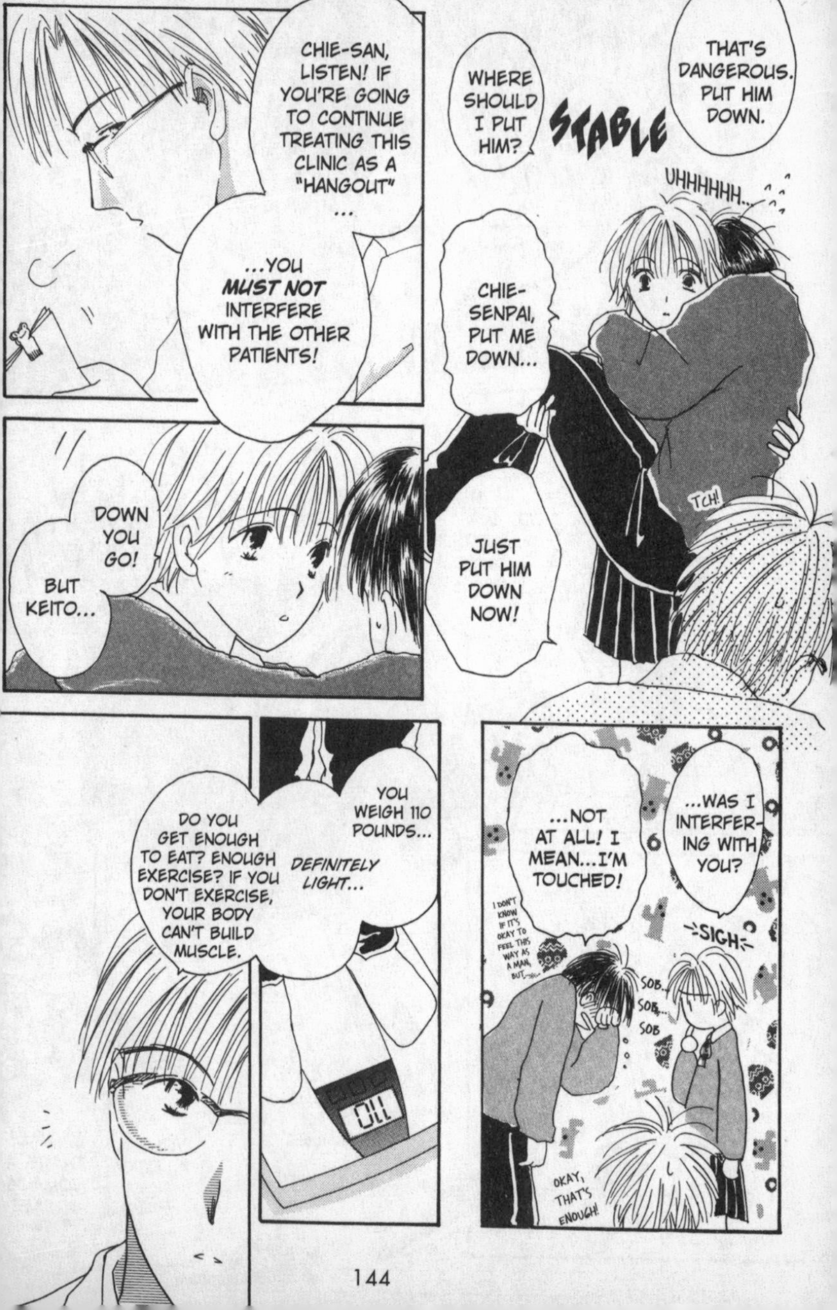
THAT'S DANGEROUS. PUT HIM DOWN.
STABLE
WHERE SHOULD I PUT HIM?
UHHHHHH...
CHIE-SENPAI, PUT ME DOWN...
TCH!
JUST PUT HIM DOWN NOW!
CHIE-SAN, LISTEN! IF YOU'RE GOING TO CONTINUE TREATING THIS CLINIC AS A "HANGOUT" ...
...YOU *MUST NOT* INTERFERE WITH THE OTHER PATIENTS!
DOWN YOU GO!
BUT KEITO...
...WAS I INTERFERING WITH YOU?
SIGH
...NOT AT ALL! I MEAN...I'M TOUCHED!
I DON'T KNOW IF IT'S OKAY TO FEEL THIS WAY AS A MAN, BUT...
SOB... SOB... SOB
OKAY, THAT'S ENOUGH!
YOU WEIGH 110 POUNDS...
DEFINITELY LIGHT...
110
DO YOU GET ENOUGH TO EAT? ENOUGH EXERCISE? IF YOU DON'T EXERCISE, YOUR BODY CAN'T BUILD MUSCLE.

GRATITUDE
****

I'VE DEFINITELY
GOTTEN A LOT
MORE LETTERS
AFTER VOLUME 1
CAME OUT. AAAH...
I'M SO LUCKY...

I FEEL
LIKE I
COULD
FLY. ♡

THANK YOU FOR
WRITING, EVERYONE.
I PROMISED TO
ANSWER ALL OF MY
FAN MAIL SO I CAN'T
BACK OUT ON THAT.
I'M IN THE PROCESS
OF ANSWERING, BUT
I'M SO BUSY RIGHT
NOW, IT'S ALL I CAN
DO TO ANSWER ONE
PIECE OF MAIL. SORRY
TO THE FANS WHO'VE
WRITTEN ME MULTIPLE
TIMES, BUT I'M ONLY
GOING TO BE ABLE
TO RESPOND ONCE!

I DO LOVE
READING ALL OF
YOUR LETTERS,
THOUGH!

I'VE BEEN THINKING
ABOUT REPLYING
WITH SEASONAL
POSTCARDS, SO ANY
FANS WHO WANT ONE,
LET ME KNOW (JUST
WRITING "I WANT
ONE!" IS FINE) AND
I'LL BE HAPPY.*

SEE YOU
AT THE END
OF THE VOLUME!
THANK YOU
TO THE READER
WHO MADE THIS
DOLL.

*(CMX EDITOR NOTE:
OFFER NOT VALID IN
NORTH AMERICA)

AND I CAN'T HELP THINKING HOW LUCKY YOU ARE, SENSEI, GETTING TO SEE CHIE-SENPAI'S BODY EVERY SINGLE DAY!

IT'S KEITO-KUN!

WHY DO YOU LOOK SO ANGRY, KAIO-KUN?

...SHE'S BEEN MY PATIENT SINCE JUNIOR HIGH SCHOOL...

AT LEAST TRY TO GET MY NAME RIGHT!

WHAT ARE YOU TALKING ABOUT? IT'S NOT SOMETHING I'M ESPECIALLY THRILLED ABOUT!

AND ANYWAY...

REALLY? YOU'RE PRETTY COOL ABOUT IT, SENSEI.

IWASA-SENSEI IS 'A' 'COOL' 'CUSTOMER,' ALL RIGHT.

BUT...

...FEBRUARY TWO YEARS AGO...

-KOFF-

-KOFF-

UNFRIENDL...

SERIOUS...

IWAS
INTER

MEDICA
SURGE
8:30A
3:30P

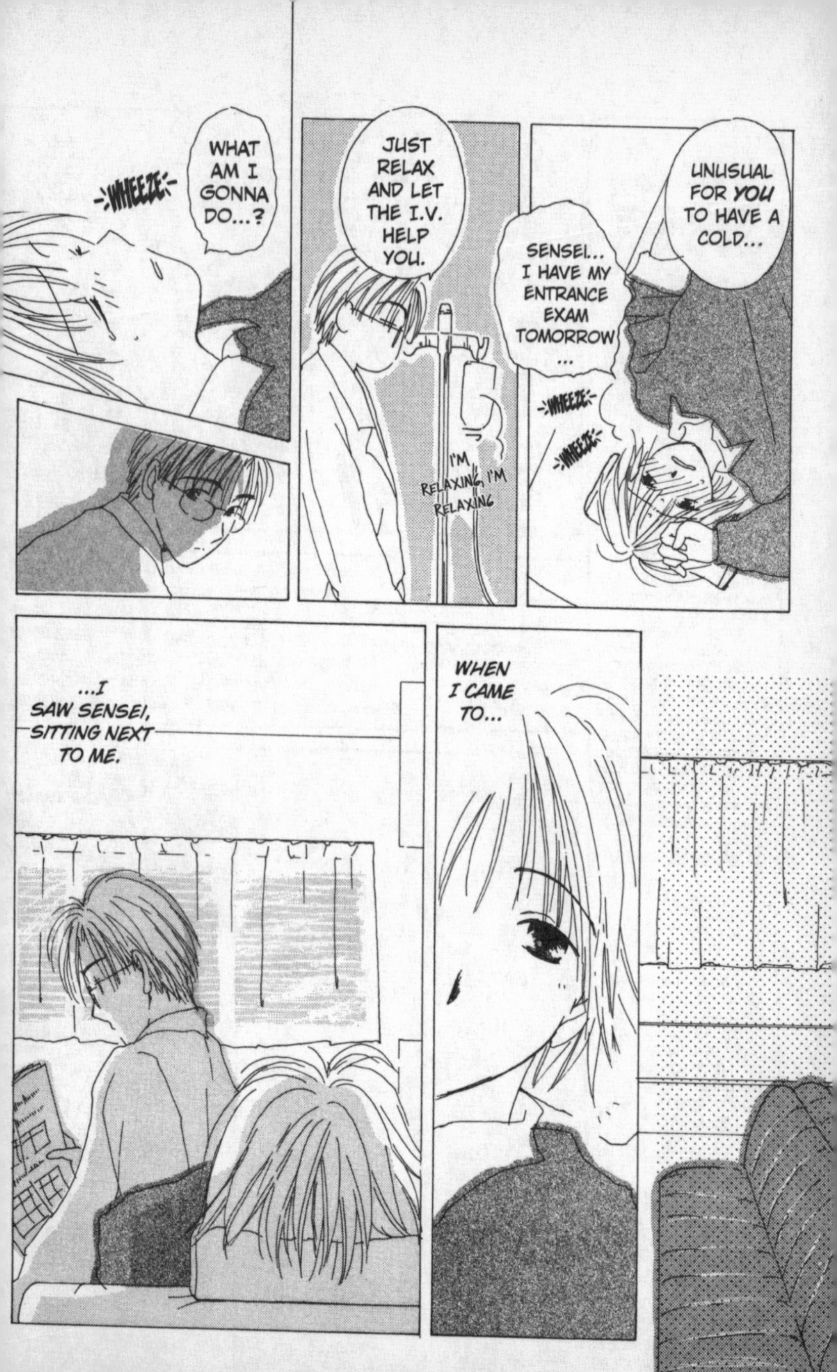
UNUSUAL FOR YOU TO HAVE A COLD...
SENSEI... I HAVE MY ENTRANCE EXAM TOMORROW ...
WHEEZE
WHEEZE
JUST RELAX AND LET THE I.V. HELP YOU.
I'M RELAXING, I'M RELAXING
WHEEZE
WHAT AM I GONNA DO...?
WHEN I CAME TO...
...I SAW SENSEI, SITTING NEXT TO ME.

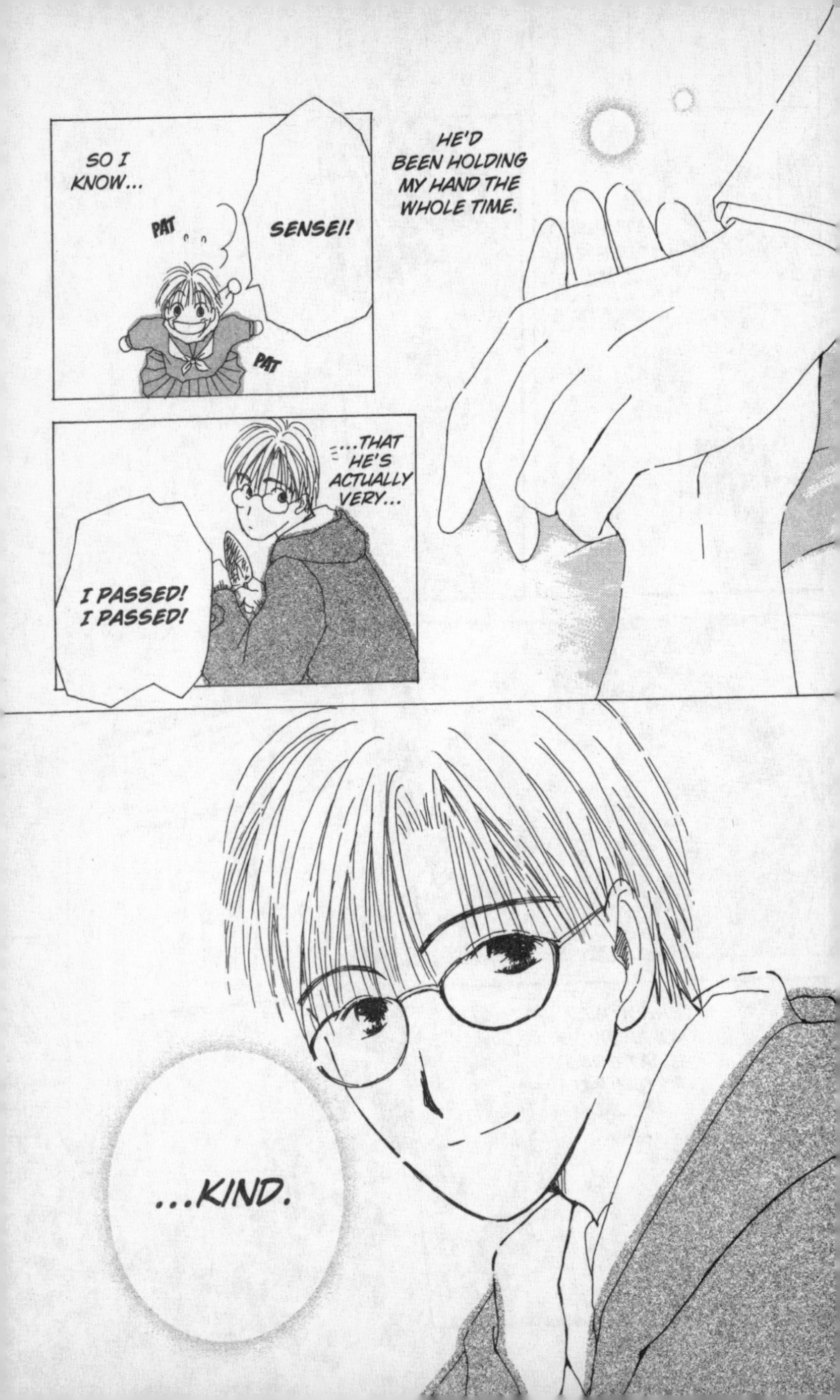
HE'D BEEN HOLDING MY HAND THE WHOLE TIME.
SO I KNOW...
SENSEI!
PAT
PAT
...THAT HE'S ACTUALLY VERY...
I PASSED! I PASSED!
...KIND.

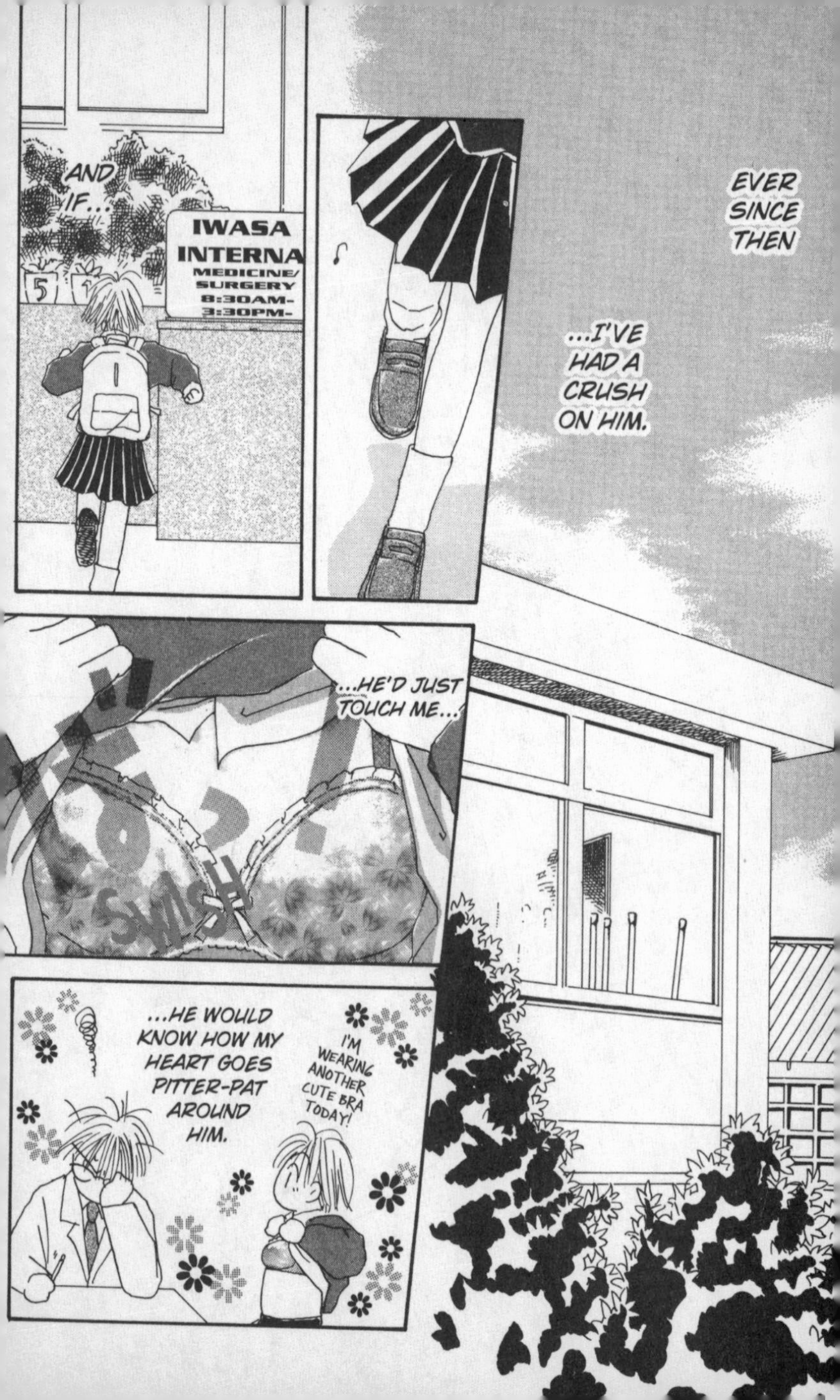
EVER SINCE THEN
...I'VE HAD A CRUSH ON HIM.
AND IF...
IWASA INTERNA
MEDICINE/ SURGERY
8:30AM-
3:30PM-
5
...HE'D JUST TOUCH ME...
SWISH
...HE WOULD KNOW HOW MY HEART GOES PITTER-PAT AROUND HIM.
I'M WEARING ANOTHER CUTE BRA TODAY!

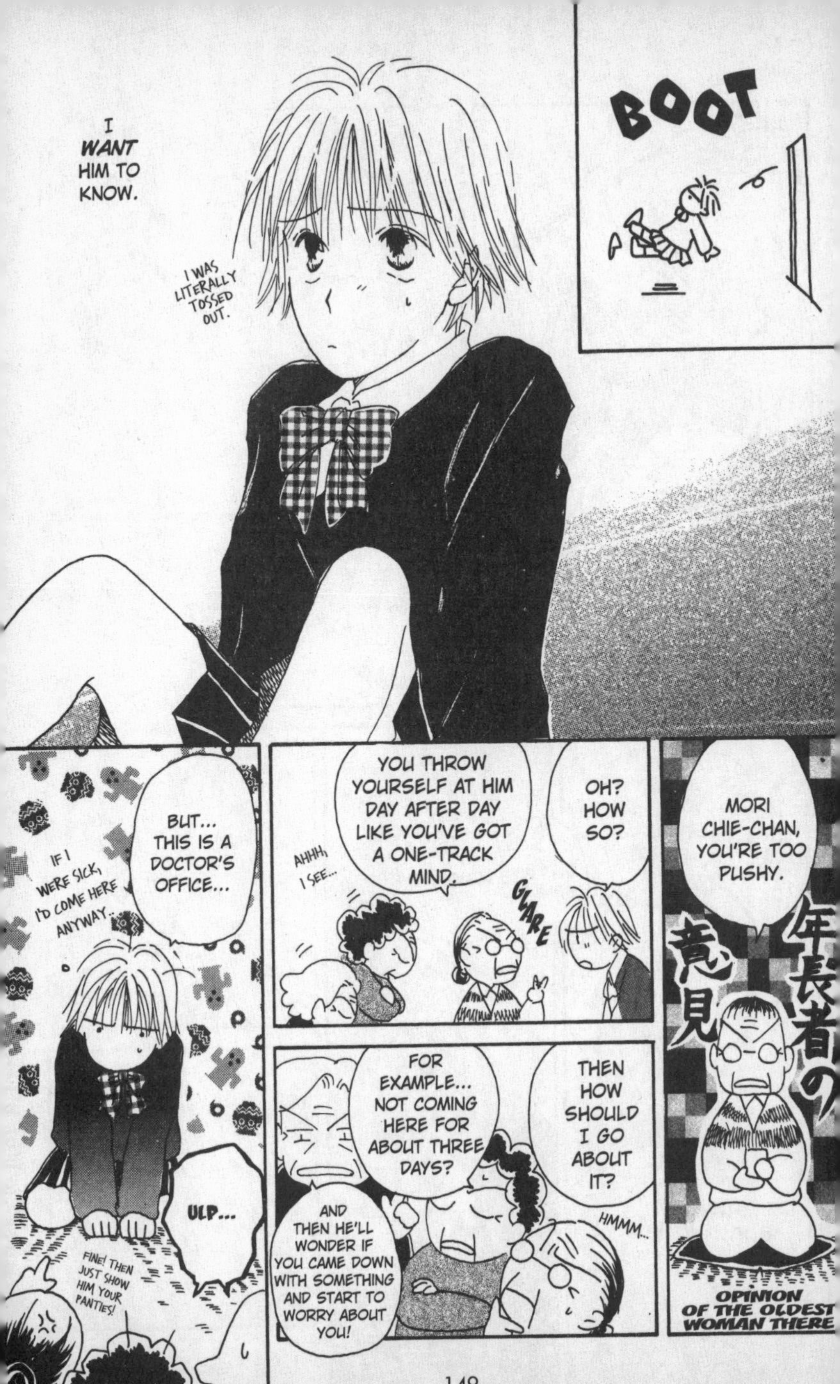
BOOT
I WANT HIM TO KNOW.
I WAS LITERALLY TOSSED OUT.
MORI CHIE-CHAN, YOU'RE TOO PUSHY.
年長者の意見
OPINION OF THE OLDEST WOMAN THERE
OH? HOW SO?
YOU THROW YOURSELF AT HIM DAY AFTER DAY LIKE YOU'VE GOT A ONE-TRACK MIND.
GLARE
AHHH, I SEE...
THEN HOW SHOULD I GO ABOUT IT?
FOR EXAMPLE... NOT COMING HERE FOR ABOUT THREE DAYS?
AND THEN HE'LL WONDER IF YOU CAME DOWN WITH SOMETHING AND START TO WORRY ABOUT YOU!
HMMM...
BUT... THIS IS A DOCTOR'S OFFICE...
IF I WERE SICK, I'D COME HERE ANYWAY...
ULP...
FINE! THEN JUST SHOW HIM YOUR PANTIES!

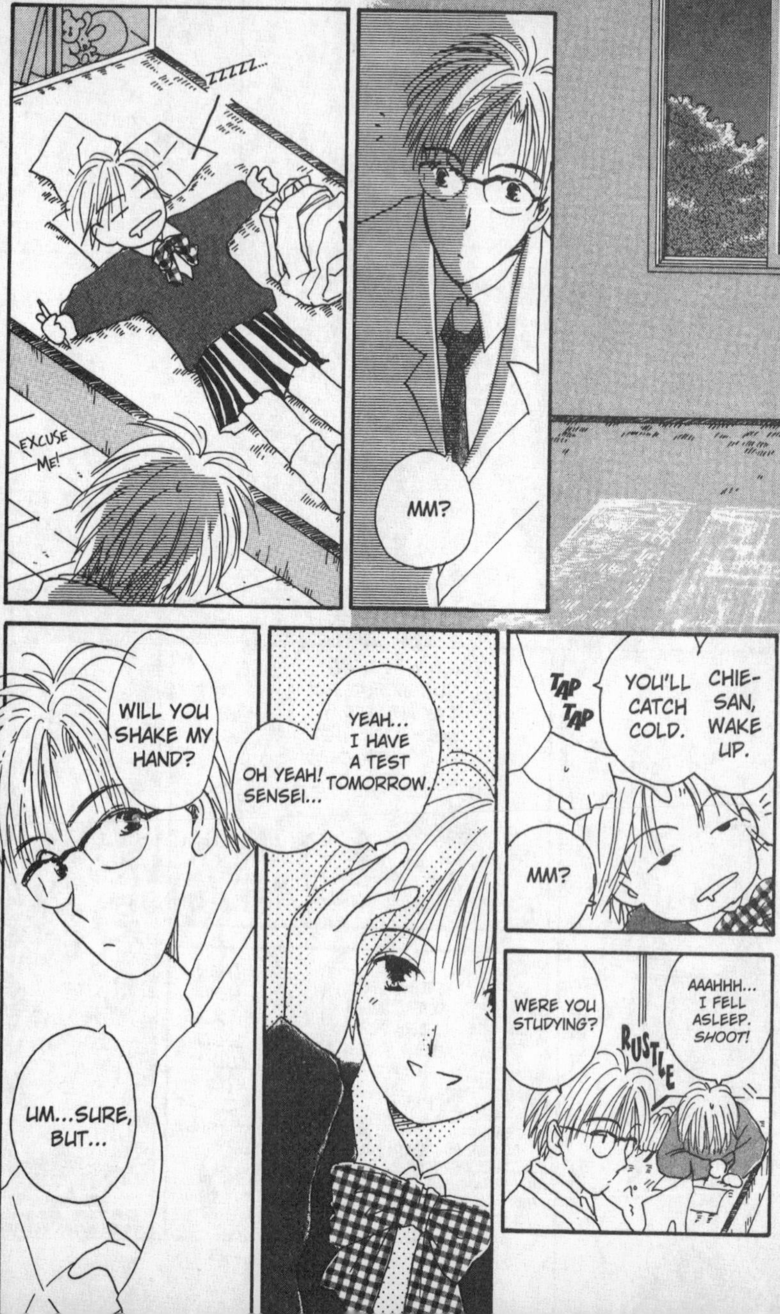
MM?
ZZZZZ...
EXCUSE ME!
CHIE-SAN, WAKE UP.
YOU'LL CATCH COLD.
TAP TAP
MM?
AAAHHH... I FELL ASLEEP. SHOOT!
RUSTLE
WERE YOU STUDYING?
YEAH... I HAVE A TEST TOMORROW...
OH YEAH! SENSEI...
WILL YOU SHAKE MY HAND?
UM...SURE, BUT...

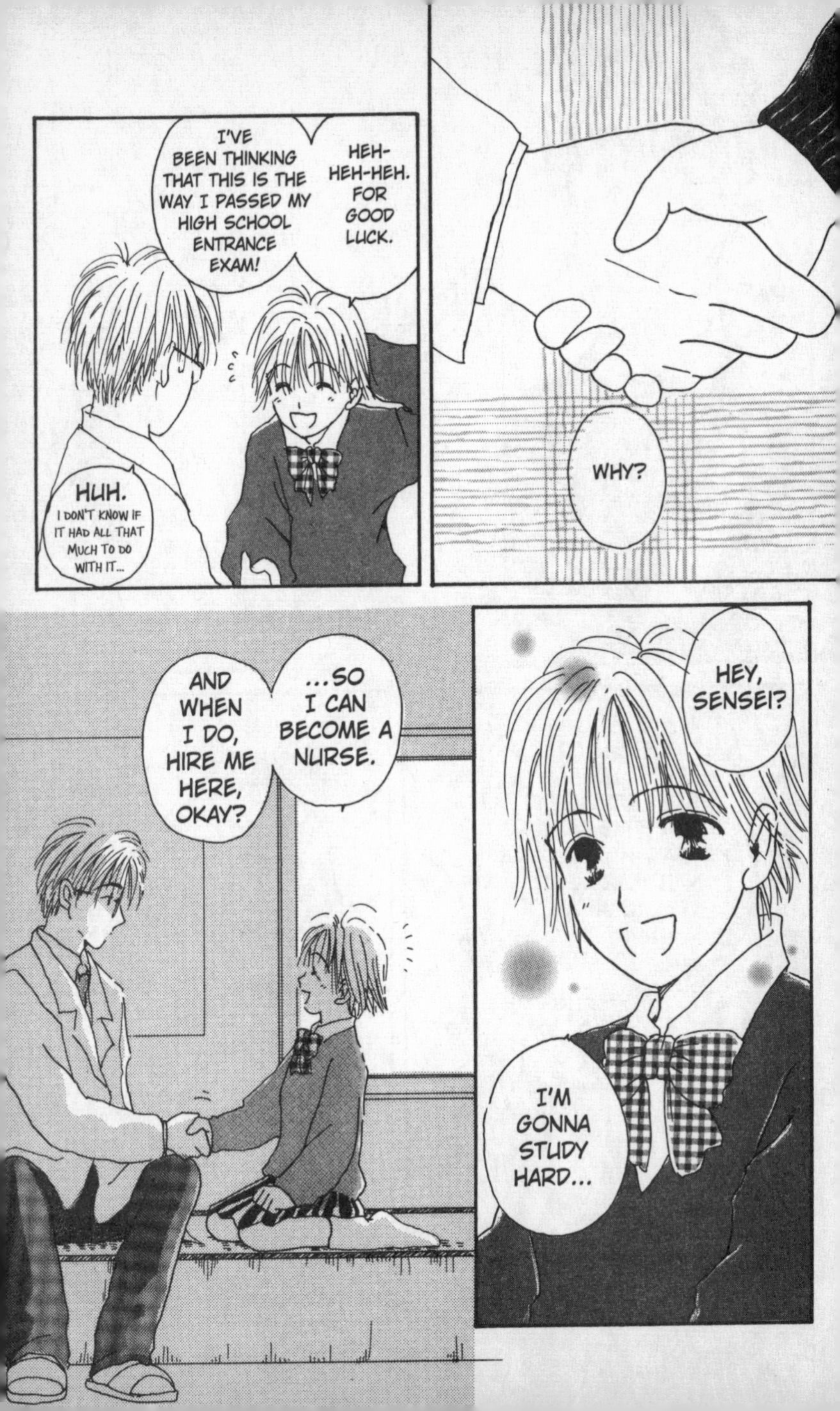
WHY?
HEH-HEH-HEH. FOR GOOD LUCK.
I'VE BEEN THINKING THAT THIS IS THE WAY I PASSED MY HIGH SCHOOL ENTRANCE EXAM!
HUH. I DON'T KNOW IF IT HAD ALL THAT MUCH TO DO WITH IT...
HEY, SENSEI?
I'M GONNA STUDY HARD...
...SO I CAN BECOME A NURSE.
AND WHEN I DO, HIRE ME HERE, OKAY?

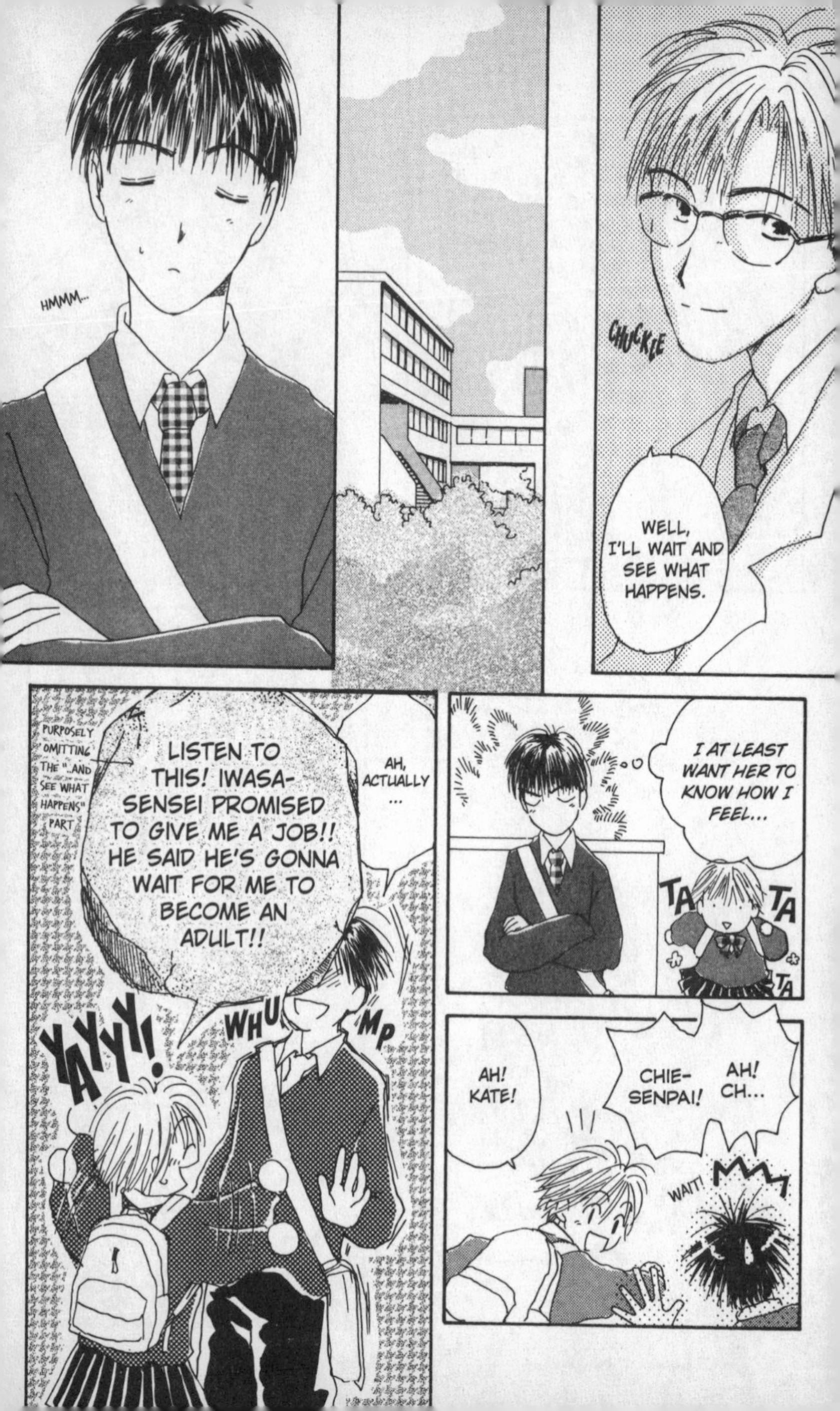
CHUCKLE
WELL, I'LL WAIT AND SEE WHAT HAPPENS.
HMMM...
I AT LEAST WANT HER TO KNOW HOW I FEEL...
TA TA TA
AH! CH...
CHIE-SENPAI!
AH! KATE!
WAIT!
AH, ACTUALLY ...
LISTEN TO THIS! IWASA-SENSEI PROMISED TO GIVE ME A JOB!! HE SAID HE'S GONNA WAIT FOR ME TO BECOME AN ADULT!!
PURPOSELY OMITTING THE "...AND SEE WHAT HAPPENS" PART
WHUMP
YAYYY!

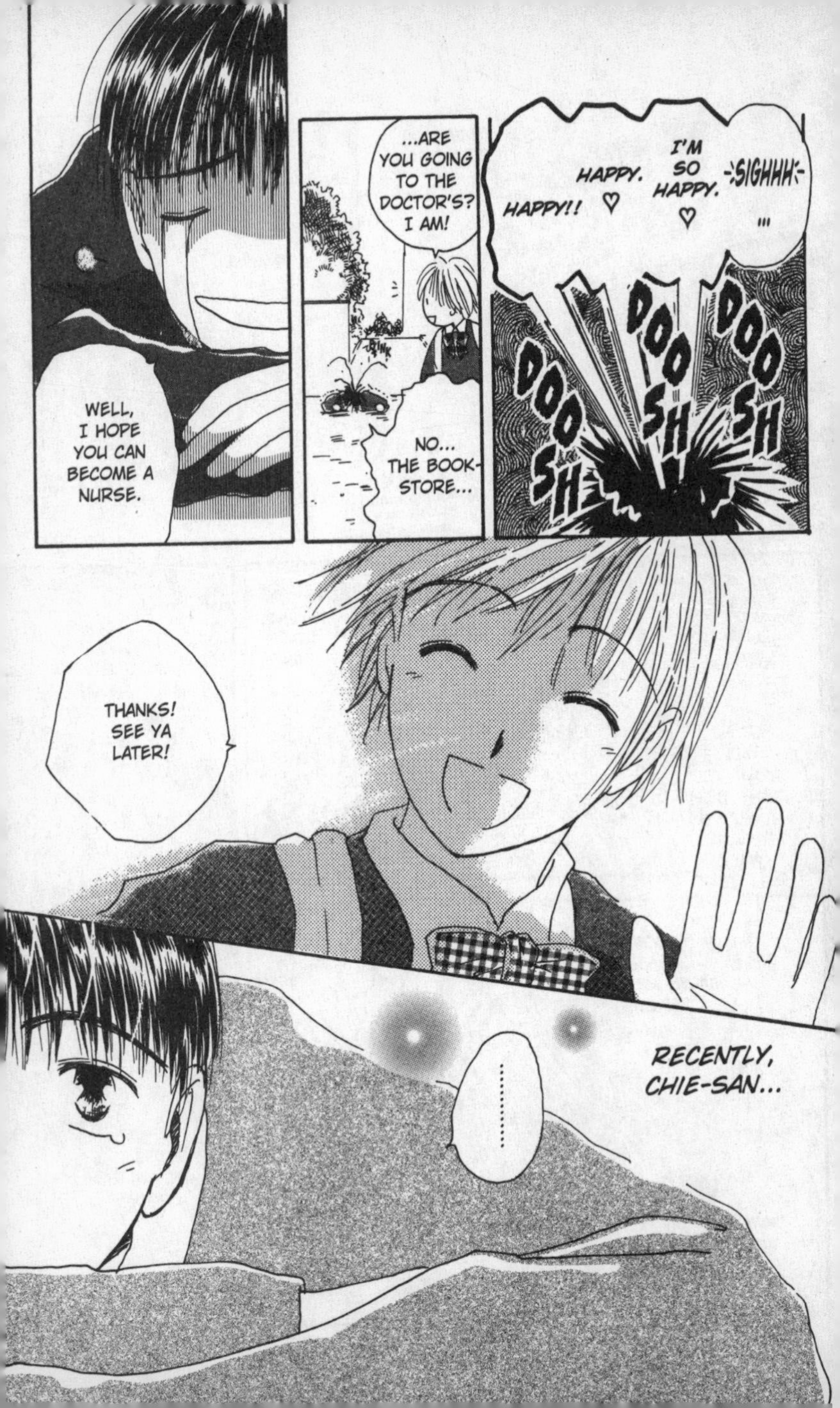
-SIGHHH-
...
I'M SO HAPPY. ♡
HAPPY. ♡
HAPPY!!
DOOSH
DOOSH
DOOSH
...ARE YOU GOING TO THE DOCTOR'S? I AM!
NO... THE BOOK-STORE...
WELL, I HOPE YOU CAN BECOME A NURSE.
THANKS! SEE YA LATER!
RECENTLY, CHIE-SAN...
......

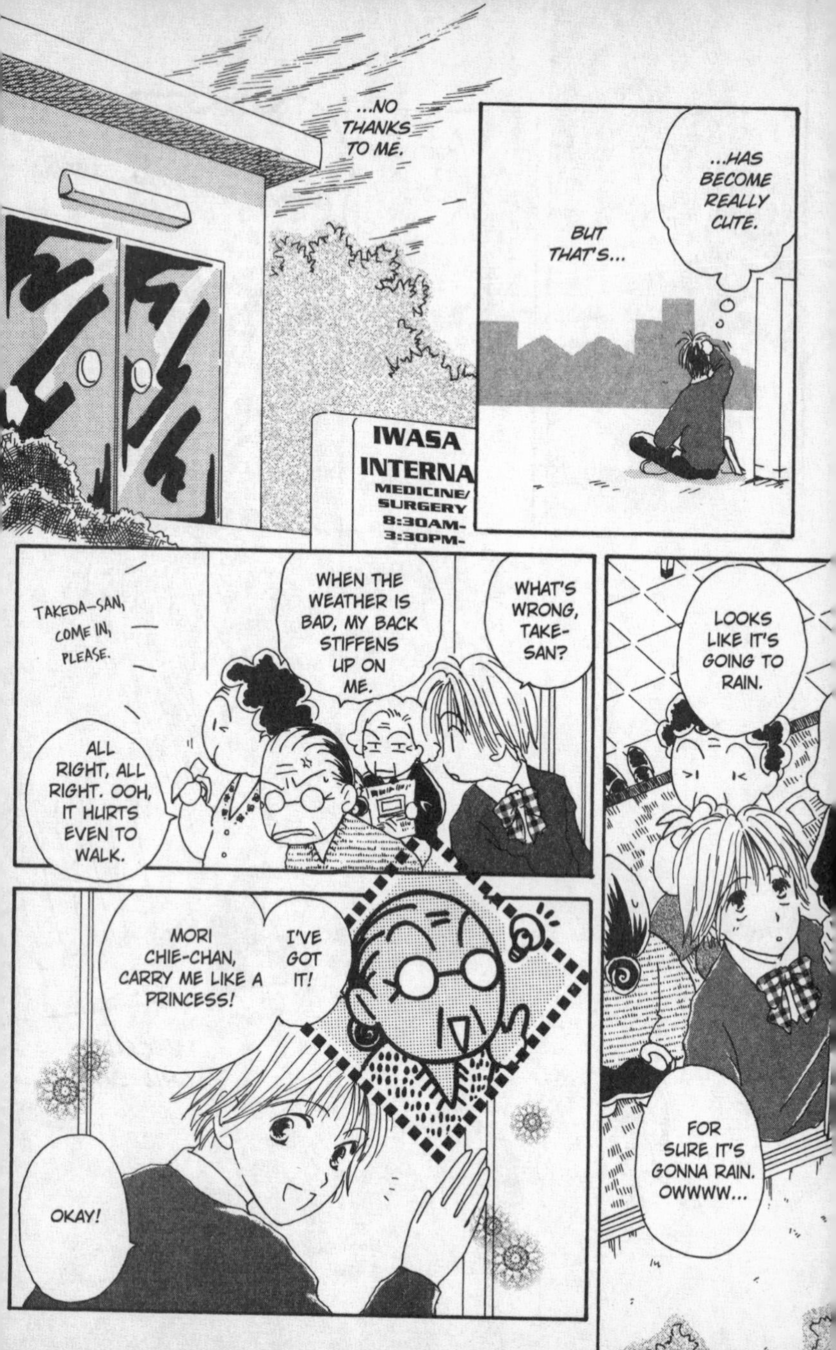

...HAS BECOME REALLY CUTE.
BUT THAT'S...
...NO THANKS TO ME.
IWASA INTERNA
MEDICINE/ SURGERY
8:30AM- 3:30PM-
LOOKS LIKE IT'S GOING TO RAIN.
FOR SURE IT'S GONNA RAIN. OWWWW...
WHAT'S WRONG, TAKE-SAN?
WHEN THE WEATHER IS BAD, MY BACK STIFFENS UP ON ME.
TAKEDA-SAN, COME IN, PLEASE.
ALL RIGHT, ALL RIGHT. OOH, IT HURTS EVEN TO WALK.
I'VE GOT IT!
MORI CHIE-CHAN, CARRY ME LIKE A PRINCESS!
OKAY!

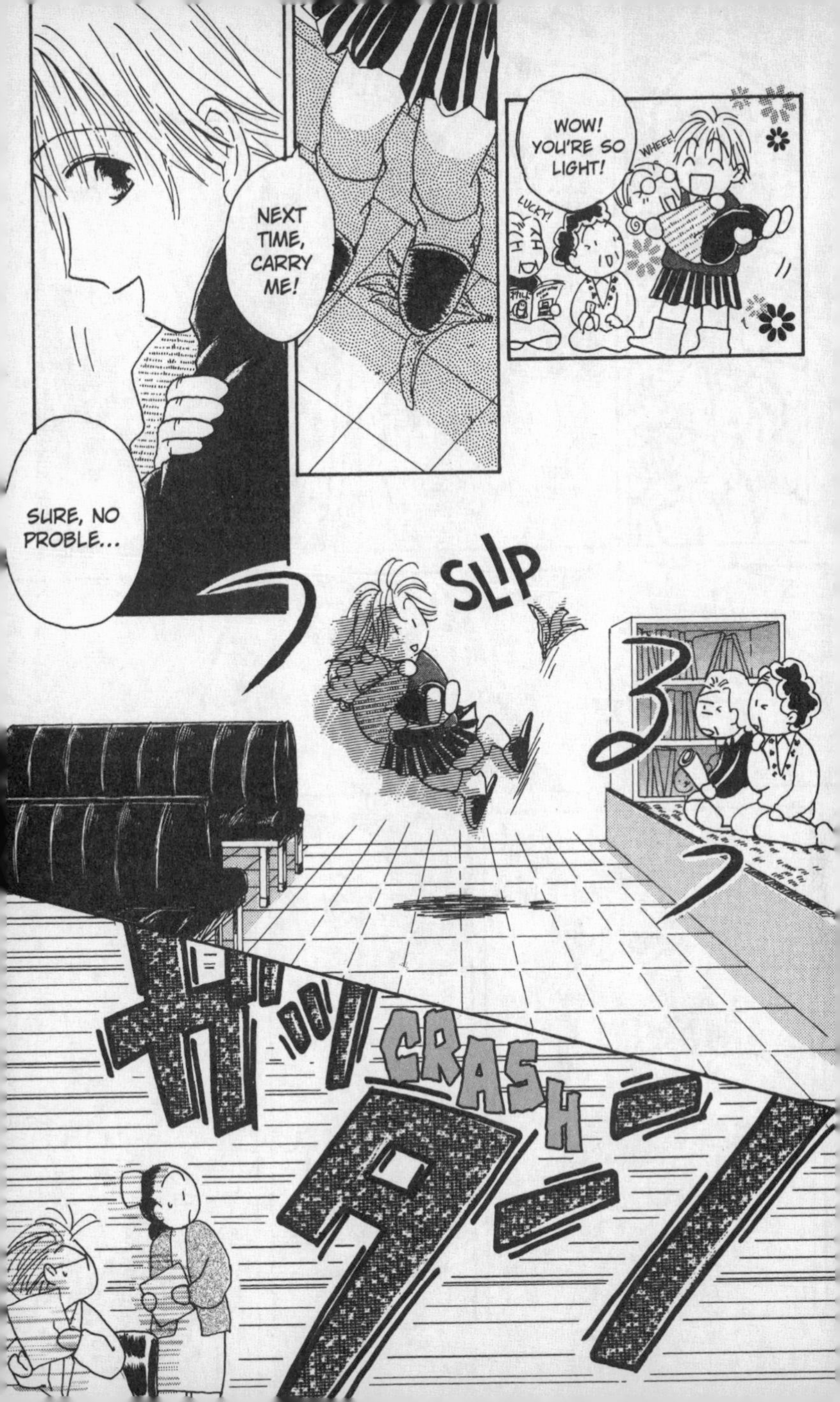
WOW! YOU'RE SO LIGHT!
WHEEE!
LUCKY!
NEXT TIME, CARRY ME!
SURE, NO PROBLE...
SLIP
CRASH

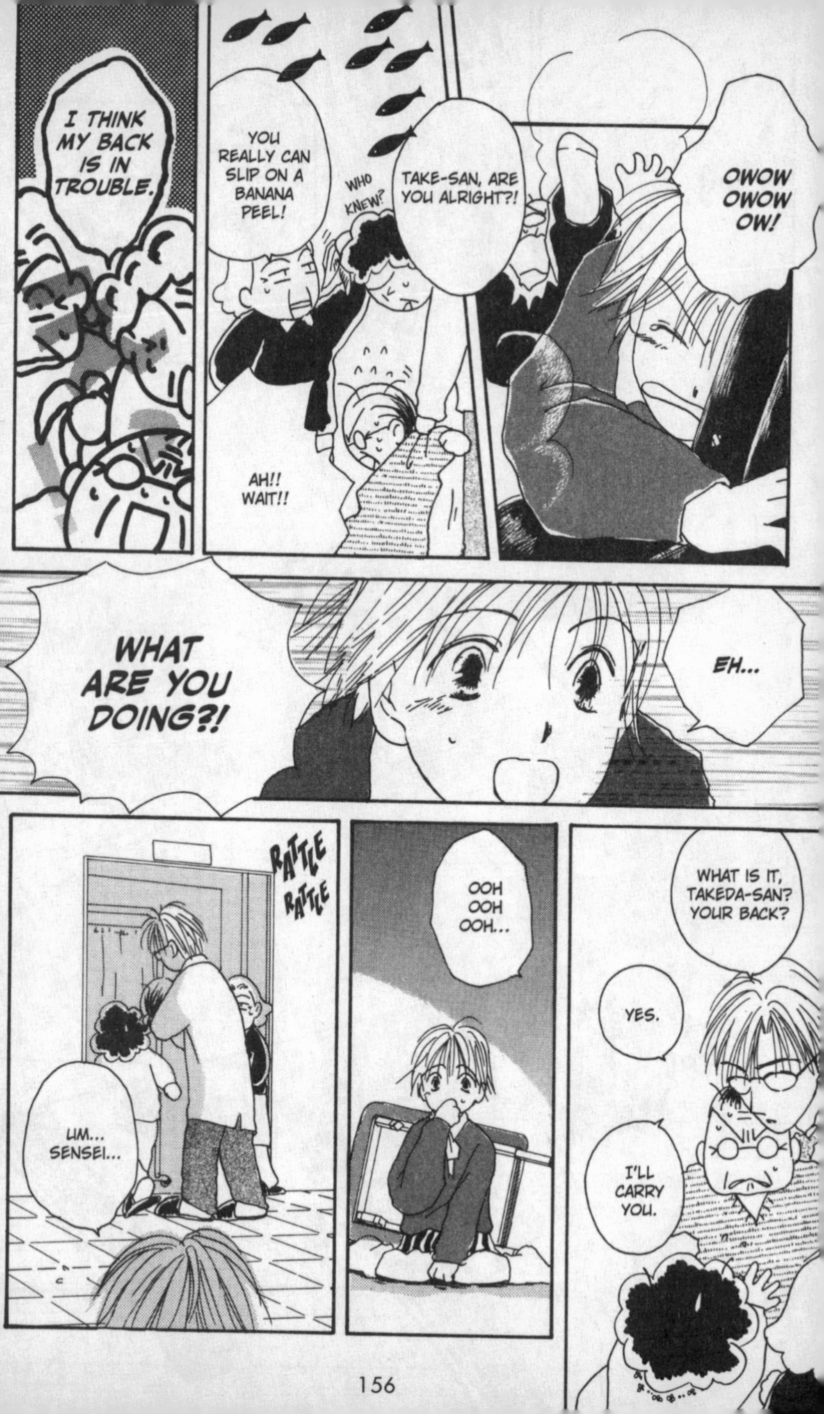
OWOW OWOW OW!
TAKE-SAN, ARE YOU ALRIGHT?!
WHO KNEW?
YOU REALLY CAN SLIP ON A BANANA PEEL!
AH!! WAIT!!
I THINK MY BACK IS IN TROUBLE.
EH...
WHAT ARE YOU DOING?!
WHAT IS IT, TAKEDA-SAN? YOUR BACK?
YES.
I'LL CARRY YOU.
OOH OOH OOH...
RATTLE RATTLE
UM... SENSEI...

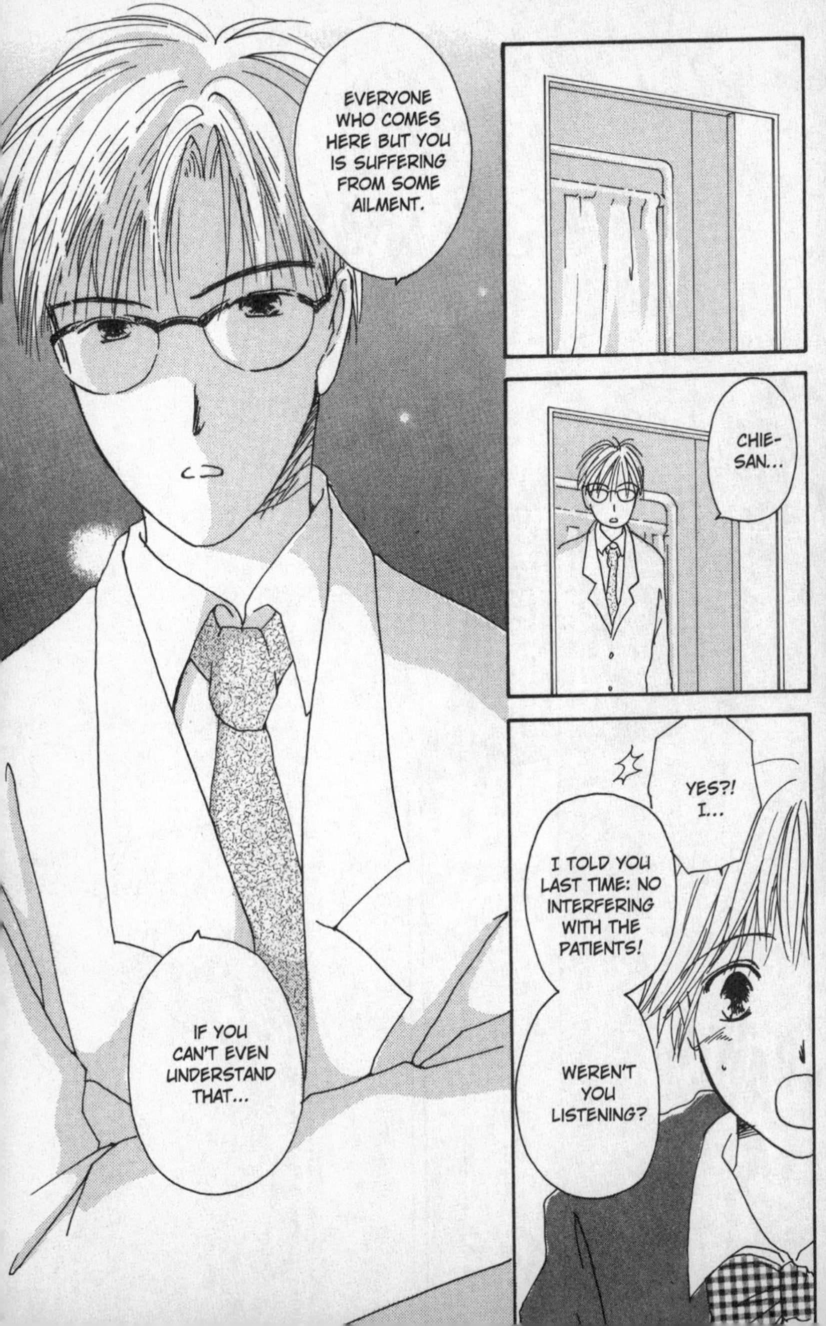
CHIE-SAN...
YES?! I...
I TOLD YOU LAST TIME: NO INTERFERING WITH THE PATIENTS!
WEREN'T YOU LISTENING?
EVERYONE WHO COMES HERE BUT YOU IS SUFFERING FROM SOME AILMENT.
IF YOU CAN'T EVEN UNDERSTAND THAT...

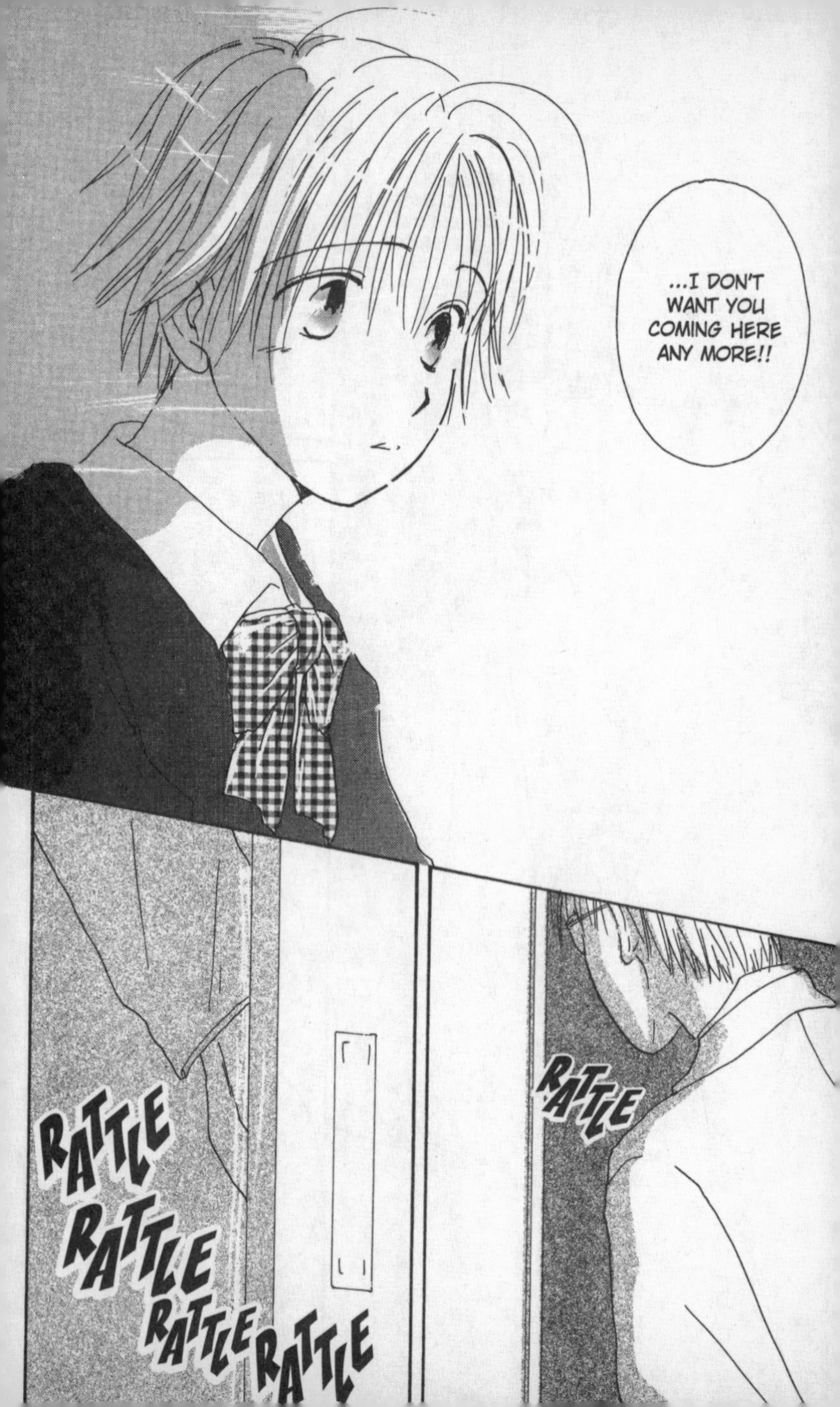
...I DON'T WANT YOU COMING HERE ANY MORE!!
RATTLE
RATTLE RATTLE RATTLE RATTLE

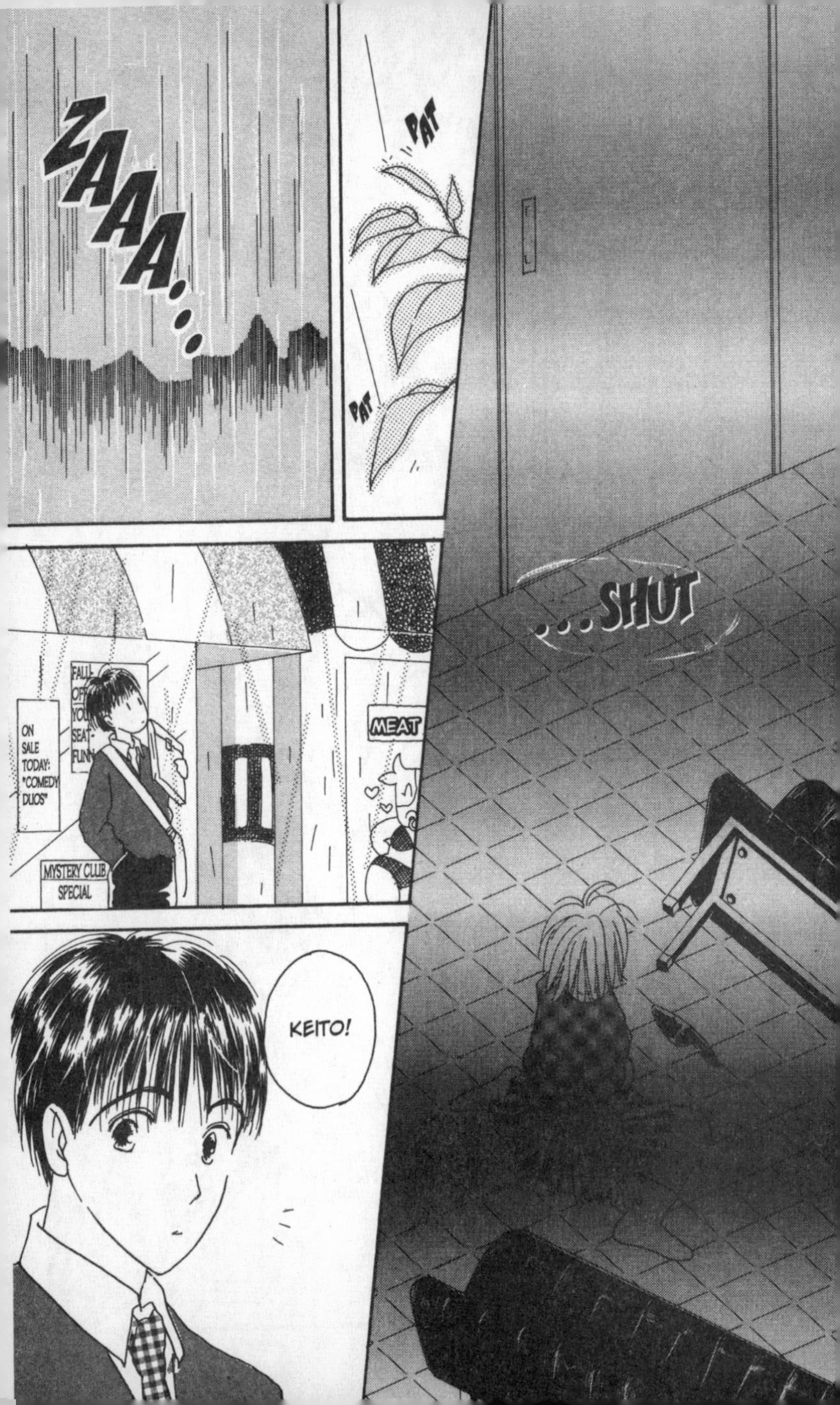
...SHUT
PAT
PAT
ZAAA...
MEAT
ON SALE TODAY: "COMEDY DUOS"
MYSTERY CLUB SPECIAL
KEITO!

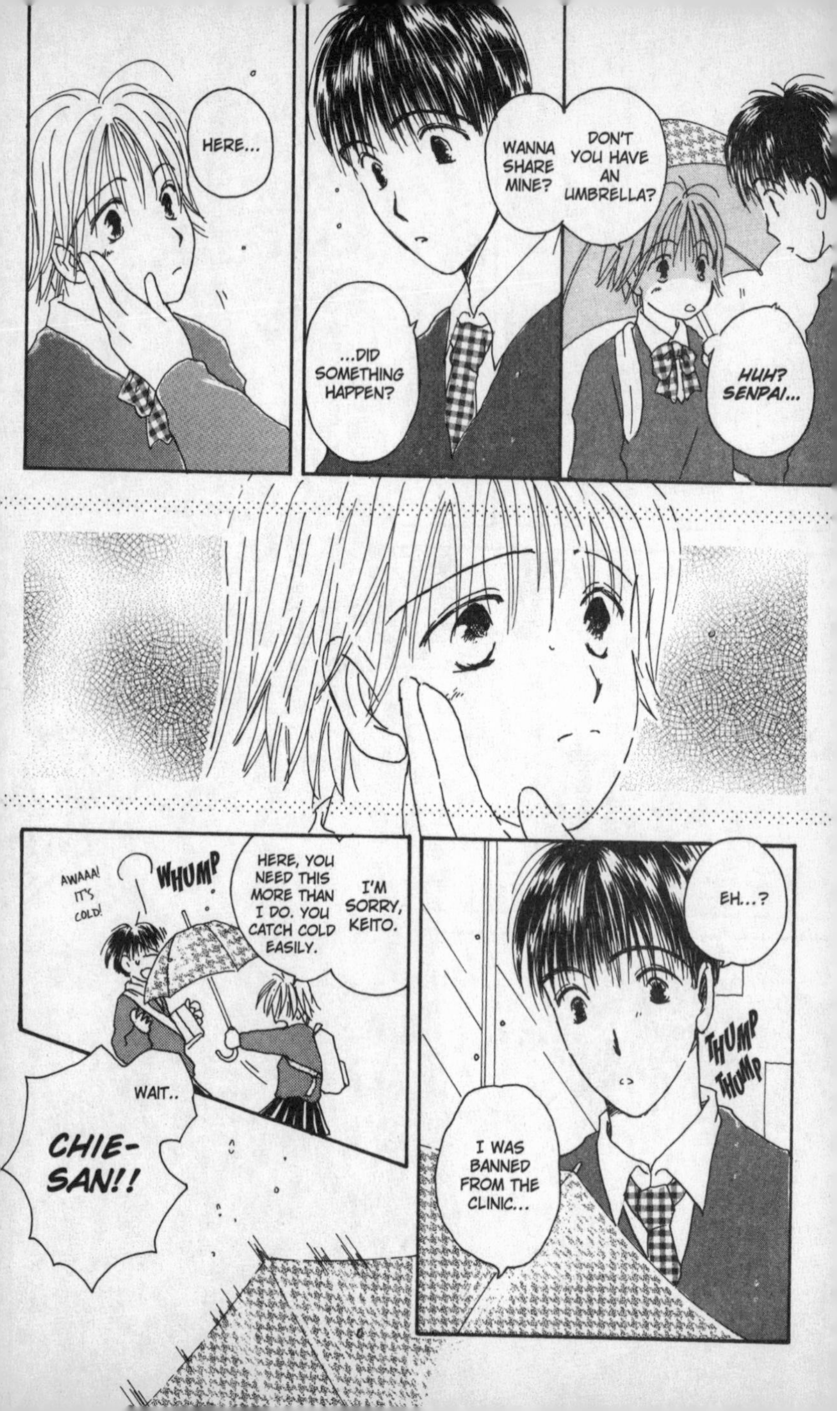
DON'T YOU HAVE AN UMBRELLA?
WANNA SHARE MINE?
HUH? SENPAI...
...DID SOMETHING HAPPEN?
HERE...
EH...?
THUMP THUMP
I WAS BANNED FROM THE CLINIC...
I'M SORRY, KEITO.
HERE, YOU NEED THIS MORE THAN I DO. YOU CATCH COLD EASILY.
WHUMP
AWAAA! IT'S COLD!
WAIT.. CHIE-SAN!!

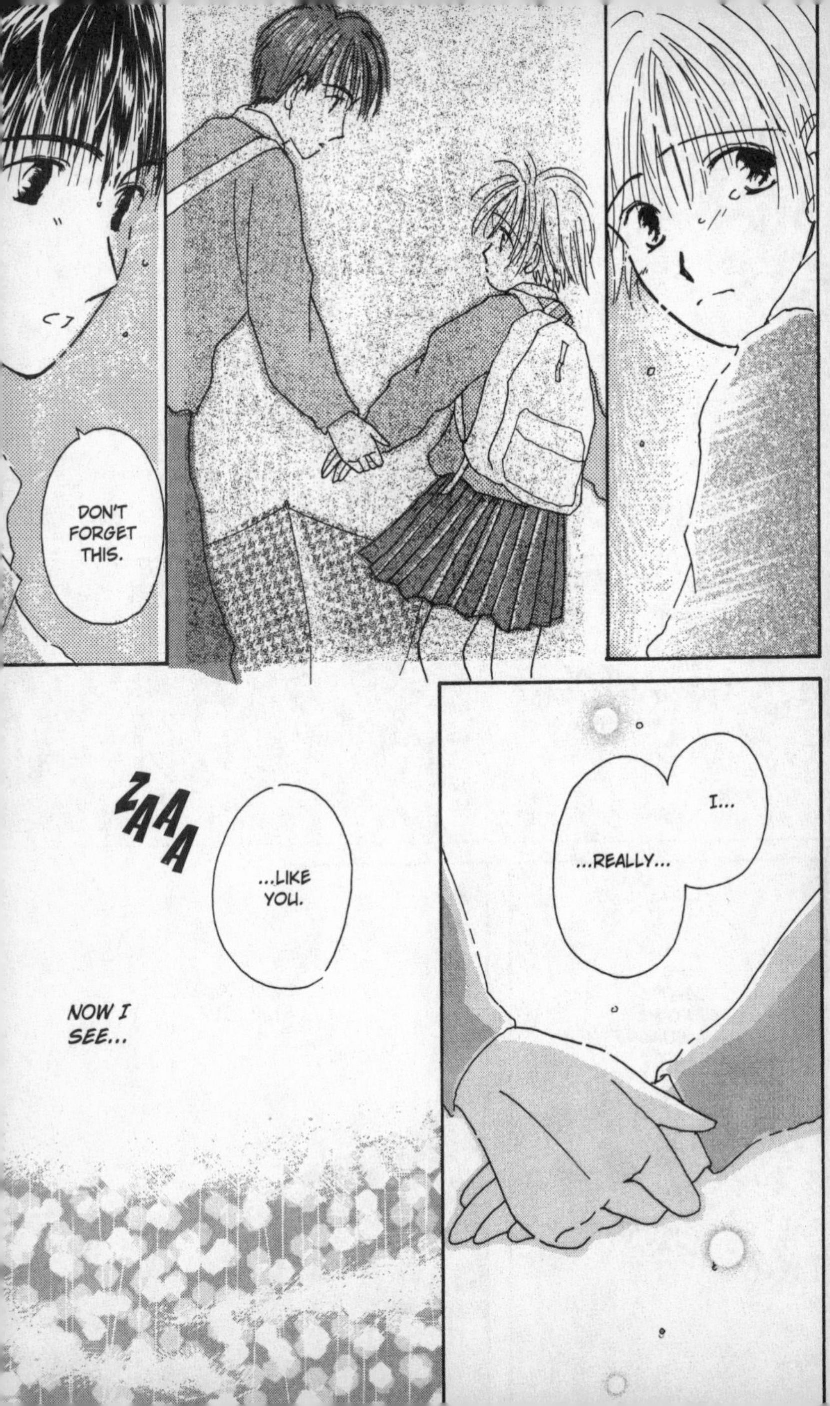
DON'T FORGET THIS.
I...
...REALLY...
...LIKE YOU.
ZAAA
NOW I SEE...

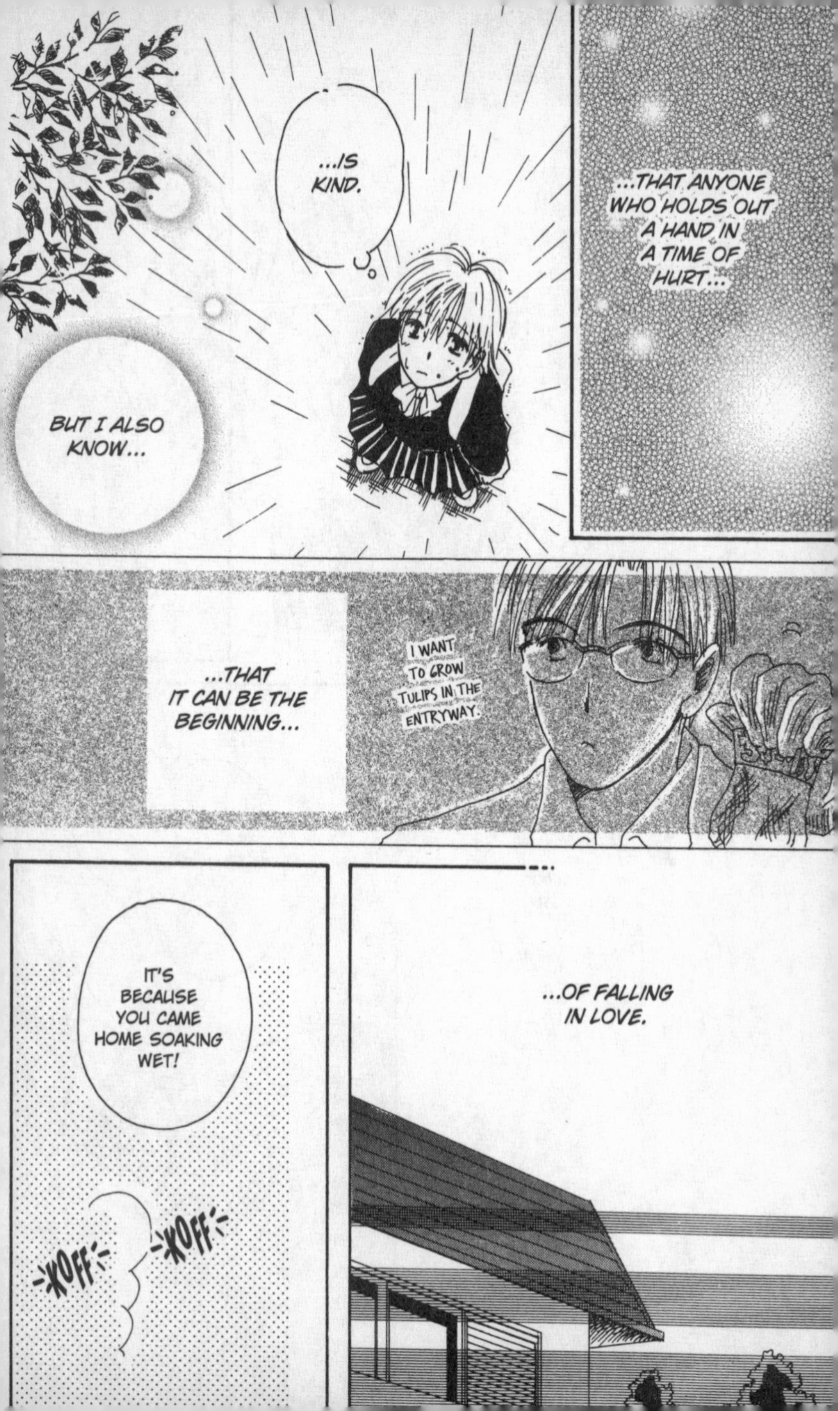
...IS KIND.
BUT I ALSO KNOW...
...THAT ANYONE WHO HOLDS OUT A HAND IN A TIME OF HURT...
I WANT TO GROW TULIPS IN THE ENTRYWAY.
...THAT IT CAN BE THE BEGINNING...
...OF FALLING IN LOVE.
IT'S BECAUSE YOU CAME HOME SOAKING WET!
KOFF
KOFF

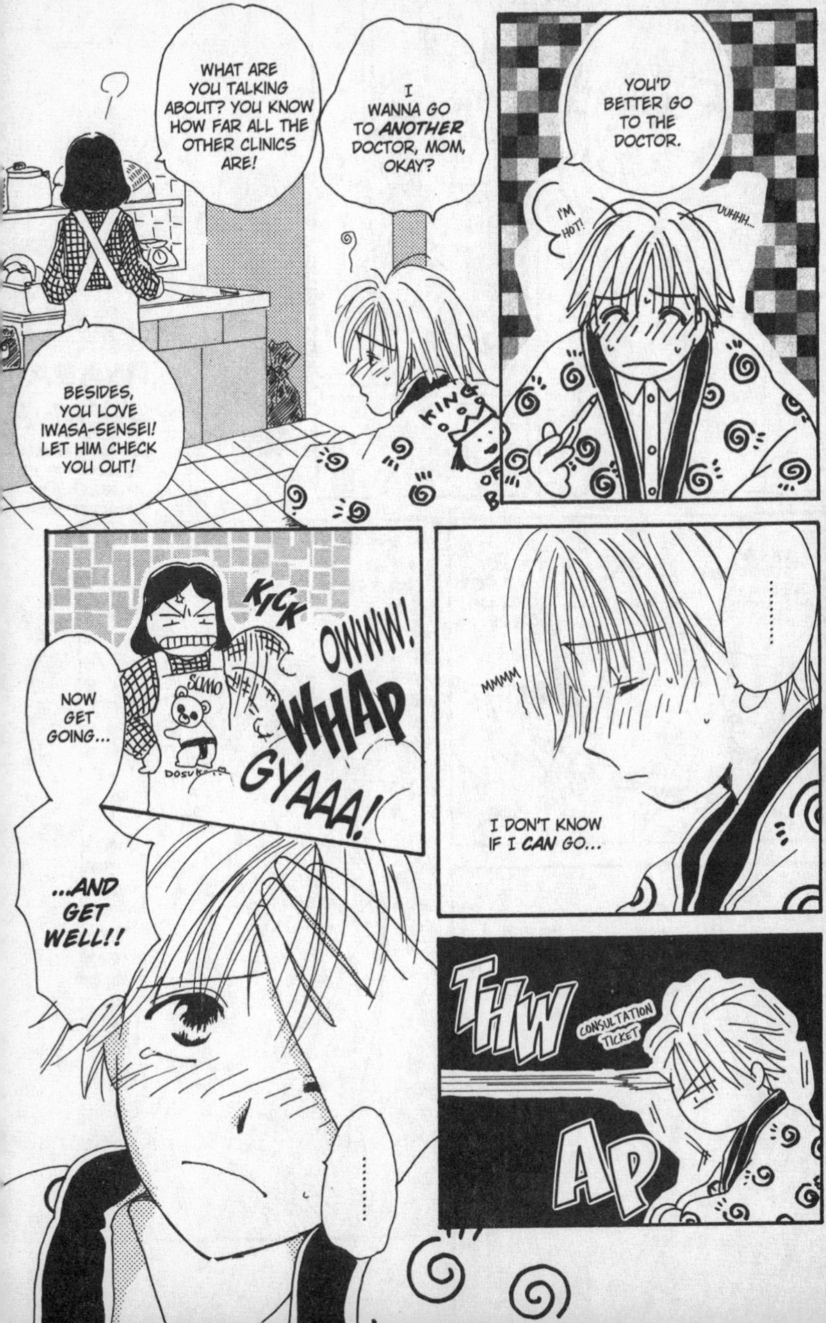
YOU'D BETTER GO TO THE DOCTOR.
I'M HOT!
UUHHH...
I WANNA GO TO ANOTHER DOCTOR, MOM, OKAY?
WHAT ARE YOU TALKING ABOUT? YOU KNOW HOW FAR ALL THE OTHER CLINICS ARE!
BESIDES, YOU LOVE IWASA-SENSEI! LET HIM CHECK YOU OUT!
KING OF B
......
MMMM
I DON'T KNOW IF I CAN GO...
THWAP
CONSULTATION TICKET
NOW GET GOING...
KICK
OWWW!
WHAP
GYAAA!
SUMO
...AND GET WELL!!
......

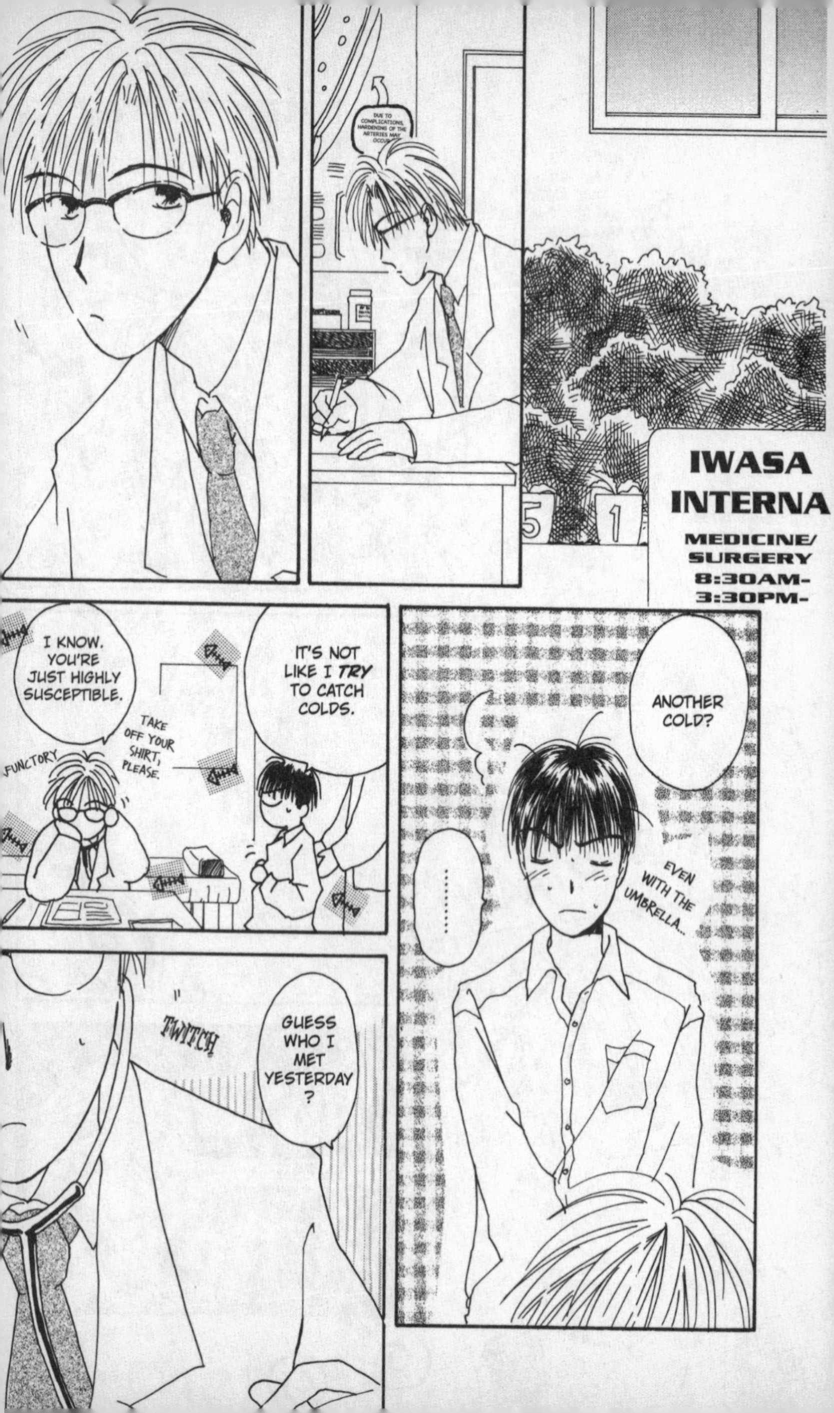
IWASA INTERNA
MEDICINE/ SURGERY 8:30AM- 3:30PM-
DUE TO COMPLICATIONS, HARDENING OF THE ARTERIES MAY OCCU
ANOTHER COLD?
......
EVEN WITH THE UMBRELLA...
IT'S NOT LIKE I *TRY* TO CATCH COLDS.
I KNOW. YOU'RE JUST HIGHLY SUSCEPTIBLE.
TAKE OFF YOUR SHIRT, PLEASE.
FUNCTORY
GUESS WHO I MET YESTERDAY?
TWITCH

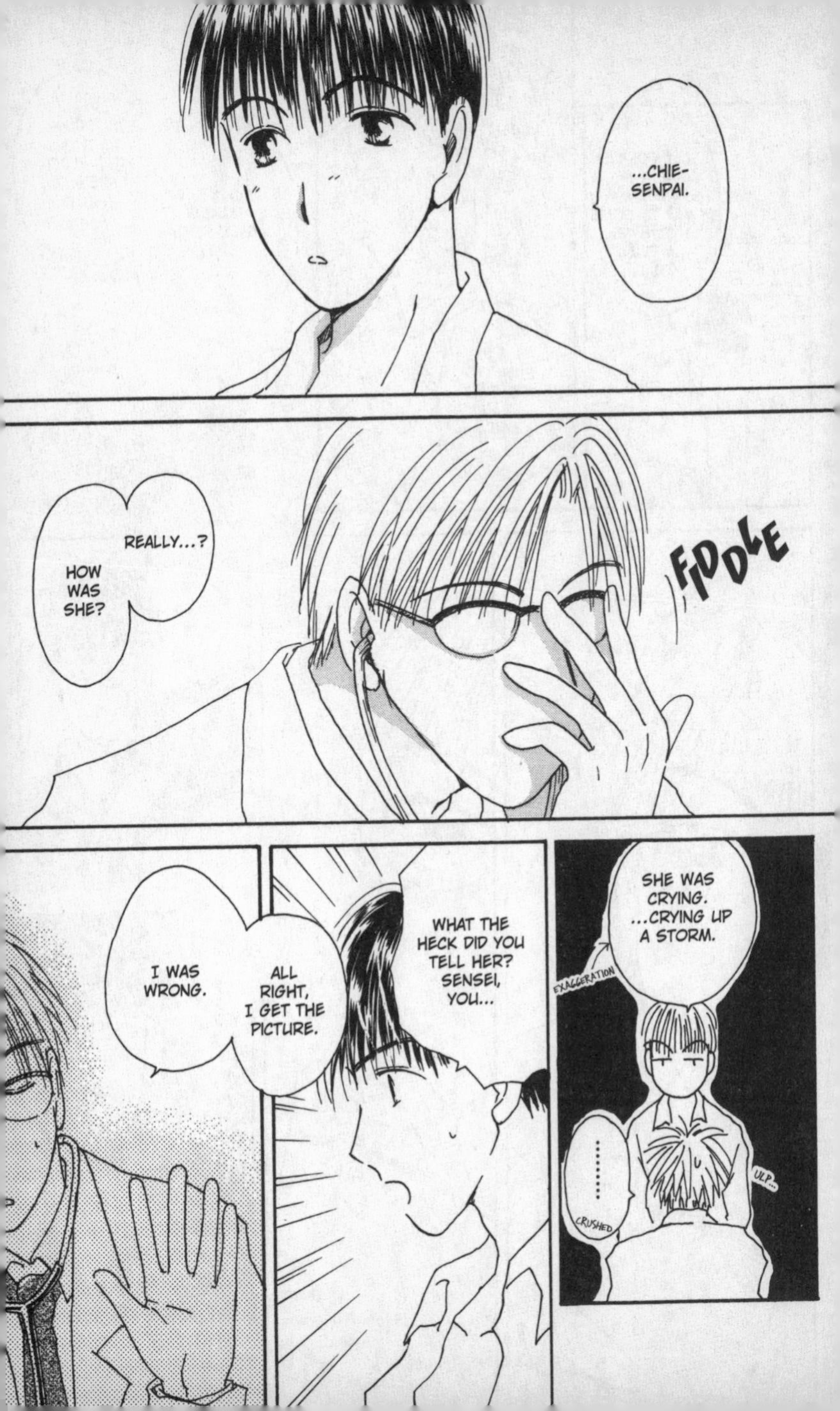
...CHIE-SENPAI.
FIDDLE
REALLY...?
HOW WAS SHE?
SHE WAS CRYING. ...CRYING UP A STORM.
EXAGGERATION
......
CRUSHED
ULP...
WHAT THE HECK DID YOU TELL HER? SENSEI, YOU...
ALL RIGHT, I GET THE PICTURE.
I WAS WRONG.

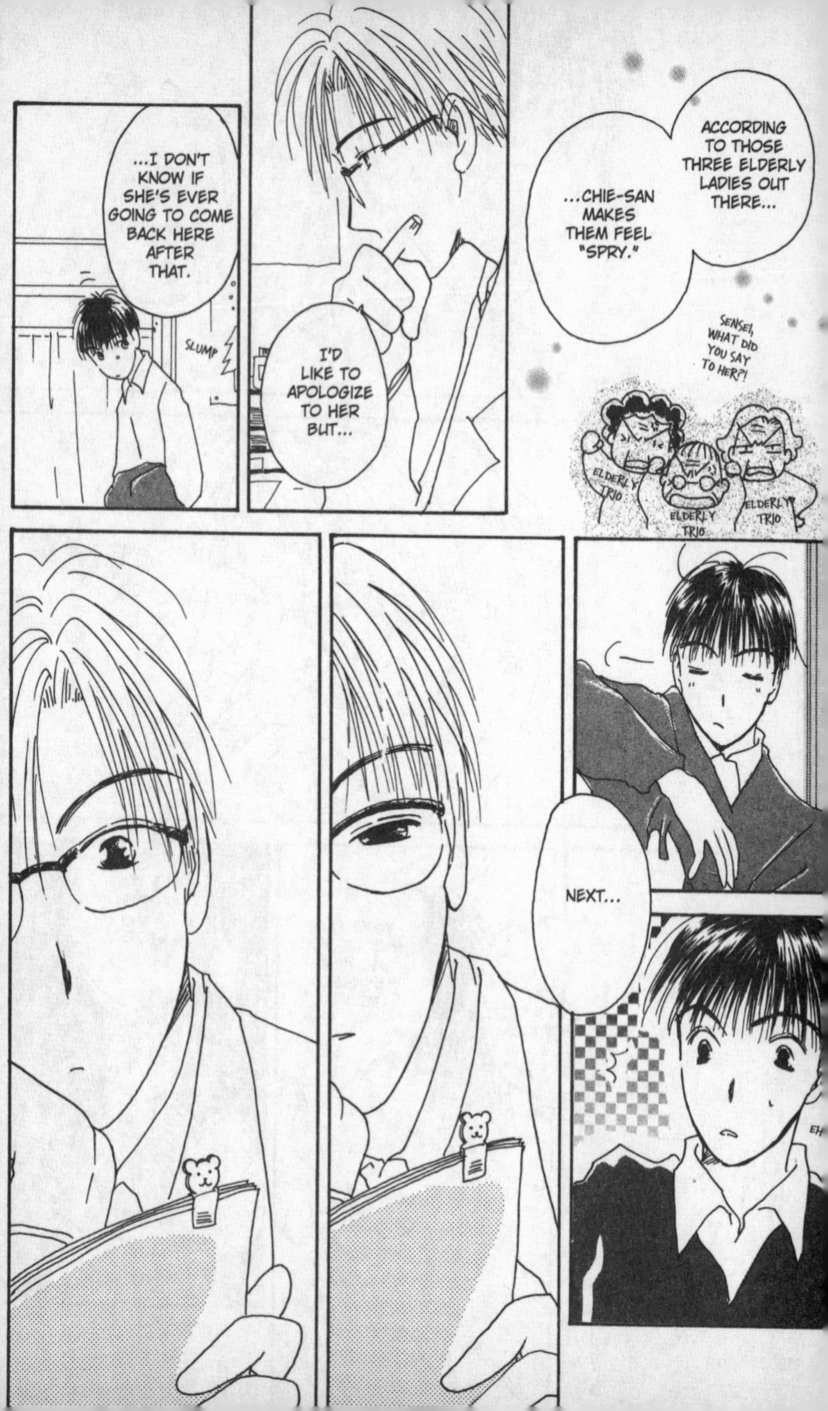
ACCORDING TO THOSE THREE ELDERLY LADIES OUT THERE...
...CHIE-SAN MAKES THEM FEEL "SPRY."
SENSEI, WHAT DID YOU SAY TO HER?!
ELDERLY TRIO
ELDERLY TRIO
ELDERLY TRIO
I'D LIKE TO APOLOGIZE TO HER BUT...
...I DON'T KNOW IF SHE'S EVER GOING TO COME BACK HERE AFTER THAT.
SLUMP
NEXT...
EH

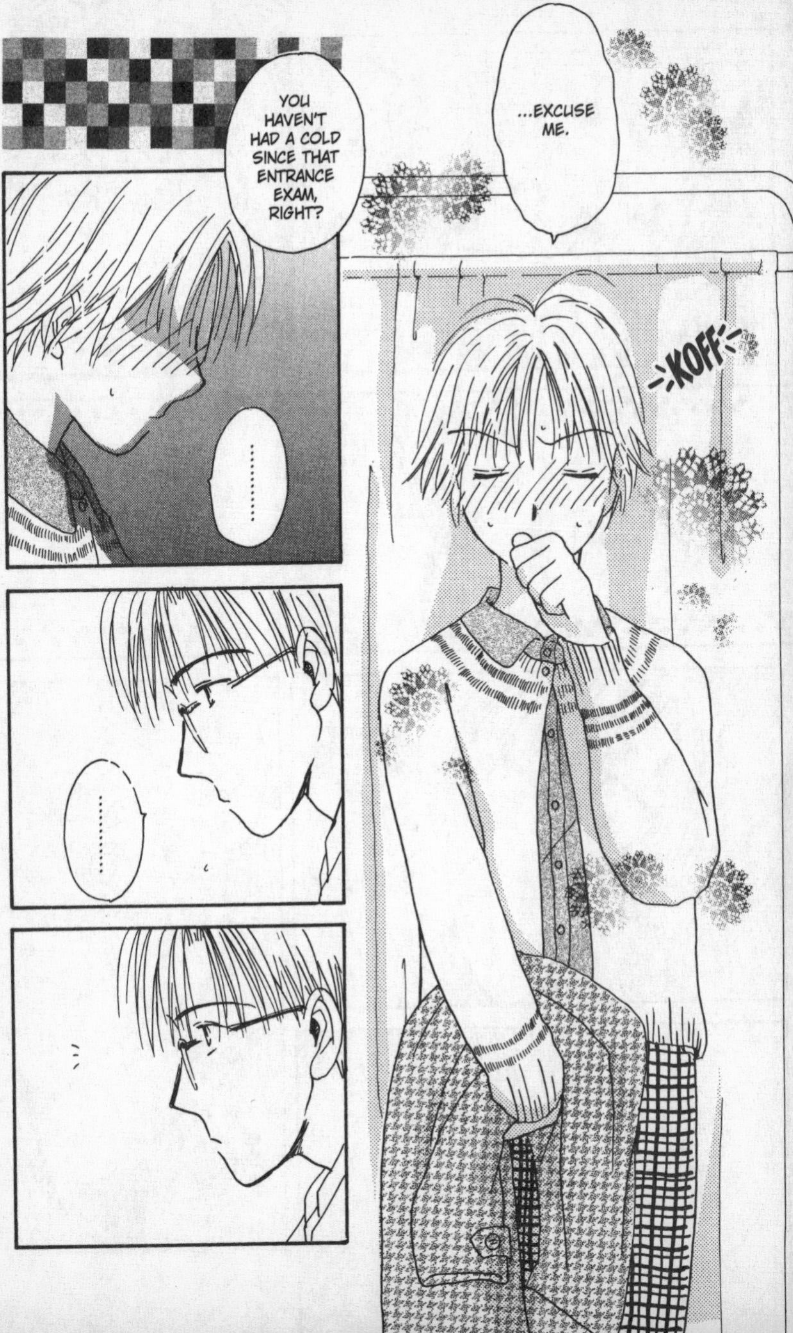
...EXCUSE ME.
KOFF
YOU HAVEN'T HAD A COLD SINCE THAT ENTRANCE EXAM, RIGHT?
......
......

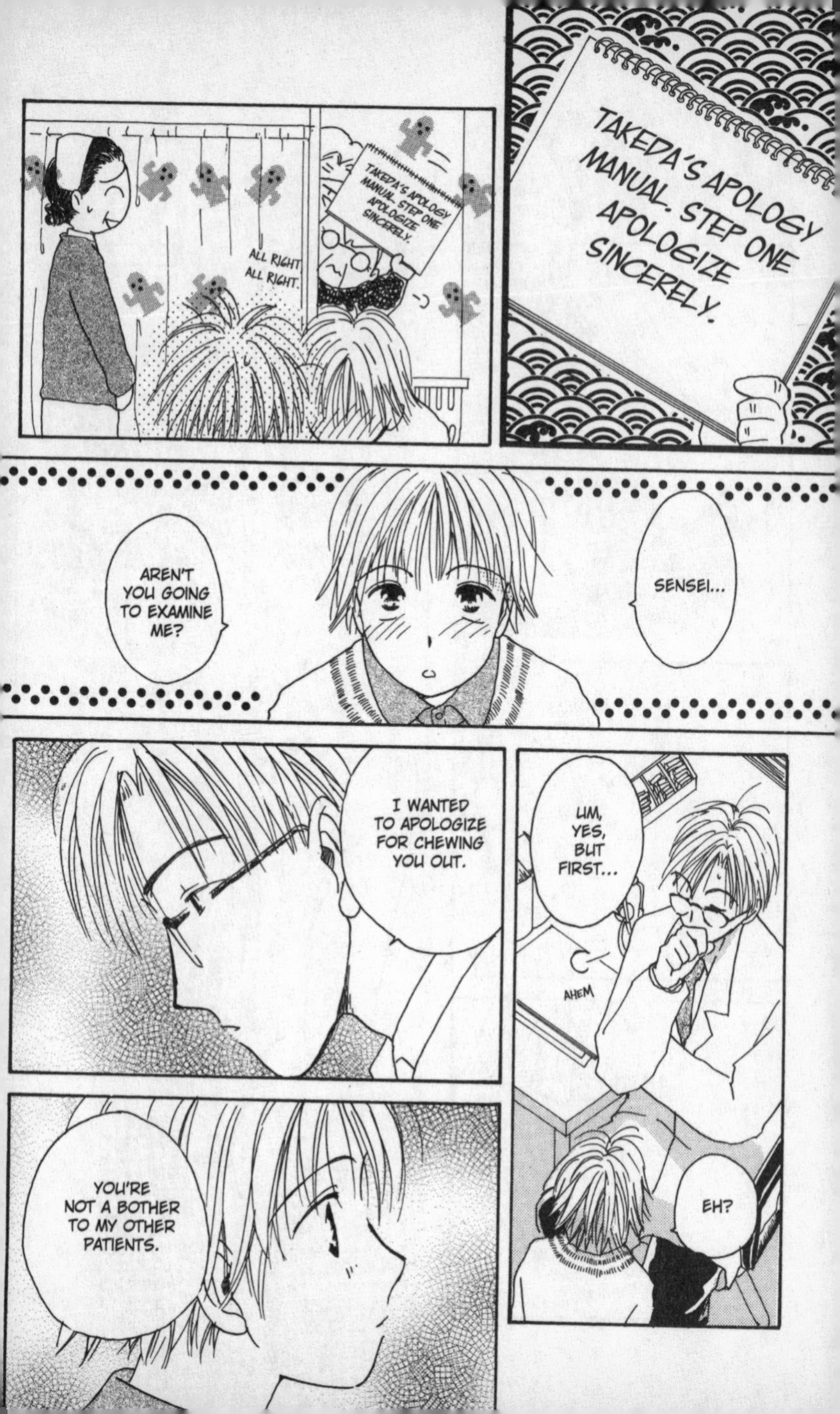
TAKEDA'S APOLOGY MANUAL. STEP ONE APOLOGIZE SINCERELY.
TAKEDA'S APOLOGY MANUAL. STEP ONE APOLOGIZE SINCERELY.
ALL RIGHT ALL RIGHT.
SENSEI...
AREN'T YOU GOING TO EXAMINE ME?
UM, YES, BUT FIRST...
AHEM
EH?
I WANTED TO APOLOGIZE FOR CHEWING YOU OUT.
YOU'RE NOT A BOTHER TO MY OTHER PATIENTS.

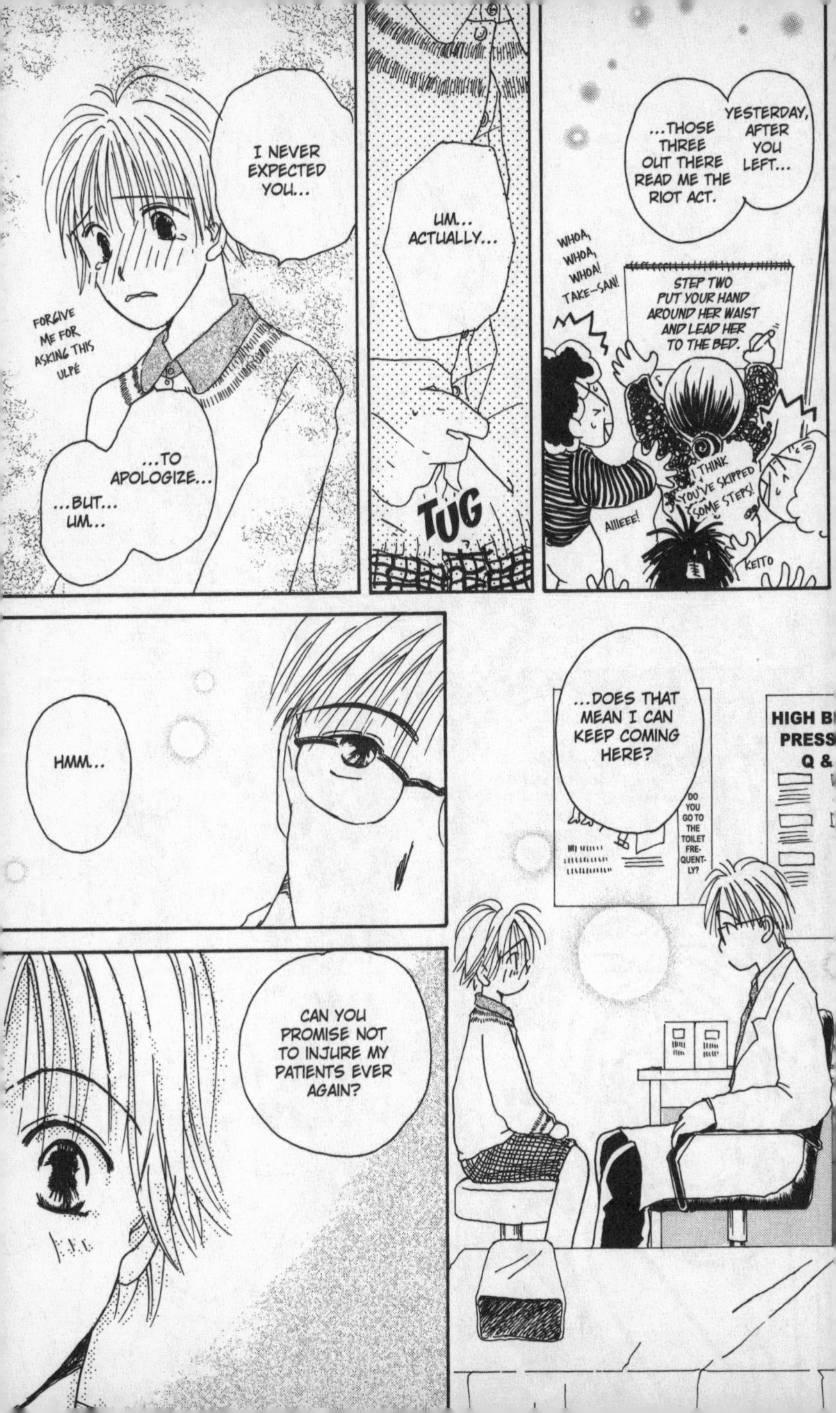
YESTERDAY, AFTER YOU LEFT...
...THOSE THREE OUT THERE READ ME THE RIOT ACT.
WHOA, WHOA, WHOA! TAKE-SAN!
STEP TWO PUT YOUR HAND AROUND HER WAIST AND LEAD HER TO THE BED.
I THINK YOU'VE SKIPPED SOME STEPS!
AIIIEEE!
KEITO
UM... ACTUALLY...
TUG
I NEVER EXPECTED YOU...
FORGIVE ME FOR ASKING THIS ULPÉ
...TO APOLOGIZE...
...BUT... UM...
...DOES THAT MEAN I CAN KEEP COMING HERE?
HIGH B
PRESS
Q &
DO YOU GO TO THE TOILET FRE-QUENT-LY?
HMM...
CAN YOU PROMISE NOT TO INJURE MY PATIENTS EVER AGAIN?

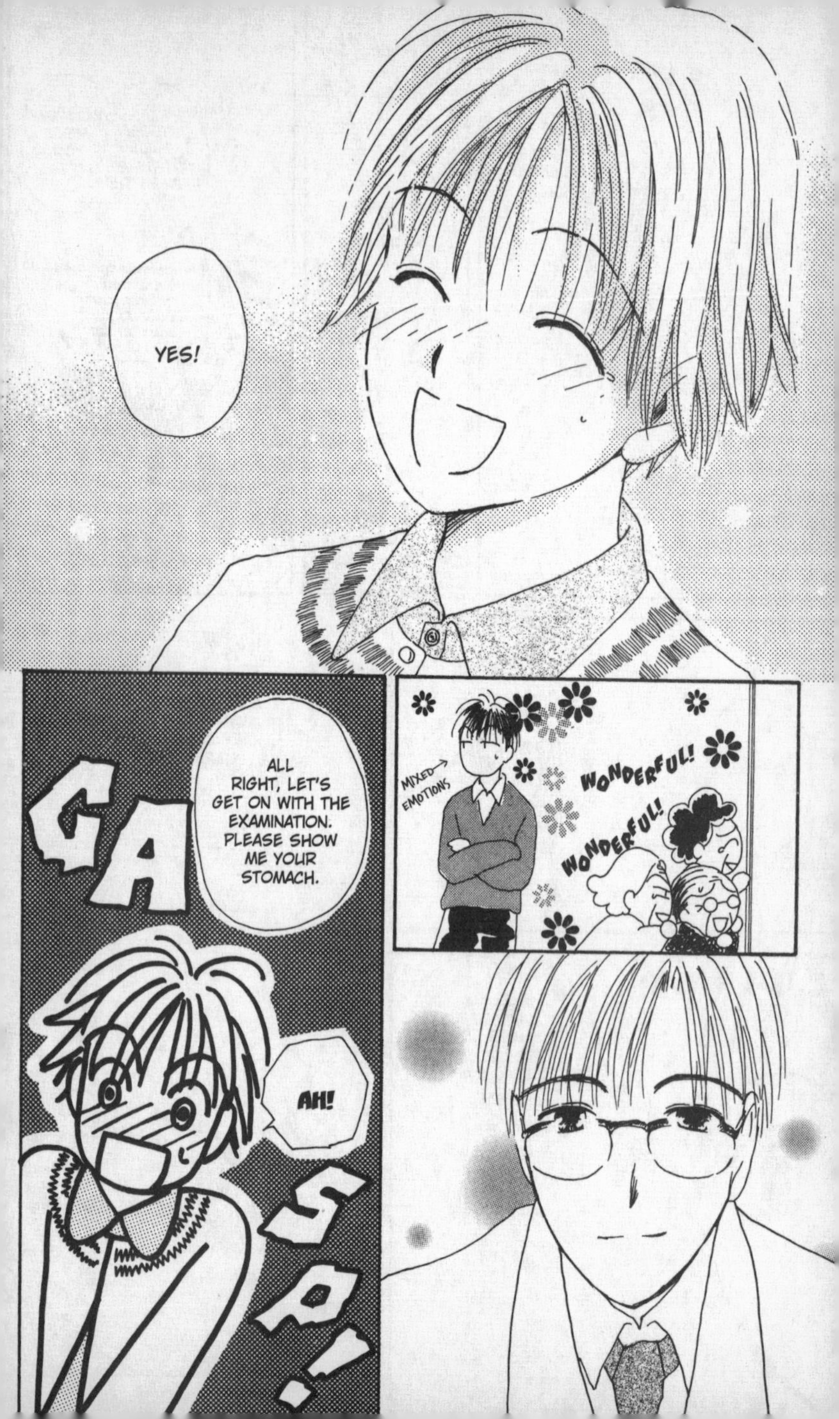
YES!
MIXED EMOTIONS
WONDERFUL!
WONDERFUL!
ALL RIGHT, LET'S GET ON WITH THE EXAMINATION. PLEASE SHOW ME YOUR STOMACH.
GA
AH!
SP!

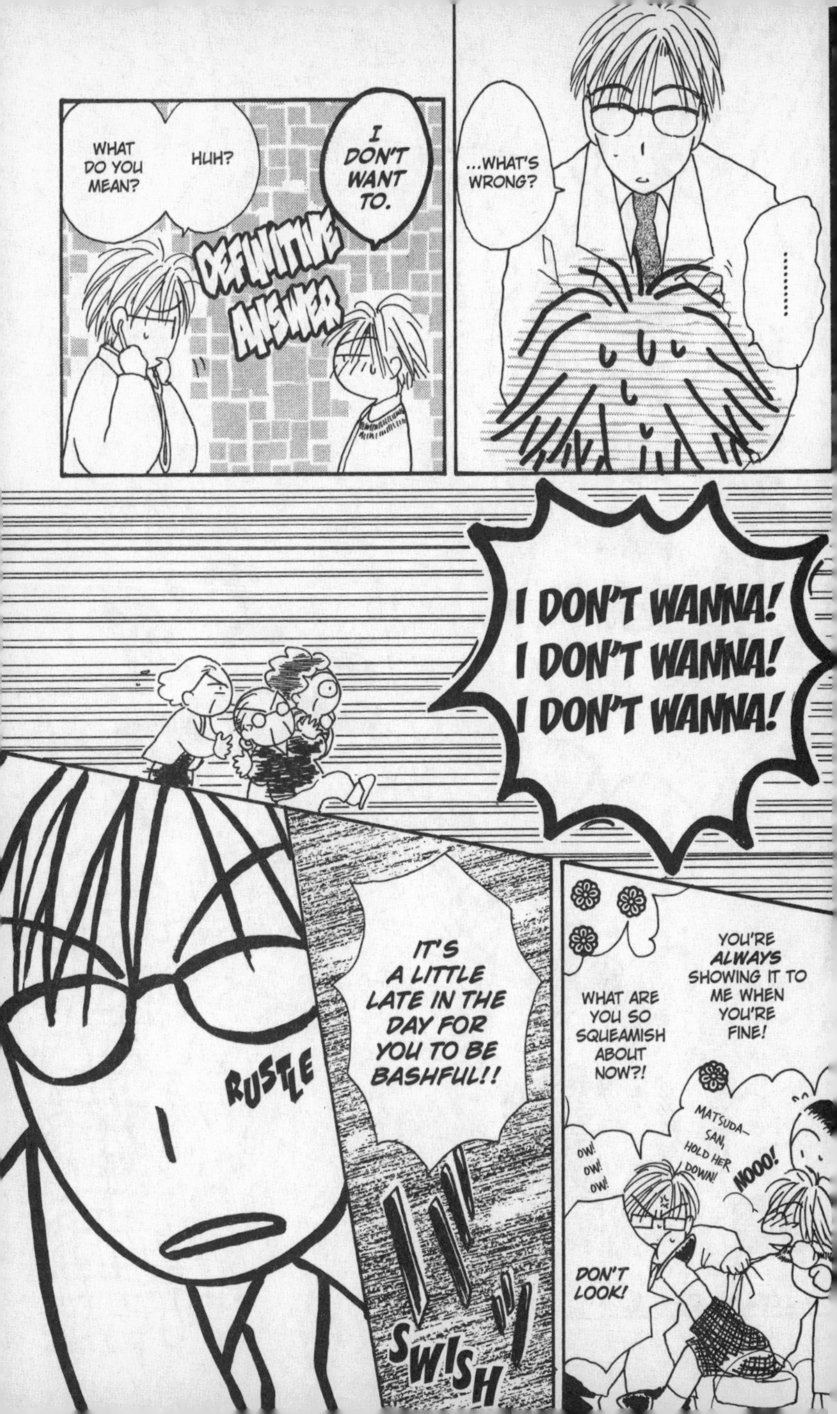
...WHAT'S WRONG?
......
I DON'T WANT TO.
DEFINITIVE ANSWER
HUH?
WHAT DO YOU MEAN?
I DON'T WANNA! I DON'T WANNA! I DON'T WANNA!
YOU'RE ALWAYS SHOWING IT TO ME WHEN YOU'RE FINE!
WHAT ARE YOU SO SQUEAMISH ABOUT NOW?!
NOOO!
MATSUDA-SAN, HOLD HER DOWN!
OW! OW! OW!
DON'T LOOK!
IT'S A LITTLE LATE IN THE DAY FOR YOU TO BE BASHFUL!!
SWISH
RUSTLE

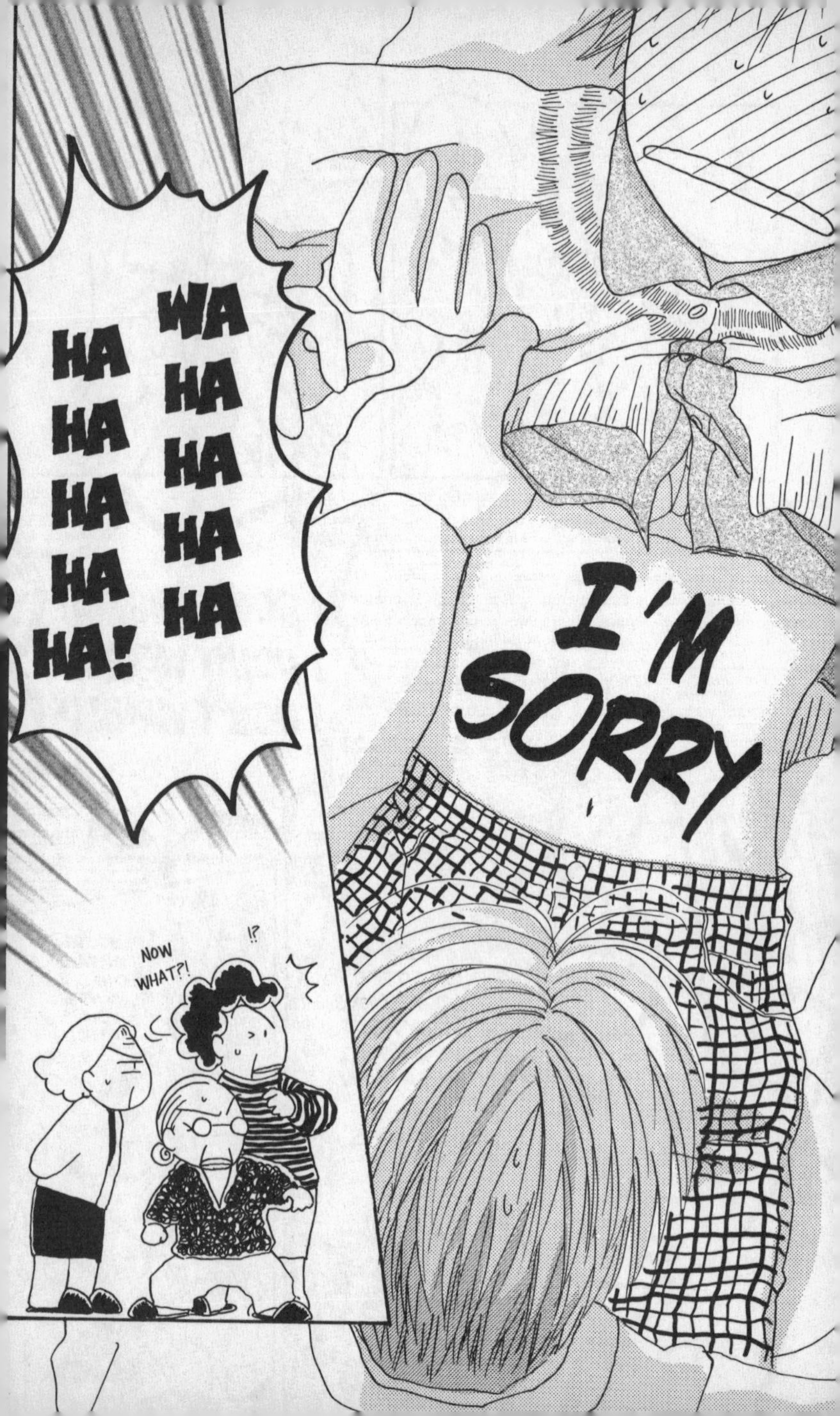
I'M SORRY
WA HA HA HA HA HA HA HA HA HA HA HA HA!
!?
NOW WHAT?!

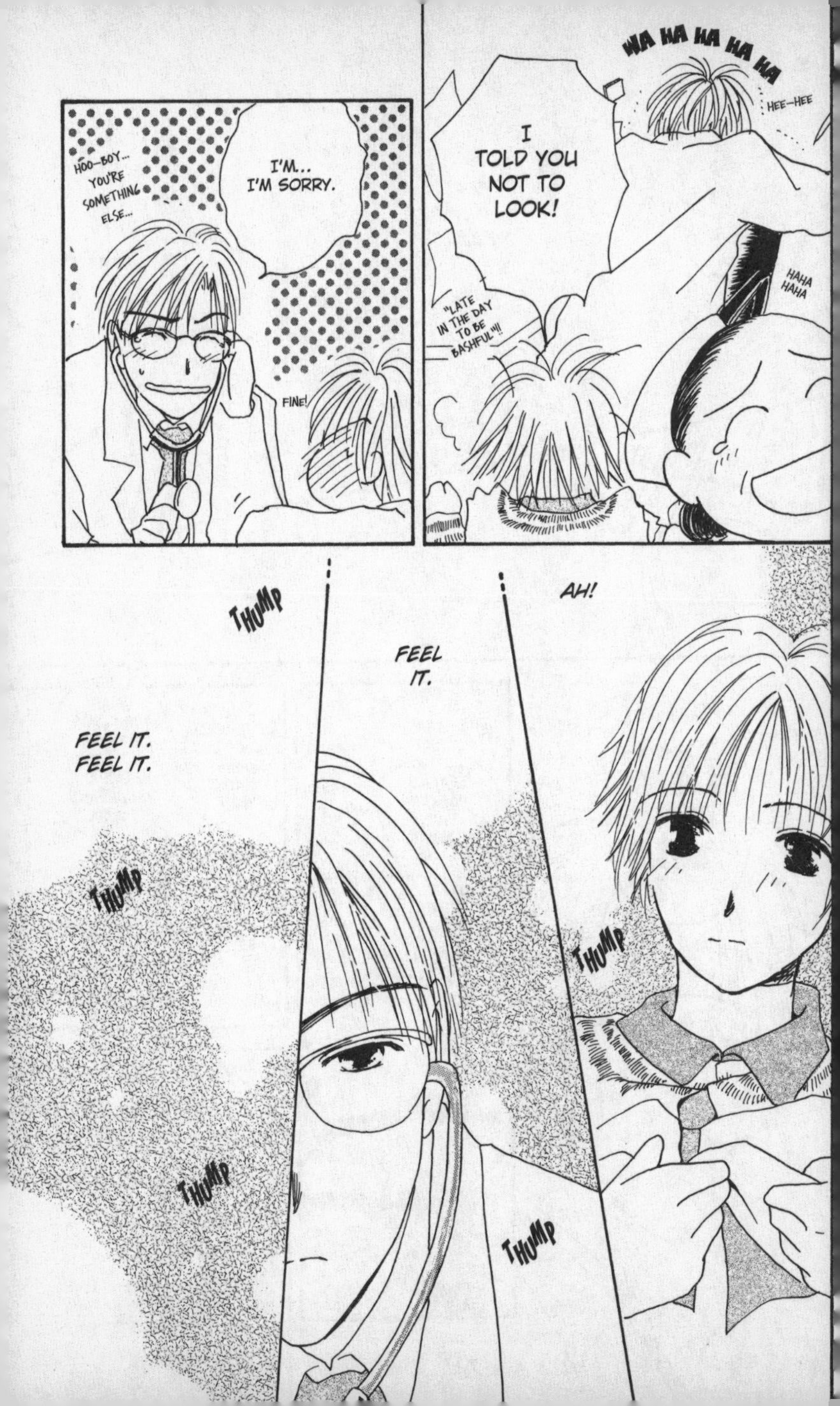
WA HA HA HA HA
HEE-HEE
I TOLD YOU NOT TO LOOK!
HAHA HAHA
"LATE IN THE DAY TO BE BASHFUL"!!
I'M... I'M SORRY.
HOO-BOY... YOU'RE SOMETHING ELSE...
FINE!
AH!
FEEL IT.
THUMP
FEEL IT. FEEL IT.
THUMP
THUMP
THUMP
THUMP

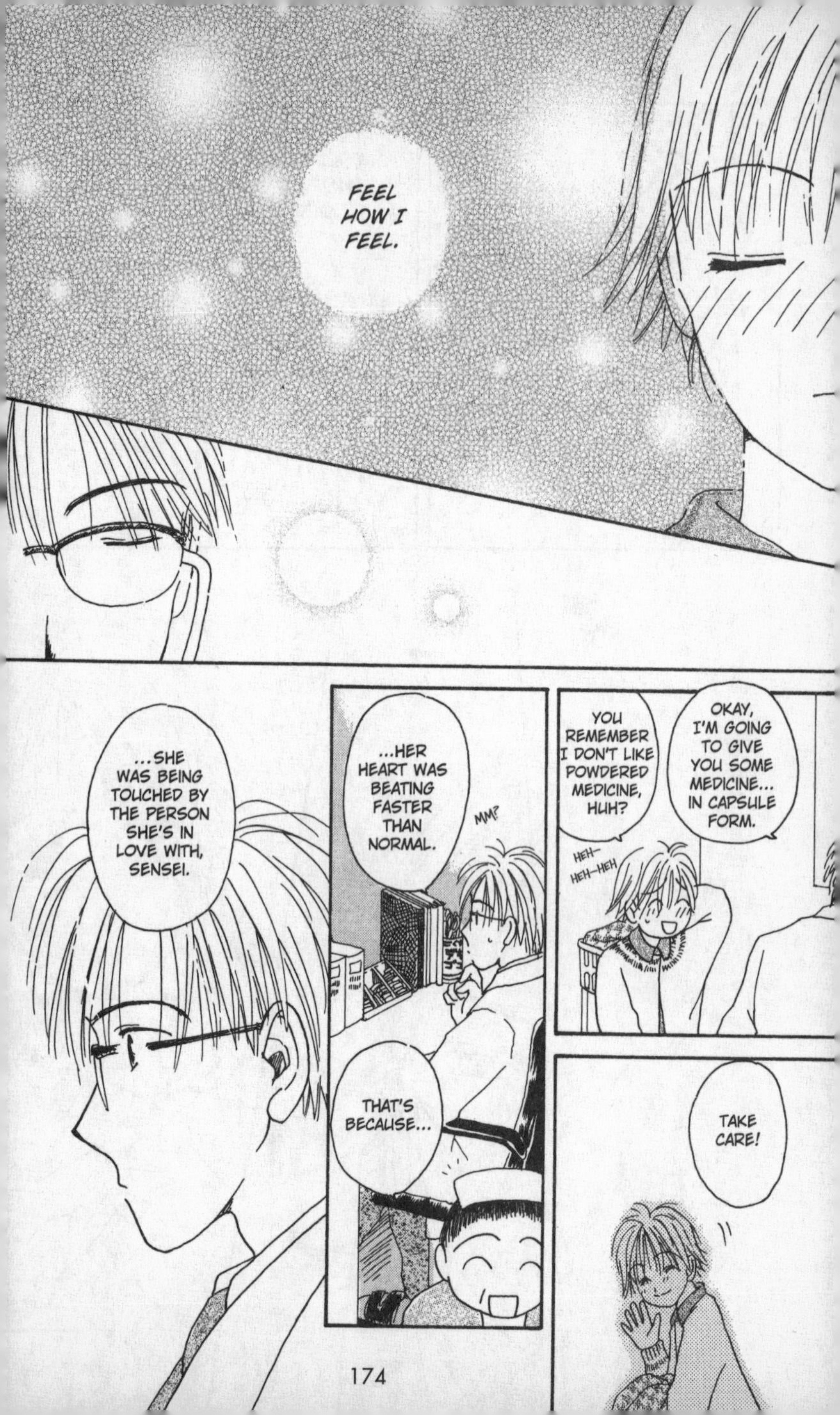
FEEL HOW I FEEL.
OKAY, I'M GOING TO GIVE YOU SOME MEDICINE... IN CAPSULE FORM.
YOU REMEMBER I DON'T LIKE POWDERED MEDICINE, HUH?
HEH-HEH-HEH
TAKE CARE!
...HER HEART WAS BEATING FASTER THAN NORMAL.
MM?
THAT'S BECAUSE...
...SHE WAS BEING TOUCHED BY THE PERSON SHE'S IN LOVE WITH, SENSEI.

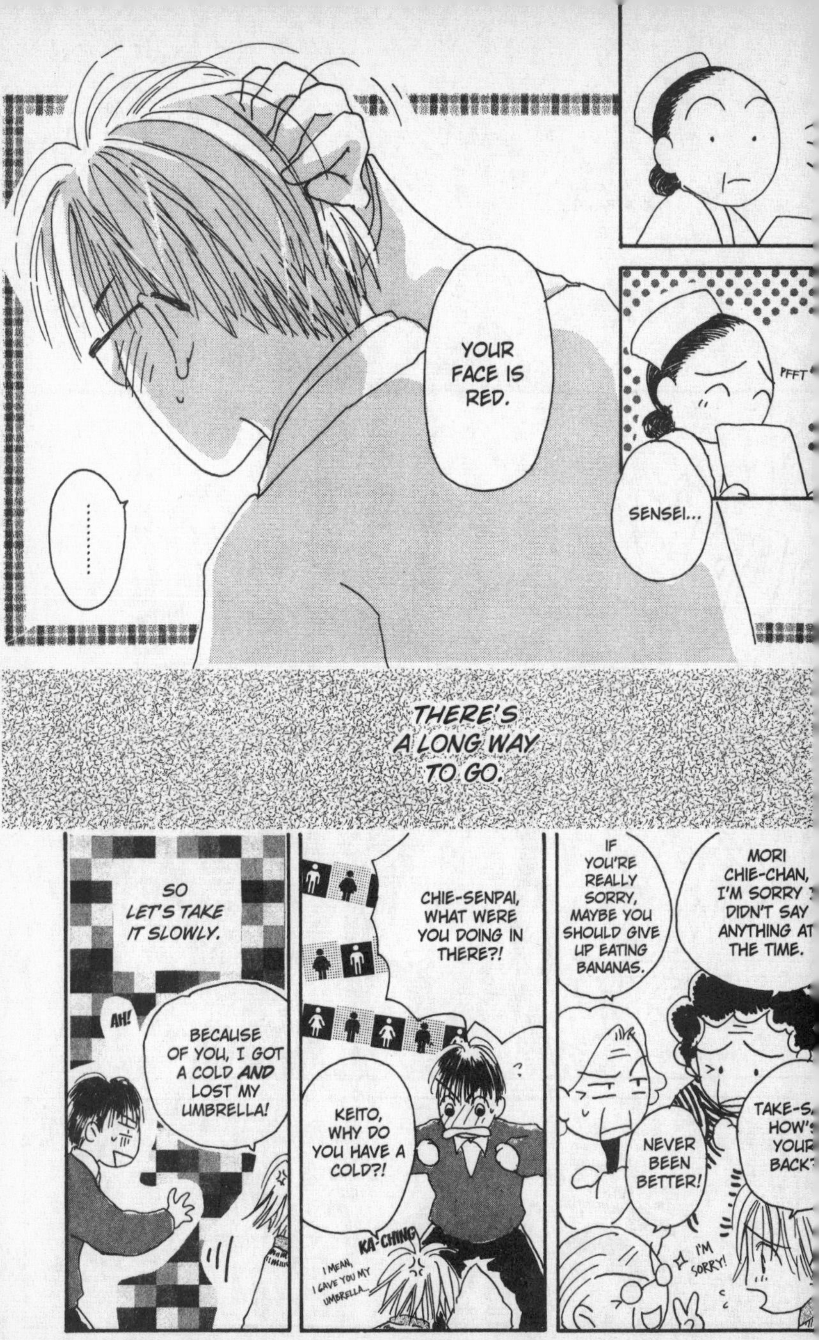
PFFT
SENSEI...
YOUR FACE IS RED.
......
THERE'S A LONG WAY TO GO.
MORI CHIE-CHAN, I'M SORRY I DIDN'T SAY ANYTHING AT THE TIME.
IF YOU'RE REALLY SORRY, MAYBE YOU SHOULD GIVE UP EATING BANANAS.
NEVER BEEN BETTER!
I'M SORRY!
CHIE-SENPAI, WHAT WERE YOU DOING IN THERE?!
KEITO, WHY DO YOU HAVE A COLD?!
KA-CHING
I MEAN, I GAVE YOU MY UMBRELLA...
SO LET'S TAKE IT SLOWLY.
AH!
BECAUSE OF YOU, I GOT A COLD AND LOST MY UMBRELLA!

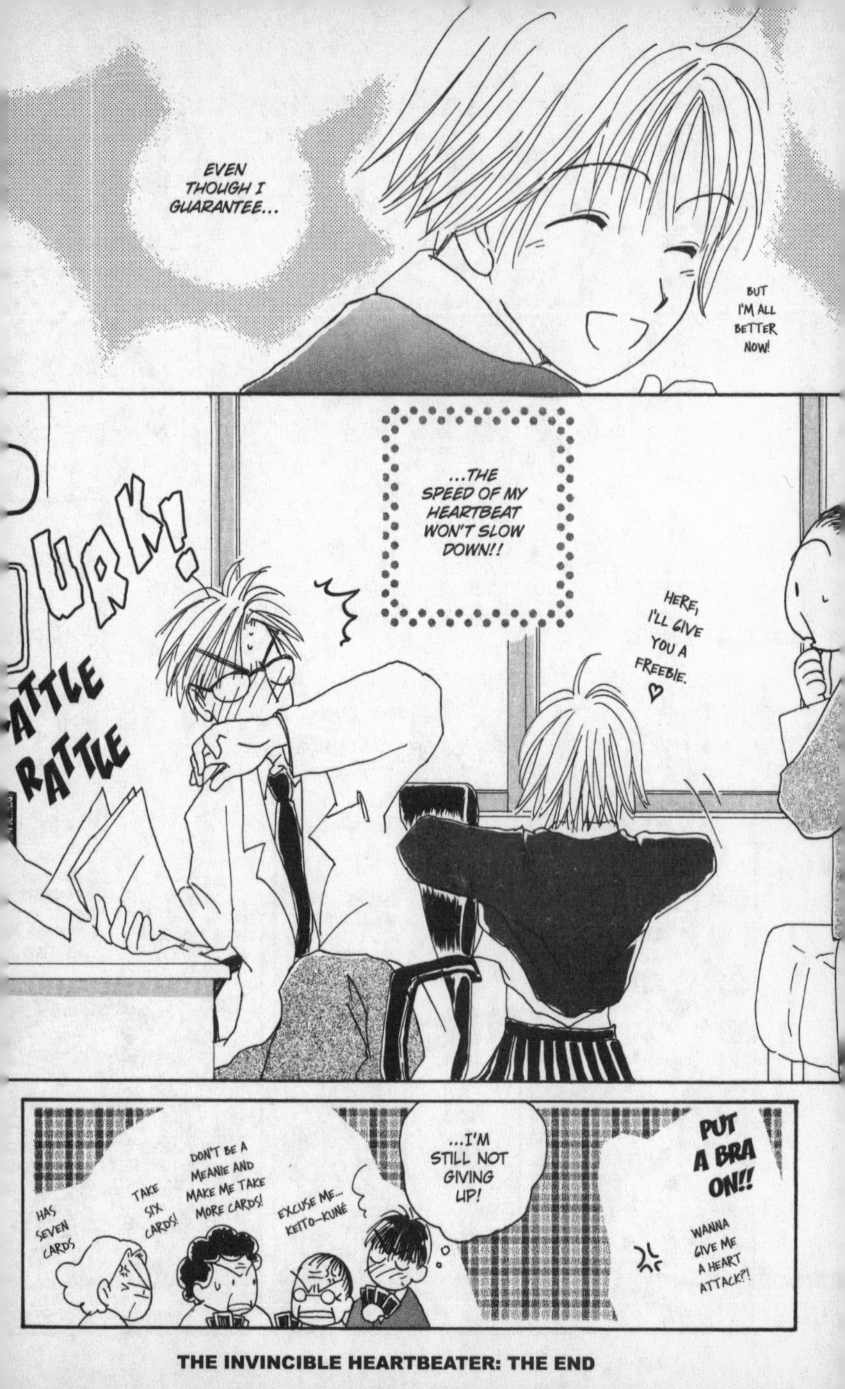
BUT I'M ALL BETTER NOW!
EVEN THOUGH I GUARANTEE...
HERE, I'LL GIVE YOU A FREEBIE. ♥
...THE SPEED OF MY HEARTBEAT WON'T SLOW DOWN!!
URK!
ATTLE RATTLE
PUT A BRA ON!!
WANNA GIVE ME A HEART ATTACK?!
...I'M STILL NOT GIVING UP!
EXCUSE ME... KEITO-KUN
DON'T BE A MEANIE AND MAKE ME TAKE MORE CARDS!
TAKE SIX CARDS!
HAS SEVEN CARDS

THE INVINCIBLE HEARTBEATER: THE END

NATURAL CENTRIPETAL FORCE ALPHA

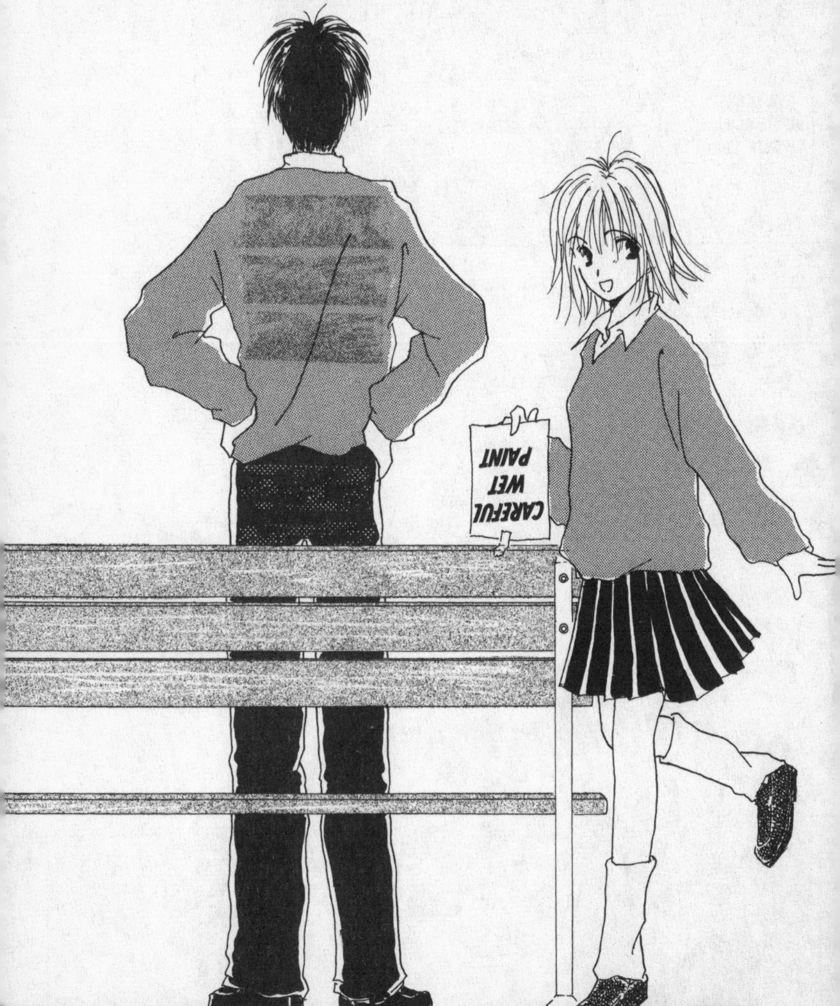
CAREFUL
WET
PAINT

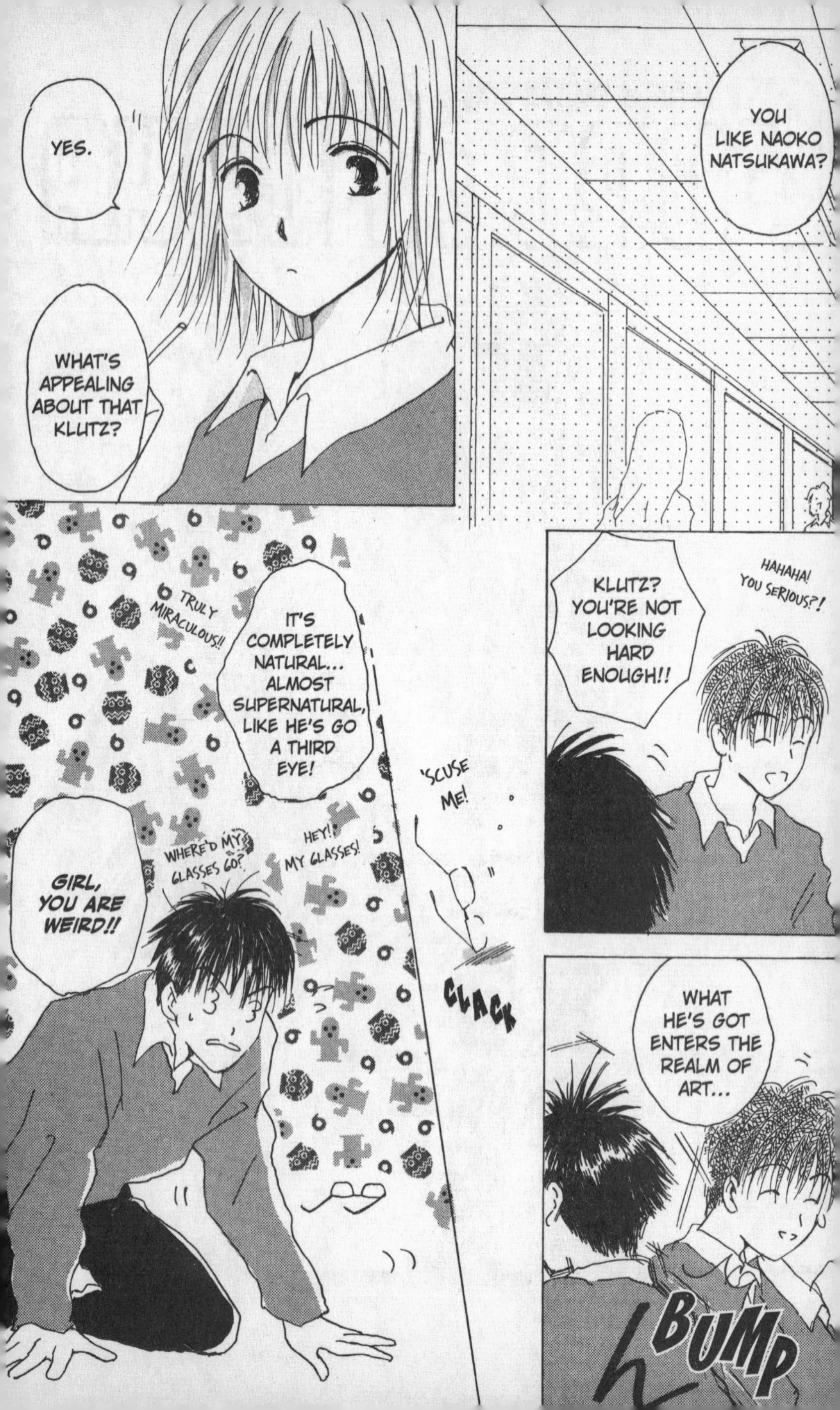
YOU LIKE NAOKO NATSUKAWA?
YES.
WHAT'S APPEALING ABOUT THAT KLUTZ?
HAHAHA! YOU SERIOUS?!
KLUTZ? YOU'RE NOT LOOKING HARD ENOUGH!!
WHAT HE'S GOT ENTERS THE REALM OF ART...
BUMP
IT'S COMPLETELY NATURAL... ALMOST SUPERNATURAL, LIKE HE'S GO A THIRD EYE!
TRULY MIRACULOUS!!
'SCUSE ME!
CLACK
HEY! MY GLASSES!
WHERE'D MY GLASSES GO?
GIRL, YOU ARE WEIRD!!

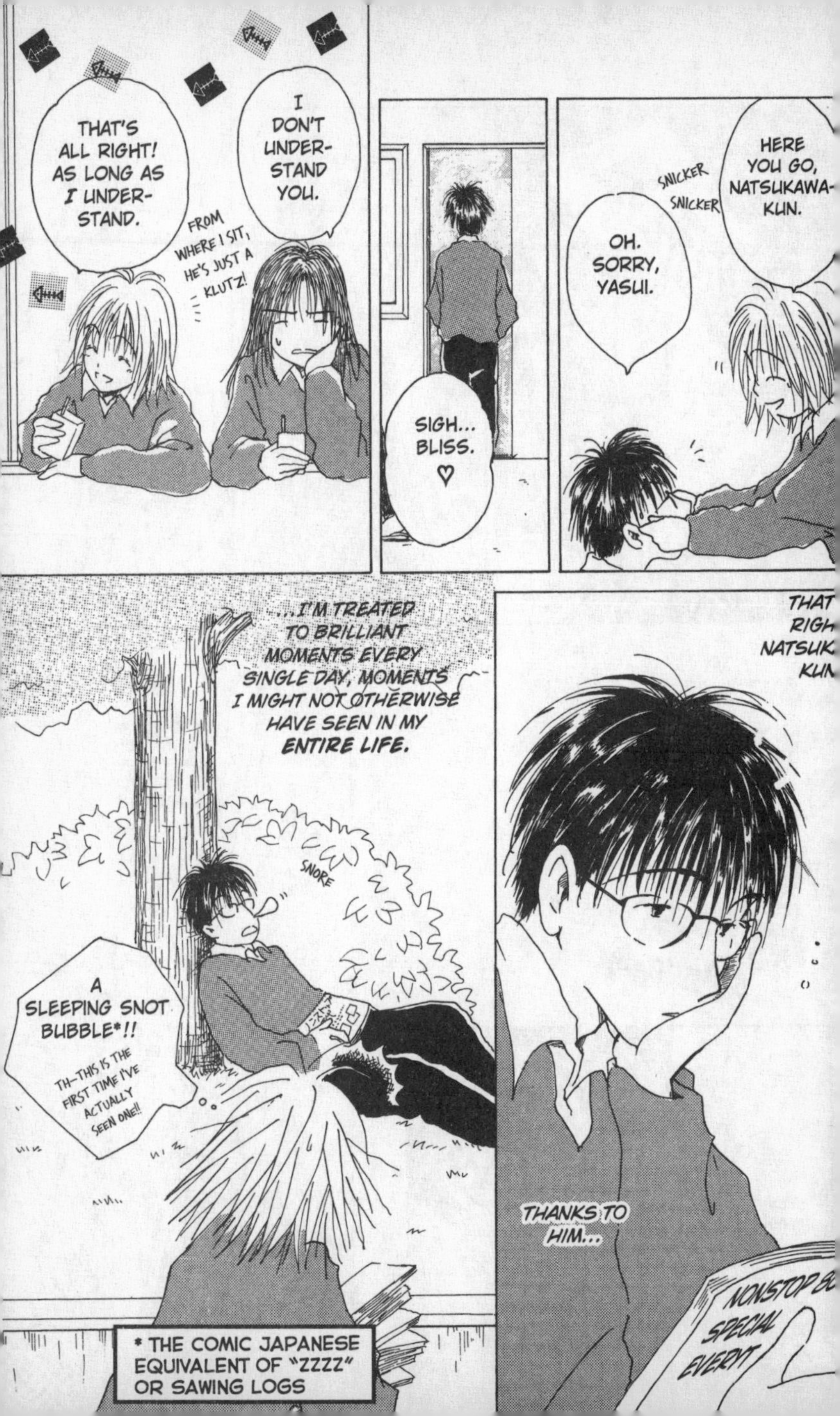
HERE YOU GO, NATSUKAWA-KUN.
SNICKER SNICKER
OH. SORRY, YASUI.
SIGH... BLISS. ♥
I DON'T UNDERSTAND YOU.
THAT'S ALL RIGHT! AS LONG AS I UNDERSTAND.
FROM WHERE I SIT, HE'S JUST A KLUTZ!
THAT RIGH NATSUK KUN
THANKS TO HIM...
NONSTOP SPECIAL EVERYT
...I'M TREATED TO BRILLIANT MOMENTS EVERY SINGLE DAY, MOMENTS I MIGHT NOT OTHERWISE HAVE SEEN IN MY ENTIRE LIFE.
SNORE
A SLEEPING SNOT BUBBLE*!!
TH-THIS IS THE FIRST TIME I'VE ACTUALLY SEEN ONE!!
* THE COMIC JAPANESE EQUIVALENT OF "ZZZZ" OR SAWING LOGS

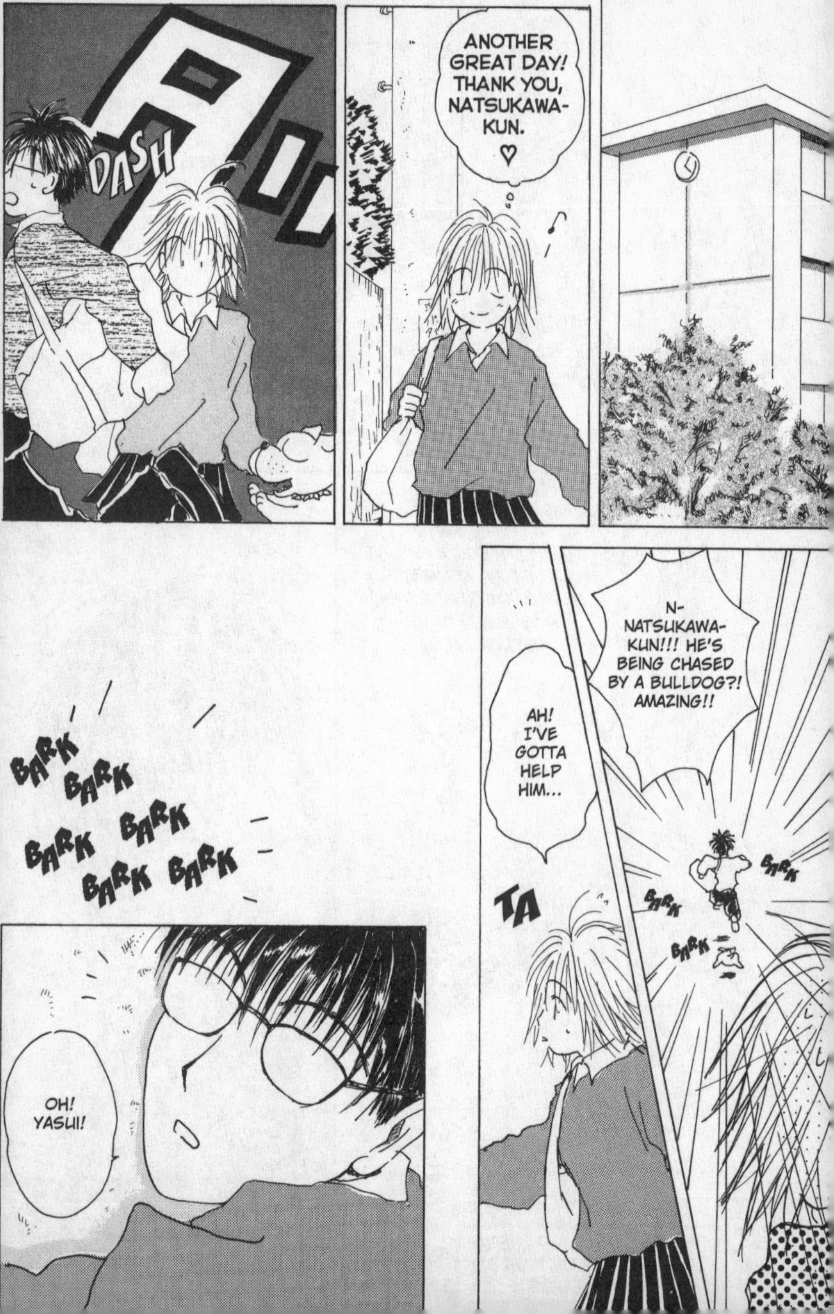
ANOTHER GREAT DAY! THANK YOU, NATSUKAWA-KUN. ♥
DASH
N-NATSUKAWA-KUN!!! HE'S BEING CHASED BY A BULLDOG?! AMAZING!!
BARK
BARK
BARK
AH! I'VE GOTTA HELP HIM...
TA
BARK BARK
BARK BARK
BARK BARK
OH! YASUI!

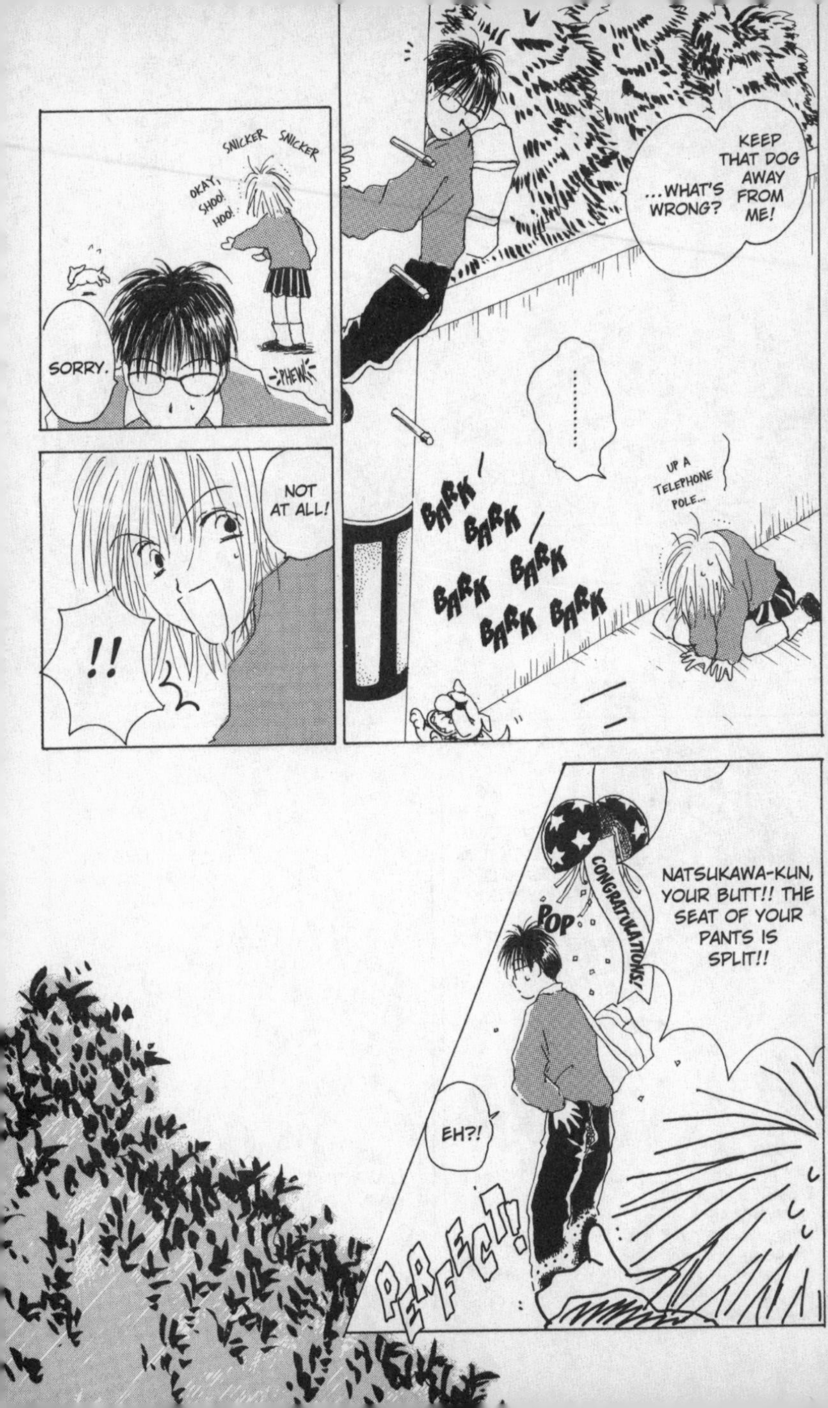
KEEP THAT DOG AWAY FROM ME!
...WHAT'S WRONG?
......
UP A TELEPHONE POLE...
BARK BARK BARK BARK BARK BARK
SNICKER SNICKER
OKAY, SHOO! HOO!
PHEW
SORRY.
NOT AT ALL!
!!
NATSUKAWA-KUN, YOUR BUTT!! THE SEAT OF YOUR PANTS IS SPLIT!!
CONGRATULATIONS!
POP
EH?!
PERFECT!!

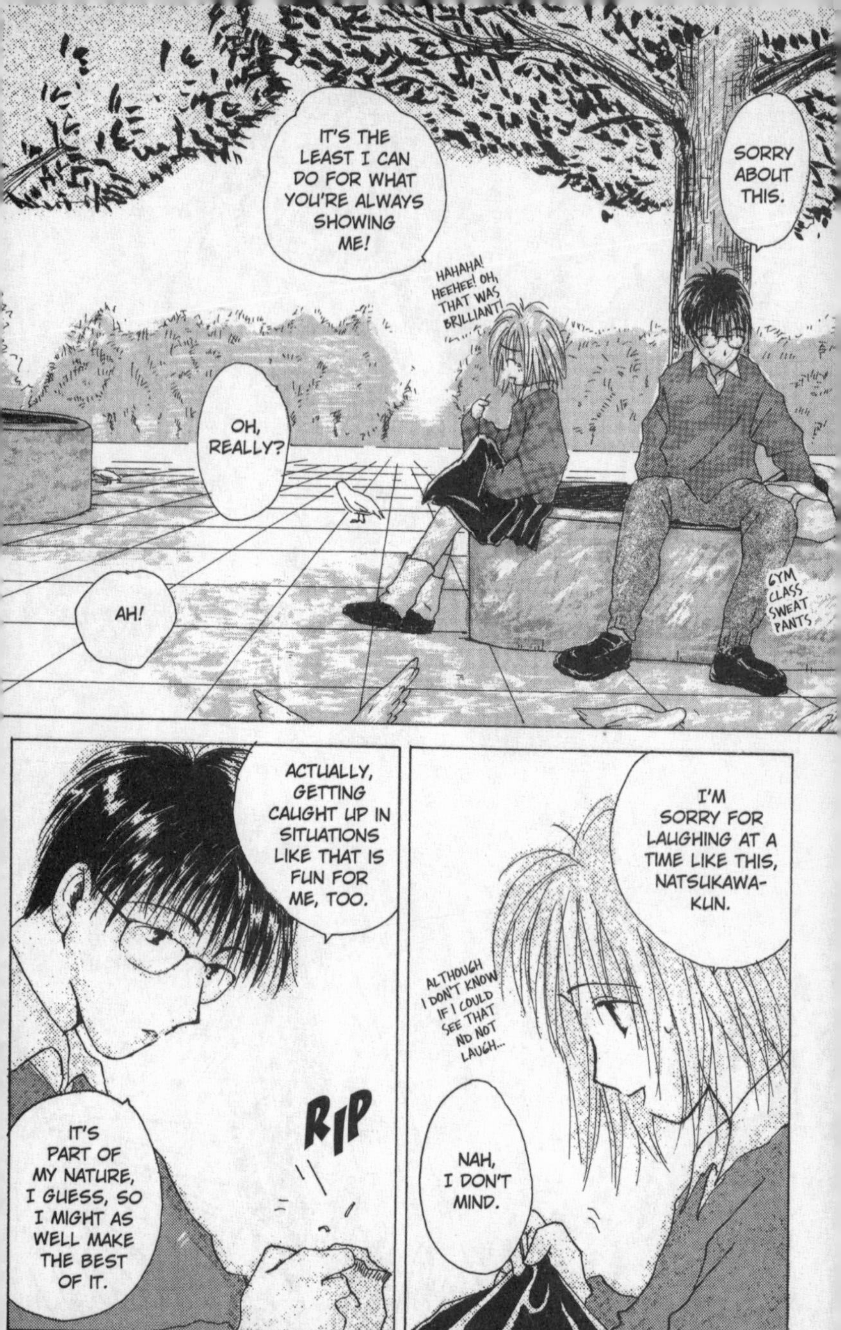
SORRY ABOUT THIS.
IT'S THE LEAST I CAN DO FOR WHAT YOU'RE ALWAYS SHOWING ME!
HAHAHA! HEEHEE! OH, THAT WAS BRILLIANT!
OH, REALLY?
GYM CLASS SWEAT PANTS
AH!
I'M SORRY FOR LAUGHING AT A TIME LIKE THIS, NATSUKAWA-KUN.
ALTHOUGH I DON'T KNOW IF I COULD SEE THAT ND NOT LAUGH...
NAH, I DON'T MIND.
ACTUALLY, GETTING CAUGHT UP IN SITUATIONS LIKE THAT IS FUN FOR ME, TOO.
RIP
IT'S PART OF MY NATURE, I GUESS, SO I MIGHT AS WELL MAKE THE BEST OF IT.

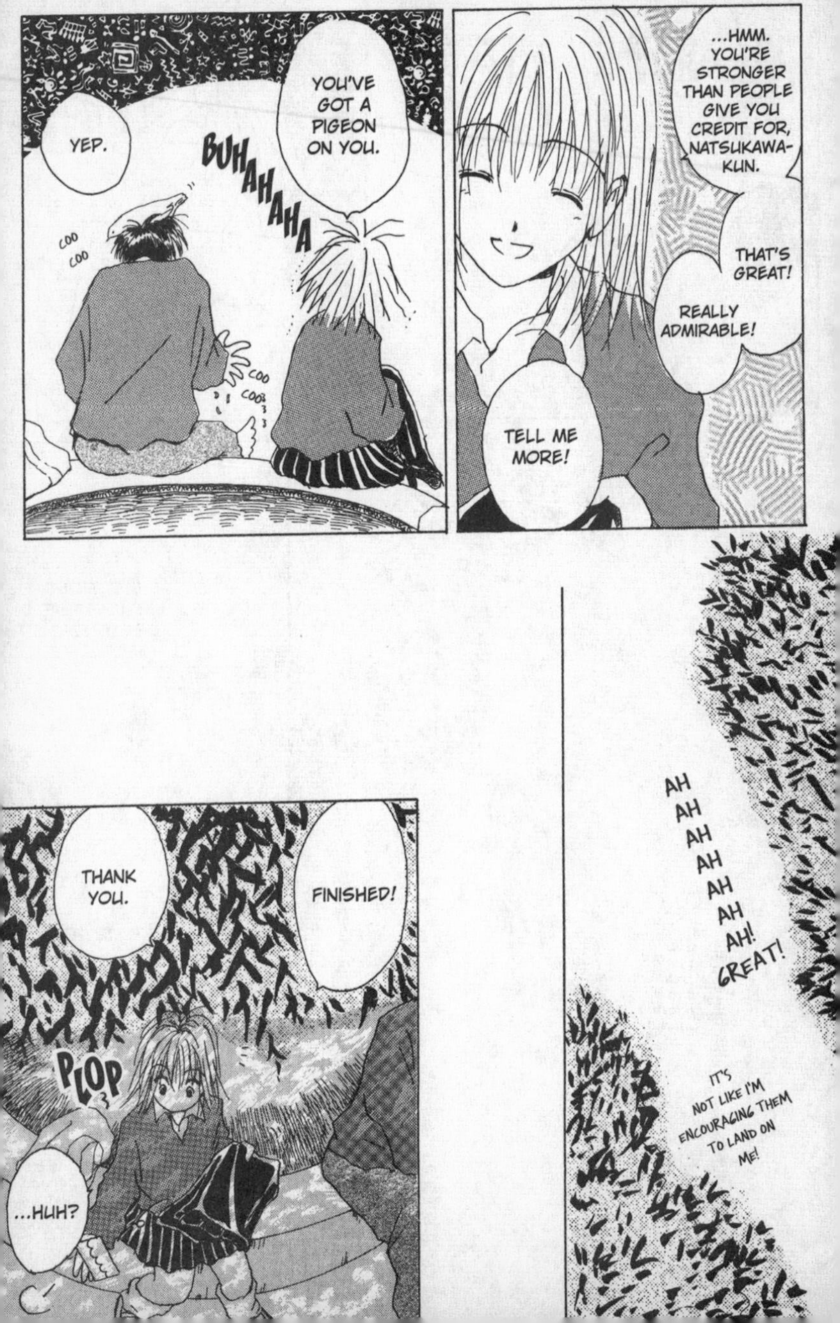
...HMM. YOU'RE STRONGER THAN PEOPLE GIVE YOU CREDIT FOR, NATSUKAWA-KUN.
THAT'S GREAT!
REALLY ADMIRABLE!
TELL ME MORE!
YOU'VE GOT A PIGEON ON YOU.
BUHAHAHAHA
YEP.
COO COO
COO COO
AH AH AH AH AH AH AH! GREAT!
IT'S NOT LIKE I'M ENCOURAGING THEM TO LAND ON ME!
FINISHED!
THANK YOU.
PLOP
...HUH?

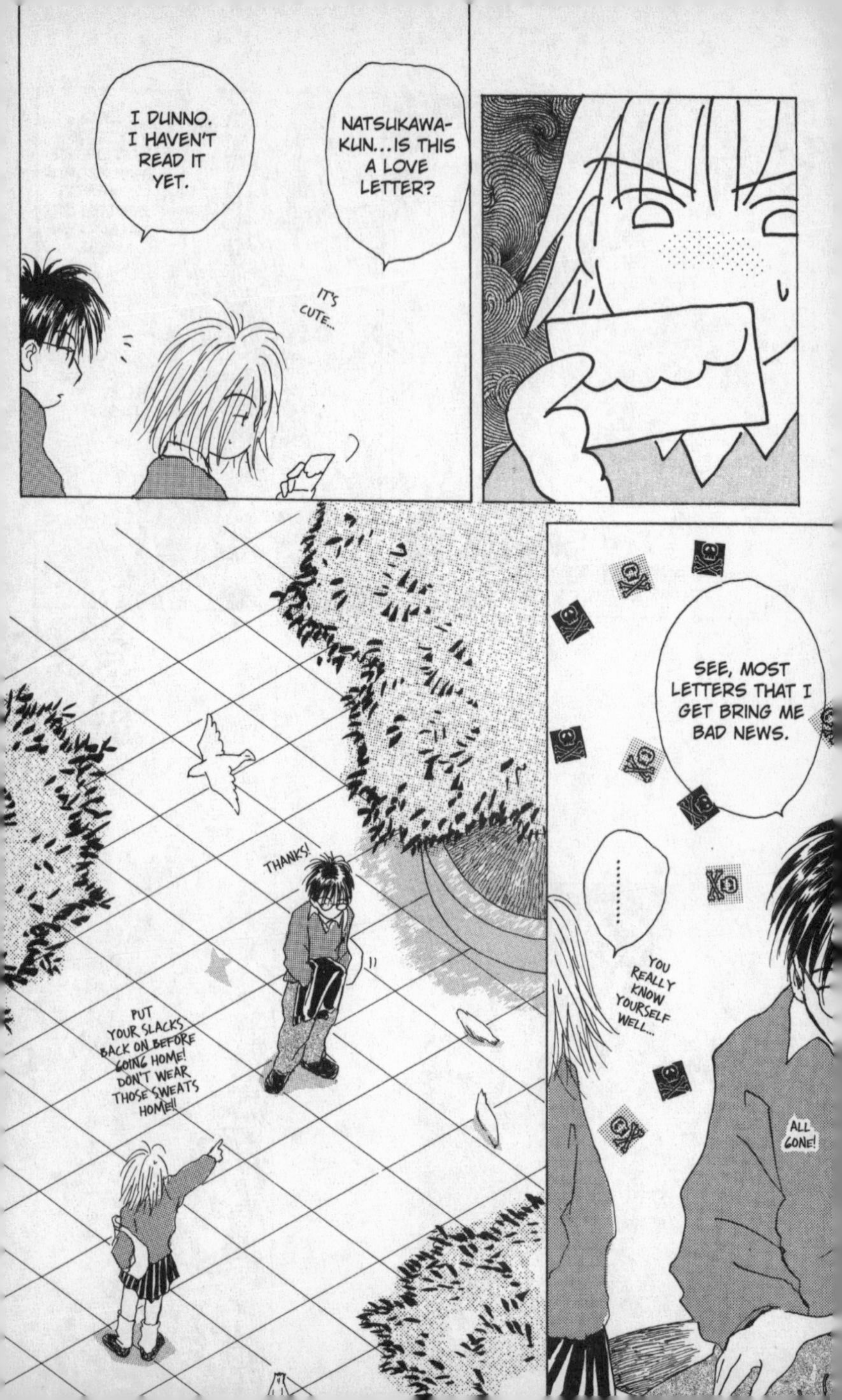
NATSUKAWA-KUN...IS THIS A LOVE LETTER?
I DUNNO. I HAVEN'T READ IT YET.
IT'S CUTE...
SEE, MOST LETTERS THAT I GET BRING ME BAD NEWS.
......
YOU REALLY KNOW YOURSELF WELL...
ALL GONE!
THANKS!
PUT YOUR SLACKS BACK ON BEFORE GOING HOME! DON'T WEAR THOSE SWEATS HOME!!

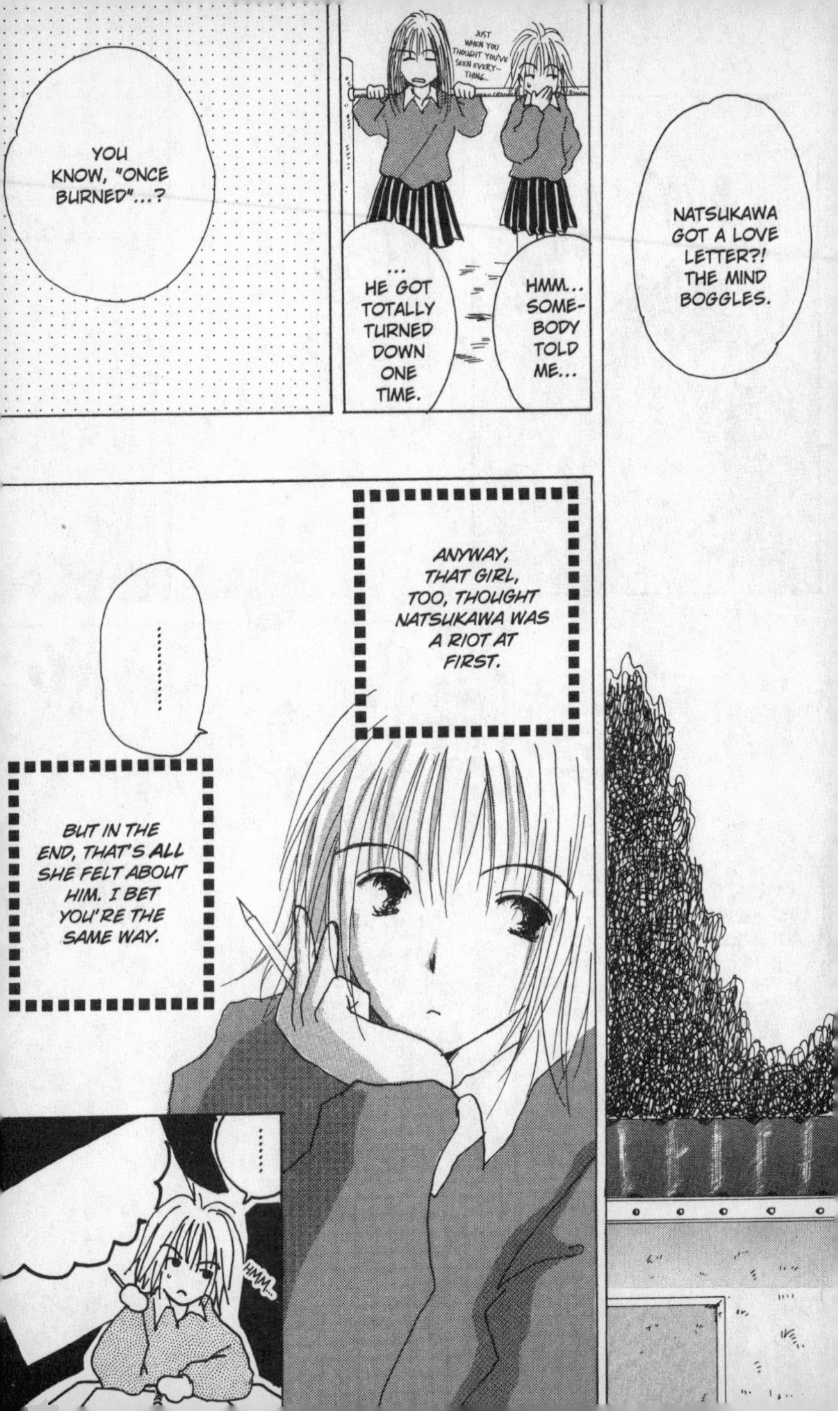
NATSUKAWA GOT A LOVE LETTER?! THE MIND BOGGLES.
JUST WHEN YOU THOUGHT YOU'VE SEEN EVERYTHING...
HMM... SOMEBODY TOLD ME...
...HE GOT TOTALLY TURNED DOWN ONE TIME.
YOU KNOW, "ONCE BURNED"...?
ANYWAY, THAT GIRL, TOO, THOUGHT NATSUKAWA WAS A RIOT AT FIRST.
......
BUT IN THE END, THAT'S ALL SHE FELT ABOUT HIM. I BET YOU'RE THE SAME WAY.
......
HMM...

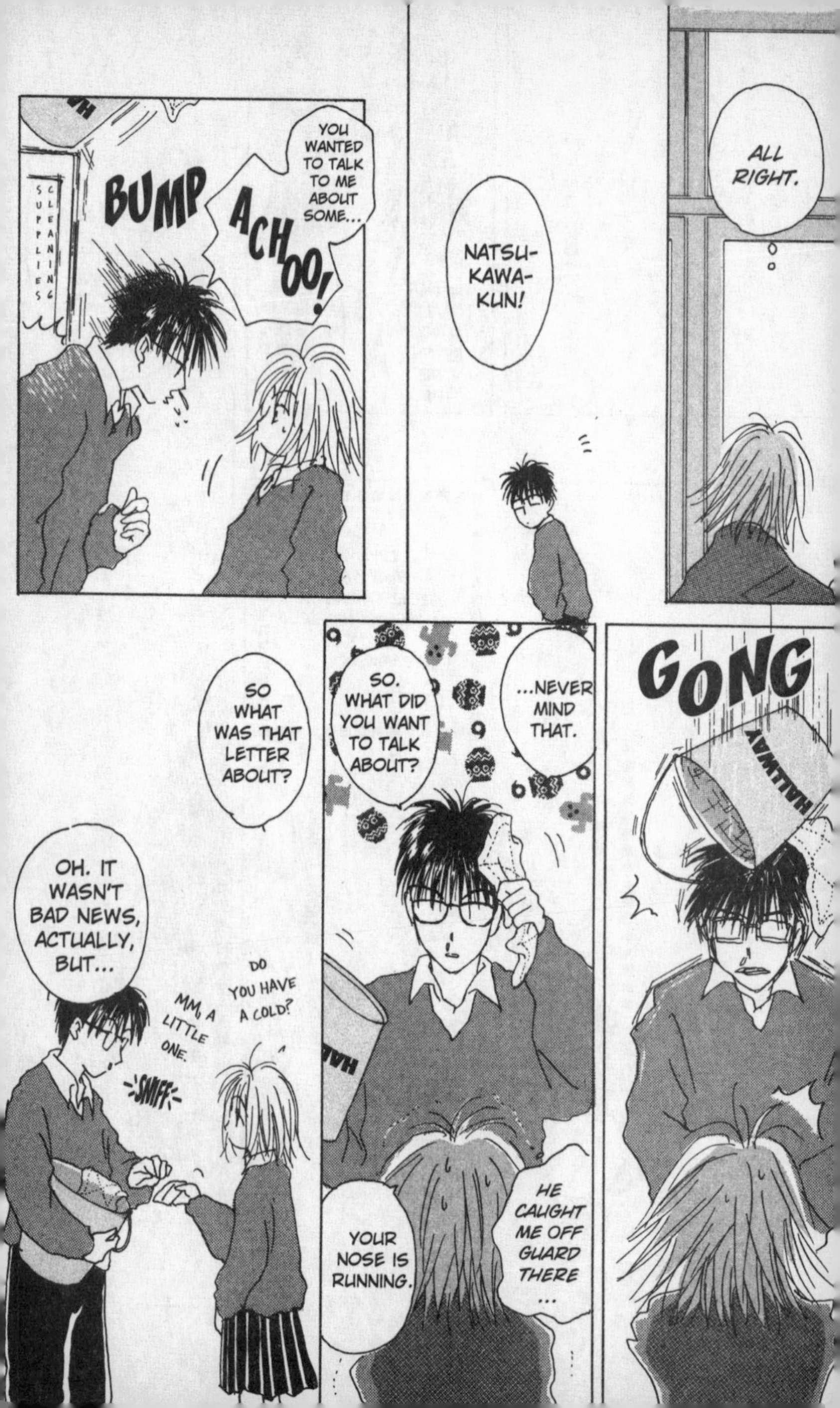
ALL RIGHT.
NATSU-KAWA-KUN!
YOU WANTED TO TALK TO ME ABOUT SOME...
ACHOO!
BUMP
CLEANING SUPPLIES
GONG
HALLWAY
...NEVER MIND THAT.
SO. WHAT DID YOU WANT TO TALK ABOUT?
HE CAUGHT ME OFF GUARD THERE...
YOUR NOSE IS RUNNING.
SO WHAT WAS THAT LETTER ABOUT?
OH. IT WASN'T BAD NEWS, ACTUALLY, BUT...
DO YOU HAVE A COLD?
MM, A LITTLE ONE.
SNIFF

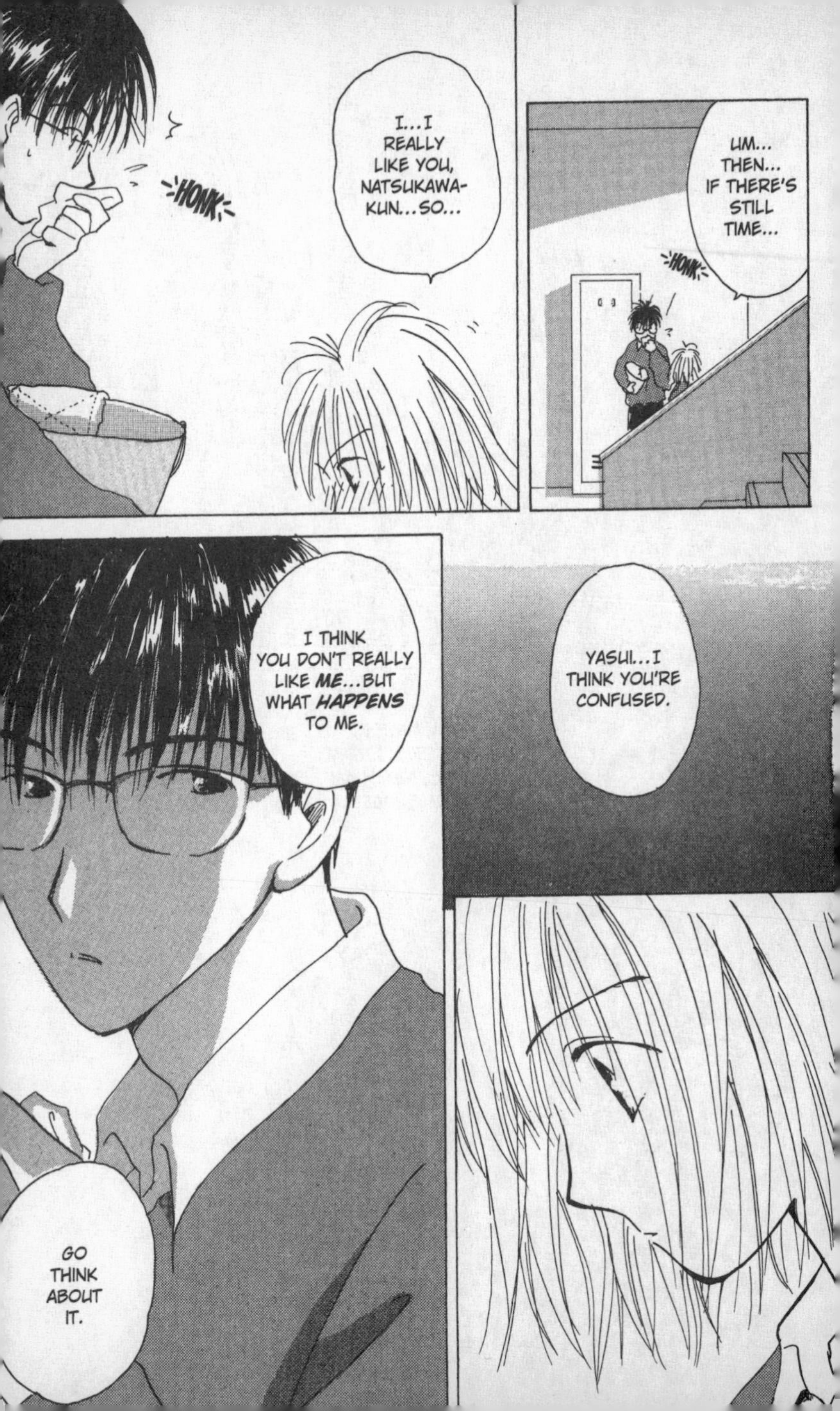
UM... THEN... IF THERE'S STILL TIME...
HONK
HONK
I...I REALLY LIKE YOU, NATSUKAWA-KUN...SO...
YASUI...I THINK YOU'RE CONFUSED.
I THINK YOU DON'T REALLY LIKE *ME*...BUT WHAT *HAPPENS* TO ME.
GO THINK ABOUT IT.

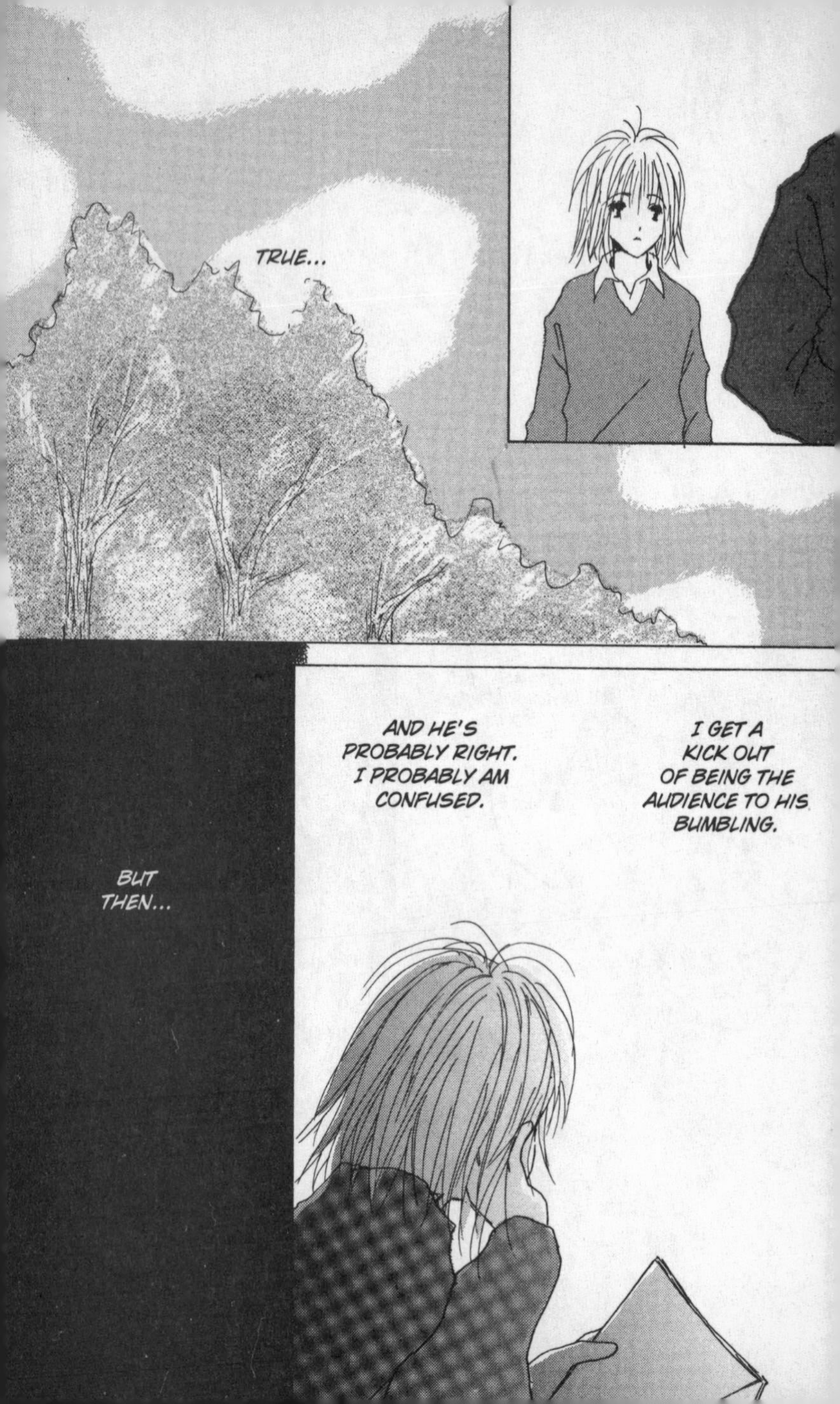

TRUE...
I GET A KICK OUT OF BEING THE AUDIENCE TO HIS BUMBLING.
AND HE'S PROBABLY RIGHT. I PROBABLY AM CONFUSED.
BUT THEN...

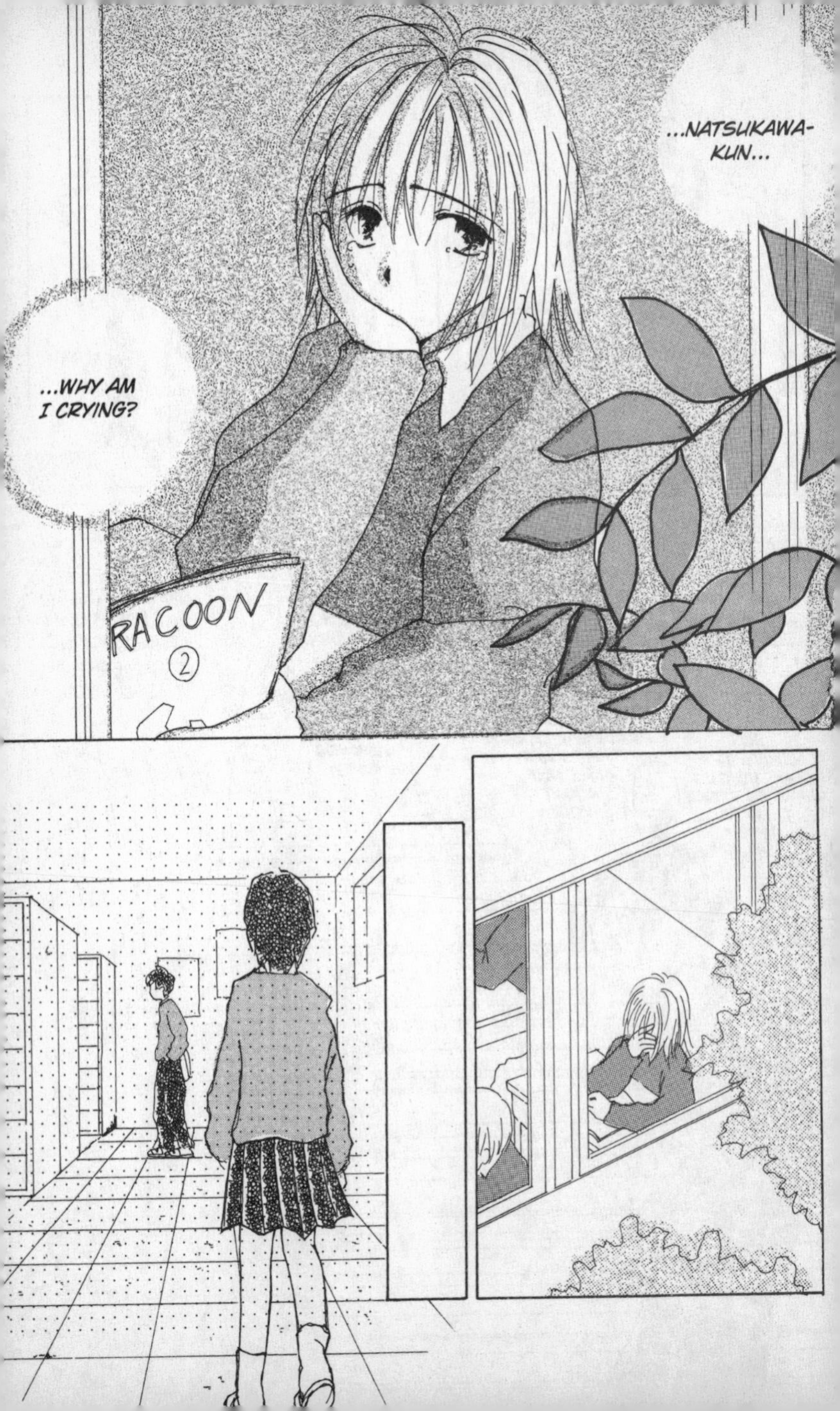
...NATSUKAWA-KUN...
...WHY AM I CRYING?
RACOON
2

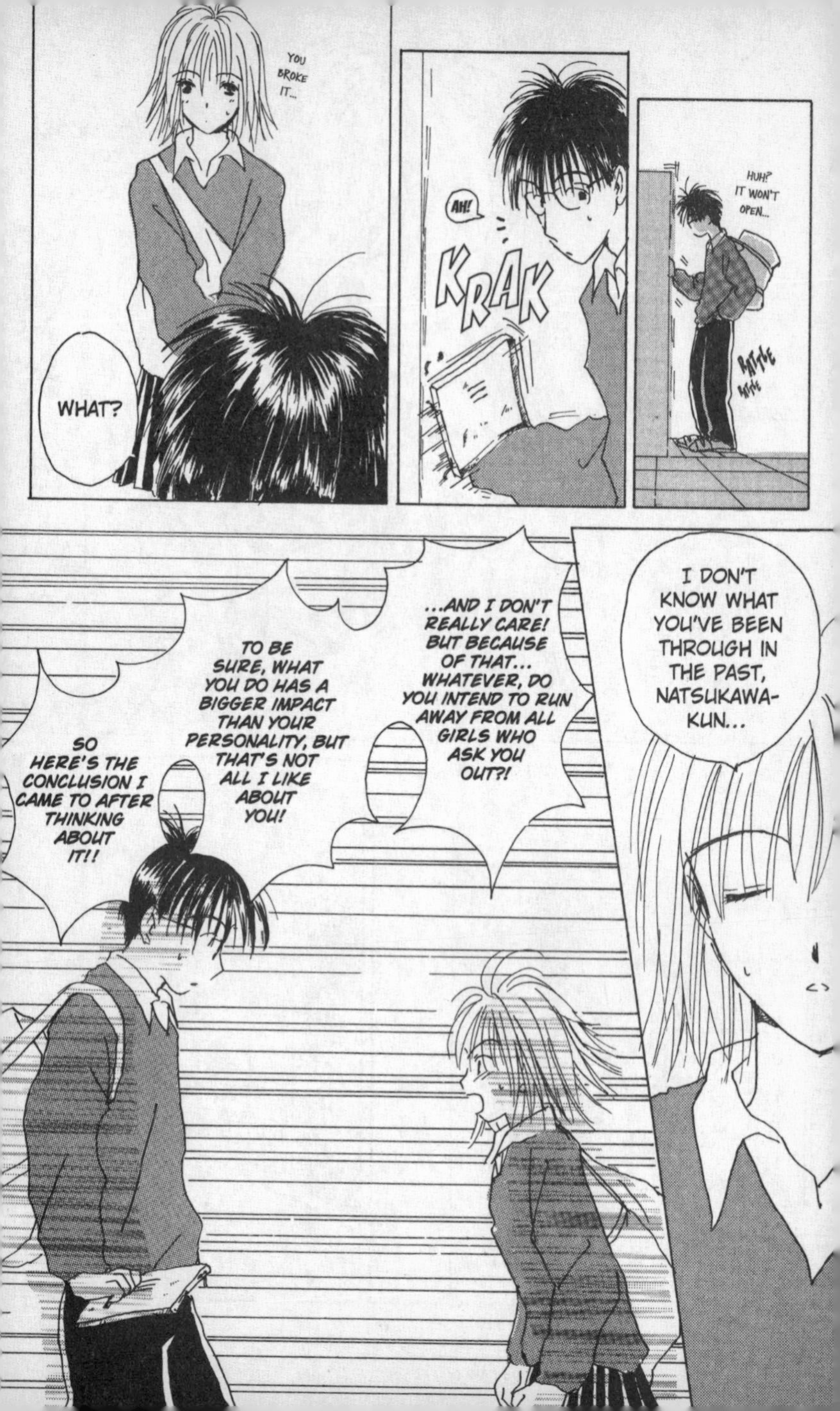
HUH? IT WON'T OPEN...
RATTLE RATTLE
AH!
KRAK
YOU BROKE IT...
WHAT?
I DON'T KNOW WHAT YOU'VE BEEN THROUGH IN THE PAST, NATSUKAWA-KUN...
...AND I DON'T REALLY CARE! BUT BECAUSE OF THAT... WHATEVER, DO YOU INTEND TO RUN AWAY FROM ALL GIRLS WHO ASK YOU OUT?!
TO BE SURE, WHAT YOU DO HAS A BIGGER IMPACT THAN YOUR PERSONALITY, BUT THAT'S NOT ALL I LIKE ABOUT YOU!
SO HERE'S THE CONCLUSION I CAME TO AFTER THINKING ABOUT IT!!

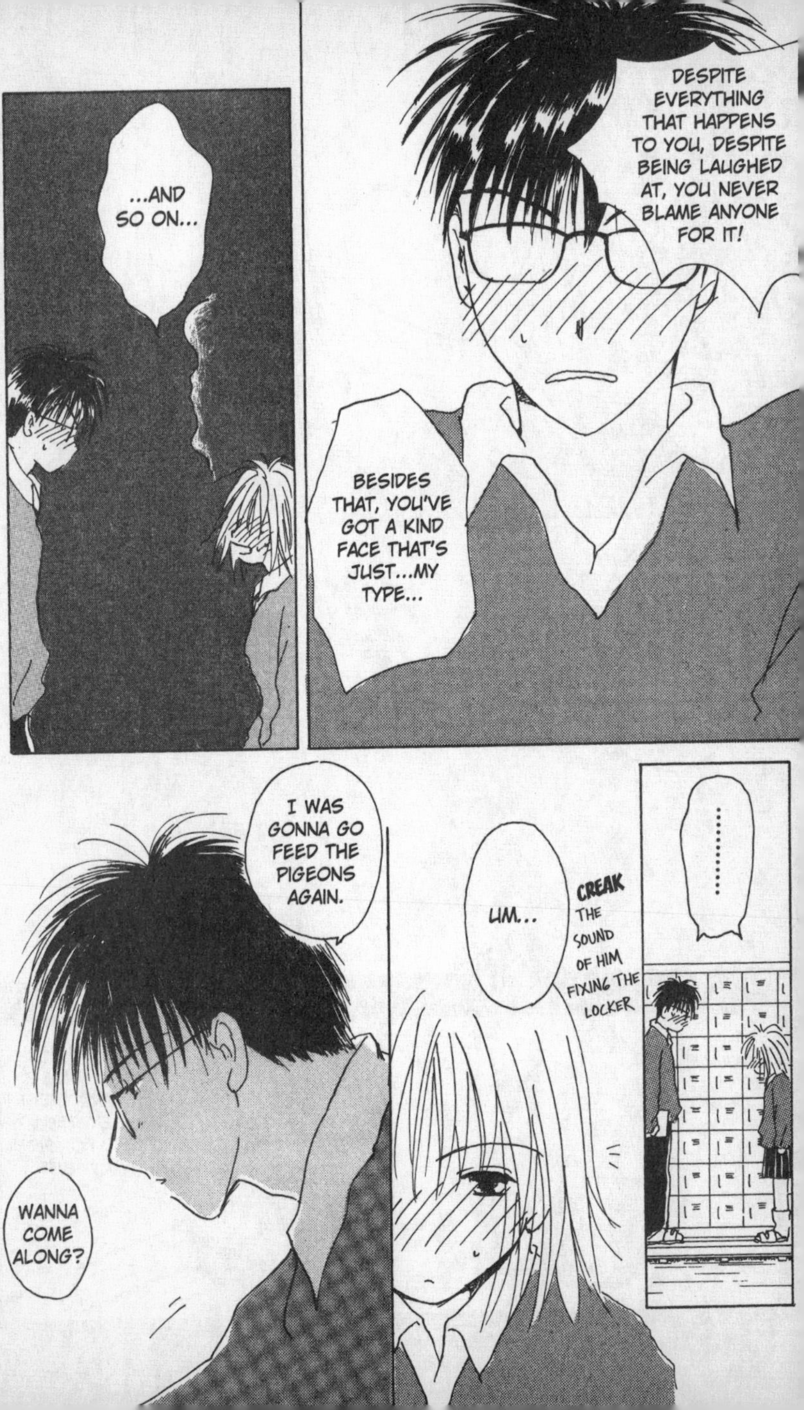
DESPITE EVERYTHING THAT HAPPENS TO YOU, DESPITE BEING LAUGHED AT, YOU NEVER BLAME ANYONE FOR IT!
BESIDES THAT, YOU'VE GOT A KIND FACE THAT'S JUST...MY TYPE...
...AND SO ON...
......
UM...
CREAK
THE SOUND OF HIM FIXING THE LOCKER
I WAS GONNA GO FEED THE PIGEONS AGAIN.
WANNA COME ALONG?

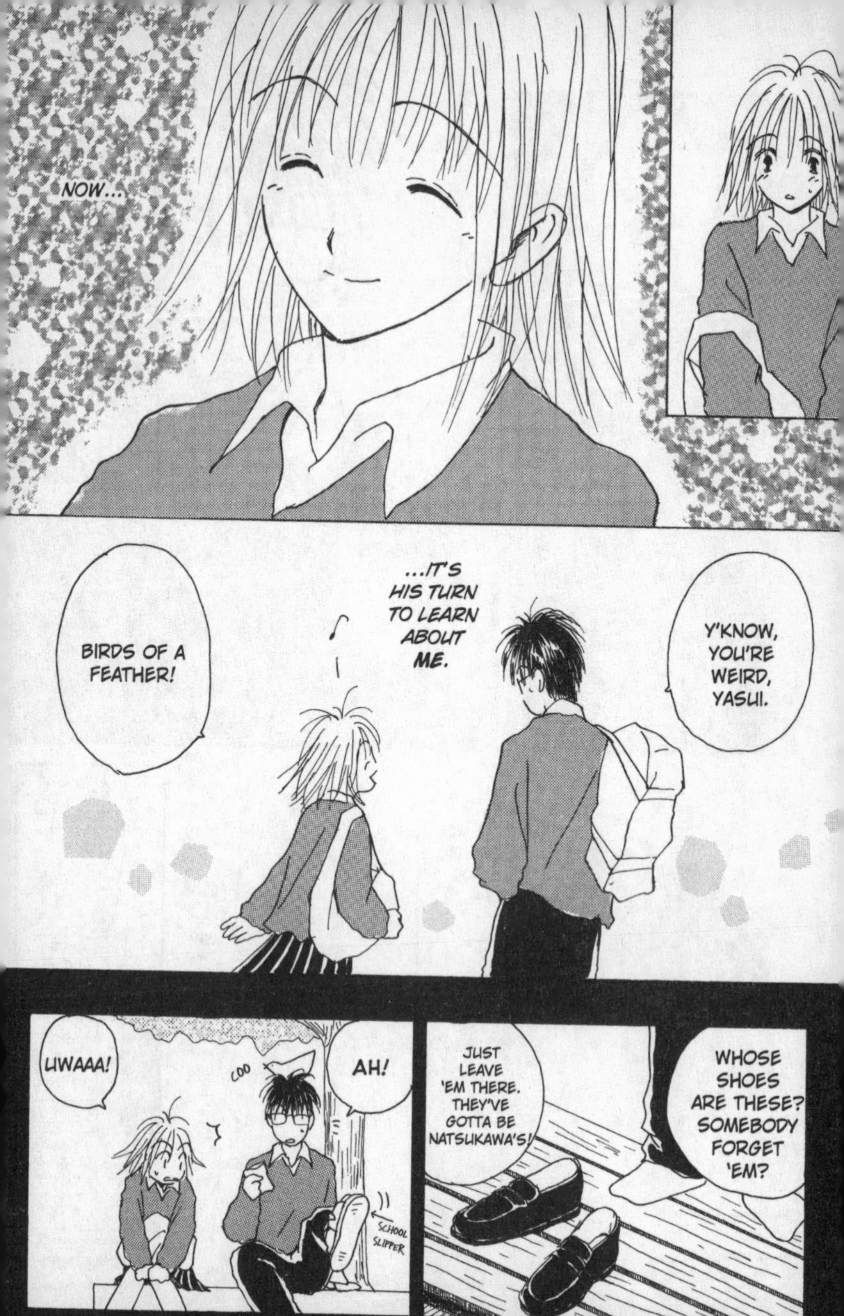
NOW...
Y'KNOW, YOU'RE WEIRD, YASUI.
...IT'S HIS TURN TO LEARN ABOUT ME.
BIRDS OF A FEATHER!
WHOSE SHOES ARE THESE? SOMEBODY FORGET 'EM?
JUST LEAVE 'EM THERE. THEY'VE GOTTA BE NATSUKAWA'S!
AH!
COO
UWAAA!
SCHOOL SLIPPER

NATURAL CENTRIPETAL FORCE ALPHA: THE END

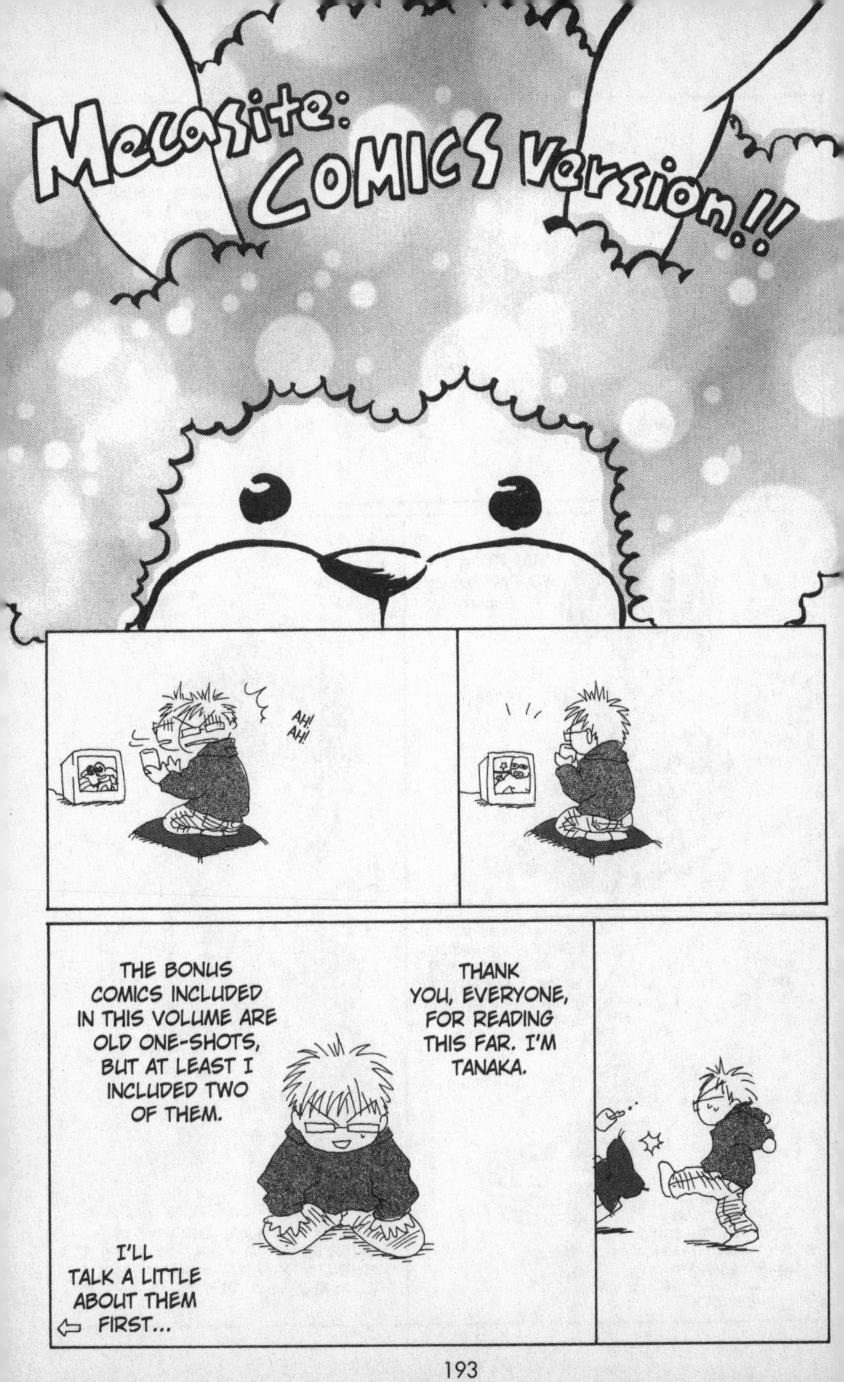
Mecasite: COMICS version!!
AH! AH!
THANK YOU, EVERYONE, FOR READING THIS FAR. I'M TANAKA.
THE BONUS COMICS INCLUDED IN THIS VOLUME ARE OLD ONE-SHOTS, BUT AT LEAST I INCLUDED TWO OF THEM.
I'LL TALK A LITTLE ABOUT THEM FIRST...

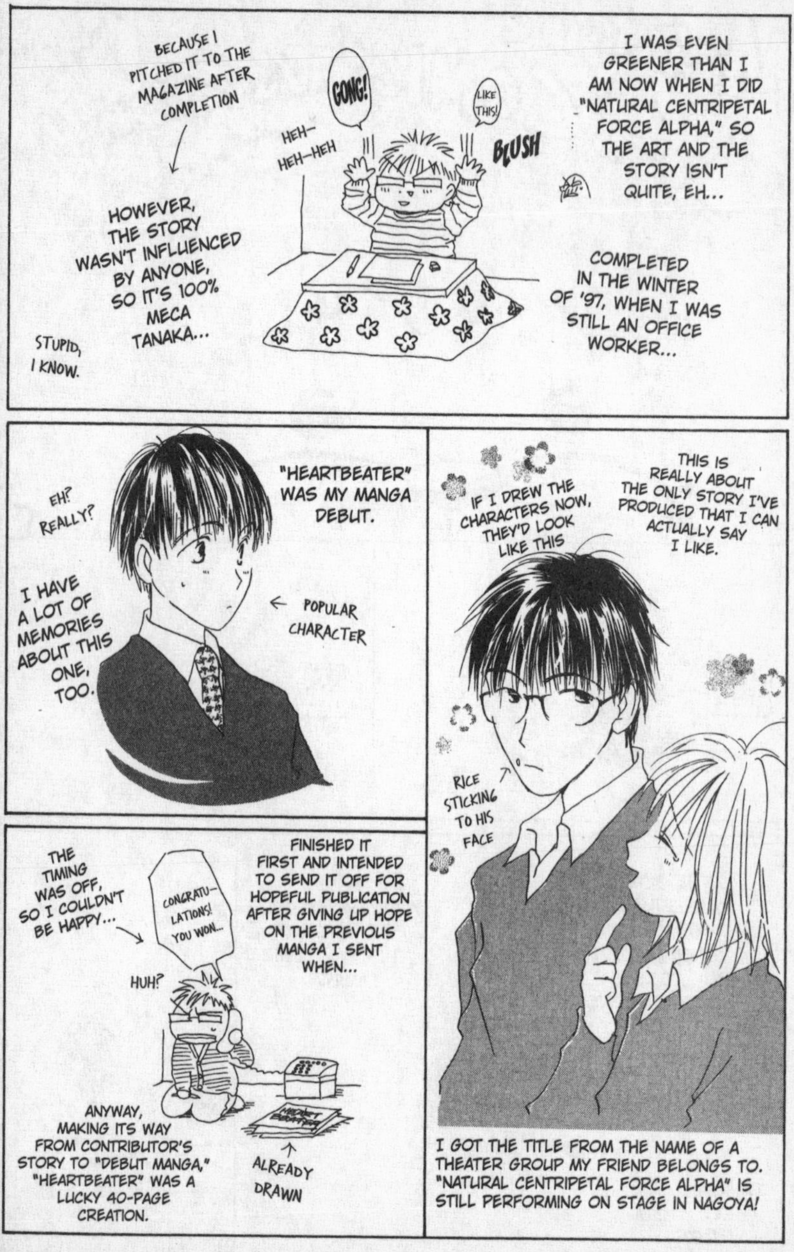
I WAS EVEN GREENER THAN I AM NOW WHEN I DID "NATURAL CENTRIPETAL FORCE ALPHA," SO THE ART AND THE STORY ISN'T QUITE, EH...
COMPLETED IN THE WINTER OF '97, WHEN I WAS STILL AN OFFICE WORKER...
LIKE THIS!
BLUSH
GONG!
HEH-HEH-HEH
BECAUSE I PITCHED IT TO THE MAGAZINE AFTER COMPLETION
HOWEVER, THE STORY WASN'T INFLUENCED BY ANYONE, SO IT'S 100% MECA TANAKA...
STUPID, I KNOW.
THIS IS REALLY ABOUT THE ONLY STORY I'VE PRODUCED THAT I CAN ACTUALLY SAY I LIKE.
IF I DREW THE CHARACTERS NOW, THEY'D LOOK LIKE THIS
RICE STICKING TO HIS FACE
I GOT THE TITLE FROM THE NAME OF A THEATER GROUP MY FRIEND BELONGS TO. "NATURAL CENTRIPETAL FORCE ALPHA" IS STILL PERFORMING ON STAGE IN NAGOYA!
"HEARTBEATER" WAS MY MANGA DEBUT.
EH? REALLY?
POPULAR CHARACTER
I HAVE A LOT OF MEMORIES ABOUT THIS ONE, TOO.
FINISHED IT FIRST AND INTENDED TO SEND IT OFF FOR HOPEFUL PUBLICATION AFTER GIVING UP HOPE ON THE PREVIOUS MANGA I SENT WHEN...
CONGRATULATIONS! YOU WON...
THE TIMING WAS OFF, SO I COULDN'T BE HAPPY...
HUH?
ALREADY DRAWN
ANYWAY, MAKING ITS WAY FROM CONTRIBUTOR'S STORY TO "DEBUT MANGA," "HEARTBEATER" WAS A LUCKY 40-PAGE CREATION.

Mecasite: Comics Version!!

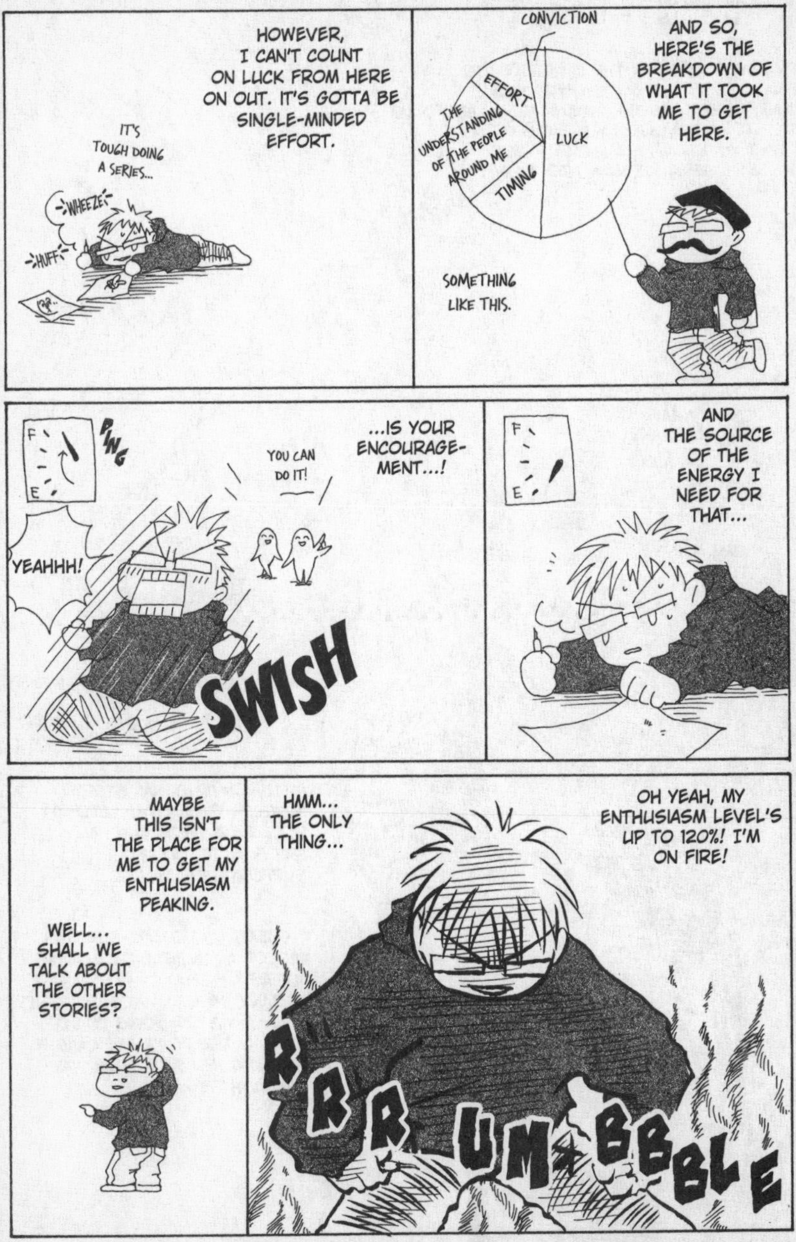
AND SO, HERE'S THE BREAKDOWN OF WHAT IT TOOK ME TO GET HERE.
CONVICTION
EFFORT
THE UNDERSTANDING OF THE PEOPLE AROUND ME
TIMING
LUCK
SOMETHING LIKE THIS.
HOWEVER, I CAN'T COUNT ON LUCK FROM HERE ON OUT. IT'S GOTTA BE SINGLE-MINDED EFFORT.
IT'S TOUGH DOING A SERIES...
WHEEZE
HUFF
AND THE SOURCE OF THE ENERGY I NEED FOR THAT...
F
E
...IS YOUR ENCOURAGE-MENT...!
YOU CAN DO IT!
PING
F
E
YEAHHH!
SWISH
OH YEAH, MY ENTHUSIASM LEVEL'S UP TO 120%! I'M ON FIRE!
HMM... THE ONLY THING...
RRRUMBBBLE
MAYBE THIS ISN'T THE PLACE FOR ME TO GET MY ENTHUSIASM PEAKING.
WELL... SHALL WE TALK ABOUT THE OTHER STORIES?

HERO=RED?

RIGINALLY, I INTENDED THE CHARACTER TO E A NARCISSIST BUT SOMEWHERE ALONG E LINE, HE BECAME THE HANDSOME YOUNG "BLUE". THIS STORY, WE LEARN YUZUKO'S TYPE. W THAT WE KNOW SHE LIKES "PRETTY YS," LET'S ASK HER: HOW ABOUT BESHIMA-SAN?

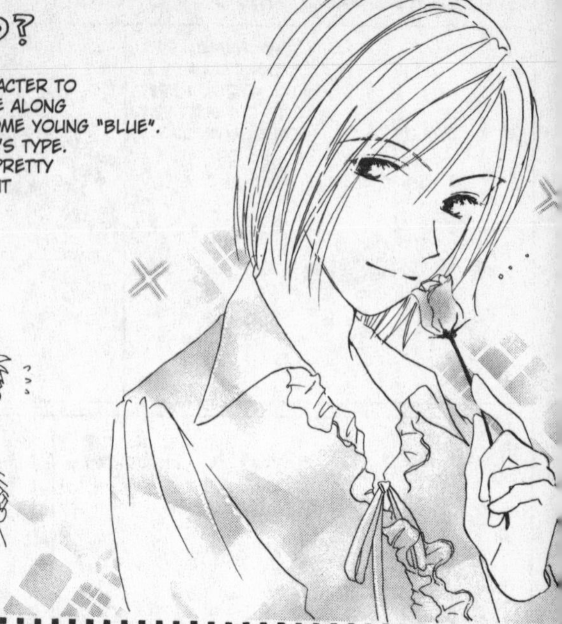

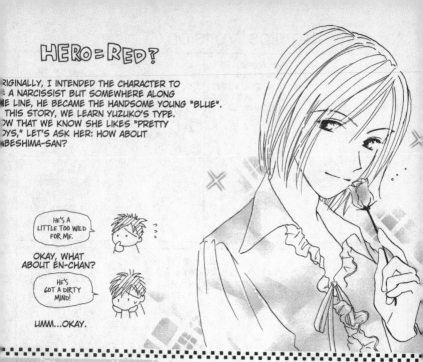

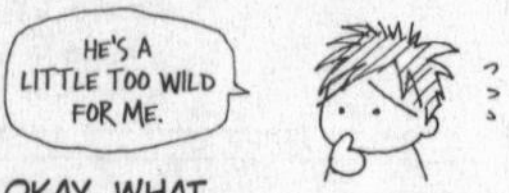
HE'S A LITTLE TOO WILD FOR ME.

OKAY, WHAT ABOUT EN-CHAN?

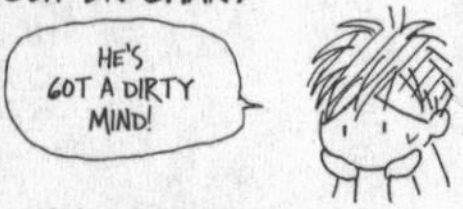
HE'S GOT A DIRTY MIND!

UMM...OKAY.

HIGH-SCHOOL TEACHER

AN UNCONVENTIONAL STORY, IN WHICH I TOOK THE LEADING ROLE AWAY FROM EN-CHAN AND GAVE IT TO THE SUPPORTING PLAYERS.

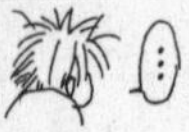
...

IT SEEMS LIKE TSUDA-KUN WAS KIND OF A JUVENILE DELINQUENT, BUT AS A FRIEND OF EN-CHAN, HE CAN'T BE ALL THAT BAD, RIGHT? STILL, IF YOU'RE GOING TO DO WHAT HE DID, DON'T GET CAUGHT. LEARN TO NAVIGATE YOUR WAY THROUGH THE WORLD.

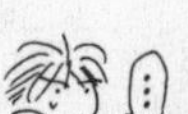
...

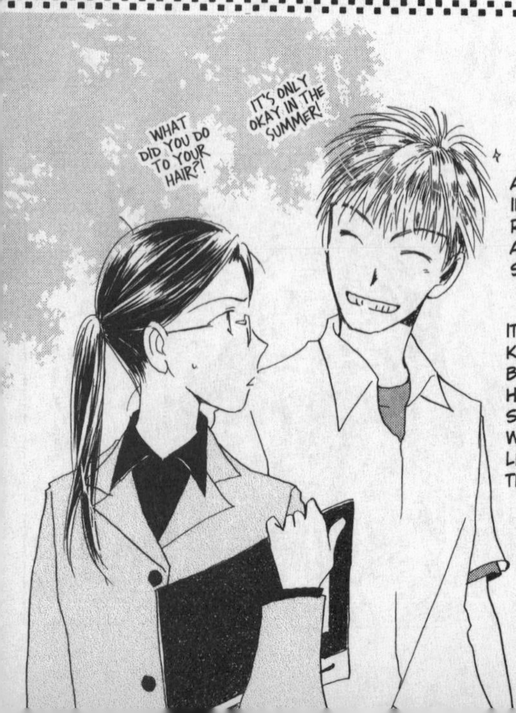
IT'S ONLY OKAY IN THE SUMMER!
WHAT DID YOU DO TO YOUR HAIR?!

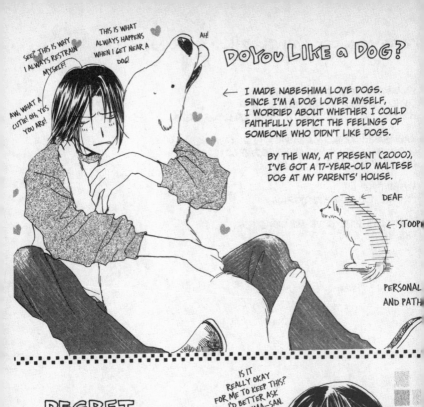

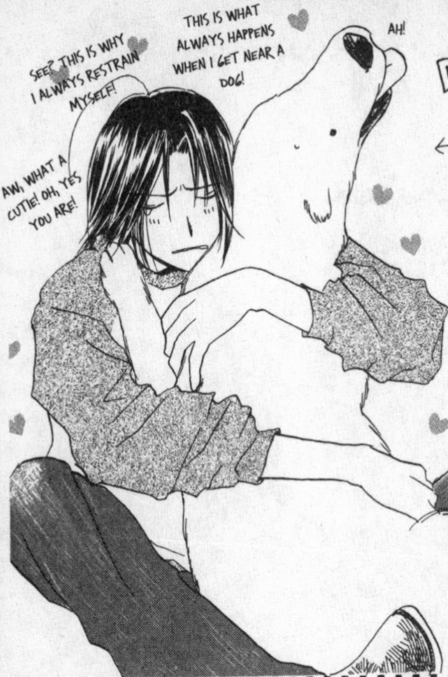
THIS IS WHAT ALWAYS HAPPENS WHEN I GET NEAR A DOG!
AH!
SEE? THIS IS WHY I ALWAYS RESTRAIN MYSELF!
AW, WHAT A CUTIE! OH, YES YOU ARE!

DoYou LIKE a DOG?

← I MADE NABESHIMA LOVE DOGS. SINCE I'M A DOG LOVER MYSELF, I WORRIED ABOUT WHETHER I COULD FAITHFULLY DEPICT THE FEELINGS OF SOMEONE WHO DIDN'T LIKE DOGS.

BY THE WAY, AT PRESENT (2000), I'VE GOT A 17-YEAR-OLD MALTESE DOG AT MY PARENTS' HOUSE.

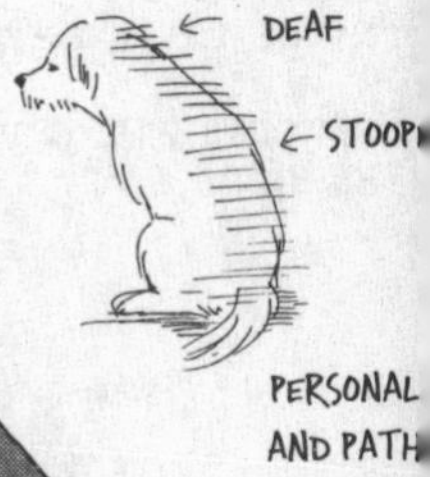
DEAF
STOOP
PERSONAL
AND PATH

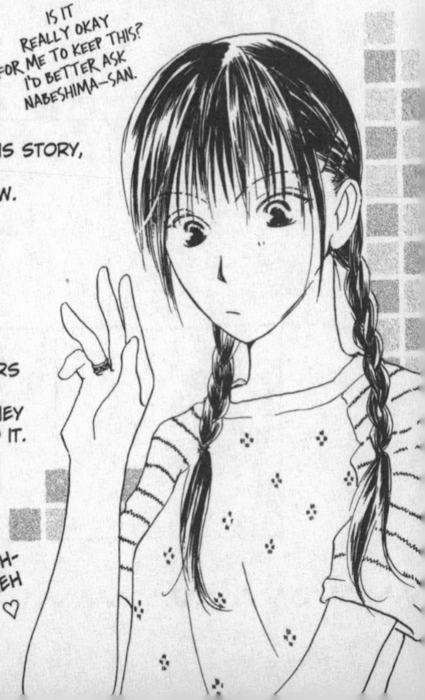
IS IT REALLY OKAY FOR ME TO KEEP THIS? I'D BETTER ASK NABESHIMA-SAN.

REGRET

I SCARED MYSELF WHEN, DURING THE COURSE OF CREATING THE ART FOR THIS STORY, I GOT INTO A MINI-SLUMP BECAUSE I COMPLETELY LOST THE ABILITY TO DRAW.

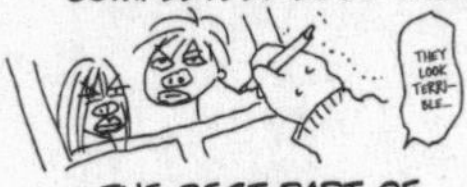
THEY LOOK TERRI-BLE...

THE BEST PART OF THIS STORY WAS THIS.

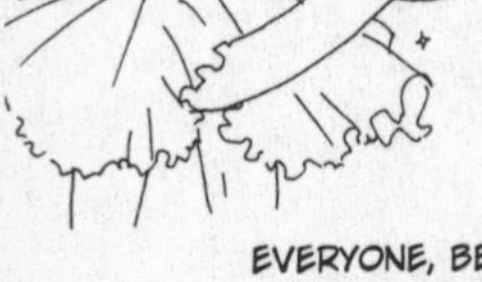

I THOUGHT READERS WOULD BE DIVIDED OVER THIS, BUT THEY WERE REALLY INTO IT.

EVERYONE, BE AWARE THAT I LOVE THIS KIND OF THING!

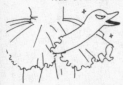

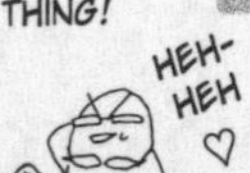
HEH-HEH ♡

THANKS!

YAMAMOTO CHIE-SAMA
(WHO CO-CREATED V5 WITH ME AND
HELPED ME COME UP WITH THEIR RALLYING CRIES)

KAWASAKI WAKAKO-SAMA WITH FURUKAWA-KUN
(HOMEPAGE ADMINISTRATOR...CONGRATULATIONS
ON YOUR MARRIAGE)

MY EDITOR
(THANK YOU FOR EVERYTHING)

EVERYONE WHO GAVE ME IDEAS FOR
THE BUNNY SUIT

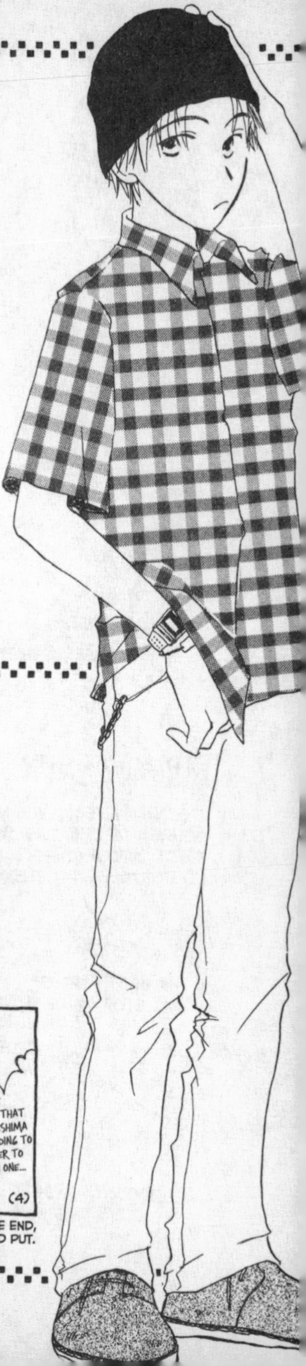

THE FIRST APPEARANCE OF THE BOSS: SOUL GSG

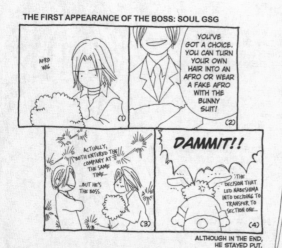

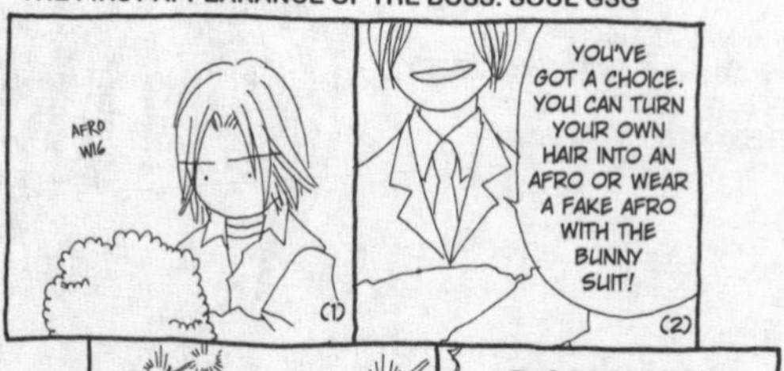
AFRO WIG
(1)
YOU'VE GOT A CHOICE. YOU CAN TURN YOUR OWN HAIR INTO AN AFRO OR WEAR A FAKE AFRO WITH THE BUNNY SUIT!
(2)
ACTUALLY, BOTH ENTERED THE COMPANY AT THE SAME TIME...
...BUT HE'S THE BOSS.
(3)
DAMMIT!!
:THE DECISION THAT LED NABESHIMA INTO DECIDING TO TRANSFER TO SECTION ONE...
(4)

ALTHOUGH IN THE END,
HE STAYED PUT.

MECASITE HTTP://WWW.AURORA.DTI.NE.JP/-WAKA/

(*CMX EDiTOR NOTE: ABOVE URL iS NO LONGER VALiD)

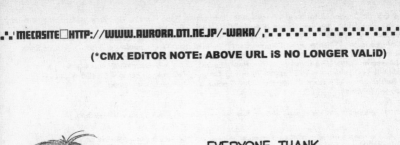

EVERYONE, THANK YOU VERY MUCH...

...FOR SUPPORTING ME AND READING MY COMICS. WELL, THAT'S ALL FOR NOW!

MECA TANAKA

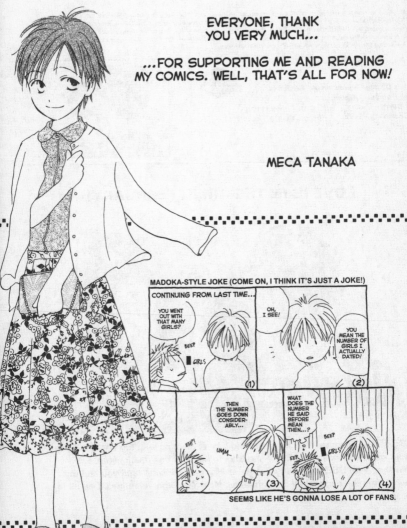

MADOKA-STYLE JOKE (COME ON, I THINK IT'S JUST A JOKE!)

CONTINUING FROM LAST TIME...
YOU WENT OUT WITH THAT MANY GIRLS?
BEEP
GIRLS
(1)
OH, I SEE!
YOU MEAN THE NUMBER OF GIRLS I ACTUALLY DATED!
(2)
THEN THE NUMBER GOES DOWN CONSIDER-ABLY...
EH?!
UMM...
(3)
WHAT DOES THE NUMBER HE SAID BEFORE MEAN THEN...?
BEEP
GIRLS
EEP
(4)

SEEMS LIKE HE'S GONNA LOSE A LOT OF FANS.

MECASITE: COMICS VERSION!!: THE END

509

MUKAEDESU. Volume 2 © 1998 Meca Tanaka. All Rights Reserved. First published in Japan in 2000 by HAKUSENSHA,
., Tokyo.

UKAE DESU. Volume 2, published by WildStorm Productions, an imprint of DC Comics, 888 Prospect St. #240, La Jolla,
92037. English Translation © 2007. All Rights Reserved. English language translation rights in the United States of America
Canada arranged with HAKUSENSHA, INC., Tokyo, through Tuttle-Mori Agency, Inc., Tokyo. The stories, characters, and
dents mentioned in this magazine are entirely fictional. Printed on recyclable paper. WildStorm does not read or accept
solicited submissions of ideas, stories or artwork. Printed in Canada.

Comics, a Warner Bros. Entertainment Company.

eldon Drzka – Translation and Adaptation
lson Ramos – Lettering
rry Berry – Design
n Chadwick – Editor

ISBN:1-4012-1117-8
ISBN-13: 978-1-4012-1117-2

LOVE IS IN THE AIR IN FEBRUARY!

OMUKAE desu.
Volume 3

By Meca Tanaka. Yuzuko is allowed a brief meeting with the boyfriend she had when she was alive. But if she tries to rekindle this relationship, she's finished with GSG. A ghostly girl stalks Madoka, and wait until you find out why. And the gang takes on Christmas, New Year, and Valentine's Day all in one volume!